To Robin
with High Regard
and Deep Affection.
                        Jack
2/95

D1559450

INDIVIDUAL

JUSTICE

IN

MASS TORT

LITIGATION

JACK B. WEINSTEIN

INDIVIDUAL
JUSTICE
IN
MASS TORT
LITIGATION

THE EFFECT OF

CLASS ACTIONS,

CONSOLIDATIONS,

AND OTHER

MULTIPARTY DEVICES

NORTHWESTERN UNIVERSITY PRESS

EVANSTON, ILLINOIS

Northwestern University Press
Evanston, Illinois 60208-4210

Copyright © 1995 by Jack B. Weinstein
All rights reserved. Published 1995 by Northwestern University Press
Printed in the United States of America

Library of Congress Cataloging-in-Publication Data

Weinstein, Jack B.
    Individual justice in mass tort litigation : the effect of class
actions, consolidations, and other multiparty devices / Jack B.
Weinstein.
       p.   cm.
    Includes index.
    ISBN 0-8101-1188-8
    1. Torts—United States. 2. Class actions (Civil procedure)—
United States. 3. Complex litigation—United States. 4. Justice,
Administration of—United States.
KF1250.W45   1995
347.73'53—dc20
[347.30753]   94-33789
                       CIP

The paper used in this publication meets the minimum requirements of
the American National Standard for Information Sciences—Permanence
of Paper for Printed Library Materials, ANSI Z39.48-1984.

This book is dedicated to

Evelyn Weinstein, MSW, ACSW, who

has devoted her professional life to

individual justice in medical and

other nonlegal settings.

CONTENTS

PREFACE

Before I was introduced to mass torts, I had a number of cases with large numbers of plaintiffs joined together through a class action. That is an action brought by a few parties representing many persons under Rule 23 of the federal Rules of Civil Procedure. One or a few attorneys appear for the class. Often, many of those being represented—and bound by the action—are not even aware that their rights have been violated; they have no say in choosing the attorney purporting to represent them. There are provisions for close supervision of these cases by the court to ensure fairness and adequate representation by the attorneys with controls over their fees. My class action cases, up to the early 1980s, involved securities, labor matters, and various school and prison constitutional issues.

The first major multiple-party tort case I had involved children from all over the country injured by explosive caps. I shall advert to it briefly in the book because the theory of industry-wide liability for not warning children of the dangers of playing with the caps by markings on the devices bore on my later thinking with respect to mass torts involving a number of defendants, particularly in the Agent Orange case.

The Agent Orange case was assigned to me in the early 1980s by the Federal Multidistrict Panel, a group of federal judges with power to transfer related cases in all federal courts to one transferee judge who has power under section 1407 of title 28 of the United States Judicial Code to control the litigation before trial. Discovery through such devices as depositions, written interrogatories, requests for documents, and the like provides information to the parties. Motions, such as those to amend pleadings, to dismiss all or part of the case on the ground of legal or factual deficiencies, to allow class actions to proceed or not, and to transfer the case to appropriate courts for trial, including to the transferee judge, for convenience under section 1404 of title 28 of the United States Code are decided by the one transferee judge.

Hundreds of thousands of former United States, Australian, and New Zealand armed forces personnel *thought* that the spraying of herbicides—commonly referred to as Agent Orange because barrels of the substance had an orange stripe on them—in Vietnam to clear brush in which the enemy might hide had caused serious injuries to themselves and their offspring. Had it not been settled, the Agent Orange case would have had to be dismissed since there was insufficient evidence that the sprayings had caused illness to particular persons and because under various Supreme Court cases, neither the government nor the companies from whom the herbicides had been purchased could be sued for discretionary acts of the government in waging the Vietnam War.[1] I was particularly interested in the case, partly because of the many suits involving potential draftees that I had heard, most resulting in dismissals. Cases against the young men involved were based on conscientious objector status and other grounds.

As a result of being involved in the complexities of the Agent Orange case I began to reflect on how our legal system deals with disasters—whether real or imaginary. This resulted in an article published in the Columbia Law School's Environmental Law Journal. It is chapter 2. Since there has been little shift in my views, only a few minor changes have been made.

I should add a few words here about the nature of law school scholarly journals. They are edited by students who often—as in the case of major parts of chapters 3–8 originally published as studies on Ethics and Mass Torts—make helpful suggestions to the author and carefully check all citations and textual statements for accuracy. The writing style in these journals does tend to be somewhat terse and legalistic. To reduce the burden on the reader and make the text slightly more tolerable, I have transferred the footnotes to the end of the volume.

Subsequently, in the mid-1980s I became heavily involved in the cases of workers who had fallen ill because of asbestos exposure in the 1930s and 1940s. Trying some eighty of these cases before juries and helping to settle thousands of others, I found myself continuing to consider new procedures and new substantive law. To try to understand why our American judges could use their powers so flexibly, I began to consider powers of the Equity judges, the chancellors of Medieval England, and how their techniques were carried over to modern times. My interest in this subject was particularly piqued because the Development of Legal Institutions in Medieval England was the first law course I taught—then under Professor Julius Goebel at Columbia. This study resulted in an article published in the proceedings of an international conference on equity in Israel and an article written with one of my law clerks for the Illinois Law Review. Revisions, except in the most minor particulars, have not been necessary. These writings appear as chapter 9 of the book.

In the early 1990s I had before me many cases involving diethylstilbestrol (DES) and worker stress syndromes. The DES cases resulted from the taking of a drug manufactured by many companies for use during pregnancy to inhibit involuntary abortion. Many of the daughters (as well, probably, as sons and grandchildren) suffered severe damage to their reproductive organs. The stress syndrome cases arose from allegations by workers that steady use of computer keyboards and other repetitive tasks caused carpal tunnel syndrome and other diseases.

During all this period I was teaching and working with scientists and others to improve our handling of these mass cases. While I had written on the teaching of ethics[2] and embodied ethical issues in my teaching of criminal law, civil practice, evidence, and trial practice when I was on the faculty or an adjunct professor at Columbia University and elsewhere, ethical issues, generally, seemed subservient to the procedure and substance students were most interested in. Yet, increasing exposure to mass torts left me with the sense that ethical issues were critical and pervasive; they had to be faced directly. The result of these studies was a series of lectures[3] and an article on Ethics and Mass Litigation in the Northwestern University Law Review.[4] Expanded, the article appears as ethical issues in chapters 3 (ethics generally), 4 (lawyers), 5 (judges), 6 (scientists), 7 (parties), and 8 (legislators).

Chapter 10 consists in large part of my 1991 lecture at the Administrative Conference of the United States. A number of scholars met to consider the possibility of administrative and other methods of dealing with mass cases. My views are still tentative, but they build on the initial article in chapter 2.

I have not included the thousands of printed pages of my relevant decisions on mass torts. For the reader who wants further exposure to this material, citations to the printed opinions are gathered in this preface. Nor have I quoted extensively from the tens of thousands of pages of hearings and colloquies with counsel and parties. Most of my decisions are unpublished, deep in the filed records and docket entries of many cases dealing with these matters. It seemed only merciful to spare the reader these details, however much the individual litigants, their lawyers, the judge, and an occasional law professor may savor them.

My law clerks have been particularly gracious in sharing their wisdom with me on this and other subjects. They are: Professor Margaret A. Berger (1967), William D. Siegel (1967), Stephen L. Cohen (1967–1968), Professor Paul J. Spiegelman (1967–1968), Professor Paul I. Sherman (1968–1969), Richard J. Davis (1969–1970), Dale L. Matschullat (1970–1971), Wayne A. Cross (1970–1971), Paul S. Ryerson (1971–1972), Professor Rand E. Rosenblatt (1971–1972), Mark C. Morril (1972–1973), Susan Price Carr (1972–1973) (deceased), Steven I. Shulman (1973–1974), Professor Michael J. Perry (1973–1974), Leslie G. Fagen

(1973–1974), William C. Bonvillian (1974–1975), Professor Joan Wexler (1974–1975), Keith Secular (1975–1976), U.S. District Judge Denise Cote (1975–1976), Professor Steven S. Nemerson (1976–1977), Professor Diane L. Zimmerman (1976–1977), Tom A. Bernstein (1977–1978), Willys H. Schneider (1977–1978), Paul W. Bartel (1978–1979), Wayne S. Braveman (1978–1979), Daniel J. Cooper (1979–1980), Bonnie Kayatta-Steingart (1979–1980), Emily M. Altman (1980–1981), Jamie Lehman (1980–1981) (deceased), Professor Guyora Binder (1981–1982), Jo-Anne Weissbart (1981–1982), Abbe Leon Dienstag (1982–1983), Lani Aloha Adler (1982–1983), Allen R. Friedman (1983–1984), Laura S. Schnell (1983–1984), David A. Brittenham (1984–1985), Gay A. Crosthwait Danforth (1984–1985), Professor Anita Bernstein (1985–1986), Simon Arieh Zak (1985–1986), Martin S. Lederman (1986–1987), Marie V. O'Connell (1986–1987), Professor Jonathan B. Wiener (1987–1988), Ann Alexander (1987–1988), Peter Woodin (1988–1989), Claudia Lewis (1988–1989), Robert Kushen (1989–1990), Eileen Hershenov (1989–1990), Vineet Bhatia (1990–1991), Robin E. Abrams (1990–1991), John Goldberg (1991–1992), Professor Jessica Vapnek (1991–1992), Samuel W. Buell (1992–1993), Laraine Pacheco (1992–1993), Judith G. Federbush (1993–1994), and Frances E. Bivens (1993–1994). Many clinical students from Columbia, Cardozo, and Brooklyn Law Schools have assisted them and me.

The law school seminars include: "Equality and the Law," given with Professor R. Kent Greenawalt (Columbia); "Individual Justice in a Mass Society," given with Professor Arthur Murphy (Columbia); "Complex Litigation, Jurisdiction and Choice of Law," given with Professor Harold L. Korn (Columbia); "Complex Litigation and Science," given with Professor Margaret A. Berger (Brooklyn); and "Mass Torts," given with Professor Kenneth R. Feinberg (Georgetown). The many papers produced by my students have not been cited or relied upon, although they obviously affected my views. A private seminar in settlement of cases was given to me by practicing attorneys David Shapiro and Kenneth R. Feinberg. Michael Marchetti assisted in final cite checking. Dorothy Rosenberg was most supportive.

My main articles and books directly relevant to mass torts include the following:

"Individual Justice in Mass Litigations," 88 Nw. U. L. Rev. 90 (1993).

"Preliminary Reflections on the Law's Reaction to Disasters," 1 Colum. J. Envtl. L. 1 (1986).

"The Effect of Equity on Mass Tort Law," 1991 U. Ill. L. Rev. 269 (with Eileen B. Hershenov).

"Procedural and Substantive Problems in Complex Litigation Arising from Disasters," 5 Touro L. Rev. 1 (1988).

[Administrative Compensation in Mass Torts] "A View from the Judiciary," 13 Cardozo L. Rev. (1992).

ALI/ABA "Expert Testimony and Novel Scientific Evidence in Toxic Tort Litigation" (June 1988).

ALI/ABA "Scientific Evidence in Complex Litigation" (July 1991).

ALI/ABA "Role of Expert Testimony and Novel Scientific Evidence in Proof of Causation" (Nov. 1987).

"Rule 702 of the Federal Rules of Evidence Is Sound; It Should Not Be Amended," 136 F.R.D. 631 (1991).

"Improving Expert Testimony," 20 Rich. L. Rev. 473 (1986).

"After Fifty Years of the Federal Rules of Civil Procedure: Are the Barriers to Justice Being Raised?," 137 U. Pa. L. Rev. 1901 (1989).

"The Ghost of Process Past: The Fiftieth Anniversary of the Federal Rules of Civil Procedure," 54 Brook. L. Rev. 1 (1988).

"Modern Teaching at Brooklyn Law School—The Example of Toxic Torts," 52 Brook. L. Rev. 329 (1986).

"Of Sailing Ships and Seeking Facts: Brief Reflections on Magistrates and the Federal Rules of Civil Procedure," 62 St. John's L. Rev. 429 (with Jonathan B. Weiner) (1986).

"The Role of the Court in Toxic Tort Litigation," 73 Geo. L. J. 1389 (1985).

Mass Torts, Cases and Materials (with Kenneth R. Feinberg) (1993).

The Law Reacts to a Nuclear Explosion in Brooklyn and Love Triumphs (1991) (a novelette used in teaching ethics, mass torts, and other subjects).

Reading materials for the seminars (years 1978–1994).

The directly relevant written opinions include:

AGENT ORANGE

781 F. Supp. 934 (1992) (civil plaintiffs—remand to state)
139 F.R.D. 581 (1991) (compensation to attorney)
781 F. Supp. 902 (1991) (binding parties)
707 F. Supp. 1368 (1988) (insurance)
689 F. Supp. 1250 (1988) (distribution scheme)
104 F.R.D. 559 (1985) (secrecy of records)
611 F. Supp. 1267 (1985) (scientific proof)
611 F. Supp. 1396 (1985) (fairness of settlement)
603 F. Supp. 239 (1985) (class certification)
611 F. Supp. 1296 (1985) (attorney's fees)
611 F. Supp. 1293 (1985) (scientific proof)
597 F. Supp. 740 (1984) (analysis of substantive law)
590 F. Supp. 690 (1984) (conflict of laws)

99 F.R.D. 645 (1983) (secrecy)
100 F.R.D. 735 (1983) (management and appeals)
100 F.R.D. 718 (1983) (certification of class)
1992 and subsequent annual reports on expenditure of monies for
veterans and families.

ASBESTOS

129 B.R. 710 (1991) (history of Manville Trust)
726 F. Supp. 426 (1989) (computation damages)
120 B.R. 648 (1990) (class certification)
123 B.R. 7 (1990) (joint administration)
737 F. Supp. 735 (1990) (Special Master ethics)
134 F.R.D. 32 (1990) (power over state cases)
769 F. Supp. 85 (1991) (consolidation)
772 F. Supp. 1380 (1991) (computation of damages)
Findley v. Falise, NYAL Index No. 4000, No. 90-3973
(E.D.N.Y. 1993) (memorandum to parties on questions for
decision after remand)

DES

789 F. Supp. 552 (1992) (theories of jurisdiction)
789 F. Supp. 548 (1992) (market share)
825 F. Supp. 475 (1993) (lack of disqualification of trial judge)
814 F. Supp. 305 (1993) (remand issues)

REPETITIVE STRESS AND HEALTH

142 F.R.D. 584 (consolidation)
Luther v. The 65 Security Plan, 831 F. Supp. 1008 (E.D.N.Y. 1993)
(health program financing; methods of consolidation)

LILCO—ATOMIC PLANT

710 F. Supp. 1485 (1989) (qui tam action)
710 F. Supp. 1477 (1989) (fee awards)
710 F. Supp. 1428 (1989) (settlement fairness)
710 F. Supp. 1422 (1989) (settlement and certification)
710 F. Supp. 1407 (1989) (intervention and opt-out issues)
710 F. Supp. 1387 (1989) (RICO and rates)
685 F. Supp. 38 (1988) (class action standing)

Jack B. Weinstein
April 1994

....

CHAPTER 1

OVERVIEW

Traditionally, the tort law and lawyers have been devoted to dealing with individuals and their problems on a retail basis. Modern disasters affecting large numbers of people make that approach impossible except at unacceptable transactional costs and inefficiencies that would prevent vindication of most people's rights. Yet, we want to retain the sense of individual justice and control of their cases by the parties, as well as devotion to the individual client by attorneys that stamps this country's approach to the law. In the field of mass torts, the courts have made pragmatic choices in devising procedures and remedies in an attempt to preserve the essence of our prior conceptual approach to the law while devising effective remedies for the injured.

Every person has a sense of justice. Every person wants to be treated fairly. In this country fair treatment usually includes the right to be heard in court by a judge and usually a jury.

Effective justice has traditionally required individual counsel and a judge with the time and inclination to listen and decide case by case. The huge growth in population, in complex technology, and in the number of court cases makes it increasingly difficult to provide individuals with equal access to the court system.

Our judicial system is widely admired throughout the world, particularly where tyranny prevails. One reason is that federal and many state courts, particularly in the post–World War II period, have held out the prospect of empowerment through the courts of the disadvantaged. In a period of increased frustration with the inability to be treated as an individual rather than as a number in a computer, the sense that a court is concerned with individual problems is essential to the health of our democratic society. In our tripartite system the legislature and executive have responded to the voices of the many; the courts have responded primarily to the voice of the individual.

Courts dealing with large numbers of individual complaints have increasingly turned to mass processing of cases through such devices as class actions and consolidations. Complaints such as those about school discrimination, voting abuses, prison cruelties, toxic poisons, and dangers from pharmaceuticals appear to have required some kind of mass procedures.

The huge influx of criminal cases, particularly drug-related matters, also puts pressure on the courts to reduce the time devoted to single criminal cases. Sentencing guidelines designed to produce uniformity reduce the opportunity of the court to treat defendants individually.[1]

Increased caseloads have led to procedures for discouraging use of the courthouse by many who seek help. A rich and increasingly conservative society denies legal assistance to many who need it.

Are the ideals and possibility of individualized justice largely outmoded? I answer with a qualified "no." We can provide individual justice in a mass society if we wish to, and we should try to do so if we want to maintain a vital democracy.

In some kinds of claims, individual justice can be effective if there is adequate legal assistance, particularly to indigent parties. Such cases include those involving charges of race, sex, or age discrimination, social security benefits, habeas corpus petitions brought by prison inmates, and criminal defense.

Other cases call for more effective court reforms if we are to accord justice to all litigants. Sometimes mass treatment, either by the courts or through Congress and administrative agencies, yields a more effective individual remedy. Included in this category are mass tort cases, possible nuclear disasters, black lung cases brought by miners, childhood vaccine cases, and workers' compensation cases.

Taking some cases out of the system, for example, by eventually either partially or fully decriminalizing sale and possession of some drugs which are now illegal, would free resources that could be redirected on behalf of individual litigants in other cases. The effects of decriminalization on the large minority populations of our inner cities may weigh against across-the-board efforts in this area; in any event, possible adverse effects of standing down from the war on drugs must be taken into consideration.

These problems do not lend themselves to easy answers, nor can they be fully addressed by the courts alone. But, to the extent that the courts can provide more resources and increased efficiency, offer better sensitivity training, and help take some disputes out of the system, they might go a long way toward finding a solution.

My approach to these problems consists of two prongs: first, by the courts and lawyers through institutions, and second, by the judge and lawyer establishing an empathetic relationship with those seeking justice. Both can be illustrated by examples from cases over which I presided.

Steps should be taken to ensure that courts provide individual justice, even in a mass context. Examples are: certification of classes of litigants who could not afford to bring individual cases; establishment in the Agent Orange case of the Appeals Office and telephone answering service that enable complaints to be heard, as well as a judicial policy of answering all letters sent to the court, and other innovative procedures developed in the mass tort context; alternative dispute resolution; use of magistrates and special masters and other increases in court personnel; and legal representation for the poor.

A personal approach in individual cases cannot be readily reproduced, codified, or institutionalized by rule or statute. The best guarantee in the courts is judicial appointees to the federal bench who are people of quality, sensitivity, and imagination, and who are able to maintain their independence from the political process to as great a degree as possible. Examples of many judges' out-of-the-ordinary responses to particular litigants include attempts to be creative about sentencing while keeping within congressionally mandated parameters, efforts to provide social security benefit applicants with pro bono funds so they might go to a doctor of their choosing for a second medical opinion, and efforts to provide individual prisoners and civil rights plaintiffs with a chance to be heard.[2]

We need seriously to readdress the problems of mass toxic tort litigation. Improvements are possible. Litigations involving large numbers of plaintiffs, such as Agent Orange, Dalkon Shield, heart valves, atomic weapons pollution sites, Bendectin, repetitive task syndromes (particularly carpal tunnel problems), breast implants, and the like, require us to treat a wide variety of problems—jurisdictional, scientific, substantive, and administrative, as well as philosophical and ethical—differently from the way we have met them in the traditional one-plaintiff-one-defendant case.[3]

Chief among our current concerns should be the "individual" aspect of mass litigations. How can we provide each plaintiff and each defendant with the benefits of a system in mass torts that treats him or her as an individual person? How can each person obtain the respect that his or her individuality and personal needs should command in an egalitarian democracy such as ours?

Before turning to these challenging questions, a brief review of the current status of other aspects of mass tort litigation provides necessary background.

The scientific problems remain troubling. Much of the current indictment of science and the courts is exaggerated and not reflective of what happens in our courtrooms. Yet there is much room for improvement. Courts need to be able to turn to some neutral body or bodies to recommend scientists who do not work on behalf of litigants to help us evaluate available information, utilizing Rule 706 of the Federal Rules of Evidence or special master appointments or other techniques. Courts also need to be able to call on the scientific community for assistance in conducting timely relevant research and analysis.

The National Academy of Science recently produced excellent studies on statistics and on DNA in the courtroom. The Federal Judicial Center is producing an analysis of judges' roles in cases in which DNA is used for identification. In Agent Orange, the court relied upon Centers for Disease Control studies. In a whole-cell pertussis vaccine case national studies of respected pediatricians' groups were utilized. The Environmental Protection Agency (EPA), Occupational Safety and Health Administration (OSHA), Food and Drug Administration (FDA), and other independent scientific groups also can help.

At what we can call the administrative-procedural level, the problem remains one of operating a system which is fairly speedy and efficient and of reducing transaction costs. The means involved include consolidating cases before one judge, applying a single substantive rule, providing lead counsel on both sides to conduct the basic litigation, furnishing prompt and effective scientific research and testimony, and arriving at a method of payment using relatively fixed and simple criteria for compensation.

Efficiency is a worthy goal. Opinions in cases involving Agent Orange, DES, asbestos, and carpal tunnel syndrome relate primarily to methods of ameliorating the burdens these enormous cases present for the parties, attorneys, and courts.

Insofar as possible, alternative dispute resolution arrangements for avoiding litigation, such as in the recent Pfizer Heart Valve settlement, need to be encouraged. This settlement provided for, in effect, an insurance policy for those with heart valves, medical monitoring, payment for replacement, and reasonable damages, where the valves proved defective. Traditional tort suits were discouraged.

Nonlitigation settlements giving effective help to those who think they have been injured, without destroying those believed to be at fault, are the wave of the future. Traditional tort-lottery lump sum payments can cause great damage to a community and even successful plaintiffs; the attorneys and insurance industry take most of the money. Given transactional and other costs, somewhere in the order of 20 percent of each dollar paid by industry or society probably goes to the victim in the DES cases.

The proposed national health care system together with more effective control of toxic substances and other pervasive health hazards will reduce the need for reliance on our tort compensation-deterrence system. For mass torts a federal legislative scheme replacing the hodgepodge of the fifty state systems will be required.

In the future, for those injured by mass tort events, expansion of social security disability benefits to cover the entire population can be expected to provide the equivalent of tort compensation for loss of capacity to work. National health plans can be expected to provide medical services. Better administrative control of dangerous substances and more sensible evaluations of risks and benefits *before* the harm occurs will provide the protection now assumed to be afforded by the deterrent effect of torts.[4]

Given adequate disclosure by industry to government regulatory agencies, industry which follows government strictures on design safety, production and labeling, and the like should receive the protection of federal preemption doctrine. Where the government does not enforce its own regulations, qui tam actions—that is, private actions brought on behalf of the government agencies—should be permitted.

Pain and suffering will probably not be directly compensated. These elements can, unfortunately, be deemed the normal aspects of life in our mass technological society; first-party insurance for pain and suffering is not generally available because of this common assumption—that is, except in tort law. On the whole, speaking only of health, the steady increase in life expectancy in our nation suggests that the benefits of mass technology and chemistry far outweigh the risks.

Those industries and manufacturers who do create extra hazards should be directly fined or taxed by the government to pay for the extra costs of health care and disability pensions.[5] Those individuals who want additional protection above the health care system and social security disability system may be able to purchase some forms of first-party insurance directly or, in the case of workers, bargain with their employers either for extra pay for hazardous work or extra protection for injuries.[6]

The main losers, were such an integrated system adopted, would probably be the legal profession and insurance industry. Since the transactional costs for lawyers' fees—both defendants and plaintiffs—and insurance overhead of our mass tort system run into many billions annually, the effect in reducing the income of the legal profession and insurance providers of a more rational system will be enormous. There is, however, ample, more modest work for lawyers in helping people improve their status and obtain benefits.

For the present, the courts must assume the current system will remain in operation, and they must do what they can to make it more effective. Until the national legislature acts on the substantive side, the issue in mass cases is how to modify the law of torts to provide a just system of compensation and deterrence. Recent work suggests that tort law is somewhat better at deterrence and overdeterrence than at fair compensation.[7] M. F. Peretz illustrated the point in his essay "The Fifth Freedom" on contraceptives:

> One factor that makes the extensive research needed for development of [a contraceptive or abortion] pill uneconomic in the United States is a widespread public misunderstanding of the effects of the prolonged use of any drug on a large population. Genetic diversity insures that there will always be some people in whom even the safest drug produces adverse effects. If the percentage of such people is substantial, then the adverse effects show up in clinical trials carried out on several hundred people before the drug is released on the market; but if the adverse effects manifest themselves in only, say, one person out of 10,000, then the probability of their showing up in clinical trials is negligible. When the drug is later used by millions, and affected persons sue the manufacturers for negligence, then litigation and damages may cost that firm many millions of dollars. These costs and the accompanying adverse publicity are some of the factors that have discouraged further development of contraceptives.[8]

That the tort system is still needed for some deterrent functions—however crude—is illustrated by *Corrosion Proof Fittings v. E.P.A.*[9] After all the adverse information about asbestos revealed by litigation, OSHA, and the Consumer Products Safety Commission, EPA adopted a final rule banning the use and sale of most products containing asbestos. The Court of Appeals reversed the EPA's decision in 1991 because all the regulatory "t"s had not been crossed. Saving 148–202 lives at a cost of $450–$800 million was not, it held, justified by the statute. But how else will we prevent those probable deaths? How will we, or can we, find out who died as a result of continued production of asbestos products and compensate their families? We cannot under our present system. That these are undifferentiated hazards of our modern life suggests that a general health care system as a safety net to back up the tort and regulatory systems is desirable.

Traditionally the courts have properly focused on compensation of the plaintiff shown to have been harmed by a particular defendant because that is the direct issue before the court in a tort action. Deterrence is an indirect result of compensation.

The philosophical questions raised by mass tort cases require us to consider the challenge of providing individual justice. Our pragmatic judicial system has an eclectic view of philosophy. We simultaneously rely on Kant, Bentham, Rawls, Nozick, and others without shame at inconsistencies in their work and critiques by other philosophers.

Useful is the analysis of Professor Seyla Benhabib,[10] who suggests reliance by courts on an approach stressing dialogue among those affected by jurisprudential decisions. She writes, "[The t]hree strands of

[1] a neoconservative social diagnosis, [2] a politics of community and philosophical ethics [and] [3] a historically informed practical reason form the core elements of the contemporary neo-Aristotelian position."[11]

These three strands assist in judicial analysis. A social diagnosis stressing individualism more curbed than in the past, in part because of a declining economy, appears to be one direction in which we are going. It suggests less stress on high individual awards even though the academically respected critics of our tort system argue that the system is substantially sound and does provide necessary protections for our society.[12] The politics of community is important, as in the Buffalo Creek class action and others referred to in the discussion in chapter 2. A historically informed reason is one of the key methods of the judicial system in making and applying substantive and procedural law and in handling practical situations.

From a short-term historical point of view we might examine a number of cases that suggest where a changed approach might lead. The first case is the Hawk's Nest Tunnel litigation in West Virginia in the early 1930s in which many unprotected laborers were victims of acute silicosis (over seven hundred died). By today's standards the lawyers sold out.[13] Settlements ranged from $30.00 to a Black family to $1,600.00 to a White family. The lawyers agreed not to reveal what they had found and took the bulk of the settlement. This, on a 0 to 10 scale, represents about 0.1 for the legal system.

A second example is the Buffalo Creek disaster described in the book of the same name by Gerald M. Stern.[14] Stern worked for Arnold and Porter, which took a reasonable 25 percent contingency fee. It settled much of the litigation for $13.5 million, which was quite good for 1972. Nothing, however, was done for the communities that were destroyed.[15] By today's standards this case would rate a 5 on a 0 to 10 scale.

We can use Agent Orange (7), Dalkon Shield (8), DES (6), and the heart valve settlement with Pfizer in 1992 or the 1994 breast implant tentative settlement (9) as illustrative of the trend in the law.

A hypothetical case indicates where that trend puts us today. Given a modern case like Buffalo Creek with an ethical firm like Arnold and Porter handling it, how should it proceed? A class action would be brought to represent everyone. Probably subclasses of property owners, families of the dead, the physically injured, and the psychologically injured would be certified. The settlement would be much higher—on the order of ten times, or $135 million in 1975 dollars. It would include psychiatric services, the rebuilding of homes, and the transfer of property for community development from the state and the coal company. The state and the coal companies in the real case pushed people off their land. Communities were broken up. New schools, medical facilities, and the rebuilding of communities would be part of a modern settlement, as would medical monitoring and treatment for those "shocked" by the occurrence. Much of the settlement would be paid by the insurance companies, the government through federal emergency funds, the Small Business Administration, and others. The state would, by road building and other means, also provide capital and ongoing supervision.

Compensation would be made on a grid using bureaucratic models with individual attention in internal administrative appeals to special masters and the like. The attorneys would hold meetings and hearings with their clients while negotiations went forward. Groups of clients would, through paraprofessionals and their own representatives, maintain close contact with the lawyers, the courts, and other agencies. There would be public fairness hearings held by the judge in connection with settlement of the Rule 23 class action.

The Exxon Valdez case needs to be examined carefully. It involves federal, state, municipal, and private interests. Communities include fishery workers and the populace of the United States interested in preserving Alaska for future generations. How is this case proceeding? What are the problems? Is it moving swiftly enough on criminal and civil tracks and at reasonable transactional costs? Are the criminal and civil tort laws the best vehicles for handling such a complex case? Neither the traditional criminal laws nor the traditional tort laws seem apt vehicles for dealing with a case with such broad implications. Even a portion of the civil proceedings require, for example, tens of millions of dollars in investments by plaintiffs' attorneys to get through the discovery-settlement stages.

After this brief survey of the lay of the land today in the various aspects of mass tort litigation, the challenge of individual justice may now be addressed. Two preliminary points should be made.

First, there will be a serious cost in cash and time should we require more individual contact with litigants by the court or attorneys, or both. Whether the effort and cost are justified is a matter warranting serious discussion.

Second, the proper amount of effort to increase contact with, and understanding of and by, the litigants will vary with the nature of the injury. At one end of the spectrum are the Dalkon Shield, Agent Orange, and DES cases. In these cases, the plaintiff feels that serious harm has occurred as a result of defendants' action, and there may be an element of outrage. At the other end of the spectrum are many purely commercial cases where each of those injured suffered only a small financial loss, but the sum of the losses may be huge. Here, the litigant probably is unaware of the potential claim until a class action is brought and settled and the time for distribution of funds or other assets arrives. Illustrative are some of the securities cases and the recent settlement of consumer claims against airlines. As we move along this spectrum, the more the litigant is "hurt," the more individual care by the legal system is required.

Three distinct areas comprise the heart of the matter of individual justice. First is the relationship between lawyers and clients. This area presents ethical issues not often addressed. Our rules of ethics tend to assume a one-to-one relationship between client and attorney in a relatively simple case.

Second is the relationship of court-administered compensation distribution schemes set up in mass product cases, such as Dalkon Shield and Agent Orange, with individual claimants. Where pro se litigants are involved, the relationship with litigants may be easier to solve.

Third is the obligation of the court itself to individual litigants. The judge should, it is submitted, expose himself or herself on a person-to-person basis to the emotional and other needs of the litigants. This proposition requires a shift from the traditional Anglo-American jurisprudential view that the common law judge is an oracle on high, muffled in the black robe of anonymity, uttering the law and deciding the facts without involvement.

We need to rethink the obligation of the judge to our society in mass torts under the present system. Many people, particularly those caught up in mass cases, feel alienated and dehumanized when dealing with our institutions. Their participation in the system is too often, from their view, ineffective. They are items, things, rather than persons. Instead of being treated with the dignity and inviolability deemed essential by philosophers such as Kant or Buber, they are anonymous recipients of a form of justice they do not understand—players in a kind of lottery of awards and rejections from our system of law.

We can ameliorate the baneful effects of our sometimes cold and dispassionate system without losing too much desirable efficiency in handling mass cases. We have spent great resources and time thinking about the efficiency issues as reflected, for example, in the American Law Institute's work on complex litigation, mass torts, and compensation, in the American Bar Association's and others' attempts to deal with disasters, and in our cases on class actions, bankruptcy, and other forms of consolidation.

The ethical area has received little attention except indirectly in connection with fees. Even fees are treated primarily as an aspect of transaction costs. Reasonableness hearings in class actions also often skirt the ethical and caring issues.

Aside from a few studies by the Rand Corporation on what clients expect of litigations—and these were made in connection with traditional single tort claimants' cases—and in the few reports indicating how relatively few persons who might make claims actually do sue, there is almost no research in this field. Further research and thinking are required.

Let us touch upon a few aspects of attorney-client problems in mass torts. In the extensive *Manville* asbestos bankruptcy proceedings, one opinion contains reports indicating administrative settlement of hundreds of cases at once. This experience was duplicated in settlements in litigated asbestos matters involving the Brooklyn Navy Yard and power station cases, as well as in DES cases. A deal is struck between plaintiff's counsel and defendant's counsel for a total sum to be allocated for all of the "inventory" of the plaintiff's attorney. How is that sum to be divided among all the clients? At this point, conflicts of interest arise. Some attorneys use a court-appointed special master to assist in the division and to immunize the attorney against future complaints of clients.

Many attorneys do maintain appropriate contact with their clients even in mass cases. The close rapport between attorney and clients in some of the DES cases is patent. At the same time, there is reason to be dubious about whether this relationship is maintained where there are hundreds or thousands of clients or in large class, bankruptcy, or like actions.

An article on the profession's role, in the National Law Journal's special edition on Environmental Matters and Lack of Due Process of September 1, 1992, provides anecdotal material about clients' bitterness at lawyers' lack of communication with them. There appears, for example, to have been lack of effective communication between members of the class and their attorneys in the settlement of the Reichhold Chemical Company plant explosion in Columbia, Mississippi.

The recent research by Rand and others indicates that, to a large degree, satisfaction or dissatisfaction of litigants with the justice system is based on their expectations that they will participate in a litigation. They seem to prefer a formal trial or arbitration to settlement, even where that might lead to less money or more delay. Settlement and dignity of litigations are, however, not inconsistent.

How is the lawyer for the plaintiffs to keep in touch with all the clients while he or she is working out a reasonable settlement? Will he or she permit one or a few objectors to put the whole settlement at risk?

An example from the asbestos cases is the conflict attorneys face when they have both seriously injured—for example, mesothelioma cases—and potentially injured—for example, pleural plaque—clients. Shall the attorney push all cases at once or advocate first for the most seriously injured? In the Boston settlements, the cases sent to Philadelphia by the Multi-District Litigation Panel and in the *Manville* settlement, this was and is a key issue. Some attorneys and judges want the less serious cases put on the "back burner."

An even more difficult problem arises in the asbestos matter. How shall attorneys provide for present, as opposed to future, claimants? In the original *Manville* settlement, attorneys insisted on paying people in full in the order of claims they had filed. All the available money was quickly exhausted, leaving nothing for the hundreds of thousands of claimants that would come later—most represented by attorneys who, with their earlier clients, had received almost all available trust funds. Eventually, all the separate bankruptcy and other trust funds should be combined in a single administration providing less overhead, and therefore more assets for those injured.

Turning to the court's responsibility, in the Agent Orange case, for example, hearings were held all over the country. The judge listened to some six hundred people and received hundreds of telephone and written communications. He was struck by the deep emotional underpinnings of the litigation. The fact that the science did not support a viable cause of action did not warrant ignoring those cries from the heart for justice.

In administering the funds available from the Agent Orange settlement, the court tried to take these matters of claimant distress into account. It has, for example, a large bank of telephones run by Aetna, the disbursing agent, to receive inquiries from veterans. It tries to assist veterans in obtaining compensation under the scheme set up by the court as well as from the government's Veterans Administration program. It has provided an appeal system set up under a sympathetic former corporation counsel of New York City, W. Bernard Richland, to take account of the special problems of the veterans most in need of help. It has funded a national legal service for veterans in Washington, D.C., that has produced explanatory materials and treatises to assist veterans in obtaining help from the court-administered funds, from the VA, and from other agencies. There is a hot line to help families obtain services from over seventy funded family social and medical service programs throughout the country and from other agencies. Over 140,000 people have received these medical-social services. The system is expensive, but necessary. How it should be improved in future cases is not evident.

In the Dalkon Shield cases, where many of the claimants proceed pro se, the administering court agency has trained paraprofessionals to work with the claimants and explain procedures. It has produced literature designed to give individual claimants a sense of participation. How well this works is not clear.

In Agent Orange, Dalkon Shield, and like cases a modified technique of ombudspersons serving independently of the court, the compensating agency, or any party is worth considering.

In the asbestos cases, where some attorneys have thousands of clients, there is good reason to believe that many clients are not in contact with their attorneys and that they have little understanding of the nature or status of their cases. There is little of the traditional one-to-one client-attorney relationship.

The court assigned the Manville Trust reorganization found from unsolicited letters that in many instances clients felt abandoned. The Trust does communicate with the relatively small number of pro se claimants to explain the present state of the settlement, but it has felt inhibited about communicating directly with those who were formally represented by attorneys. That some of these attorneys do not keep in touch with their clients is evident from the many settlements long since entered into that have never been consummated because the attorneys, having had no real continuing contact with the claimant, could not fill out the simple final forms giving details of the claims. We need to rethink the rules against the court going past the lawyer, directly to the client. Perhaps materials jointly produced by the plaintiffs' attorneys and the Trust, under the aegis of the court, might be useful. With more than two hundred thousand claims made on the Manville Asbestos Trust to date, and hundreds of thousands more likely, the matter is not insignificant.

In the Agent Orange case, more than a half million telephone calls have been logged, and tens of thousands of people have been contacted by letter and hot line in administering help to tens of thousands of people through the social agencies funded in every state and Puerto Rico. Over ten thousand appeals from decisions of the disbursing agent have been heard by the Special Appeals Master.

In the Dalkon Shield litigation, there are hundreds of thousands of cases. As indicated, attempts are made to contact individual clients by trust employees.

In the proposals made in connection with possible atomic plant explosions by the President's Commission, we potentially deal, as in Bhopal and Chernobyl, with millions of claimants. This issue of personal contact and explanation was not covered in the Commissioner's final report. Presumably in such a disaster, radio, TV, and the print press would constitute the communication nexus.

If the costs of communicating become too great, efficiency will be adversely affected. Yet the problems of individual contact cannot be ignored.

We need to think of the relationship between plaintiff and attorney or plaintiff and court in a less inhibited way than we have in the past. For example, one federal judge has suggested that class action representation by attorneys be put up for bid. If this method of choosing class counsel is used, one of the conditions of the request for bids should be to explain how individuals in the class will be kept informed and provide input. Judges need to consider how class action hearings can more effectively integrate the claimants into the proceedings. As a practical matter, of course, getting more people involved in settlement may make a peaceful disposition much more difficult.

In the LILCO-Shoreham case, a number of hearings were held throughout the district, both at night and during the day, so that people involved in the Shoreham atomic plant controversy could be heard. The hearings might have been more productive had the attorneys, judge, and special master produced a document to explain to those who were to appear what was involved and what the difficulties were. It would have helped focus the discussion.

In DES cases, with the assistance of a special master, hundreds of cases were settled. After the settlements, one judge sat down with many of the DES claimants in chambers and heard their harrowing stories. The ability to address the court, with a reporter present, seemed to provide a catharsis for those who believed themselves harmed by DES. Many of them complained that they could not get health insurance for themselves or their children; a class action would have provided for this contingency and other needs of the group.

The problem of empathy versus impartiality and aloofness is not an easy one for the courts. Even in a medical model, empathy may be dangerous since subjectivity may interfere with dispassionate analysis and good judgment required of the professional. The problems are compounded and may be more difficult in the legal setting. Nevertheless, we must consider parting from a traditional colder model.

The sense that we must address the matter is confirmed by what has happened, and is happening, in connection with sentencing, where the courts and the law appear to be going in a direction contrary to the one here proposed for mass torts and disasters. The one-to-one relationship of the sentencing judge to the defendant has been largely eroded by mechanical guidelines and harsh minimum sentences that may have had a disastrous impact on the soul of the courts and justice. In the fields of drugs and crime, the legislatures' solutions seem largely designed on public relations grounds rather than on the utilitarian needs of our society and of individuals.

What further research on mass cases should be done by organizations such as Rand, the American Law Institute, the American Bar Association Foundation, and the law schools? What is happening out in the field between clients and attorneys in mass cases? What is, and should be, the role of the courts in mass cases?

Finally, is it sound to conclude that even when a judge has no great discretion to affect what happens in individual cases, he or she must still strive to be more sensitive to the people before him or her and to their needs in mass cases? In this time of increasing public alienation from lawyers and the law, the legitimacy of our legal institutions depends upon the individual's belief that he or she counts in the system and that we lawyers and judges are here to serve all the people.

Should not judges and lawyers continue to reiterate in some organized and systematic way their sense that there but for the grace of God go we? Must we not stand for a moment in the shoes of the people we serve and judge if we are to meet our responsibility to ourselves, the law, and society?

Traditional tort concepts are only the starting point in attempting to solve the numerous thorny problems which arise when thousands of plaintiffs sue multiple defendants in federal and state jurisdictions throughout the nation. How our courts, as well as the other branches of our federal and state governments, are able to cope with this mushrooming caseload is, in a real and important sense, a test of the ability of our political institutions to meet the challenge of a unique type of litigation. The problems associated with mass tort litigation range all the way from issues of jurisdiction and conflicts of law, to perplexing determinations of causation, to unique ethical dilemmas. The last category—ethical issues confronting judges, plaintiffs, and defense counsel—is the main focus of the discussion in the next few chapters.

If the reader has the impression from the forceful way that I state some of my views in the following chapters that I am certain of either the broad or narrow details, he or she would be mistaken. I have the greatest respect for the views of those judges, lawyers, and academics who believe that case-by-case treatment of claims must be preserved as against class actions and consolidations as a way of deciding large numbers of cases more quickly, cheaply, and with more uniform and predictable results for both the injured and the injuring.[16]

CHAPTER 2

THE LAW'S REACTION TO DISASTERS[1]

Men and women are responsible for events, technology, and products that cause masses of people to suffer death, disability, and large property losses. These disasters are routine in the sense that they are bound to occur—the only questions are when and how. The disasters we create are growing in severity and frequency. Dangers are intensified by increases in world population, concentration of people in urban areas, manipulation of the environment, creation of new products through chemical and biological engineering, and closer links between various parts of the world through trade and exchanges of technology.[2] Differences in sophistication, economic power, and access to government between those creating the new technology and those who are exposed to it also enhance the dangers.[3]

For the purpose of this discussion we will put aside the ultimate disasters such as war, particularly nuclear war, and such horrors as famine and pestilence—though even the latter are now probably attributable as much to human folly as to nature's occasional cruelties.[4] This discussion is concerned with disasters for which a legal entity may be found financially responsible.

Disasters are of particular concern to lawyers[5] because we, like the law, are dedicated to the general proposition that people should be compensated when they are harmed by others. Our goal has been to provide prompt and full payment to those who are harmed, by those who caused the harm, while minimizing the overall costs to the system.[6] We fall far short of this goal in connection with many disasters. Compensation is often delayed, expensive, and erratic.[7]

The question is: given our current legal, technical, social and political development, can we handle claims arising from mass tort disasters more effectively? The power exists: the federal government can legislate in problem areas.[8] But whether and how federal—or state—power should be exercised in the area of disaster claims management is not at all clear.

The goal of this chapter is to help pose this issue more precisely and aid in formulating ways of addressing it. First, from a litigator's point of view, there is described a typology of disasters and some of the problems the legal system has had with each type. Then, from a judge's point of view, there is indicated what is required to manage litigations arising from mass torts. Noted are some of the many bits and pieces of judicial procedure, common law practice, and legislation we have developed in meeting disasters in the past and some thoughts on how those tools can be improved to deal more effectively with the problems of the future. Finally, there are some proposals for going forward with the inquiry.

I conclude that, in dealing with disasters, a national system of health and disability insurance for all is desirable. Absent such a thorough change, the law can handle small- and medium-scale disasters such as airplane crashes with relatively modest changes in substance and procedure. Massive disasters, such as those caused by asbestos, mandate major changes in substance and practice, such as the creation of a National Disaster Court if the tort system is continued for mass torts, or the use of administrative remedies and of international tribunals.

Classification of disasters either for purpose of analysis or for the purpose of triggering the operation of special substantive or procedural rules is to a large degree arbitrary. For example, whether and for what purposes events such as the deaths and injuries resulting from the gas leak at Bhopal, India, should be treated as mass disasters rather than normal tort cases are largely matters of judgment.

Although I emphasize procedure and practice, the primacy of tort theory in deciding how disastrous events should be treated by adjudicative and legislative bodies must be acknowledged.[9] Questions such as who should bear the risks, how the risks should be shared or shifted, and what role insurance should play are central to any sound analysis. Traditional tort theories provide some answers to these questions. There are times, however, when practical administrative problems and costs may overwhelm present substantive theory. In some respects, a mass tort disaster presents this situation.

A. TYPES OF DISASTERS

1. CLEAR CAUSE—SINGLE EVENT—INJURIES PROXIMATE IN TIME AND SPACE

Disasters may result from a cataclysmic event in which the connection between the injury and the event is clear. Typical of this category are airplane crashes, leaks of poisonous gas from industrial plants like that in Bhopal, and explosions at petrochemical plants and storage facilities like that in Mexico City.[10] The Beverly Hills Supper Club fire and the Kansas City Skywalk collapse might also be placed in this category.[11]

In this class of disasters there is usually no serious question about what injuries resulted from the event. Causation in the broad sense is obvious. Even though the question of why the calamity occurred may be unanswered, and may determine the ultimate assessment of financial responsibility for damages, there is no doubt that someone should pay —putting aside the fraudulent claimants who place themselves in harm's way *after* the harm has occurred.

In order to facilitate compensation, some serious legal questions may have to be addressed. For example, a decision on choice of substantive law may be required if the nationality or state citizenship of those injured or responsible is different from the place of injury or the forum of adjudication. The present system of choice of law answers this sort of question with difficulty.

The issue of government liability has also arisen in this category of disasters. The 1947 Texas City disaster, in which ships containing ammonium nitrate fertilizer exploded, is a well-known example. The 273 suits brought against the government on behalf of the eight thousand persons injured were dismissed because of limitations in the Federal Tort Claims Act based on the government's prerogative to immunize itself from suit.[12] Such limitations seem difficult to justify. In their study Catastrophic Accidents in Government Programs,[13] Professors Rosenthal, Korn, and Lubman call the Texas City case a "discouraging example" of how these matters should not be handled.[14] It is congressional policy to provide compensation for a peacetime incident involving a United States nuclear-powered ship.[15] Why not for any government ship? Why not for any government-caused disaster?

Some disasters in this category, such as major airplane crashes, have been handled relatively effectively by our tort system.[16] Lawyers have utilized consolidation procedures, class actions, collateral estoppel techniques, and informal agreements among themselves in order to speed resolution of claims.[17] Nevertheless, in many cases compensation remains uncertain, expensive, and delayed.[18]

2. CLEAR CAUSE—MULTIPLE EVENTS—INJURIES NONPROXIMATE IN PLACE

Some mass torts may result from a single product manufactured by one or a small group of producers where the link between the damage to any individual and the product is highly probable. In this category, widespread but precise injuries are usually revealed shortly after the event. The most notorious case involved the drug thalidomide. It was produced by a relatively few European chemical plants and caused an unusual syndrome of birth defects all over the world.[19] A few of the infants might have been born with the same birth defects even if their mothers had not taken the drug, but in the majority of cases proof of causation was not a difficult problem once the necessary scientific studies had been made. Some of the claims brought by toxic shock syndrome victims against tampon manufacturers[20] and the cases involving intrauterine contraceptive devices[21] may also fall into this category.

The legal system has not been wholly successful in its treatment of this class of cases, in part because of difficulties in establishing causation and in part because of limitations on consolidation and other litigation management devices.[22] Variations in law among forums have made these problems particularly vexing.

3. UNCLEAR CAUSE—MULTIPLE EVENTS—INJURIES NONPROXIMATE IN TIME AND PLACE

Serious causation questions may arise in cases in which an individual suffers an injury which is common to the general population but which may be the result of exposure to a particular product. Compensation must turn on whether the person would have sustained the injury had there been no exposure. Such serious causation questions have been litigated in the radiation cases arising from above-ground test explosions of nuclear devices by the United States Army, with some plaintiffs establishing causation and some failing to do so.[23] Some would put in this category (as well as in category 4, below) claims of lung cancer victims that their illnesses resulted from asbestos or tobacco exposure.[24]

Scientific methods of determining causation for purposes of diagnosis and medical treatment are useful, but not easily transferable to the causal problems the law faces in litigation.[25] Plaintiffs in these cases meet serious obstacles in attempting to prove causation and in overcoming other substantive and procedural barriers, while courts deal with difficult questions in determining the admissibility of, and the weight that should be given to, causation evidence.[26]

4. UNCLEAR CAUSE—MULTIPLE EVENTS—INJURIES NONPROXIMATE IN TIME AND PLACE—IDENTITIES OF BOTH PRODUCERS AND INJURED UNCLEAR

We can expect more situations in which there appears to be an increased incidence of a fairly widespread disease, but it is not clear which, if any, persons suffer from it as a result of exposure to a particular toxic substance, and it is also not evident which of many producers is responsible for any particular injury. This is the situation that may exist in the DES cases, in many hazardous waste injury cases, and in cases where workers have moved from job to job and have been exposed to toxic substances over many years.[27]

These problems are compounded when there is a long latency period between exposure and the manifestation of symptoms. During this extended period, other factors may cause the disease, complicating the problem of proving causation. Insurance carriers and producers may change over the years, creating questions of who is responsible and who should pay.

Although some courts have used novel theories to allow plaintiffs to recover,[28] the law has had serious difficulties with these cases absent special legislation[29] or broad interpretation of workers' compensation statutes.[30] Moreover, in some states, statutes of limitations may bar a tort action before claimants even know that an injury has occurred.[31]

B. JURISDICTIONS IMPLICATED

The problems in dealing with these cases may be exacerbated depending upon the number and kinds of jurisdictions implicated.

1. INTRASTATE

The simplest disaster is one involving events and parties from only one state. The substantive and procedural law in such a case is uniform. There may be need for some procedural and substantive changes, such as further utilization of statewide consolidation of cases[32] or more realistic statute of limitations rules,[33] but these can be provided by usual methods of law reform at the state level.

Nonetheless, these conventional means cannot address all potential problems. Even when a large fire[34] or the collapse of a part of a building[35] appears to a layman to be intrastate in character, concurrent federal and state court jurisdiction may lead to cases being brought in both court systems, creating serious management problems. The relatively simple case of a liquefied gas tank explosion on Staten Island, New York, for example, ended up in federal court as well as in a number of New York state courts.[36]

2. INTERSTATE

Most disasters, particularly those for which causal attribution is difficult, involve people and institutions from many states. The cases may be initiated in state and federal courts all over the country, and the applicable substantive law and procedural practice may vary enormously. The Bendectin and asbestos litigations fall into this category.[37]

Increasingly, disasters cross national boundaries. Technology and trade send dangerous substances across national lines. Multinational companies have alter egos in many countries. What laws apply, where the suits are to be brought, and what country's standards of compensation are to be used are all important questions.[38]

The Bhopal disaster presents one example of a multinational problem. In Bhopal, technology and management were exported by a United States corporation, leading to mass injury in India and to many unanswered legal questions.[39]

Other kinds of transnational claims are in the offing. How, for example, will we treat the claims that are likely to arise in North America and Europe from the huge property and health losses that will be attributed by some to acid rain, which may be caused by a combination of many pollution sources?[40] Creation of international tribunals may be in order. Global warming attributable largely to industrialized nations or ozone layer depletion provide such hazards to the world that only international political decisions offer a means of adequate control; the tort systems of individual countries are practically useless in this geopolitical arena.

C. DESIRABLE CONDITIONS FOR DISASTER MANAGEMENT BY COURTS

Conditions for court management of claims arising from disasters might be improved in a number of ways. I shall state seven objectives categorically without extended discussion. These principles are developed further in part D of this chapter, which examines presently existing practice and procedure, and they serve as a basis for the tentative proposals made in part E.

1. CONCENTRATION OF DECISION MAKING

Power to speak for each side in a mass tort dispute needs to be concentrated in the hands of one or at most a few persons.[41] Optimally, that person or persons should be capable of making decisions and committing all the parties on one side of the case to carrying out those decisions. This requirement would extend to the representatives of the claimants, to the representatives of those against whom claims are made, and to the court or other tribunal. The difficulties in litigating asbestos cases are a prime example of the problems caused by lack of coordination among defendants.[42] Some asbestos defendants have agreed to make substantial contributions to a fund, and many are integrating their efforts as insurance runs out and more and more companies are driven into bankruptcy. Plaintiffs' counsel are under greater pressure to come to terms with each other, but questions of ego and the urge to demonstrate who can become the richest have limited cooperation.

A committee of state trial judges originally concerned only with asbestos litigation has now expanded their committee to include all mass torts.[43] Ten federal trial judges handling asbestos cases have met informally on their own initiative over the last few years. State judges also have organized to deal with asbestos cases, and the two groups remain in touch through a liaison judge.[44] The federal judges asked the Multidistrict Litigation Panel to consolidate the federal cases in one court.[45] The MDL Panel then reversed its pattern of refusing to consolidate asbestos cases and sent all cases to one federal judge as recommended by the group of ten.[46]

Unfortunately, the asbestos cases were sent by the MDL Panel to a single federal judge rather late in the litigation, only after many large corporations had been bankrupted.[47] This protracted legal struggle resulted in hundreds of millions of dollars in unnecessary fees for lawyers, overcompensated some claimants while undercompensating others, led to long delays in paying worthy claimants, and tied up our state and federal courts.[48]

2. SINGLE FORUM

The basic legal and factual decisions governing disaster claims should be made in a single forum.

3. SINGLE, KNOWN SUBSTANTIVE LAW

It is essential that there be a single, easily determined and authoritative substantive law applied to the litigation so that the parties know in advance what the law provides. Even more advantageous, of course, would be a uniform law in place *before* the disaster occurs so that the parties could take precautions such as purchasing insurance—if available at affordable rates[49]—or decline to engage in activities that may prove too costly in terms of possible future liability.[50] Proposed national product liability legislation is one attempt to achieve this goal.[51]

4. Support to Trier

The court or other tribunal needs facilities and personnel such as magistrates, special masters,[52] and clerical workers[53] to extend its reach, and to act as both buffer and conduit between the trier and the parties and other interested individuals and organizations.

5. Flexible, Controlled Fact-Finding

Reasonable fact-finding procedures are essential. This goal, however, does not imply that the jury need necessarily be eliminated. In particular, flexible rules on the admissibility of evidence, such as Rules 702 to 705 of the Federal Rules of Evidence governing the use of experts, are needed, especially in litigation in which scientific evidence is important.[54] But liberal rules on admissibility require the judge to exercise firm control to ensure that the evidence produced by experiments and data gathering is appropriate for use at trial.[55]

6. Cap on Award and Method of Allocation

Particularly large disasters probably require a cap on the total cost to defendants,[56] a method of allocating the cost among defendants, and a sure source of funds. The Superfund Group proposals for compensation,[57] the Price-Anderson Act multi-hundred-million cap for a nuclear power plant accident,[58] and the Wellington asbestos group proposals[59] might serve as models for addressing these concerns.[60] Although awkward, the bankruptcy approach represents, in part, an attempt to meet this and other needs.[61]

7. Single Distribution Plan

The method of distribution to the claimants should require little or no further adjudication. Essentially, a workers' compensation–like scheme crafted for the individual case is necessary. Punitive damages and large claims of pain and suffering are probably impractical and undesirable.[62] The workers' compensation framework can be equitable because in return for forgoing large recoveries, workers are assured compensation even when there is insufficient proof of specific causation—provided that the plan takes account of such factors as inflation and new hazards.

Some form of a needs test might be useful to identify and compensate those who need help the most, but under our mixed capitalist-welfare system this refinement may not be a realistic possibility. There are so many collateral income sources—pensions, Aid to Families with Dependent Children, Social Security disability, workers' compensation, private insurance, and the like—that accounting for collateral benefits may create more problems than it solves.

D. PROCEDURAL TOOLS AND MODELS

Unfortunately, we already have had fairly wide experience in all types of disasters. In dealing with them on an ad hoc common law basis or through sporadic legislation, our lawyers and lawmakers have shown a great deal of ingenuity and effective pragmatism.[63] Often, however, the cost of the solutions has been very high. For example, in the asbestos cases, of the tens of billions that will be expended by defendants, insurers, and courts, considerably less than a third will go to the injured.[64]

A systematic approach to existing tools and models might suggest treatment under, at least, the following headings: (1) Who will bring and defend claims, and how shall these activities be controlled and financed? (2) What tribunals have jurisdiction and how can they acquire power over all claimants and defendants? (3) What substantive law applies and how can it be made uniform in the dispute? (4) What procedural law applies and how can it be used to minimize transaction costs such as attorney fees and court time? (5) What compensation scheme can be utilized—for example, one based upon need, damage, prefixed sums, lump-sum or periodic payments, or individually determined awards? (6) What are the sources of the awards?

The following discussion in this chapter takes a somewhat different perspective, asking: What are some of the devices that have been used in the past? What possibilities do they present for improving our handling of mass disasters? Can we combine the devices already tested in new ways to meet our new problems?

1. MULTIDISTRICT LITIGATION AND OTHER CONSOLIDATION PROCEDURES

The use of a multidistrict judicial panel to switch cases from all federal courts to one federal judge for control of preliminary motions, discovery, and settlement has proven useful in many cases.[65] Transfer of cases within the federal system for full trial under the multidistrict litigation statute for the convenience of the parties and in the interest of justice would be a helpful auxiliary.[66]

It may be desirable for states to consider analogous provisions for transfer and consolidation of pretrial procedures when consolidation for the complete trial might prove to be unmanageable. Some of our large states have judicial divisions and departments almost as complex as those in the federal system. In New York, cases have been assigned to single judges providing effective consolidation. In the DES cases the single issue of market share was assigned to one judge to control decisions throughout the state.

Cases commenced in state courts cannot be included in the present federal multidistrict mechanism unless they can be removed to federal court. Under the Commerce Clause,[67] Congress has the power to transfer to the federal court those state cases not presently removable, on the ground that in disputes of this size and nature, national issues predominate.[68] Stays of competing state litigation are also possible.[69]

In some instances it might be more sensible to send all the cases to the court system of the state with the predominant interest. In part this can be accomplished through federal stays, application of *forum non conveniens* concepts, and deferential refusals to accept jurisdiction. A more direct and comprehensive approach could be provided by Congress, based on its constitutional power to regulate federal court jurisdiction,[70] its authority to legislate in matters affecting interstate commerce[71]—including matters within the province of state and local governments[72]—and the obligation imposed on states by the Supremacy Clause.[73] Under such a scheme, federal and state cases would be transferred to a single state forum, provided perhaps—as a matter of comity—that the state court consented.

The American Law Institute approved in 1993 an extensive plan that would allow a federal panel of judges to transfer both state and federal cases to a single federal or state judge. It provides for a choice of law decision by the transferee judge that would permit application of one substantive law to any issue and, in effect, would afford national service. The transferee courts would supervise the case for all purposes, including trial. In theory at least, the present federal multidistrict transferee judge only has power over pretrial phases of the case. The ALI proposal was not limited to mass cases. While I would fully support adoption of the ALI plan for mass litigations as a masterful and elegant solution of many of the procedural problems, it seems doubtful that any political support can be generated for them in their present form, applicable to all cases.

It seems improbable that, absent national legislation, voluntary cooperation among the state and national judicial systems can streamline disaster litigation. The National Center for State Courts, for example, organized an excellent "Judicial Administration Working Group on Asbestos Litigation."[74] It made many useful suggestions for facilitation of insurance claims, use of alternative dispute resolution methods, pretrial and trial procedures, and model standing orders on such matters as the form of complaints, standard interrogatories, and the like.[75] But the impact of its work on the sprawling asbestos personal injury litigation seems to have been marginal at best, and it has had no apparent effect on the second wave of asbestos problems involving removal of asbestos from schools and other buildings.[76] Similar well-intentioned efforts by the Federal Judicial Center probably will also turn out to have had only minor impact on controlling this litigation.[77]

Some methods that rely on federal-state coordination and cooperation are feasible. Joint management of state and federal cases is possible. There is no reason why a state judge and a federal judge cannot jointly decide discovery issues, assigning a single magistrate or special master to both the state and federal cases. In cooperation with state judges I have used this technique in the asbestos and the DES litigations. Lawyers may press their discovery in one tribunal and arrange in one court by either stipulation or order of the presiding judges for a test trial or settlement that will control the entire federal-state litigation.

Some formal guidelines or procedures are desirable to avoid the lack of consensus present in some cases, such as the Kansas City Skywalk case,[78] that leads to unnecessary conflicts and disputes. Federal-state judicial councils,[79] existing in many of our states, might provide an appropriate forum, equivalent to that of the present federal multidistrict panel, for switching cases. Legislation is desirable to resolve disputes that cannot be mediated about forum choice.

Even if procedural problems are dealt with, there remain potentially serious choice of law problems. It is clearly desirable to have one substantive law applicable to all related disputes. Modern conflict of laws concepts such as "center of gravity," "national consensus," or "better law" provide a limited basis for uniformity in some instances,[80] but the uniformity problem often presents serious obstacles.[81] For example, in the asbestos cases, differences among the federal circuits and states about the effect of insurance coverage under a variety of policies and insurers have made global settlements more difficult.[82]

State rulings on questions certified by federal courts are sometimes possible,[83] but the difficulties of coordination between the two court systems and the resulting delay are considerable. A federal conflicts of laws in mass torts to replace the often barren and mechanical reference to state law is desirable under the Federal Constitution's Full Faith and Credit Clause.[84]

One solution that has been proposed is federal product liability legislation.[85] That answer has been opposed by many.[86]

An alternative would limit federal legislative action to the circumstances of some mass tort disasters.[87] How such a disaster would be defined, and who or what bodies would make the decision to characterize a series of litigations as warranting special treatment, are among the serious issues that must be considered in deciding whether this approach is practicable.

A victims' compensation fund financed on the basis of market share by producers and divided on some statistical basis among those injured has its attractions.[88] Such a solution may work better if a special tax and compensation scheme is devised. The Superfund toxic waste cleanup fund's provision of a tax reflects one side of this equation.[89] Suggestions have been made for federal legislation to compensate hazardous waste site victims whose medical bills are not covered by insurance.[90]

It may well be desirable to limit federal legislation to the most difficult class of problems—those involving mass cases in which the injuries are nonproximate in time and place and the identities of both the injured and the injuring parties are not clear. These are essentially the toxic tort and pharmaceutical cases. The federal government is so heavily involved in regulation and cleanup of toxic substances that creation of a national substantive policy on toxic mass disasters seems a reasonable step. Control of pharmaceutical and health-related devices is already a duty of the Food and Drug Administration. A limited national product liability statute would have the advantage of leaving most of tort law to be handled in traditional ways pursuant to state law.

2. CLASS ACTIONS

The class action furnishes a useful way of bringing together many plaintiffs and defendants in a single litigation that will bind all the parties. It has limits, required in part by due process. One such limit is the right to opt out. The Bendectin litigation demonstrated that this right may make full use of the class action device impossible under current rules.[91] As a practical matter, however, experienced plaintiff and defense counsel can usually avoid the problem of plaintiffs' opting out of a settlement. Defendants insist on the power to cancel the settlement if enough plaintiffs opt out, but almost never take advantage of such a "walk away" clause. Moreover, the right to opt out does not extend to class actions that seek punitive damages beyond the ability of any company to satisfy, or when the defendant's assets constitutes a limited fund insufficient to pay all claims.[92] The class action may prove useful in controlling such damages—assuming that they are not eliminated as a matter of policy.[93]

We must also remember that class actions are not as well developed in most states as they are in the federal courts. There is, too, the unresolved question in most states of whether state law will permit a state class action judgment to bind out-of-state class members.[94] Such issues can be laid to rest by state legislation and court rule. The Supreme Court in Phillips Petroleum Co. v. Shutts[95] has made it clear that the

Federal Constitution provides no substantial barrier to state expansion of class actions. Congress arguably can extend state court jurisdiction—including personal service—to the limits of fully expanded federal court jurisdiction.[96] After all, Congress theoretically has the power to eliminate all the federal courts except the Supreme Court, and to leave all jurisdiction in the state courts except for the Supreme Court's limited original and appellate jurisdiction.[97]

There are a series of dark and arcane issues on the border of procedure and ethics that need to be addressed in the class action area. How are these mass tort cases to be financed? How are the lead lawyers to be selected?[98] How paid?[99] How is liaison with class members to be maintained? Who decides when and how to settle? The answers to date are far from satisfactory. Whether better answers are possible is not clear.

3. Attorney Cooperation—Specialists and Lead Attorneys

In many instances, attorneys have learned to cooperate among themselves and to select specialists as lead attorneys. They coordinate a series of cases and potential cases with little or no assistance from the courts.[100]

4. Private Settlements—Ad Hoc and Institutional

A number of institutions for mediation and settlement have assumed an increased role in dispute resolution. How successful they will be in cases involving many claimants whose only relationship with each other is the common disaster is not clear. But the attempt to work out private settlements in the asbestos cases or the breast implant cases, for example, is worth studying.[101] Work on dispute management at the Center for Public Resources and various arbitration agencies has been useful in shifting some litigations to Alternative Dispute Resolution procedures (ADR).[102]

One difficulty raising serious questions about private settlements in multiparty cases is determining who can speak with authority for each side. The jockeying among plaintiffs' attorneys for control and for fees is well known.[103] On the defendants' side similar struggles also take place, with insurance companies often fighting for control of litigation and protection from liability exposure.

5. Court Administration and Added Personnel

Federal courts in particular have enhanced their capacity to manage complex litigations through the use of masters and magistrates to supervise discovery,[104] decrees, and settlement.[105] Availability of special funds for added clerks and secretaries also makes it easier to supervise a major litigation. The ability to call in special court-appointed technical experts under Rule 706 of the Federal Rules of Evidence is helpful.[106] A state judge who takes responsibility for a joint federal-state litigation must be given necessary aid and facilities. But how is financing to be arranged when state court budgets are tight? How should the financial burden be allocated between federal and state budgets? Such mundane problems need consideration. The matter is returned to again in chapter 10, The Future.

6. COMPENSATION SCHEMES AND LEGISLATED LIMITS ON LIABILITY

A variety of legislative compensation schemes have been developed.[107] The workers' compensation model is useful, but modest compensation provisions combined with a failure to adjust for inflation and new kinds of injuries have unfortunately led to increased pressure to circumvent the statutes by suing persons other than employers.[108] It is, I think, shocking that only 40 percent of workers' wages lost due to occupational diseases are replaced and only 5 percent of the replacement comes from workers' compensation.[109] Still, the workers' compensation model was helpful, for example, in designing legislation to compensate coal miners for black lung disease.[110]

Were workers' compensation legislation modernized, workers injured by products such as asbestos would collect only workers' compensation, albeit at more realistic payment levels. Third-party suits against asbestos suppliers could then be eliminated without shocking our sense of fairness.

A general compensation plan is feasible. In New Zealand, for example, a form of socialized medicine provides protection.[111] Other compensation can be provided for victims who meet a means test, and additional protection could be made available through insurance carried by those who can afford it. In the United States, actual and threatened litigation attributable to asbestos, toxic substances, and other pollutants has stimulated proposals for legislation with a compensation component.[112]

The cost of the black lung legislation has apparently caused some members of Congress to become disenchanted with this approach. Any general compensation plan as broad as that of New Zealand would seem to be similarly unpalatable to our present leaders. In addition, complex overlapping collateral benefits available through workers' compensation, pensions, private insurance, fringe employment benefits, Medicare, Medicaid, Aid to Families with Dependent Children, Social Security disability, Supplemental Security Income, and other programs make devising a rational scheme of compensation for those in the United States who need help difficult. A small damage award, for example, may cause loss of social welfare benefits worth more than the recovery.

The Superfund Study Group proposed a two-tier system for hazardous waste cases that would provide victims with a workers' compensation–type scheme while allowing those more seriously injured to sue using standard tort law.[113] This proposal is interesting but flawed by its failure to resolve the conflict between the two systems.[114] Moreover, the combination of federal substantive compensation law with a state compensation bureaucracy would be clumsy. To date, there has been no proof that a sufficient number of cases exists to warrant such a scheme.[115] Given the small environment of cases in which causality can be shown— even with the aid of presumptions—federal courts, alone or together with state courts, can handle the situation at the moment. This is true whether a tort or compensation plan is adopted so long as the cases arising from any one local toxic dump are consolidated. Huge increases in cases in the future, however, could overburden the courts, making the Superfund proposal or similar schemes more attractive.

The viability of a compensation scheme would probably depend on the ability of the distribution system to cap liability and to limit recovery. Any limitation on liability constitutes to some extent a subsidy to the industry protected because those injured will not collect compensation otherwise chargeable as a cost to that industry. A cap is a kind of internal tariff paid by the injured. Like a tariff or subsidy, however, it may be justified as a matter of national policy when the insurance industry is refusing adequate liability policies at affordable premiums.[116]

Many of the proposed compensation schemes and plans for limitation of overall liability probably do not fully take into account municipal and other governmental costs such as welfare, disability compensation, and hospital and civic emergency services. Because they shift costs from those who cause harm to government entities, schemes like New Zealand's function as a general public subsidy to those causing harm.

Some payback mechanism seems desirable to ensure that those causing harm pay a substantial portion of their share of the cost. This is partly for reasons of deterrence, but mainly to internalize costs to society within the industry. Any such cost-shifting scheme should channel costs to one or a few parties at fault, with further cost shifting among other parties also at fault—as between suppliers and a manufacturer, for example—handled privately.[117]

Differences in the amount of compensation received by those injured in relatively minor incidents and those injured in mass disasters could raise equal protection objections. Such objections do not seem persuasive in view of court approval of the distinctions drawn in no-fault automobile and workers' compensation plans, the Supreme Court's approval of the Price-Anderson nuclear disaster compensation cap,[118] and the strong support the Supreme Court has given to legislation designed to protect our national economy.[119]

7. CLAIMS COMMISSIONS

A variety of claims commissions have been used in the past to resolve disputes. The claims commission mechanism is particularly suited to dealing with multinational disasters. The Micronesian claims commission, for example, was created to compensate the "losses of Micronesians directly caused by the hostilities of World War II."[120] In its first stage the commission was a binational organization with representatives from Japan and the United States. Each country donated the equivalent of $5 million. In the second phase, a five-person commission composed of two Micronesians and three Americans adjudicated claims against the United States, paying those claims from a $20 million fund provided by the United States. Awards were based upon preestablished values, for example, $50 for a 14-foot ocean-going outrigger sailing canoe, and $5 for a ukulele.[121] The Iranian Claims Commission is another illustration of the use of the claims commission mechanism in an international context.[122]

In the United States, a claims commission was used in connection with the dispute over Tris, a chemical fire retardant used in clothing. The government, through misguided regulations, caused business losses and paid the bill through special Claims Court procedures.[123]

Claims commissions have usually involved either a large fund available in advance or a government's large resources. Can this device be adapted to situations in which the price is paid by private litigants and is not ascertainable at the outset of the litigation? As in the compensation scheme area, fixing maximum liability by legislation could work. We must decide whether a limit on the total amount of liability can be justified and, if so, at what level.

8. INTERNATIONAL CONVENTIONS

On an international scale, there is a trend toward individual nations taking more responsibility, through treaties and agreements, for actions that have international implications. The Bhopal disaster will probably increase pressure in this direction. The International Convention on Civil Liability for Oil Pollution requires nations that own or license oil tankers to be strictly liable for damages resulting from spills.[124] Such nations are required to make contributions to a fund that will be used to compensate those suffering accident damage. The 1960 Paris Convention in the Field of Nuclear Energy covers a number of European states much as the Price-Anderson Act governs liability in the United States.[125]

International efforts in pollution liability have not been entirely successful outside the oil spill area.[126] Despite Canadian and Scandinavian efforts, no agreement has been reached on assessing liability for acid rain damage.[127] The 1979 Convention on Long-Range Transboundary Air Pollution includes pledges by each nation to limit air pollution emissions.[128] No specific emission limits are set, however, and no liability is imposed for violation of the pledges. Many similar agreements exist, but it is questionable whether any of these provide appropriate vehicles for compensation if injuries occur.[129]

9. HYBRID GOVERNMENT-SPONSORED PROTECTION PLANS

A number of proposed or existing pieces of legislation furnish useful models for dealing with disasters. For example, many statutory safeguards exist for the operation of nuclear reactors, including use of standing advisory committees and provisions for evacuation plans. The United States government requires detailed insurance plans of reactor operators and provides indemnification of up to $500 million for "a nuclear incident" in this country and $100 million for "incidents occurring outside the United States."[130] A "tax" on nuclear power plants pays part of the cost of the government insurance.[131] Congress has empowered federal district courts to provide "a plan for the disposition of pending claims and the distribution of remaining funds" when "public liability may exceed" coverage.[132] Such provisions are reminiscent of proposed European Economic Community proposals to limit liability for any single product liability disaster.[133]

The Legislative Drafting and Research Fund of Columbia University has done extensive work providing studies and draft legislation to deal with the escape of radioactive substances from nuclear power plants and injuries from toxic chemical dumps.[134] We may be at a stage where we can generalize beyond these special cases to other situations.

The proposals of the "Superfund Section 301(e) Study Group" on methods of improving legal remedies for injuries and damages from hazardous wastes are useful though, as I have indicated, inadequate. The 1982 report to Congress resulted from the work of a distinguished panel of lawyers and scholars. The report concludes that there are "identifiable barriers to recovery, and that available remedies may not be adequate to deal with many valid claims that may emerge."[135] It includes a number of separate proposals, including a compensation scheme involving insurance based on an industry tax, a no-fault remedy, changes in state law, and individual suits combined with a compensation system.[136] Some of these proposals may be adaptable to other forms of disasters.

10. SPECIALIZED COURTS

Use of specialized courts to assume jurisdiction over a series of related disputes is possible. Congress, for example, has provided for a special court to handle railroad reorganization, and an Emergency Court of Appeals staffed by regular federal judges to deal with price-fixing issues during and after World War II.[137] A Temporary Court of Appeals of the United States dealing with oil and gas matters was created.[138] A special federal court to handle disasters, with judges assigned by the Chief Justice, the Judicial Panel on Multidistrict Litigation, or some other body, is worth considering.

Litigation such as that in asbestos might be handled more easily in this manner. Judges from various parts of the country could sit en banc or try cases individually as needed. Appeals would then be taken to one court of appeals. One possible appellate toxic tort court is the Court of Appeals for the Federal Circuit, which specializes in patents but has a great deal of scientific expertise. It has the best technical-scientific library of any court in the country, and its five members typically hire lawyers with scientific backgrounds as clerks.[139] From this perspective, use of the bankruptcy court as a way of centralizing many asbestos litigations was an interesting initiative that achieved part of the goal of a single trial and appellate court.[140]

There has always been a reluctance in the bar and Congress to create specialized courts that may outlive their usefulness and leave federal judges without posts. The objection would not apply to a single national disaster court staffed by generalist judges assigned only as needed. Regular court of appeals judges could constitute a majority of the appellate panel of such a court—though Federal Circuit judges experienced in science might play a useful role.

E. PROPOSALS FOR CHANGE

All would agree that we can and should improve safety devices and government and private regulation both here and abroad to limit the frequency and magnitude of disasters. Government regulation and control must serve as the first and main line of defense. The prospect of huge tort recoveries, of course, can be a strong factor in inducing large responsible manufacturers to exercise care. But the threat is unlikely to have any significant deterrent effect on thinly capitalized, "fly-by-night" operators who may be responsible for a disproportionate number of disasters. Moreover, it can have the undesirable effect of keeping valuable drugs and other products off the market when the benefits to society outweigh the risks.[141] When the public benefits from such products, it should pay a large part of the costs incurred by the relatively few unlucky enough to be injured.

If dangerous products are to be taken off the market and dangerous situations remedied quickly, society must promptly receive and act upon information about injuries.[142] Government regulation and warning label requirements offer the best initial mechanism, one based on information such as that available from Centers for Disease Control studies and from injury reports required by the Food and Drug Administration and other government agencies.

Nevertheless, we must recognize that this prophylactic approach cannot be perfect. Government agencies are often underfunded; the effects of our scientific and technical initiatives are not fully knowable; risks must be taken to obtain the benefits of new advances; and carelessness, ignorance, and greed sometimes interfere. Watchdog private consumer and advocacy groups are helpful, but they are generally underfunded, limiting their effectiveness.

Disasters inevitably will occur. Will the law be prepared to meet them in the best way possible?

Some of the proposals for reform that should be considered are relatively simple—for example, the Superfund Study Group's suggestion that obstacles to state court actions be removed.[143] As already indicated, many procedural devices for dealing with such cases have already been developed.[144] Other more innovative approaches need to be considered as well.

At least in instances in which the effect of a toxic substance is potentially widespread, but the causal connection between exposure and specific injuries is uncertain, a national plan of health insurance and comprehensive disability insurance providing limited protection should be considered. Such a plan would expand upon already existing Social Security and Supplemental Security Income programs. The cost of any increased incidence of disease attributable to a specific product such as benzene or asbestos could be charged back to the industry by the government as a tax. Present workers' compensation and unemployment insurance schemes have such mechanisms. Additional protection would be optional: the middle class could purchase first-party insurance for loss of high earnings, and workers could receive added coverage in the form of employment fringe benefits.

It seems likely that over time such a rational compensation scheme can generate significant support in the United States. Industry, faced with huge liabilities and lack of reasonably priced insurance, may rethink its opposition to comprehensive compensation plans. Despite the many problems with the proposal, in my opinion it offers the most elegant—and in the long run the most equitable—solution. The poor would continue to get less than the rich, but they would, as a group, receive more than they do now.

Other steps can and should be taken during the interim period before comprehensive health insurance and general disability payment legislation is adopted. The following proposals should be considered to meet the immediate need.

1. NATIONAL DISASTER COURT

At the national level, a Federal National Disaster Court could be authorized. No judges or personnel need to be assigned to it on a permanent basis. The Chief Justice of the Supreme Court could assign Article III judges with expertise in the particular type of litigation involved for temporary duty as needed. In especially difficult cases, a number of trial judges could be assigned at the same time. Clerical and other personnel could be authorized by the Administrative Office of the Federal Courts. Experience already exists in transferring judges and personnel, as, for example, in the antidrug program in southern Florida and in the visiting judges program in the federal courts.[145]

This proposal would also conform to the Bar Harbor Resolution.[146] That policy statement recognized the need to assign particular judges with requisite experience to unusually difficult cases.

The questions of what circumstances and what body would trigger the Disaster Court's operation could be handled in a number of ways. The triggering criteria would need to be spelled out.[147] They should be broader than those in the present federal multidistrict litigation law,[148] under which the asbestos litigation was denied multidistrict treatment for many years until 1992.[149] The Disaster Court's great power over procedure and choice of law should be activated only in the most extraordinary cases. A disaster sufficient to trigger its operation should be substantial—for example, one that causes at least $500 million in potential damages, injures more than five hundred people, and involves the laws of at least two jurisdictions. These parameters—used here only for illustrative purposes—are substantially more than is required to constitute an "extraordinary nuclear occurrence," which triggers such matters as waivers of defenses by the nuclear plant operator.[150]

The President and governors now declare disasters for many purposes, including loans and emergency services.[151] Nevertheless, allowing the executive to determine the existence of a disaster for judicial purposes might create too many political pressures and implicate separation of powers issues.

The present multidistrict panel would be an appropriate body to decide whether the criteria have been met for Disaster Court operation. Once the panel made the determination, the Chief Justice could immediately transfer judges to the case as needed.

The transferee judge or judges could be authorized to compel immediate temporary emergency payments to those in need, similar to the way payments were authorized following the Three Mile Island incident.[152] A well-run system would, in the Bhopal case, have made similar payments and paid basic medical and death benefits within days of the occurrence.

Compensation should be limited to exclude punitive damages. Pain and suffering awards beyond fixed limits must be excluded for policy as well as practical reasons.[153]

Where the trial should take place would be up to the new court. Knowing in advance who would hear appeals and that there is a requirement that appeals be expedited could save months or years of litigation. Appeal to a single court would be desirable. A panel of judges could be preselected by the Chief Justice, or an appeals court could be designated by law—either the United States Court of Appeals for the District of Columbia Circuit or a special appellate court with some particular scientific expertise should be considered. In some cases, directing appeals to the circuit in which most of the trials are centered might be desirable.

The advantage of using a temporary Disaster Court staffed by temporarily assigned judges, rather than seeking more radical reform or federalization of the toxic tort system, is that a special disaster court would operate only where the present system was not doing an acceptable job. Hence the Disaster Court probably would not be convened for airplane crashes and other situations that are successfully handled under a conventional multidistrict referral system.

2. SWITCHING CASES AMONG STATE AND FEDERAL COURTS

When disasters are involved, a body such as the Judicial Panel on Multidistrict Litigation should have power to switch cases to and from federal and state courts. The panel could include representative state judges for this purpose in addition to its normal membership of federal judges. Why should there not be joint federal-state trials? So far as the public is concerned we have one judicial system, which should be integrated to improve efficiency. Joint federal-state tribunals might be put in place by the Chief Justice of the United States and the Chief Judge of an affected state's highest court.[154] The American Law Institute recommended such an approach in 1993.

3. Binational and Multinational Tribunals

At the international level, there should be a joint Canada–United States tribunal prepared to try cases in either country according to the tribunal's own choice of law rules.[155] Rights such as trial by jury arguably could be implicated, but as indicated in the Iranian cases, the treaty-making power can be used to channel disputes into international tribunals without offense to such constitutional procedural rights.[156]

Who could invoke the jurisdiction of such a tribunal? Perhaps a case could be referred to a binational tribunal by a joint proclamation of the Chiefs of State of the two nations. The Chief of State's control over foreign relations makes this locus of control desirable.

Use of one nation's courts by other nations and their nationals is possible and has been utilized in a number of instances.[157] India adopted a law authorizing the central government to sue in United States courts on behalf of all those injured in Bhopal.[158] But, as the Wetstone and Rosencranz study of acid rain problems indicates, such recourse to national courts has not generally been helpful in massive pollution or tort situations.[159] Some bilateral or multilateral planning for these contingencies among the nations of the world seems necessary.

4. Planning for Disasters

Within the limits of due process and equal protection, we need to consider new ways of handling immense new problems. Failure to grow and change may create far more serious dangers to our legal system than would new ideas that are consistent with historical patterns.

Would it not be useful for the American Bar Association with its hundreds of thousands of responsible members to set up a special committee to consider this issue of disasters in its most general as well as particular aspects? Many of its committees are already working in related areas.

Academic input can be helpful. Among the institutions that have taken a leading role in addressing the mass tort problem are Columbia Law School, through the Legislative Drafting Research Fund under the direction of Professor Frank Grad, which was responsible for many of the studies leading to the nuclear power plant insurance act and the Superfund Report, and the Parker School of Columbia University, which reviewed the Bhopal problem; Yale Law School, which has held conferences on tort law; the Institute for Health Policy Analysis of Georgetown University, which held conferences on Causation and Financial Compensation; and the American Law Institute.

Any study group probably should include scientists, political scientists, and sociologists, in addition to lawyers, judges, and law professors. Inclusion of representatives from Mexico, Canada, and other countries might be helpful as well.

It is particularly fitting for American lawyers to take the lead. Our bar and adversarial system, our high awards for damages, our contingent fee system, and our encouragement of plaintiffs through small cost barriers and broad discovery all encourage litigation to flow toward our courts whenever an American connection exists. Given our general view that plaintiff's choice of forum prevails, even concepts of *forum non conveniens* provide only a limited barrier to litigation here.

Colleagues from other nations of the world, whether from the Napoleonic Code European countries or Mexico, or common law countries such as Canada or England, may wish to participate on some basis. Draft binational treaties to address such problems as the Bhopal incident or transnational boundary pollution with Canada or Mexico would need to be considered by representatives of these other countries.

F. CONCLUSION

Substance and procedure at the state, national, and multinational levels are implicated in answering some of the questions posed by forthcoming disasters. Sometimes the American bar is chided for being too strong, too talented, and too expensive. Is this, perhaps, a field where its great skills can help serve all mankind?

....

CHAPTER 3

General Problems of Ethics in Modern Cases[1]

A. The Changing World of Mass Cases

The ethical issues present in mass tort cases are numerous, troubling, and complex. They have not been given the special attention they deserve. Lack of analysis has led to tensions that need to be resolved by open and candid discussions of differences between these cases and traditional single-party disputes.[2]

One wise scholar told me, "Mass torts are public interest cases." He confirmed what I see in the courts.

Our current general code of ethics assumes a Lincolnesque lawyer strongly bonded to an individual client. In mass torts the facts do not fit this picture, this conceptual framework.[3] As one commentator observed, the difficulties of mass tort litigation "typify the recurrent problem of legal rules that perform fairly well in commonplace settings but, like Newton's laws of physics, lose their ordering power under extraordinary conditions."[4]

When Lincoln took office there were about 30 million people in the United States.[5] The population had increased about ten times since 1776. Today it is approximately one-quarter of a billion, soon to be ten times what it was in Lincoln's time.[6] In the Gettysburg Address Lincoln challenged the nation: could the principles, as he saw them, of union, equality, and obligation to future generations stated by Jefferson in the Declaration of Independence endure?[7] And John Henry Wigmore insisted, beginning with his first treatise on evidence at the end of the last century, that we seek the truth in painstaking case-by-case analysis.

We face again the question of whether a structure of government and justice crafted for three million and conceived in individual liberty can continue to serve us well in our time and beyond. Contrast the individual client of Lincoln with the more than ten thousand represented by one attorney in asbestos cases in Maryland,[8] the ten thousand claimants represented by one law firm against the Manville Personal Injury Settlement Trust,[9] the 45,000 present claimants represented by a consortium of lawyers in asbestos cases mostly in Texas,[10] or the representative in

Manville of future claimants estimated to number in the hundreds of thousands.[11] Can we handle the problems now presented while preserving the sense of individual justice that Jefferson and Lincoln assumed? Can we apply Wigmore's assumptions about individual litigants and evidentiary analysis to the massive multiparty litigations of today, more likely to be decided outside the courtroom than in it?

I address one aspect of this problem—ethics and mass torts—in this and following chapters. The term "ethics" is used in the broad sense of morality and humankind's obligation to create a just society,[12] as well as in the narrower sense of the standard of professional conduct guiding lawyers, judges, and other participants in the legal system.

The problems are thorny. The issues of ethics in mass tort cases cannot be addressed through mere tinkering with rules. The ethical problems, I submit, suggest the need for modifying the legal process to match the technological, economic, and sociological conditions of today. Fortunately, we have in our legal tradition strong foundations of fairness upon which to remodel procedural, substantive, and ethical structures.[13]

It should be noted at the outset that both plaintiffs' and defendants' attorneys specializing in mass torts are, in the main, more highly skilled, no less ethical, and as interested in the public welfare as the average attorney or layperson. It was partly out of respect for the importance and difficulty of their work that I began a study of ethics in mass tort litigations.[14]

While much of the discussion that follows seems tipped against the plaintiffs' bar, that is primarily because its problems have been more open and observable. On balance, taking a global view of mass torts, there is reason to criticize and to praise all of us who are involved in these cases.

The defendant corporations have not, with respect to many products, adequately tested and warned. Their executives often have delayed taking protective action. Their attorneys often have stonewalled and encouraged a huge discovery system to fund large defense firms and to break the financial backs of plaintiffs' attorneys. Plaintiffs' counsel often have been greedy for fees, have not connected emotionally with their clients, and have not adequately screened their cases. Judges often have failed to deal effectively with a huge flood of cases. The scientific community often has been less than helpful. Regulatory agencies often have not adequately protected the public against dangerous substances and processes. The legislative and executive branches have avoided the issues. And the public itself often has overestimated the capacity of the legal, medical, scientific, political, and managerial systems to protect against and compensate for every possible hazard of life.

The ethical issues in mass tort cases are numerous, troubling, and complex. They have not, in my view, been given the special attention they deserve. Lack of analysis has led to tensions that need to be resolved by open and candid discussions of differences between these cases and traditional single-party disputes.[15]

Mass tort cases are akin to public litigations involving court-ordered restructuring of institutions to protect constitutional rights.[16] In dealing with such mass tort cases[17] as Agent Orange,[18] asbestos,[19] and DES,[20] I have sensed an atmosphere similar to that of public interest cases I have supervised such as the Mark Twain school desegregation case,[21] the reform of the Suffolk County Developmentally Disabled Center,[22] and jail and prison[23] reform litigation.[24]

In the Agent Orange cases, I heard from hundreds of terrified veterans and their families concerned that herbicides sprayed in Vietnam had crippled them and their children. In the asbestos cases, men, women, and children wept when they spoke of how they or their loved ones had been struck down forty years after they worked in asbestos dust while building our navy during World War 2. In the DES cases, women sobbed in my chambers while telling me how the destruction of their reproductive systems had ruined their marriages, their hopes for children, and their dignity as persons. In the Mark Twain school desegregation case, I walked the streets of Coney Island examining decayed buildings and segregated schools with despondent parents and demoralized students. In the reform of the Suffolk County Developmentally Disabled Center, I saw children lying naked in their feces on cold floors, and parents frantic with concern and guilt.[25]

Mass tort cases and public litigations both implicate serious political and sociological issues. Both are restrained by economic imperatives.[26] Both have strong psychological underpinnings. And both affect larger communities than those encompassed by the litigants before the court.

Like many of our great public cases, mass torts often embody disquieting uncertainties about modern society and the individual's relation to our institutions. School desegregation cases involve underlying issues of racial and social prejudice, sexual fantasies, and concern about safety, property values, and power. Prison reform cases raise questions about the role of punishment and theological assumptions about the inherent badness or goodness of humanity. Cases such as the Exxon Valdez oil spill or the New York City World Trade Center bombing of 1993 may seriously affect a town, a state, or an entire country.[27] Many constitutional cases dealing with privacy, sexuality, hate, or abortion require analysis in terms of group psychology or psychiatry and sociology.

So, too, with many mass torts.[28] Despite the fact that life expectancy keeps climbing, many fear the effects of strange chemical, electromagnetic, atomic, and pharmaceutical products on our bodies and those of our children.[29] There is often a near paranoid terror of an unknown malefactor in the large corporation, interest group, or government agency. A sense of extreme anxiety sometimes surfaces in these cases. All these subliminal—and sometimes overt—forces require great sensitivity and understanding by the courts and lawyers to prevent potentially reasonable resolutions from dissolving in irrational disagreements.[30] Supervising such cases, the judge is often faced with the reality that people do not always act consistently with the model of the "reasonable economic person." Irrationality and emotion often intrude in and out of court.

While resolution of public institutional litigation depends upon the availability of cash, the improvement of living conditions underlies the litigation. Mass tort cases usually are driven by more obviously venal influences; that is to say, payment of money is more clearly at issue. Nevertheless, mass tort litigations often have an underlying, if less focused, purpose which goes beyond mere transfers of wealth—they deal with the health and sense of security of many individuals and the viability of major economic institutions.

B. ADMINISTRATIVE-PROCEDURAL LEVEL

As pointed out in chapter 2, at the administrative-procedural level, the problem in mass torts is one of providing a fair and speedy compensation system that also reduces transaction costs.[31] In summary, these principles include consolidating cases before one judge[32] (with the option of calling on other judges to assist in settlements, trials, and other proceedings), applying a single substantive, evidentiary, privilege, ethics, and procedural law; providing lead counsel on both sides to coordinate and conduct the basic litigation and organize and simplify discovery; furnishing prompt and effective scientific research and testimony; and developing a method of speedy and efficient payment using relatively fixed and simple, although equitable, criteria for compensation.[33]

We have spent great resources and time thinking about the efficiency issues as reflected, for example, in the American Law Institute's work on complex litigation,[34] mass torts, and compensation,[35] in the American Bar Association's and other attempts to deal with disasters,[36] and in cases on class actions, bankruptcy, and other forms of consolidation.[37] Judges and court-related institutions have begun to devote an extraordinary amount of attention to the cost-effectiveness aspect of the problem. The Chief Justice of the United States appointed a special committee to make recommendations to Congress.[38] The Federal Judicial Center and various groups of state judges have also addressed the problem of mass torts generally.[39] Limitations on the ability of the Multidistrict Litigation Panel to deal with state cases—a defect that would be rectified by proposals developed by the American Law Institute[40]—have led plaintiffs' lawyers to shift more cases to the state courts, where they are free of federal integrated calendar, discovery, fee, and other controls.

The law has learned to take speedier and more efficient action—at least in some cases—in the last decade. In the breast implant cases, for example, the Multidistrict Litigation Panel consolidated all federal cases in one federal court almost immediately after it became apparent that there was great potential for massive litigation.[41] The assigned transferee judge has exercised firm control. He has appointed lead counsel, a special master, and a magistrate judge; provided for a special document depository; required the use of computers and television technology to control document and expert costs; and sought to coordinate state and federal pretrial activity, even arranging for state judges assigned to breast implant cases to attend joint meetings at which he explained the pretrial process he had set up.[42]

The speed with which the number of breast implant cases exploded on the scene is attributable in part to a well-organized plaintiffs' bar, which now has the capital, the organizational skills, and the advertising techniques to seek clientele.[43] As in so many other mass tort cases in their early stages, little is yet known about the science involved—harm, causation, and prognosis—and it will take years to understand fully the legal basis and validity of many of the claims. Nevertheless, it is likely that these cases will be largely disposed of by settlement before the key issues of science have been definitively decided.

The breast implant cases show, too, the conflicts among attorneys and the difficulty of handling these cases. For example, some attorneys desired the cases consolidated so they could settle large numbers of both sound cases and marginally viable cases more readily. Others brought class actions so they could control the litigation as representatives of all claimants and work out sensible and quick global resolutions. A third group, operating in a more traditional manner, wanted to be retained in only those cases they thought had particular merit so they could forcefully represent relatively few clients on a one-on-one basis.

Consolidation of these breast implant cases clearly had efficiency benefits. But such consolidations do tend to encourage the commencement of suits of questionable merit. Since consolidated cases probably will be settled in large groups, the less defensible claims are likely to obtain more than they would if they were litigated (assuming they would have been brought at all), while the more serious claims will probably be settled for less than they would in individual trials.

What is clear from the huge consolidations required in mass torts is that they have many of the characteristics of class actions. In a class action the attorneys as well as the court have special obligations to see that all members of the class are fairly treated, are not overcharged by their lawyers, and are not subjected to inadequate legal work on their behalf.

It is my conclusion, as indicated below, that mass consolidations are in effect quasi-class actions. Obligations to claimants, defendants, and the public remain much the same whether the cases are gathered together by bankruptcy proceedings, class actions, or national or local consolidations. Efforts have been made to amend Rule 23[44] to make it easier to use in mass torts, by, for example, giving the court more explicit power to provide less expensive notice through indirect service on individual members and by limiting the right to opt out.[45] Many of these powers already are exercised,[46] but explicit changes in the rules could overcome some appellate hostility based on an outdated notion that class actions are not appropriate for mass torts.[47] Intertwined with these important procedural matters are serious ethical concerns.

C. TRADITIONAL ETHICAL RULES

Even as late as 1969 (two years after I became a judge), the drafters of the ABA Code of Professional Responsibility fashioned their "new" set of ethical rules after principles first codified at the turn of the century.[48] They did not envisage a lawyer never meeting the many clients he or she represented. It has been properly noted that "much of the intellectual effort in the field of legal ethics during the past quarter century has been an attempt to reevaluate the rules that emerged during the 'golden age' of the solo practitioner and the small firm."[49] Yet, the current American Law Institute project on Restatement of the Law Governing Lawyers ignores mass torts and largely restates the old models of the one-lawyer, one-client relationship and the two-litigant case.[50]

My own experiences on the bench have led me to conclude that we need to go beyond the rules of the past and provide more realistic guidance to today's lawyers and judges. The ethics issues inherent in litigation of mass torts warrant consideration of whether lawyers can, or judges should, continue to try to adapt their behavior to conform strictly to traditional ethical rules. Do we need a modified set of ethical guidelines to assist us in dealing with these massive cases just as we have special class action rules of civil procedure? For the attorney, the viability is placed in question of such ethical imperatives as the duty to communicate with each client effectively, to maintain confidences, and to avoid conflicts of interest in client representation.[51]

The judge, too, is faced with nontraditional ethical dilemmas. To what extent should the judge relinquish the role of passive, neutral mediator in favor of a more activist, managerial stance, particularly when creative solutions to complex problems require intervention?[52] What steps can a judge reasonably take to educate him- or herself about highly technical scientific matters without losing the appearance or fact of impartiality? Should the judge look beyond the case at bar and consider the needs of society in resolving a matter—and how should the judge resolve the inconsistencies among the needs of the parties and the public? How much leeway should judges have in communicating with clients and the public, particularly about matters affecting public health and safety?

Of course, every lawsuit implicates the public interest. It is the nature of a common law system that judges, and sometimes jurors, consider the impact of their decisions beyond the parties before them. In mass tort cases the public interest takes on much greater significance. The process involves more than the routine theoretical calculation of the effect of a particular decision or rule on future cases through stare decisis. What renders a mass tort case different is the degree to which all participants—judges, lawyers, and litigants—must deal with the case as an institutional problem with sociopolitical implications extending far beyond the narrow confines of the courtroom.

Once this quality is recognized in a particular case, a duty attaches to all participants to be aware of, and responsive to, the needs of the entire community as well as subcommunities, and at least to the broad number of people and interests directly affected. This responsiveness cannot be ensured by a narrow view of the adversarial system and the ordinary rules that govern its operation. Advocates cannot rely upon a fair and zealously contested proceeding to automatically produce the most appropriate result. And judges cannot rely upon a narrow application of law to fact to yield justice.

The problem of ethics in mass torts can be seen from two perspectives. From outside the legal system, it appears to be one of the responsiveness of our legal institutions to the needs of the community. From inside, it involves the ability of the present procedural system to manage the moral pressures exerted by mass tort cases. Without serious rethinking and reformulation of traditional precepts, our legal institutions are not likely to succeed either in managing the enormous burdens which confront them, or in meeting the needs of the respective communities involved. Members of the bench and bar are obligated to answer the calls for help by many who claim injury as well as requests from defendants, their insurers, and their employees.[53]

Mass tort cases require us to distinguish between positive rules of law and ethical precepts. When members of the legal profession speak of "legal ethics," they generally refer to the rules of law regulating the conduct of lawyers and judges.[54] Within the legal community, when a particular practice is decried as "unethical," it is usually sanctionable, that is, it subjects the actor to liability or discipline. Our mandatory law school courses on "legal ethics" and the component of the bar exam that tests "professional responsibility" deal narrowly with these rules in the same way we teach rules of procedure or substantive law,[55] leaving extralegal considerations to the individual's own judgment.

When the legal community speaks of "legal ethics," then, it refers to positive law, not morality.[56] This positive law has devolved from some important moral precepts, including fundamental beliefs about fair process, the right to be heard, and access to justice within an ordered society. Some would argue that the traditional adversarial system of dispute resolution, with all its governing rules of conduct, is fundamental to our conception of democracy.[57]

It is my belief, however, that this positive law no longer functions well when applied in the modern context of mass tort cases. The law is usually sensible in adjusting wherever possible to achieve a workable arrangement with the real world. It does not insist on its own inutility. When rules of positive law break down in application, we do not ignore their lack of congruency with life. We try to change them. The common practice in mass tort cases, in my own experience and as related to me by my colleagues in the field, unfortunately has been to ignore ethical problems in the name of expediency. A principled system of laws cannot long tolerate such a practice. In regulating conduct in a practicable way, positive law must stay in touch with both the actual world at work and our sense of what is moral and just.

In reforming positive law, we return to and reexamine our sense of justice. We must rely on our concept of ethics in the sense of "the good" in Aristotelian terms to avoid being swept away in swiftly changing social conditions and assumptions. The challenge of ethics in mass tort cases can be met in either of two ways: we can fashion a new set of positive rules of law to apply in these cases, or we can institutionalize a practice of granting "variances," allowing workable relief from the ordinary operation of the positive law.[58] In either case, we first must find a set of ethical principles to guide our selection of the rules or exceptions we will apply in practice. Without such a moral compass, we may lose our way as we seek the answers to the difficult problems we face.

D. COMMUNITARIAN AND COMMUNICATARIAN ETHICS

Because of the political, sociological, economic, and technological implications of many mass tort cases, we must consider not only the individual litigant and lawyer, but entire communities. We assume, properly I believe, that dignity is enhanced by individual control of litigation for each person's own benefit. Our legal system highly values individual interests and prerogatives. But just as individualism run riot can be damaging in social matters, so too may it need checking in mass litigations.[59]

Each of us lives in many communities if we define this term as a group of people having common rights and privileges or common interests.[60] Sometimes the community is defined by status, as in a community of prisoners or of schoolchildren. Often it consists of a diffuse group having little continuing physical connection, as is the case with women from all parts of the country suffering reproductive organ impairment because their mothers took a drug during pregnancy. At other times it is defined by geography, as when a group of homes in a valley is swept away by a flood.

To deal with such groups it is helpful to consider some of the insights of communitarian ethicists.[61] We need to look not only to the individual's hurt but also to similar harm suffered by others in the community, and suggested solutions for those who may be secondarily affected—including workers who may lose their jobs if the business they work for is bankrupted.[62] Compensation to the individual is not the end-all of modern mass tort law; the effects of remedies on the community cannot be ignored.

The field of communicatarian ethics also should be consulted.[63] As applied, the communicatarian ethic traces at least to the work of Mill on liberty and the American legal-constitutional scheme.[64] We need to ask whether an opportunity to discuss and ventilate views of those aggrieved is required in mass litigations.[65] Dialogue may lead to more satisfying solutions because many of those affected will have played some role in the process. The felt needs and reasoning of those directly concerned may provide insights otherwise overlooked.[66] Dialogue also increases the sense of dignity of the participating person as an important entity, one who counts and will be heard.[67] We also need to improve communication within the system, particularly with respect to our jurors,[68] but this important matter is beyond the scope of this book.

George Sharswood's work of the last century—upon which our current legal ethics codes are based—assumed a communitarian bent. He exhorted a "[h]igh moral principle [as] the [lawyer's] only safe guide, the only torch to light his way amidst the darkness and obstruction."[69] The lawyer's primary obligation, as he perceived it, was to the common good.[70] In balancing this "republican" role with the lawyer's adversarial role, Sharswood apparently understood that the system "could not require each individual lawyer to represent any client and to seek the greatest success for every client represented."[71] Accordingly, he endorsed the view that "the lawyer was a public officer with duties to the public and the court as well as the client."[72]

The case of the Buffalo Creek disaster adverted to in chapter 1 illustrates why we need to consider both the impact on a community and the need to communicate with those affected.[73] An improperly designed and maintained coal company dam broke, destroying the small settlements of an entire valley. Lawyers worked out a good all-cash settlement with individual dollar awards to many of those injured in person or property. The old communities, however, were utterly destroyed and never rebuilt; residents began to live a more barren, less community-centered life.[74]

A more communitarian-communicatarian approach would have required active consultation—including public hearings in and out of court—with the clients, the local, state, and federal authorities, the coal company, and the insurers. Agreement on a package of schools, health facilities, job opportunities, roads, parks, and new houses as well as individual compensation would seem to have been warranted.

As a general rule, the need for more intense court intervention is in inverse proportion to the effectiveness of the community in dealing with disasters. This was illustrated by the asbestos tragedy: it was the long-term failures of government, management, and the medical and engineering professions that allowed a dangerous situation—installation of asbestos with inadequate ventilation and masks for workers—to fester and grow long after it should have been checked.[75]

A more recent example is the New York City World Trade Center disaster. The explosion threatened the viability of the city as a financial center and could have costs tens of thousands of critical jobs as well as the lives of many businesses. Acting swiftly, the political,[76] commercial,[77] and medical[78] communities provided temporary space, communication facilities, and psychiatric support. Insurance and other claims will be made; in the main they will be dealt with by quick out-of-court voluntary arrangements and arbitration. Most of the relatively few cases coming to the courts should be processed through the courts' mediation, settlement, and arbitration channels.[79] Should the cases prove more numerous than expected, a single federal judge to coordinate the New Jersey and the Southern and Eastern District cases, together with a single state judge for the state cases and a jointly appointed special master, can help dispose of the disputes quickly.[80] Theoretically, many of the fifty thousand or so people affected by the explosion could sue the Port Authority for ignoring its own reports about the security dangers of public parking under the Trade Center complex, but their recovery likely will be small, except in the relatively few cases of death or serious injury where substantial awards are warranted.[81] Lawyers should be discouraged from bringing de minimis cases; courts will not be likely to encourage global settlements that allow large fees for cases which should not be brought. New Yorkers are tough, resilient, and proud of their city; many of the less seriously injured will prefer the memory of survival and a letter of thanks from someone in authority to a small check shared with a class attorney. Key to the community's work, of course, are the immediate efforts of emergency fire, police, engineering, and hospital facilities.[82] A more extensive disaster such as a full atomic energy plant explosion would present similar but much more intense problems.[83]

Comprehensive solutions are hard to devise. Special masters and others might well be needed to supplement the judge and to act as brokers among the various interested groups. I assigned this role to special masters in resolving a considerable number of cases, including the Mark Twain Junior High School case in Brooklyn and the national Agent Orange Vietnam veterans case.

Resolutions of mass torts exert pressures on clients, attorneys, and judges that are different in kind from those attendant on traditional one-on-one cash settlements or even structured settlements with payment over time. Courts, however, have equity powers[84] to provide alternative forms of awards and to encourage settlements that appropriately address the various communities' and parties' needs.[85] Where standing rules inhibit those elements of the relevant communities who are not parties to the lawsuit from being heard, courts can exercise their discretion to invite appearances as amicus curiae.[86]

How, you may ask, can we expect lawyers to act in the public interest when a communitarian approach may not result in maximum cash advantage to their clients and to themselves in fees? Are most lawyers cognizant of their obligation to wider communities?[87] In these mass cases the answer has to be that the lawyer must think in terms of community as well as client. After all, lawyers are public servants given special privileges and monopoly status. The law is not merely a fee-making machine. It is a profession with public responsibilities.

In mass tort litigations the nature of the community varies from case to case.[88] Unlike the Buffalo Creek communities, disputes such as the one involving the Dalkon Shield intrauterine device involve a scattered mass of people with no prior personal relationships. By contrast, in the Agent Orange case the plaintiffs, who had been members of the armed forces in Vietnam, had a strong sense of shared sacrifice. This common experience and community made it easier for the veterans to establish effective advocacy groups to communicate with each other and with the courts and ultimately to obtain congressional help.

It is my impression that few of the groups of plaintiffs I have dealt with in the Agent Orange, asbestos, or DES cases were helped systematically or sympathetically as communities by lawyers handling their cases. Most lawyers were focused on getting cash for the individual client, obtaining a large fee, and closing the file as quickly and with as little effort as possible. Yet, however we may criticize the tort system, we must not forget that without the plaintiffs' tort bar, the injured would have received no help. Neither the government nor defendants assisted except under great pressure generated by massive litigations.

Ethics requires us to deal with individual client dignity as well as with group and community needs.[89] How can we provide plaintiffs and defendants with the benefits of a system that treats them as individual persons, even in mass torts?[90] How can they communicate with each other and us, and we with them? How can each person obtain the respect that individuality and personal needs command? In considering ethics in mass torts, we must keep in mind both the individual's needs and the community's needs.[91]

Three areas of ethics need consideration:

The first area is the relationship among lawyers and clients. Our rules of ethics still tend to assume a one-to-one relationship between client and attorney in a relatively simple case. Problems of communication and conflicts between attorney and client, however, arise in their most troubling form in large complex cases. Related are problems of lawyers on either side cooperating with each other, creating issues such as secrecy or infighting, making it difficulty to control the litigation.

The second area is the relationship between court-administered compensation distribution schemes and individual claimants.[92] Where pro se litigants are involved, connection with litigants may be easier since the plaintiff has a direct relationship with the court. Special problems of trusts and of companies in effect controlled by plaintiffs' attorneys also need consideration.

The third area is the obligation of the court itself to individual litigants as well as to lawyers and the community. The judge must, I suggest, expose himself or herself to the emotional and other needs of the litigants. This proposition may be the most controversial aspect of my present thinking on ethics. It requires recognition that there has been a shift from the traditional Anglo-American view that the common law judge is an oracle on high, muffled in the black robe of anonymity, spewing out the law automatically and deciding the facts dispassionately.

The judge in mass tort as well as public institution reform cases has an obligation to assist both attorneys and clients. The court has a duty to insist that lawyers act appropriately toward their clients—in terms of adequacy of representation, communication, and fees. But the court also needs to consider how what is done affects the larger community. Mass cases require us to rethink the obligation of the judge in our society. Laypersons caught up in such disputes often feel alienated and dehumanized,[93] as their participation in the legal system is too often, from their viewpoint, ineffective. Instead of being treated on a person-to-person basis with dignity and inviolability, they are treated as passive recipients of a form of justice they do not understand—players in a legal lottery of arbitrary awards and rejections.[94]

I do not advocate imposition of a new rigid jurisprudence against which all our ethical rules and decisions must be strictly judged. The greatest virtue of our common law system is its fact-oriented flexibility.[95] Rules are the basis of an ordered society. Yet, the capacity to make exceptions is what defines an ordered society as humane. As Professor Harry W. Jones put it,

> The moral problem of the judge, the prosecutor or the practicing lawyer is only rarely, "Is this a just general rule?" Far more commonly the painful question is "What is justice in this concrete situation?" . . . I propose, therefore, that we [must] seek the moral dimension of law not in precepts and rules but in the process of responsible decision which pervades the whole of law in life.[96]

In ethics, as in many other areas, we strive for general rules supplemented by the flexibility necessary to treat like cases alike and unlike cases differently.[97] Too rigid an adherence to formal ethical-legal rules constitutes a violation of the basic rule of ethics itself, requiring a practicable humane regime in which the needs of the public, the parties, and the law are in reasonable balance.[98]

By way of analogy, consider the problem of feeding residents in a nursing home. Were every resident permitted to demand an individual cook to meet individual desires, the institution would lose all capacity to feed its charges at reasonable cost. A single chef is necessary. To maintain individual dignity and satisfaction, however, provision should be made for each resident to supplement the fixed institutional diet with his or her own preferences. Family members should be allowed to bring in their own foods and individuals should be permitted some leeway to complain and have special arrangements.[99]

Similarly, in the Manville settlement the litigants are trying to provide a matrix for payment by disease, with escape valves for special cases within a lower and upper range. Any increased flexibility has costs in time to decide whether a departure is necessary. Thus far I have been satisfied that a rigid matrix in asbestos cases is not necessary.[100]

We are primarily interested in process—however "messy" in practice. We need not adopt a metaethical, transcendental, self-contained theory—a categorical, hermeneutically consistent system that explains everything. Our questions are "Does it work in resolving conflicts with a maximum of satisfaction to those involved in a dispute in the court?" and "Does it offend our sense of morality?"[101] The law has the same characteristic Arthur Schlesinger recently attributed to the great diplomat George

Kennan: it has an "incorrigible preference for the concrete over the abstract and for life over theory."[102]

We can provide methods of ameliorating the baleful effects of our sometimes cold and dispassionate system without losing too much efficiency in handling mass cases. Simultaneously, we must address the problems of efficiency and ethics—two sides of justice.

I shall try to highlight some of the issues and how they might be addressed in the chapters that follow.

CHAPTER 4

ETHICS OF LAWYERS

Perhaps most fundamental to our model of professional ethics is the lawyer's duty of loyalty to his or her client.[1] We have constructed an adversarial system in which, for the most part, the individual does not stand alone but is represented by a trained officer of the court. The lawyer is required to be an absolutely loyal surrogate for the client.[2] This ensures that justice is served and that the client receives the full and fair hearing to which he or she is entitled.[3]

Nevertheless there is a concomitant duty to the court and society independent of obligations to client.[4]

Loyalty to client is promoted through two basic rules. First is the duty of the lawyer to be a zealous and effective advocate. The ABA's Model Rules of Professional Conduct state in their preamble that "when an opposing party is well represented, a lawyer can be a zealous advocate on behalf of a client and at the same time assume that justice is being done."[5] The rules require that a lawyer provide competent representation and act with diligence and promptness.[6] The precepts against serving clients under conditions that present conflicts of interest ensure that the lawyer's loyalty is not compromised.[7]

Second is the duty to communicate with the client. The rules direct the lawyer to keep the client "reasonably informed" of the status of the case and to explain the matter to the extent necessary for the client to make informed decisions.[8] In addition, a lawyer is required to abide by the client's decisions concerning the objectives of the representation.[9] Dispositive decisions, such as whether to enter a guilty plea or accept a settlement, are for the client.[10]

The theory of dispute resolution by adversarial proceeding is founded upon this conception of the lawyer's role. The lawyer supplies his or her professional expertise and skill while standing, to the extent possible, in the shoes of the client. The lawyer must argue the client's case with the same commitment and zeal as would the individual client were he or she trained in the law. The client enjoys the best of both worlds: the benefit of the legal expertise of the lawyer, which the client does not possess, and the commitment and zeal of the client as embodied in the loyal attorney.

When we impose this adversarial model—the lawyer as fiduciary to the client—on the mass tort case, we find that the notion of the lawyer standing in the shoes of the client is sometimes ludicrous. In asbestos litigation, for example, some lawyers represent more than ten thousand plaintiffs. In other mass torts, such as DES or Dalkon Shield or toxic dump pollutions, lawyers routinely have carried many hundreds of clients at a time.[11] The efficiency advantages due to economies of scale in such circumstances are obvious. Amassing large numbers of cases in the hands of relatively few specialized lawyers can greatly facilitate settlement and afford plaintiffs the benefit of attorneys experienced in complex cases.[12]

But plaintiffs in mass cases pay a price for these advantages. Many of these lawyers do not maintain meaningful one-to-one contact with their clients, nor can they represent these people as individuals, each with his or her own needs and desires.[13] The client becomes no more than an unembodied cause of action. Defendants, as will be pointed out below, also pay a price in inflated recoveries for large numbers of questionable cases (although they may pay less in transactional costs in far more serious cases).

At best these plaintiffs' lawyers construct small bureaucracies including paralegals, newsletters, and phone banks to maintain contact with their clients. At worst the lawyers neglect their clients. Injured persons may find that they have surrendered their rights to a system in which they have little or no input. Even with the best-intentioned lawyers, some alienation of the individual seems inevitable. There is a vast difference between the boutique law firms that take relatively few strong cases and those that, like a vacuum cleaner, suck up good and bad cases, hoping that they can settle in gross.

A. COMMUNICATION

Let us first consider the duty to communicate. This duty requires the lawyer to explain the progress of the litigation so that the client will have sufficient information to participate intelligently. In the so-called golden age, when cases were treated one at a time, such a mandate presented no ethical dilemma. In the context of the mass tort, however, client communication, effective or otherwise, is a considerable problem.

Two preliminary points about communication should be made. There will be a serious cost in terms of cash and effort if we require more individual contact with litigants by the court or attorneys, or both. Whether the expense is justified merits serious discussion. Second, the effort required to increase contact with the litigant should vary with the nature of the injury to the litigant. At one end of the spectrum are the Dalkon Shield, Agent Orange, and DES cases, where the plaintiffs feel that serious bodily harm has occurred as a result of defendants' actions. There may be an element of outrage because the person and personality of an individual has been breached and harmed by the delict of a faceless, distant corporate power. At the other end of the spectrum are purely commercial or security cases where the litigant probably was unaware of the claim until a class action was brought and the time for distribution of funds or other assets arrived, as illustrated by some of the fraud cases[14] and the recent apparent settlement of consumer claims against airlines.[15] The more the litigant believes he or she is "hurt," the more care from the system is required—a sound rule for parceling out "TLC" in all situations.

Whether the selection and training of lawyers makes them useful, as a class, for emotional support is not clear.[16] But the system can provide some outlet for the venting of emotions.

1. THE PROBLEM

Lawyers who carry numerous clients may not always be able to meet the ethical requirements of effective communication. The language of the rules does not appear to create an insurmountable problem. A lawyer who is careful to establish mechanisms for communication with clients, such as mass mailings, newsletters, large group meetings, use of client leaders to speak for other clients, and phones staffed by paralegals, theoretically can give clients enough information to let them make the important strategic decisions for which the rules require client direction and consent.[17] As the numbers of clients extend into the thousands, however, even these forms of communication may be insufficient.[18] Newsletters can help.[19] But newsletters are less vehicles for communication than self-serving devices for the lawyers to minimize the risk that clients will "jump ship."

Some attorneys rely heavily on paralegals to handle the "relationship work" because they are less expensive and may communicate more effectively. Paralegals may sit in on client interviews and serve as a bridge between the legal and the lay worlds, often functioning as quasi social workers. If adequately supervised this practice can work reasonably well. Even if clients take the initiative and contact their attorneys, there is simply not enough attorney power to satisfy the communication needs of hundreds or thousands of clients.

I have no doubt that some attorneys do maintain appropriate contact with their clients even in mass cases; for example, I have observed the close rapport between one plaintiff attorney and her clients in DES cases.[20]

At the same time, I am dubious about whether this relationship is effectively maintained where there are hundreds or thousands of clients, or in large class, or bankruptcy, actions.[21] In cases involving large distribution vehicles such as the Manville Trust or the Dalkon Shield Trust, attorneys may actually hamper effective communication with claimants, because when claimants are represented by counsel, the compensation entity generally is prohibited from communicating directly with them.[22] Anecdotal evidence suggests that some attorneys do not give important information to their clients.[23]

Even if the communication rules are technically complied with, clients may not be satisfied with these forms of contact with their lawyers.[24] Much depends on the style of the lawyer, the nature of the case, and the kinds of clients. Studies indicate that plaintiffs value the result yielded by a lawsuit more if they believe that they have participated meaningfully in the system and that their voice has been heard.[25] Plaintiffs, as I have noted, may be even happier with a somewhat lower settlement if it results from a process in which they participated and in which they had significant input.[26]

We would be reckless were we to ignore litigant satisfaction.[27] Public confidence in our system of justice depends on the system's responsiveness to people's needs.[28] From that public confidence flows the power of our courts.[29] Some clients are extremely bitter over their lawyers' failure to communicate.[30] In the case of the Reichold Chemical Co. plant explosion in Columbia, Mississippi,

> Residents charge that [attorneys] took 50 percent or more of meager personal-injury and property-damage settlements; neglected to provide copies of hurriedly signed contingency fee contracts; failed to get promised medical tests; never explained the progress of their cases; and ultimately presented them with take-it-or-leave-it offers.[31]

Where large numbers of people are represented, the group can be more effective if it has leadership and can become more active in discussions with attorneys. But this kind of democracy can lead to intragroup conflicts and lay struggles for power. And, of course, it complicates the lawyer's role to have to deal not only with individual clients but also with representatives who may challenge the lawyer's leadership and sometimes have an egocentric need to control the litigation.

At public hearings on settlement of the Manville asbestos case there was an obvious antipathy between the lay White Lung Association groups purportedly speaking for workers injured by asbestos and many attorneys actually representing workers claiming injury from asbestos. I saw the same kind of conflicts in the Agent Orange and LILCO litigations at public hearings and in written communications from aggrieved clients.

Appellate courts have preferred bankruptcy rather than class action modes of settling large mass tort cases against defendants with assets insufficient to satisfy all claimants.[32] Theoretically classes of creditors, including tort claimants, have the right to vote on a bankruptcy plan. But in mass cases bankruptcy is of little value as a vehicle for communication to future claimants. Even as to present claimants, experience suggests considerable doubt about how much discussion takes place. My own view is that a much more beneficial participatory procedure is possible in class actions or consolidated actions with repeated court fairness sessions at which claimants are heard, as in the Agent Orange litigation. Strong control by the court, as required by Rule 23 of the Federal Rules of Civil Procedure to ensure fairness, is, I believe, a more effective vehicle for communication and settlement of mass cases. Bankruptcy fees are, in addition, enormous[33] and less likely to be controlled than in class actions. In the Manville case, for example, some plaintiffs' attorneys used their control to amass huge fees for themselves, stripping the trust of its assets, despite the efforts of the courts supervising the trust to limit the fees to reasonable amounts.

2. FOSTERING COMMUNICATION IN A MASS SOCIETY

Available forms of communication offer considerable promise of improving fair administration of mass torts in these areas: first, among attorneys and their clients; second, between attorneys charged with leading the litigation and attorneys representing individual clients; and, third, between the court and any of the above groups.

Most attorneys, whether representing a few or many people, have local or regional clients. They can keep in touch by telephone, through face-to-face meetings in the attorney's office, or through group meetings in public and private halls. The "800" number offers a convenient way of encouraging clients to call attorneys or their paraprofessionals. Public meetings with a group of clients are sometimes preferable because the give-and-take with the more aggressive or well-informed clients can raise issues most clients would not be aware of. However, confidentiality concerns may place some limitations on the scope of such open meetings and must be carefully considered.[34]

Courthouses should be made available without charge for such meetings, even though that use has the disadvantage of appearing to give the imprimatur of the court to the meeting. Courthouses are generally conveniently located and have at least one assembly room suitable for large gatherings. The judge in charge of the litigation might use such meetings for a brief appearance to explain the court's role to the litigants. Ultimately, cable television and telephone links permitting a wider, geographically scattered audience will be available at reasonable rates. The Federal Judicial Center and other legal, professional, and educational institutions already use television hookups to provide a kind of national town meeting that is cheaper and more efficient than having people travel to a central location. Videotapes to be used in clients' home VCRs are useful.

Modern techniques could provide an opportunity for effective communication with large groups even in the largest mass tort cases. Use of such communication procedures will add to the costs of conducting the litigation. They also will add to capitalization demands on the plaintiffs' bar. Whatever the courts can do within their budgetary constraints to make their facilities available to reduce such costs and strains on plaintiffs is appropriate. These techniques can also be used to permit clients to speak to each other and caucus among themselves, although such communication may lead to more internecine strife or permit "raids" by plaintiffs' attorneys seeking to wrest clients or control from other attorneys.

Among attorneys charged with leading a mass litigation, present practice calls for national meetings among attorneys, telephone calls, training sessions, and exchange of correspondence. This aspect of communications has been well developed by the Association of Trial Lawyers of America and ad hoc attorney organizations. Publishers currently produce literature for substantial fees in regular publications devoted to such litigations as asbestos or breast implants. These means of communication encourage national consensus and control by the attorneys for plaintiffs.

What of the attorney who represents just one or a few clients and who will not be able to afford the trips and publications utilized by the national leaders?[35] Making litigation information readily available to outlying single practitioners at little marginal costs is highly desirable. Those lawyers can then interpret the data and represent clients in a more traditional way. The most modern devices can thus be utilized to give us, in mass cases, the advantages of traditional one-on-one representation. It is submitted that those placed in charge of the national litigation have a responsibility to keep these lawyers apprised of developments. Correspondence can do most of the work. So can electronic mail, which is available for very little cost now that many attorneys have computers and modems. Recent advances in the breast implant cases have used computer disks to make all discovery available to individual attorneys at a relatively low cost.[36]

In the Agent Orange case, the Director of the Agent Orange Class Assistance Program utilizes electronic mail, local phone calls, quick message loading devices, and a satellite phone system to keep in touch with the more than seventy organizations that currently receive Agent Orange funds.[37] In the breast implant cases, documents and other data are available through the West publishing system as well as through a depository with space at the federal courthouse in Cincinnati.[38] These facilities are financed by the defendants' and plaintiffs' counsel. Suitable coding of information can be used to permit limited groups of attorneys access, thus facilitating communication among them.

Since ultimately the client, defendant, or taxpayer will pay, completion and operation of storage and accessing facilities should be put out for bid. The skill of independent contractors and their ability to cut costs must be considered. Judges will tend to think of Westlaw or Lexis since we are most familiar with these services, but others may be more efficient for individual cases. The Administrative Office of the United States Courts, the Federal Judicial Center, state judicial centers, or other government agencies should be able to assist a court in finding the right services.

These techniques can also be utilized to permit the court to keep in touch with attorneys and, where necessary, clients. For example, the judge in charge of the breast implant consolidation traveled to various regions of the country to meet with attorneys. In the Agent Orange case and LILCO class actions, I used similar peregrinations to keep in touch with claimants in fairness hearings. The court can, when necessary, use television, conference calls, or electronic mail to conduct national hearings and motion practice.[39] These devices could have been used in the Manville case, and they may be utilized in the future. The extensive telephone contacts among judges as well as their physical travel over long distances to consult with each other in coordinating control of state and federal cases should be paid for by the state and federal court systems. It is inappropriate to permit the parties, even by stipulation, to pay a judge's expenses.[40]

Such coordination techniques should also be encouraged in connection with administration of funds and special forms of relief after settlement or judgment. In the Agent Orange case, for example, the use of an 800 number with as many as forty incoming lines has permitted possible claimants to get help and a sympathetic hearing from trained laypersons.[41] More than six hundred thousand calls have been logged.[42] A "hot line" run by the National Information System for Vietnam Veterans and Their Families at the University of South Carolina has sent tens of thousands of letters and received thousands of calls putting claimants' families in touch with the appropriate helping agencies. Persons who answer calls use computers with extensive data on individual clients and available facilities. Coordination among the Agent Orange service agencies has also been useful in improving delivery of services at minimum cost. Printed pamphlets prepared for claimants and treatises as well as training programs for lawyers on veterans' and children's rights are funded by the Agent Orange Class Assistance Program.[43]

Having the plaintiffs and defendants split the costs of a joint document depository in a federal courthouse, as ordered in the breast implant litigation, also facilitates communication. Such an arrangement should be viewed as a form of alternative dispute resolution. The federal court system should in theory be paid for by taxpayers only so that it remains independent of the litigants. But given budget limitations, it may become a quasi-public institution financed partly out of tax funds and partly by litigants.[44]

Use of litigant-paid special masters to control discovery may raise a constitutional issue because Congress must approve appropriations. The practice is analogous to the National Park Service deciding that, if it does not have enough money to run a park, it will charge a new user fee without specific statutory authorization. Taken to the extreme, the constitutional argument might mean that a court must deny plaintiffs access if they cannot pay certain expenses.[45] Perhaps there are litigations, such as the Texaco-Pennzoil case or the Exxon Valdez oil spill, that are so costly that the public should not have to pay for them. Such matters warrant explicit consideration by appellate courts or the legislature. The models of private-public institutions we are developing in mass torts and alternate dispute resolution seem appropriate, but they probably should be authorized in a more formal way.

All these potential forms of communication—both the traditional and the innovative—should be explored, tested, and mined for the benefits they offer in mass cases. Despite our understandable impatience to achieve the benefits of centralized management and control in mass cases, we must insist on maintaining the essential aspects of our fundamentally individual system of justice, including communication and participation. Communication and participation from the earliest stages of the litigation are especially important in mass litigations because settlement will be the result in close to 100 percent of the cases. Individual court appearances by clients at trials are unlikely to occur in a well-run litigation.

The variety of communication devices discussed above, especially the promise of new technologies, offer means for combining the efficient resolution of cases with a meaningful hearing of individual voices. The increasingly popular form of political communication utilized by President Clinton and other politicians, in which citizens are invited to participate in a dialogue through small representative groups chosen from the wider population,[46] is an indication of how new communication methodologies can be used to advantage. The pervasive new technologies of our modern mass society need not contribute to public alienation. They can be harnessed to break down barriers and combat the unfortunate and destructive sentiment that lawyers and judges operate in an inscrutable world distanced from, and inaccessible to, the citizenry.

B. Conflicts of Interest

Related to the question of adequate attorney-client communication are the problems of client control and the lawyer's loyalty to the client. Attorneys who prosecute hundreds or thousands of claims against a single defendant or group of defendants face potentially grave conflicts of interest.[47]

1. Lawyer-Client

Perhaps the most serious potential conflict is that between lawyer and client.[48] What are the ethical obligations of the lawyer who represents the plaintiff class? Class actions, through the device of representation, are premised upon a theory of unity of interest among class members. The attorney's interests, however, may diverge from those of the class members, particularly when it comes to settlement.[49] Usually the attorney has a financial stake in the litigation greater than that of any single litigant. Given the time value of money, the attorney has a substantial incentive to reach a settlement and collect a contingency fee sooner rather than later.[50] By contrast, if the fee is calculated on a lodestar basis (hours x hourly rates) there may be an urge to pile up litigation time before concluding the case.

Class members might have different goals. How does the attorney account for the value the class as a whole might place on nonfinancial factors such as vindication of the class members' claims, or punishment for harm by defendant, in the form of a verdict? These nonmonetary goals of the litigation were important, for example, in the Agent Orange case, when some plaintiffs resented the manufacturers of herbicides containing dioxin; and in the LILCO case, when there were some who wanted to punish the power company for building a nuclear reactor.[51]

To some extent, the present ethical rules have accounted for these conflicts. Contingency fees, of course, are a pillar of our legal system and are blessed by the Model Rules.[52] In the traditional single-client, single-lawyer case, we tolerate the conflict inherent in a contingency fee arrangement because we value highly the "American system" of financing lawsuits and the court access it provides.[53] Where a single lawyer represents one or a few clients, the lawyer's obligation to follow the clients' directions usually controls the tendency to urge settlement in order to recover a quick fee.[54]

With mass tort cases, however, this lawyer-client conflict generally cannot be held in check by the obligation to follow the client's directions. Regardless of whether large numbers of claims are formally aggregated or the lawyer merely represents many clients with similar causes in a consolidated action, the lawyer acts on behalf of a group that cannot effectively control the lawyer's conduct of the litigation. The lawyer often must form his or her own judgments about what course of action is in the best interests of many clients as a group and, perhaps more importantly, best reflects the needs and the unexpressed desires of that group.[55] In many, if not most, instances the client will not even have begun to analyze the problems in any sophisticated or informed way.

Even experienced judges sometimes are lulled by traditional models of individual client participation. In the Manville Trust case, for example, the assumption on appeal was that in the prior bankruptcy proceeding each of tens of thousands of clients participated in a vote on the bankruptcy.[56] While many clients reportedly did vote by ballot in mass meetings organized by the lawyers, the vote was necessarily effectively controlled by the attorneys' advice.[57] It is unlikely that those voting had a full and sophisticated understanding of the nature of the reorganization plan. Certainly none of them (or the courts involved) had any realistic notion of the inadequacy of the resources set aside to settle potential claims. At a minimum, the reality was something far different from the process envisioned by the bankruptcy laws.[58] The appellate courts have in mind the usual case of a limited number of creditors, each with its own counsel, not tens of thousands of unorganized claimants, some known and some unknown.

That there are risks for attorneys in seeking to represent those who claim injury in what is, or may be, a mass tort is illustrated by the Agent Orange and tobacco cases. In the Agent Orange case attorneys for plaintiffs had spent a great deal of time and money pressing the case. Those attorneys who started the litigation spent millions of dollars, ultimately running out of capital. A new financial group took over and was also accumulating large debts. The case was one that, in the court's estimation, could not be won on the merits. Settlement was useful to both sides, but was particularly necessary to counsel for plaintiffs, who would have been bankrupted had the court allowed the case to go forward at enormous unreimbursable expense to them.

The more recent tobacco litigation in New Jersey illustrates the same point.[59] While in form only a single plaintiff was suing, the courts, the public, and the parties recognized that, if the plaintiff won, many billions of dollars in a potential flood of new suits and recoveries were at stake. After the defendants obtained an important preliminary victory replacing the district judge, counsel for plaintiff sought to withdraw on the ground that his law firm could no longer afford to carry the case. The newly assigned judge recognized the public interest in continuing the litigation—treating it, in effect, as a potential mass tort. The court, in accordance with the plaintiff's wish, refused to relieve the attorneys for plaintiff. The court's intervention was justified on the basis of traditional attorney-client relationships and, perhaps, by the public policy concerns about alleged smoking dangers. When an attorney undertakes what is in essence a public litigation, he or she must be prepared for financial destruction as well as glory. The issues transcend traditional one client–one attorney relationships and conflicts. They involve whole communities.

Yet, it seems unfair to place the entire burden of this huge dispute on one attorney. If he or she succeeds, many other attorneys and clients would benefit. In such a situation a consortium of lawyers in a class action might apportion the burdens better.

In class actions where counsel representing the class is not effectively handling the suit, he or she may be replaced by the court.[60] The same power should be found to exist in a mass tort subject to consolidation or bankruptcy. If the attorney with large masses of clients cannot handle the litigation properly either because of lack of capital, managerial skills, professional competence, or as a result of psychological problems, he or she should be replaced. This is a power to be exercised gingerly, but its existence underlies the right of the court to insist that the lawyer properly conduct a litigation—particularly one tinged with the public interest.

2. CLIENT-CLIENT

A. AMONG PRESENT CLIENTS

Other potential conflicts arise between or among single clients or groups of clients represented by a single attorney or firm.[61] While the attorney representing a large number of clients might, in theory, be able to reach some approximation of the objectives of the group as a whole, that attorney cannot possibly account for the varying desires of individual members of the group. At most, a lawyer with many clients can break up a large group into subgroups that share common interests and goals. This approach is sometimes used in asbestos litigation in which plaintiffs' lawyers manage the litigation by thinking of their clients as if they were divided into groups according to the type and seriousness of the harm they claim. In a class action this sort of subgrouping can sometimes be encouraged by formal subclasses, which then must be represented by independent attorneys at greater expense and with greater difficulties in terminating the disputes.[62]

The Second Circuit Court of Appeals disapproved a settlement involving the Manville Trust partly on the grounds that such independent subclasses had to be formed to protect the interests of the various groups with claims against the Trust.[63] Formation of subclasses, however, can result in too much sacrifice in terms of efficiency and bottom-line justice. In the Manville asbestos case, for example, each of the many lawyers represented claimants from each of the many subclasses the Court of Appeals required. Should the lawyers be forced to represent only people from one subclass? Should outside counsel having no clients (and no real expertise in the litigation) be appointed to represent subclasses?[64] The nearly irreconcilable conflicts among the smaller subgroups may thwart settlement entirely, resulting in protracted and costly litigation and insufficient compensation—or, in the case of some future claimants against a limited fund, no compensation.[65]

The asbestos cases present these conflicts most clearly. Those with advanced cancer want their cases pressed first and most strongly. Clients with generally less serious asbestosis and pleural plaque symptoms do not want to wait, even though their damage is less severe. All these cases cannot be tried at once. Mixing the cases for trial and settlement may result in a lower recovery for the more seriously injured,[66] but generally it will result in a quicker fee for counsel.

In the asbestos cases a number of defendants are seeking global solutions that provide for prompt payment to those most seriously injured while at the same time providing guarantees that the less seriously injured can be paid in the future. One imaginative and seemingly sensible approach has been agreed to between the Center for Claims Resolution (CCR), representing a number of defendants, and two of the leading plaintiffs' attorneys.[67] Other attorneys object strenuously to this scheme. It should be noted that the proposed settlement uses an opt-out class action as the vehicle to provide for enforcement. The class action gives the court ultimate responsibility to consider fairness between present and future claimants and between the more and less seriously injured claimants. In view of the opposition of other distinguished members of the bar, the courts will have a chance to fully evaluate the program in public after fairness hearings. This exercise of court oversight and discretion is, I submit, the only available adequate substitute for traditional ethical rules.

B. BETWEEN PRESENT AND FUTURE CLAIMANTS

Even more pressing and difficult is the problem of future claimants who are not yet represented by a lawyer.[68] This issue is almost always present in some form in mass tort cases because long latency periods are needed to discover injuries, and a limited fund probably will not compensate everyone fully.[69] The interests of the lawyer's present clients are likely to be in conflict with the interests of future claimants.[70] In distributing funds, attorneys generally believe present clients prefer a first-in, first-out (FIFO) approach or one based on the seriousness of the claim, as long as there is enough money to pay all present clients. Potential future claimants, who we know will exist in large numbers in asbestos and other cases, require protection against depletion of limited funds before they have an opportunity to assert their rights.[71]

A humane communitarian ethic requires that future claimants be included in rather than excluded from the community of those the courts recognize as harmed and in need.[72] Blind adherence to FIFO coupled with 100 percent payment of present claims is unjust. A system that willingly turns its back on injured members of the community, even though they may not yet have names and faces, is unlikely to maintain the public confidence. Our courts belong to all the people, not just those who arrive first at the courthouse door.

In the Manville Trust case the court insisted, over the objection of plaintiffs' counsel, on appointing a representative of future claimants to see that their interests were protected.[73] Simultaneously it appointed Margaret A. Berger under Rule 706 of the Federal Rules of Evidence to consult with scientists in order to determine, as far as was possible, the probable extent and nature of future claims against the trust.[74] Both defendants' and plaintiffs' attorneys have opposed attempts by the court to obtain some scientifically based assessment of future claims. Present indications are that there are several hundred thousand potential claimants. The plaintiffs' attorneys would rather not know about this huge tail extending into the future because the courts and defendants will be likely to reserve more funds for future cases. This means less for present clients, with a lower amount for fees in the immediate future. Defendants in mass tort cases also oppose a quantification of the large number of potential claimants: first, because it may encourage counsel to look for those clients; second, because the defendants may have to list huge liabilities and reserves on their Securities and Exchange Commission statements; and third, because current executives of defendants want to present a rosy picture of potential profits to enhance their own present compensation.

Prediction itself is extremely difficult. Complex epidemiological and demographic assessments of the prospective course of the relevant diseases must be made. In addition, the question of how many potential claims will result in actual claims depends upon future interest of attorneys, possible substantive and procedural changes in the law, and a host of political decisions such as those dealing with national health insurance and sociological conditions.[75] Finally, if too much protection of possible future claimants is given, present needy people may suffer.[76]

Sometimes, as in Agent Orange, the structure of the settlement itself protects most possible future claimants by providing for a continuing right to apply for court funds as disability or disease becomes manifest. Future claimants require some representation where it is clear, as it quickly became in the Manville Trust settlement, that the available fund is too small in relation to even conservative estimates of potential claims. The conflict of interest is simply too great to expect even the most community-minded lawyer who represents a present claimant to account fully for the needs of future claimants.

Establishing registries for the least serious of asbestos-related diseases (pleural plaque and nondisabling asbestosis), which place less serious claims on a separate inactive docket, has been another means in asbestos cases of avoiding the unjust results that can be caused by a FIFO treatment of claims.[77] This technique was used, for example, in Boston[78] and has been considered in connection with the consolidated federal asbestos actions in Philadelphia.[79]

There can be a cost in creating more distinct subgroups, each with its own representation. As we have learned in the Manville Trust litigation, the more subclasses created, the more severe conflicts bubble to the surface and inhibit settlement. We must strike the appropriate balance between allowing the various voices within the community to be heard and compromising disputes in a way that provides relatively prompt succor to the injured. The resources of defendants and, ultimately, the community must not be exhausted by protracted litigation.

C. SECRECY

Let us turn now to examine how the lawyer's obligation to maintain client confidences[80] and other ethical duties are implicated by secrecy agreements in mass tort cases. In this area it becomes impossible to discuss the lawyer's obligations without also considering the role of the judge.

Many, if not all, mass tort cases involve serious public concerns in terms of safety and the prevention of future injuries from the same harm. And yet, many of these cases terminate in some form of secrecy agreement. In some instances the extensive utilization of settlements may prevent effective development of the law and the facts.[81]

Historically, the private litigant has not been required to take into account public safety in vindicating his or her rights. More significantly, the plaintiffs' attorney's duty of loyalty requires him or her to put the client's interests ahead of all others. In traditional theory, the lawyer has no ethical obligation to consider the interests of third parties. Likewise, the defendant's attorney, according to the ethical rules, is to maintain the client's confidences. There is an affirmative duty not to reveal information.

Some plaintiffs' and defendants' attorneys tell me that it is almost impossible to settle many mass tort cases without a secrecy agreement.

This has been my own experience in helping to settle thousands of cases.

Secrecy often has been, in fact, the price of settlement. It is not unusual for a defendant to "sweeten" the settlement offer to plaintiffs on condition of secrecy. The defendant may threaten the plaintiff with a lengthy and expensive trial to coerce confidentiality. Some court cases can be brought and settled without the filing of a single revelatory document.[82] Others are settled on just the threat of legal action with no public record.[83] Since the ethical rules require that attorneys obtain a swift and optimal recovery for their clients, the plaintiffs' attorney seems to have little choice but to accept a favorable settlement offer on secrecy terms.

Three categories of secrecy should be considered separately: (1) secrecy as to documents that appear to reveal a defendant's negligent or otherwise wrongful conduct, such as an engineer's report during the early development of a product indicating incipient dangers; (2) secrecy as to the amount of a settlement or terms of payment;[84] and (3) secrecy as to conversations among attorneys on either plaintiff's or defendant's side, or even between plaintiff and defense counsel.

1. DOCUMENTS AND ORAL ADMISSIONS RELATING TO MERITS

The most common form of secrecy utilized by the defendant in a mass tort case is the protective order. Federal Rule of Civil Procedure 26(c) permits a party to seek a protective order prohibiting dissemination of information produced in discovery upon a showing of "good cause." This provision does not specifically refer to the public interest. Rather, it applies primarily to commercially sensitive information that might cause the defendant some competitive harm.[85] Defendants want to avoid disclosure of damaging information. Plaintiffs desire to use this damaging information as a negotiation tool for larger settlements for clients in the future.

"Smoking gun" documents are the most damaging form of this information. They indicate defendants knew of the danger but suppressed the information.[86] Oral material obtained in depositions is also often highly useful to plaintiffs and devastating to defendants. Documents showing cover-ups or early knowledge by defendants of defects can lead to billions of dollars in punitive damages as well as to extensive liability for ordinary damages, so there is strong reason for defendants to try to keep them secret.[87] Threats by plaintiffs' attorneys to reveal them can be a powerful lever for higher settlements.[88]

The societal interest in knowing what went wrong and why is great. Yet, there is some basis for the points made by defendants' counsel that, first, the cost and time to explain a single document taken out of context by a plaintiff's lawyer creates an incentive not to write things down, and, second, what appears damning may, in context after difficult proof, be shown to be neutral or even favorable to the defendant.

Courts have broad discretion in entering protective orders and sealing records. Most agreements are uncontested,[89] and crowded calendars put great pressure on judges to move cases. As a result, judges routinely approve sealing and secrecy orders. Settlement agreements are filed under seal as a matter of course.

It has been my practice to append a note to such approvals that "this order is subject to modification by the court in the public interest." In the Agent Orange case I set aside one of these orders after settlement because the public needed to know the facts.[90]

Ultimately, if the court is faced with the question whether to seal documents, it should engage in a balancing test, weighing the interest of the plaintiff against the interests in keeping the information confidential.[91]

In addition, judges should consider the interests of litigants in other suits, the needs of regulatory agencies to have access to information, concerns of public interest groups, and the interests of future plaintiffs.[92]

In cases dealing with sociopolitical problems, the court must look to the effect on the community. The individual litigant's needs cannot be the court's sole concern. The mass tort case is, as already noted, similar to an institutional reform case in its impact. The public, which created and funds our judicial institutions, depends upon those institutions to protect it. Sometimes the needs of individual members of the community must yield to those of the community as a whole.[93]

Governmental regulatory systems designed to protect the public are generally inadequate.[94] Mechanisms such as the Occupational Safety and Health Administration (OSHA), the Consumer Product Safety Commission (CPSC), the Food and Drug Administration (FDA), and the Environmental Protection Agency (EPA) have not yet fulfilled their promise, leaving society insufficiently protected.

Although the Consumer Product Safety Act requires manufacturers to report defects that have or may cause serious injury or death, substantial underreporting appears to be the rule. Less than two hundred product hazard reports from nearly two million businesses engaged in manufacturing, distributing, or selling consumer products are received annually.[95] There is a great disincentive to report. A firm's own report may serve as damaging documentary evidence in a product liability lawsuit.[96]

In 1990 reporting requirements were strengthened to require companies to report any product that was the subject of three product liability lawsuits in a three-year period.[97] Portions of these lawsuit reports, however, remain confidential and are not subject to discovery.[98]

The CPSC, for example, has been criticized for acting more "like a lap dog" than a "pit bull" in its failure to effectively monitor such products as children's toys and all-terrain vehicles.[99] The agency has been characterized as a "reluctant accomplice of manufacturers who rely on the threat of litigation against agency action to force the CPSC to back down from ordering a recall, or agree to a token recall."[100]

OSHA's record in regulating worker exposure to hazardous substances reveals that it too has been less than dramatically successful. One study reports that the agency is only equipped to inspect workplaces an average of once every eighty-four years and high-hazard workplaces an average of once every twenty-five years.[101] Even where OSHA announces millions of dollars in fines for serious abuses, the agency often quietly forgives those penalties.[102] National surveys reveal, for example, that industrial chemical manufacturers fail to warn adequately of the hazards of their products.[103] Workers often unknowingly expose themselves to chemical dangers and chemically induced disease.[104]

The recent revelations about the possibly serious side effects associated with silicone gel breast implants demonstrate the FDA's problems. Even though the agency had years to investigate, it has been charged that it "botch[ed] its responsibility," leaving an estimated one million women with implants "in emotional and medical limbo."[105] And although the details of the dangers of silicone implants were allegedly disclosed to trial lawyers more than eight years ago, because the court kept the records confidential, the FDA was "left in the dark."[106] This is not to say that science has provided a legitimate basis for many of the pending and prospective breast implant cases. The studies are only now under way. Lawyers and judges should keep open minds. But it seems fairly clear that little adequate scientific study was sponsored or consulted by the FDA.[107] This benign neglect by agencies set up to protect the public is one of the reasons for our reliance on the tort system for protection.[108]

Should we be satisfied with a system that requires officers of the court to remain silent for years while more and more women suffer from what they think was harm caused by breast implants? If this silence is "a price we must pay," what do we receive in return?

Currently a national campaign is under way, in the name of public safety, to create a presumption of public access to all information produced in litigation.[109] Advocates claim that protective orders are being used to hide product defects and public hazards and have been pressing for legislation to restrict the courts' discretion to issue protective and sealing orders.[110] These plaintiffs' attorneys have a selfish interest in opening the files for other litigations. Yet, much can be said in favor of the public's right to know.[111]

Arguably, even out-of-court procedures such as arbitration and the like affect the public interest. A federal statute supports our national arbitration scheme.[112] Should attorneys have an ethical obligation to inform the public, or at least the appropriate government body, of dangers revealed in private arbitrations?[113] Is this sound as a matter of public policy? I think it is, under adequate judicial control.

While legislation to limit protective orders has been defeated in most jurisdictions, two states, Florida and Texas, have enacted sweeping reforms to restrict the courts' ability to seal documents. Both provisions are facing constitutional challenges. The Florida statute[114] prohibits a court from issuing a protective order that conceals "information concerning a public hazard." A public hazard is broadly defined as "a product that has or is likely to cause injury."

The Texas rule[115] establishes a presumption that civil records be open. To obtain a protective order, a party has the heavy burden of showing a "specific, serious and substantial interest which clearly outweighs a presumption of openness to the general public." A court can seal the records only after deciding that the interest at stake outweighs the public interest in access. The order, however, can always be contested after it is granted. The Texas rule is being challenged in product liability cases involving the sleep-inducing drug Halcion, the antidepressant Prozac, and the Ford Bronco II.[116]

In 1993 at least fifteen states probably considered proposals to change the rules about protective orders,[117] and action is sought at the federal level as well.[118] This sunshine approach is not without its critics. One defense attorney from a large firm who testified before a California legislative committee investigating protective orders and the public safety asserted that troops in the Persian Gulf War were fighting to prevent the type of privacy invasion that such a rule would effect.[119] Another likened forcing defense attorneys to consider the public interest in revelation of potential dangers to asking a criminal defense attorney who knows his client is guilty to turn the client over to the authorities.[120]

The knowledge that secrecy cannot be depended on may discourage engineers and others from expressing doubts about a policy in written reports.[121] There is thus a possibility that less secrecy may increase dangers to society. Even some attorneys for plaintiffs admit that rules limiting protective orders make them nervous because they "inject a wild card into the settlement game."

Protective orders may have a legitimate role when there is no public impact or when true trade secrets are involved. But we can strike a fairer balance between privacy interests of corporations and the health and safety of the public.[122] A publicly maintained legal system ought not protect those who engage in misconduct, conceal the cause of injury from the victims, or render potential victims vulnerable. Moreover, such secrecy defeats the deterrent function of the justice system.

The balance, it is submitted, must involve the exercise of some judicial discretion. Yet, even judges have a conflict. They are under great pressure to clear their calendars. They will tend, therefore, to approve a secrecy agreement that encourages settlement. One law professor suggested that a remedy might be for the court to employ an ombudsperson to weigh the secrecy issue independently of the trial judge. In the federal courts a magistrate judge might do the job, although this official too would want to see the court's calendar reduced.

Whatever the method chosen, it should be a national approach whenever cases are consolidated on a national basis. It is not possible to control the litigation effectively if each state's privileges and secrecy laws are applied. Such laws should, for purposes of mass torts, be deemed procedural so that, under *Erie*,[123] the federal court does not have to apply the laws of fifty states.

2. SETTLEMENT AMOUNTS

The amount of settlement in any particular case is normally a matter of much less public interest than is evidence of the merits.[124] Sometimes a defendant will give a premium to a particularly effective advocate or appealing case because going to trial might result in an unusually high verdict, ratcheting up settlements across the board. At other times the defendant will agree to a settlement in a completely meritless case because the jurisdiction is notoriously proplaintiff and resistance is hopeless. But the defendant may not wish to provide a basis for national settlements before more neutral judges and juries. One leading defense attorney complained to me, "Plaintiffs' attorneys have misled the public into believing that the settlement amount is linked to the worth of the case." But what a willing buyer and seller agree upon is value, and a statistical analysis of jury verdicts and settlements is used in all mature litigations to set values. Here, again, some discretion by the court is called for.

These considerations appear to me to be reasonable.[125] I see no strong reason to oppose some form of secrecy as to settlement amount. Neither plaintiff nor defense counsel seem to object, and there is no great public interest.

There may, however, be occasions when only one plaintiff's attorney is aware of a problem that, if known, could result in a huge influx of cases. A secret settlement conceivably could result in great injustice.[126] This situation is highly unlikely in view of the vigilance of the press and the bar. But should it exist, the court would, I believe, be justified in refusing to suppress at least the fact—if not the amount—of the settlement.

Of course, the parties could forestall judicial intervention by settling before the suit is started. To start the suit, settle secretly, and then withdraw without informing the court of the fact that a settlement occurred seems to me to be an unethical act by attorneys for both sides. Having taken advantage of the court system paid for by the public, the attorneys should have an obligation of candor to the court and, if the court so orders, to the public.[127]

3. WITHDRAWAL OF OPINIONS

When a comprehensive opinion is destroyed as part of a settlement, so, too, are the answers to complex questions such as "the interpretation and validity of a statute, the interpretation of a contract clause regarding payment of pollution clean-up costs and the effects of hazardous substances upon individuals and the environment."[128] According to Professor Jill Fisch, "The time and effort invested in resolving these issues is a public resource" which inures to the benefit of future claimants as well.[129]

Professor Fisch has a point. Unless an error has been demonstrated, once an opinion is issued there is strong reason not to withdraw it because it can assist other courts and parties in their analysis.[130] Nevertheless, there may be rare situations where withdrawal will sufficiently defuse a situation so that a major settlement beneficial to the public will result.[131] Hard-and-fast rules in this area may be dangerous.[132]

D. BUYOUTS

Ethical dilemmas regarding secrecy go well beyond the scope of protective orders and secret settlements. Suppose a defendant conditions a more generous settlement on the plaintiffs' attorney, experienced in a particular litigation, not taking any more cases against that defendant. The attorney may be asked to give up copies of documents and depositions. He or she may be hired as a consultant to the defendant.

There is an ethical obligation to maximize the client's benefit. There is also an ethical rule that one may not restrict an attorney's right to practice.[133] What is the lawyer's obligation to a client who does not yet exist and whom he or she may never represent? Does a lawyer have a duty to future clients by virtue of having once offered his or her services? Or what happens if a defendant offers a larger settlement on the condition that the attorney say nothing publicly about the case? Is it unethical to give up the right to discuss the case or to inform the public? Does the attorney's duty to the individual client always prevail?

On April 16, 1993, the American Bar Association issued Ethics Formal Opinion 93–371 on this subject. The opinion states,

A restriction on the right of plaintiffs' counsel to represent present clients and future claimants against a defendant as part of a global settlement of some counsel's existing clients' claims against that same defendant represents an impermissible restriction on the right to practice which may not be demanded or accepted without violating Model Rule 5.6(b).

Recognizing that the problem "raises important issues regarding the intersection between a lawyer's duty to his or her present clients under Model Rule 1.2 and impermissible restrictions in the right of a lawyer to practice under Model Rule 5.6," the opinion found most persuasive the arguments under Rule 5.6. "While the Model Rules generally require that the client's interests be put first, forcing a lawyer to give up future representations may be asking too much, particularly in light of the strong countervailing policy favoring the public's unfettered choice of counsel." If an offer of this type of conditional settlement is unethical, does the plaintiffs' lawyer who receives such an offer have a duty to report the defense lawyer who makes an offer?[134]

Corporate "buyouts" of classes of claimants are not new. One of the earliest reported buyouts resulted from the deaths of more than seven hundred workers from silicosis caused by the construction of the Hawk's Nest Tunnel in West Virginia in the early 1930s.[135] Union Carbide Corporation hired black migrant laborers to work on the project without taking the most minimal safety precautions. Despite substantial resistance by defendants, eventually hundreds of suits were filed. In what was then the longest trial in the country (five weeks), a team of plaintiffs' lawyers presented 175 witnesses. Since the plaintiffs had limited resources, their attorneys made a considerable investment in the case, hoping that a favorable verdict would lead to a large number of settlements. The jury deadlocked.

Shortly before a second case was to come to trial, seventeen plaintiffs' lawyers entered into an out-of-court settlement on behalf of 157 claimants. The claimants had asked for $4 million but were given $130,000, half of which went to the attorneys. It was later revealed that the plaintiffs' attorneys had secretly signed a contract with the tunnel contractor that provided the attorneys, not the clients, with an additional $20,000 if they agreed not to engage in any further legal action. Upon learning of the agreement, the judge ordered that half that sum go to the plaintiffs. Nevertheless, the judge upheld a provision that the plaintiffs' lawyers surrender all case records to the defendants.

The second trial also resulted in a hung jury. Ultimately, a block settlement was agreed upon, and again, the plaintiffs' lawyers were required to turn over all legal papers to the defense. They were obliged to suppress all information relating to the case. These same tactics were used in an early asbestos case against Johns-Manville[136] and in the settlement of the Buffalo Creek Disaster.[137]

These "buyouts" need to be supervised by the courts in the same way as a settlement of a class action would be. The court has an obligation to the clients and to the community to see that the clients understand the arrangement and that it is fair. The court should also be able to veto any arrangement for secrecy under which files are returned to defendants and plaintiffs' lawyers agree to take no future cases. The Hawk's Nest case was a shameful episode in American jurisprudence. Without the judge's intervention it would have been even worse.[138]

E. Aggregate Settlements

Aggregate settlements present yet another problem of legal ethics.[139] There is nothing that would seem on its face more unethical (or more common) in mass litigation than for a defendant to offer an aggregate settlement of all clients' claims and for plaintiffs' counsel to take it.[140] In the asbestos, DES, and Agent Orange cases, I routinely accepted global agreements to what I concluded was the benefit of all parties and the public. Was I unethical? Were the lawyers?

Often the pressure for block settlements comes from plaintiffs' attorneys who hope to get something for a large mass of questionable cases.[141] Some attorneys are selective about the cases they take, while others will take almost any case without regard to its merit, hoping for a global settlement. The attorneys with thousands of cases are almost invariably in this second category.

Even though bulk settlements may technically violate ethical rules, judges often encourage their acceptance to terminate a large number of cases. The defendants generally prefer them because they save transaction costs and usually result in savings per case. Plaintiffs' counsel like them because they generally do not reduce their percentage fee per case so that, because of the large settlement amounts, their lawyer's hourly fees jump spectacularly. An audit of the Baltimore asbestos cases, for example, might show a net fee on the order of thousands of dollars per hour.[142] Judges occasionally have audited fees after settlement, and a few attorneys have made fee adjustments; a few judges have exerted moral suasion to shift at least some of the benefits of bulk settlements to clients.[143]

If the lawyer accepts the aggregate sum, how does he or she divide it among his clients? One attorney told me that his conscience determines the fair value of each person's claim.[144] He personally examines each case and values it. If the total demand is not obtained, each claim is reduced on a percentage basis, pro rata. In a very time-consuming process, each client then has a one-to-one conference with the attorney, and cases are reassessed if necessary. This procedure may work with tens or even a few hundred clients, but certainly not with thousands. Consider the temptations lawyers face in dividing a lump-sum settlement. Is it not human to favor the client whom you like or who has some leverage or who has a relationship with the union that referred large numbers of its members?

To help insulate themselves against claims of favoritism, some attorneys use the services of special masters to distribute lump settlement funds. Others have asked the judge in charge to mediate the division issues. These seem like useful devices which should be encouraged. I have observed their successful use in my own court.

Some commentators propose taking the valuation process out of the attorney's hands altogether by utilizing statistical claim profiles to set baseline appraisals of the value of individual claims.[145] The profiles would provide a kind of market value for different categories of claims. Data would be derived from prior adjudications and settlements in similar cases, and the court would hold a hearing to evaluate the reliability and fairness of the profiles.

The ethical rules seem to require that, where an aggregate settlement is used, each client must accept both the overall settlement and his or her own individual award. What do the attorney and the court do if there are a few holdouts among the plaintiffs?[146] Assuming that the settlement is fair, is it appropriate for either the attorney or the judge to persuade the recalcitrant person by offering him or her more money or by threatening not to find time to try his or her case? If efforts at persuasion fail, must the lawyer pursue the case to trial for that lone plaintiff? After all, the defendant settled to dispose of the case without trial. Is it ethical to ask the nonsettling plaintiff to find new counsel? Should the court allow the attorney to withdraw? Should courts permit agreements among plaintiffs under which a majority vote will control acceptance of settlement for the entire group?[147]

The theoretical answer in a nonclass, nonbankruptcy setting is that the individual client calls the tune, but I have yet to see plaintiffs successfully ignore their attorney's advice to settle an asbestos or DES case. Some in the Agent Orange case did object to settlement. Their objection was based primarily on the desire for moral vindication rather than on the merits and chance for recovery had the case been tried.

A similar problem occurs when a plaintiffs' attorney or defense counsel agrees to settle a group of cases based upon a set formula only if his or her adversary agrees to apply that formula in future cases. Such a proposal was advanced by an attorney in a case recently before me and was rejected by the other side on ethical grounds. It almost certainly violates ethical rules for an attorney to bind future clients to an automatic settlement formula. Such an agreement, however, might be necessary to settlement in some cases. In general, I think an attorney should be allowed to enter into such a deal as long as he or she obtains the consent of future clients, at the outset of the representation, to be bound by the applicable formula.

F. FINANCING

All cases require financing of some sort.[148] Apparently even Mrs. Palsgraf had difficulty financing her litigation.[149] The mass tort case, however, presents special ethical problems for plaintiffs' attorneys in meeting great expenses. In a typical tort case, where a contingency fee arrangement is utilized, the lawyer usually is able to pay for the costs of the litigation within the parameters of the ethical rules until settlement or judgment. In a mass case, however, not only are expenses often astronomical,[150] but the lag time between the beginning of the litigation and its resolution can be a decade or more. Such cases typically involve technological and policy issues, extensive discovery, expert witnesses, unusual questions of causation, and a great deal of preparation. Plaintiffs' counsel I have interviewed tell me of expending tens of millions of dollars before they receive any fee in some cases.

We must recognize, however, that the success of the mass tort plaintiffs' bar, particularly in the asbestos cases, has furnished it with so much capital, managerial skills, and expertise that it can quickly move into new fields of opportunity such as breast implants or repetitive stress syndrome. Meetings and symposia ensure that plaintiffs' attorneys across the country are kept up-to-date. Documents are put on computer and shared among plaintiffs. Experts who will be available for hire are quickly contacted. Even document analysis is for sale. What formerly might have taken years of development can now take place in a few months.

The ethical rules permit the attorney to advance the costs of litigation, but the client must remain ultimately liable for such costs. The rule, on its face, would appear to prohibit an attorney from agreeing not to seek reimbursement for costs involved if the litigation is unsuccessful.

Plaintiffs' attorneys tell me they ignore this rule—the plaintiff does not pay if there is no recovery in a mass tort litigation. In fact, if this rule were strictly enforced, it would probably paralyze class and mass litigation. Attorneys for plaintiffs advocate creating a mass tort exception to the rule. I believe these mass torts, as a way of compensating the injured, are sufficiently important to society (absent legislative action to replace them) that financing without recourse to the client should be recognized as acceptable.[151]

The contingency fee is an incentive to settle the case quickly, avoiding outlay of the large sums of money necessary to finance mass cases. Paradoxically the class action may slow down settlement because fees have, mistakenly I think, been computed almost entirely on a lodestar basis. This rule often leads to unnecessary discovery and delays so the lawyer's profit per hour can be aggregated into a large sum. Plaintiffs' attorneys generally dislike class actions because the court can control fees and because the judge has explicit power to ensure that clients are treated in a way the court thinks appropriate. Even attorneys who want only to do well by their clients and who do not overreach chafe at this judicial oversight.

If counsel is without financial resources to handle litigation, he or she may feel pressured to settle some cases quickly to finance the litigation—to prime the pump, so to speak. Attorneys with limited capital are forced to associate with other attorneys who can both manage the litigation and underwrite its costs. One court created a cooperative partial financing arrangement for plaintiffs' attorneys.[152]

No matter how the case is financed, all financial arrangements should be revealed in advance to the court. Here some secrecy through in camera, ex parte devices may be needed to prevent the opponent from learning of his adversary's financial base. If a defendant knows a plaintiff's resources can be exhausted through attrition in discovery, that defendant loses some of the incentive to settle early at a reasonable figure.

In the Agent Orange case, plaintiffs' counsel attempted a creative financing arrangement.[153] With more than $3 million already expended in the case, the plaintiffs faced a financing crisis. They agreed to allow investor attorneys to share fees based primarily upon the contribution of money rather than time. The "investors" were to receive a multiple repayment of the cash investment at the end of the case. Questions arose whether this unorthodox treble payment ran afoul of the prohibition on fee-splitting or whether it constituted an impermissible stake in the outcome of the litigation.

The trial court insisted on a reorganization of the agreement to give greater weight to the working lawyers as opposed to the investors. To overcome some ethical dilemmas, the trial judge considered the Plaintiffs' Management Committee to be an ad hoc law firm.[154] Law firms make internal arrangements giving greater financial rewards to rainmakers and partner-investors. I saw no reason to prevent a similar arrangement for the committee charged with conducting the litigation. The group was not in any way involved with forwarding clients to split fees. Moreover, it functioned like a traditional law firm in that it had common obligations of loyalty and confidentiality. Nor was the stake in the action impermissible, for the agreement served only to redistribute attorneys' fees; it did not involve the reduction of benefits to clients.

My own view was that without such an arrangement financing the Agent Orange case would have been virtually impossible. One disadvantage of the scheme, of course, was that the "investors" might favor an early settlement to recoup their profits as soon as possible, thus increasing the rate of return on their investment, but these time pressures exist in any form of financing.

The Court of Appeals rejected this approach.[155] It viewed the compensation as giving a better than average return to investors. Investing money was, the court believed, unacceptably more profitable than investing time. The court also disapproved the scheme because of its potential for diverting the loyalty of the investor-attorneys. It did agree with the trial court that the arrangement should have been revealed to the court at the outset of the litigation. Some commentators believe that the Court of Appeals did not realistically recognize the funding problems in the Agent Orange case.[156] Too narrow a view of permissible methods of financing would tend to drive these cases out of court or into the hands of the wealthiest plaintiffs' law firms, so the trial court should have considerable discretion to approve nontraditional forms of financing.

Recognizing the severe difficulties involved in financing mass cases, some commentators have suggested another creative financing approach: auctioning the rights to prosecute class actions.[157] After a claim is filed and a judge determines that the case is suitable for auction, notice would be posted in appropriate newspapers requesting sealed bids. Bidders could include nonlawyers and even a defendant in the case. The winning bidder would pay the bid amount to the court. The judge, after deducting expenses for the costs of the auction, would compensate the lawyers who initially filed the litigation and who assisted the court in "packaging" the lawsuit for sale. The remaining funds would be used for notice to the class and ultimately for distribution as in standard class action litigation. The difference from the traditional approach is that the funds would be deposited before trial or settlement. If the defendant won the bid, it could simply move for dismissal with prejudice. Otherwise, the winner would prosecute the claim. The winner would become the owner of the claim and act as his or her own agent. He or she would have the same incentive to litigate as would the sole owner of traditional litigation, and there would be no incentive to engage in a collusive settlement with the defendant. Transaction costs would presumably be reduced.

Such interesting results of economic analysis stand on their head traditional notions about champerty, but they do comport with some of the realities of mass litigation. Under this scheme, deserving persons who otherwise could not obtain help would be enabled to find attorneys with the skill and resources to contend with often well-heeled defendants.[158]

My own preference is for a more traditional method of financing, with the controlling counsel having a continuing connection with a substantial number of clients. We ought to try to avoid cutting the sympathetic connection between those injured and the lawyers and court. These are flesh-and-blood claimants, not reasonable-person economic cutouts. They deserve to be treated as people by attorneys who know at least some of them as suffering human beings.

Moreover, the entrepreneurial aspects of litigation should not be ignored. The lawyer who has invested substantial capital to develop a theory and expertise should not be replaced willy-nilly by the latecomer who has done little to bring the litigation to fruition.[159]

G. FEES

1. PLAINTIFFS

Unreasonable fees violate the attorney's ethical obligations under the disciplinary rules. Fees for plaintiffs' attorneys associated with mass tort litigation have sometimes been astronomical. In a mass tort case—unlike the typical contingent fee tort case—the lawyer's stake in the litigation is greater than each individual client's. Total fees will far exceed individual payments to plaintiffs, particularly in cases with a limited fund.[160] This is also the case in a class action where each class member may stand to recover relatively little. We tolerate the lawyer's disproportionate stake to encourage the prosecution of litigation that may produce benefits to society. At the same time, however, we must remember that unreasonable fees violate the attorney's ethical obligations.[161]

Some plaintiffs' attorneys reportedly have reaped rates of many thousands of dollars per hour.[162] Often these fees are based on a contingency arrangement when there is simply no contingency—the plaintiff is bound to recover. In these cases the plaintiff would do much better with an hourly fee retainer, but typically the plaintiff is not given the option of such an agreement. In air crash and other mass accident cases, where recovery is almost certain, some clients are signed up with contingency fees at or near the crash scene. They should at least have the right to escape such arrangements within a few months of the original retainer, when the marketplace might provide a more reasonable fee arrangement.

Abuses exist such as were reported in a Texas school bus accident, where the Coca Cola Company was the defendant.[163] Despite the fact that recovery was assured because liability and damages were clear and there was not even the remote likelihood of a trial, the lawyers received more than $30 million of the $67 million wrongful death settlement for sixteen cases.[164] The hourly rate was said to be $12,500.[165] One academic has proposed tightly controlled fees in mass cases.[166] Judges in charge of such cases should not tolerate this abuse, but we do, partly out of concern for our traditional passive role. In the *Manville* case a fee cap of 25 percent we imposed was trumped by some judges in other states who allowed millions of dollars more for individual lawyers in conformity with local practice.

Thousands upon thousands of asbestos-exposed workers are recruited for lawyers, often by union officials through the use of mass medical screening. The clients routinely sign contingency fee retainer agreements, without being apprised of the degree of risk and without being offered the possibility of paying an hourly rate. Mass settlements then result in hundreds or thousands of cases being resolved in a single proceeding with relatively little work being done per client.[167]

New Jersey has addressed this problem by limiting contingent fees when multiple clients are involved to a percentage of the aggregate sum. This arrangement could result in a dramatic saving to plaintiffs. It was orally reported to me, however, that the rule is often ignored.

In one case the plaintiffs' attorneys reportedly settled their current cases for several hundred million dollars and, allegedly, as part of the deal brought a class action to cover future claimants.[168] Without regard to the merits of the settlement, it is curious that under present practice, fees would be subject to control by the court only in the class action context. Surely fees of many tens of millions of dollars for related multi-district litigation should also be supervised by the court. There is little doubt that a contingent fee agreement is unenforceable unless it is "fair" to the client.[169] Courts have been said to have inherent authority to regulate contingency fees even outside the class action context.[170]

Both plaintiffs' and defendants' attorneys I interviewed agreed that, in a mass tort case with a contingency fee, it is reasonable to ask for fees to be reduced. On a volume basis, the reduced fee makes sense if the benefit goes to the client, not the defendant. Some responsible plaintiffs' attorneys have negotiated reduced fees when, for example, they obtain large numbers of cases from unions. Although this seems entirely sensible to me, there are some who believe that it smacks of fee-splitting.[171]

Many other ethical questions emanate from the fee issue. What is the duty of the plaintiffs' attorney to minimize fees and allocate them when the overall fee is not commensurate with the work done for each individual client? Should the attorney be required to offer the client an hourly rate? Must he advise the client of the low risk involved when settlements for a particular type of injury are common, if not guaranteed? Should the contingency fee be based solely on the aggregate amount of the settlement? A major premise of our tolerance of contingency fees, after all, is the idea that what seems often to be a huge fee must be discounted by the risk the lawyer takes of losing and recovering nothing.[172] Once an attorney undertakes the case, it may prove quite expensive and result in no fee at all.[173]

Professor Lester Brickman and his associates have developed a plan that would provide a mechanical method of reducing "excessive" contingency fees where there was no real risk.[174] In essence, the defendant would be entitled to make a prompt offer to settle. If the offer were not accepted, plaintiffs' fees would be limited to the contingency of a recovery above this assured amount.[175] While the details are ingenious, I would prefer in most mass torts a court-approved fee based on time spent plus a multiplier for risk. The problem is, of course, that when the claimant contracts with a lawyer, he or she is not in a position to bargain effectively about fees. Particularly in a mature case the lawyer is aware of limited risks and can, by settling large numbers of cases, achieve a huge hourly rate. The economic analysis as well as the effects on keeping courthouses open for people with no funds to hire lawyers on an hourly or fixed fee basis and the effects on deterrence are quite complex and difficult to predict if fee arrangements are to be changed by fiat. Given the present state of the art, freedom to contract between client and attorney with a backstop of supervision by the court to prevent grossly excessive fees seems most practicable.[176]

How aggressive should the court be in monitoring fees? In a class action the court must approve the fee. Where there are consolidations of huge numbers of cases, should fees not also be supervised by the court to prevent overreaching?[177] In my view, consolidations should be treated for some purposes as class actions to assure judicial review of fees and settlements.[178] It is only a matter of time before an aggressive attorney sues a lawyer on behalf of a frustrated class for excessive fees and incompetence in handling a mass tort.[179]

Particular care must be taken in mass tort cases to ensure that the contingency fee system and the incentives that it is founded upon operate properly and are not distorted by the nature and size of the cases. In large class actions and other consolidated litigations, the treatment of attorneys' fees often determines the shape of settlement.[180] An example of problematic contingency fee arrangements are "claims made" settlements in class actions in which the defendant sets aside a fund to meet plaintiffs' claims according to a formula, with an excess remaining after all claims are processed reverting to the defendant or its insurers.[181] The plaintiffs' attorneys often will receive a fee calculated upon a percentage of the total fund, regardless of how much of the fund ultimately ends up in the pockets of the claimants.

Should the cases be awarded to the lowest bidder? Stating that lawyers "have shown a virtual allergy to price competition,"[182] Federal District Judge Vaughn Walker of California, in a securities case, asked twenty-nine of the nation's leading class action law firms to submit to competitive bidding for appointment as lead counsel in the case.[183] Only four firms submitted bids.[184] The bids included a sliding scale of percentages that declined as the size of the recovery increased but increased as the time to effect the recovery lengthened.[185] The winning bid called for fees of 30 percent of any recovery of less than $1 million if the case lasted more than a year, declining to 15 percent for a recovery greater than $15 million and only 12 percent if that recovery was achieved in less than a year.[186] The bid also included a cap on recovery of expenses that was more than $450,000 below the cap in another competitor's bid.[187]

Competitive bidding might possibly serve as an effective screening device. One plaintiffs' attorney with whom I spoke pointed out the ethical dangers of such an arrangement: if the attorney does not have clients of his or her own, the likely motivation is to accommodate only the attorney, not the client. The clients serve as moral anchors in the litigation, and, in this respect, traditional notions of obligations to individual clients can be useful. If the attorney in charge does not act properly, a malpractice suit by the client is theoretically possible, as are disciplinary actions.

When the court appoints a committee or, in effect, approves one selected by counsel to supervise the litigation, how should fees be divided between the outlying attorneys who have actual contact with clients and the central committee members? This issue presents a difficult practical and ethical problem. I believe I gave too little attention to this subject in Agent Orange and did not fairly compensate the attorneys who represented individuals. All the fees went to members of the central committee who had almost no individual client contact. Many attorneys had spent time with individual clients and should have received compensation for this important personal relationship aspect of the litigation.[188]

The cost of these massive cases is so huge that courts must remain open to new forms of financing and sharing fees.[189] Even syndication of litigation is acceptable under some circumstances.[190] But the courts must supervise very carefully any new techniques. This implies that the attorneys must be open not only with their clients, but also the courts on what the effect of financial deals and methods of compensating cooperating lawyers are on legal fees and disbursements. Cutting fees too greatly will reduce the chance of financing these huge suits and shift the advantage sharply toward the defendants.

2. Defense

If plaintiffs' attorneys' fees are limited, should there not be some monitoring of fees to defense counsel? I have had the impression that some defendants do not settle because their attorneys are earning high fees in conducting unnecessary and overstaffed discovery or otherwise stringing out the litigation.[191] Defense counsel in mass tort cases can, in effect, profit from their clients' allergy to conceding liability even when counsel believe that such a concession is ultimately inevitable.[192] Is this practice unethical? It is hard to monitor without an audit. Fortunately, most corporations are now supervising counsel more closely to ensure that undue expenses are not incurred.[193] The court should step in and inform corporate officers when counsel for the corporation appear to be acting in their own interest.

H. Cooperation and Conflict among Attorneys

1. Plaintiffs' Attorneys

The monetary awards, the power, and the prestige associated with control of mass cases are enormous. Not surprisingly, jockeying among potential representatives becomes fierce,[194] and some lawyers engage in overt client chasing. Given the relatively small national bar capable of managing a large mass tort action, the amount of handwashing and backbiting can be substantial.

Some attorneys have recounted stories of rampant abuse, including one incident in which two lawyers solicited each other in the wake of a mass disaster.[195] Some have complained of the frustration and waste that result from struggles for leadership positions on steering committees and other plaintiffs' organizations.[196] This aspect of mass cases was seen most recently in the breast implant cases.[197] One group sought and obtained class certification in Ohio. Other groups sought to wrest control from the Ohio group by obtaining Multidistrict Litigation Panel transfers. Conflict among the attorneys ensued over who should serve as transferee judge. In the end, the Multidistrict Litigation Panel assigned the cases to a judge of its own, choosing Chief Judge Pointer of Alabama. The major contending lawyers were then, as is the usual practice, put on a coordinating committee which appears to be working well.

Deals often are made for fee sharing and for places on various committees. Vote "buying" also occurs.[198] Outside lawyers are given cases by those already involved in exchange for their support when issues of control and leadership are decided.[199]

Attorneys who engage in the most distasteful of these tactics violate their ethical duty to the community of those seeking redress. Cooperation and constructive input is essential to reaching a resolution of the complex problems involved. There will be, of course, many instances in which an attorney who seeks control of the litigation does so with the belief that it is in the best interests of his or her client and the class or group of claimants as a whole. But, in the interest of protecting the community, the court has an obligation to restrain the selfish impulses of individual attorneys when it comes time to dispense the spoils of mass litigations.

2. DEFENDANTS

Conflicts among defense clients are also a problem. It is difficult for defendants to get together to provide a sensible overall approach when some have substantial insurance or capital, some are on the brink of bankruptcy, some are major players, and others are minor participants. The breakdown of the original, broad-based Wellington claims resolution facility designed to represent asbestos defendants illustrates these problems.[200] The smaller Center for Claims Resolution (CCR) facility, coordinating the work of about twenty defendants, has been successful in reducing costs to those defendants.[201] In dealing with CCR I have had the sense that transaction costs were much reduced, to the benefit of all parties and the courts. I wonder whether the courts might not have done more to help hold together the original Wellington group and whether this action might have moderated the asbestos litigation disaster.

Defense counsel, even under a narrowly defined duty to their clients, have an obligation to cooperate and contribute to efforts at resolution. Delaying and foot-dragging serve neither the community as a whole nor corporate clients.[202] Running up fees by taking advantage of a corporate client's aversion to settlement and attempting to drive plaintiffs out of the litigation by delaying and extending discovery are unethical practices. Courts can attempt to impose order and discipline on groups of defense counsel for the same reason they can control counsel for plaintiffs: complex mass disputes require cooperation and commitment by all involved so that the public, whom lawyers and judges serve, obtains the reasonably structured resolution to which it is entitled.[203]

I. TENTATIVE ANSWERS

Questions about a lawyer's ethical choices in mass tort cases have a tendency to multiply. Problems of effective representation, zealous advocacy, communication, fees, financing, confidentiality, and conflicts of interest do not lend themselves to easy solutions. The traditional ethical rules, I believe, are inadequate due to their reliance on the single-litigant, single-lawyer model. The mass tort lawyer cannot deal with his or her clients on a one-to-one basis that permits full client participation in the litigation. This diffuse relationship inevitably will yield some level of client dissatisfaction and, because of compromises the attorney must make to formulate strategy for the group as a whole, may result in less-than-zealous advocacy for the positions of particular clients. Even if attorneys in these situations are not clearly violating the Model Rules of ethics, their conduct falls short of the ideal of the loyal advocate for an individual client envisioned by the traditional model of ethics.

Trade-offs will be required in any solution. How much dissonance between client and attorney are we willing to tolerate in the name of efficiency and practicality? Rigid adherence to traditional notions about an attorney's duty to his or her client could lead us to refuse to permit representation of large numbers of clients by single attorneys—an undesirable limitation.

The class action rules represent the rejection of such a rigid approach in the name of efficiency and economies of scale. Outside the class action context, practical considerations require that we tolerate mass representation. Where thousands of individual claims are involved, the only route to settlement is through negotiations involving a few lawyers who can speak on behalf of many claimants. The alternative is the intolerable result of thousands of individual trials monopolizing and debilitating our courts. Despite the costs of sweeping in masses of borderline cases, my own impression is that mass dispositions are cheaper and more reliable for society and defendants.

Ultimately our goal should be to maximize the level of due process and bottom-line justice each participant in the system receives. Efficiency and economies of scale are desirable not because they are inherently good, but because they result in recovery sooner and in more appropriate amounts for those who have been harmed. If justice delayed is justice denied, justice hastened is justice served. At a certain point, however, the individual participant in the system may get trampled in the rush to a solution deemed most "expedient" or "efficient" by lawyers who may have a poor understanding of their clients' interests—or an overly acute sensitivity to their own needs.

Moreover, there is always the danger that a defendant without substantial fault may be driven into huge settlements or even put out of business by the quantity of attackers, if not their quality. In the Agent Orange case, the court intervened to urge a settlement that took account of the fact that some dioxin had been negligently produced even though it could not be shown that any particular plaintiff was harmed.

In effect, both plaintiffs and defendants received protection as a group. This approach was essential, creating in effect a new rule of substantive law: costs were equitably shared among a group of indeterminate defendants, and awards were made on an equitable matrix among a group of indeterminate plaintiffs. This disposition was necessary because there was a group of possibly injured plaintiffs and a group of possibly negligent defendants, but very poor proof of causality to connect the two. Each group received and paid as a group a defensible sum based upon what was arguably the total harm to the community caused by the defendants.

In negotiations with defendants as a group, the court suggested that each defendant pay its fair share based roughly on the amount of dioxin it had produced. This was computed by the estimated degree of impurity of the defendant's herbicide multiplied by the total gallons sold to the government. Thus, the cleanest product paid proportionately less— a defensible if unique form of pro rata sharing of responsibility.

I have already adverted to some of the details of the Agent Orange distribution scheme, but I want to return to it again as illustrative of the need to look to a variety of communities in crafting dispositions in these mass cases. First, the proportion of the settlement made available for legal fees was kept to a minimum. The attorneys had done little to establish their case and would have lost it had traditional tort rules been applied.

Second, the benefits flowed to a very large community consisting of hundreds of thousands of veterans and their families—a resolution far removed from the traditional one-on-one cash tort remedy. Two funds were established. One provided for death benefits and disability benefits to veterans who served anywhere they might have been exposed to a herbicide. In effect, an insurance policy was obtained from a large insurance company which adjudicated claims and paid them, subject to veterans' appeals to a special master and the court. Veterans or their heirs have received substantial funds under this program. Before it is completed more than forty thousand claimants will have received compensation totaling some $175 million.[204]

An additional fund of more than $50 million was set up to aid the families of veterans, particularly those with children with birth defects. This fund has supported medical and social service hot lines, national legal services, and a network of some eighty service organizations with at least one branch in every state and Puerto Rico.[205] More than one hundred thousand persons have already received benefits from this fund.[206]

Even in an unusual case such as Agent Orange every effort should be made to preserve the individual lawyer-client relationship in some form. As the Supreme Court has explained in the context of criminal cases, lawyers are the often vital means by which the layperson receives a fair hearing.[207] Adequate and responsive representation is essential to both fair results and public acceptance of those results.

Once we recognize that large-scale representation in mass tort cases is both inevitable and desirable and accept the view that this form of representation makes the traditional one-on-one relationship between lawyer and client impracticable, we cannot avoid the need for a new formulation of the lawyer's ethical duty. Without such a new ethic, the lawyer will be too likely to be guided by his or her own interests where it becomes difficult to discern or follow the interests of the many clients.

A broader view of obligations to the public weal, approved by the profession and the bench, would permit exercise of this goodwill without the inhibitions imposed by the narrow traditional rules restricting the lawyer to individual client interests.[208] If the lawyer in the mass tort case understands his or her duty as running in part to the community to which clients belong, or the communities which may be affected by the result, individual needs may be better served. Such a communitarian ethic requires the lawyer to consider more than the optimal dollar recovery for the group. The lawyer must consider the impact of the benefit and harm on the communities as a whole, in both the short and the long run. The lawyer should attempt to communicate with the communities as a whole to learn their needs and desires. The lawyer should understand that the significance of the case to a community will remain long after the lawyer has left the scene.

In the asbestos cases, for example, I believe it was a mistake not to consolidate all pending cases, both state and federal, years ago in a single class action before a federal court. There were common issues of fact, such as how much producers should have known before almost all of the persons claiming disability were exposed. It should have been foreseen at least ten years ago that hundreds of thousands of claimants would be involved. A sensible national settlement with adequate funding might then have been worked out. Proper appeals to defendants—going behind the lawyers to corporate management if necessary—could have resulted in their acceptance of such an approach. The settlement might have included a pleural plaque registry, with options to take small sums pending proof of more serious diseases and guarantees of sufficient assets to pay the ultimate claims. Federal funds should have been forthcoming since much of the harm was due to inadequate government policing and deliberately hazardous activities in naval shipyards. Too early a total settlement, of course, would have underestimated both numbers of cases and their seriousness; in this field even Monday-morning quarterbacking is not easy.

Similarly, in the DES cases a national settlement could have given claimants protection such as health insurance for themselves and their children, more extensive research, and more medical advice to women. The recent Pfizer heart valve or breast implant solutions—featuring immediate partial payments and money available for replacing failed valves or implants—did much more for the concerned communities than many long drawn-out suits, which would squander most of the money in transaction costs and result in delays in receiving compensation. Even the more than $1 billion proposed fee to plaintiffs' lawyers on the $5 billion breast implant case appears justifiable since it saved at least $1.5 billion in fees and transactional costs.

Of course, such sensible results are easier, as in the Dalkon Shield, Agent Orange, heart valve, or breast implant cases, when there are only one or a few putative defendants. Probably we will need to use more Alternate Dispute Resolution (ADR) solutions with the final arrangements being validated by a binding class action. Such solutions together with a showing of concern by defendants[209] will do much to avoid the unacceptable levels of cost and dissatisfaction that often result under the present system.

These suggestions are tentative at best. Many questions are raised. Is it possible to regulate such a communitarian ethic or would we have to rely on lawyers to listen to the better angels of their nature? Is such an understanding of the lawyer's role incompatible with an adversarial system of dispute resolution? Would we be better off with a system that relies on lawyers—somewhat moderated by judges—to represent the needs of the community? Or are we better off with a system constructed primarily on lawyer's and client's self-interest?[210]

I do not pretend to have the answers. I only ask you to consider the possibility that the old rules promoting the ideal of the zealous, adversarial lawyer may be stretched beyond their limitations in the mass tort case. If that is so, some new ways must be found to light our way through this dark, uncharted territory.

CHAPTER 5

ETHICS OF JUDGES

In addressing problems of the bar, I have taken a critical empirical approach. Considering the judge's role, I am constrained to take a more normative and ideological approach. If someone were to accuse me of being less than even-handed because I refrained from publicly criticizing my own actions and those of my judicial siblings, I would have to plead nolo contendere.

A. TRADITIONAL VIEW

Central to any system of litigation ethics is a conception of the judge's role. For the most part, our traditional adversarial model has provided the basis for evaluating the conduct of judges as well as lawyers. The ABA's Code of Judicial Conduct (CJC) and the federal statute governing the conduct of federal judges[1] mandate impartiality. Many of the provisions in these codes are designed to promote the image of the judge as a detached magistrate presiding over a dispute in which he or she has neither personal interest nor predisposition.[2] The central provision in both the CJC and the federal statute requires that a judge recuse himself or herself from a matter "in which the judge's impartiality *might reasonably be questioned*."[3] The rule is prophylactic: image is deemed as important as reality.

The recent decision of the Court of Appeals for the Third Circuit ordering Judge H. Lee Sarokin off the tobacco litigation illustrates this traditional approach.[4] In the view of the Court of Appeals, Judge Sarokin, by stating his opinion that the evidence demonstrated that the tobacco industry is "the king of concealment and disinformation,"[5] had compromised the judiciary's image as impartial arbiter.[6] The forced recusals of Judge Sarokin (and of Judge James McGirr Kelly in the school asbestos cases) were extreme and unnecessary acts, wasteful of years of expensive preparation for trial, but the decisions did make the point in a striking way: even the appearance of a judge losing neutrality was seen as a serious threat to public confidence in the judiciary.

A rigid conception of the judge as presiding passively and neutrally over an adversarial proceeding in which the litigants bear the whole burden of presentation is sometimes inaccurate and unwise.[7] This is especially true in mass tort cases where, as I have noted, the traditional one-on-one adversarial model of litigation does not apply. Justice does hold true scales, but it is not blind, nor should it be.[8]

We expect that judges will bring their own experience and outlook to bear in evaluating the merits of cases before them. Justice must have a human face.[9] "Impartiality" has a clear connotation when applied to a problem of, for example, a judge's financial stake in a case. But the concept becomes far murkier and less useful when applied to a question of the appropriate effect of a judge's philosophical beliefs, personal experiences, or scientific background on his or her evaluation of a case.

In a recent Second Circuit opinion, the Court of Appeals recognized that when a judge is assigned to a complex mass tort, he or she must become involved based on the information acquired in the litigation.[10] In my view, that involvement must include concern over the various communities which may be affected by the court's decisions. Nor is it required that the judge put aside all sense of emotion and concern when the facts are disturbing.[11]

I am much impressed by the attitude of the anthropologist-sociologist-philosopher-theologian, Martin Buber. As I was readying this book for the press, wondering about the validity of some of the positions in this chapter, there came in the mail the fascinating article by Professor of Philosophy Avishai Margalit of the Hebrew University in Jerusalem, "Prophets with Honor," describing some of Buber's work.[12] Communitarian and communicatarian are reflected in Buber's writings as the following quotation from Margalit shows:

> his ultimate concern was not encounter with God but encounter with people. It is not so much God himself that is the center of his concern as the kingdom of God. Buber sees the kingdom of God as a society founded on "I-You" rather "I-It" relationships. The English translation of the book's German title, *Ich und Du,* changed the everyday word *"Du"* (the familiar form of "you") into the sublime word "Thou." This led to a skewed interpretation of Buber, as if the only thing he intended to talk about was the human relationship with the divine. . . . He was not interested in the empirical conditions of any particular society, but in "social ontology"—that is, the general conditions for creating a community. The term "society" as he used it derived from traditional German sociological Romanticism, and is ambiguous between *Gesellschaft* and *Gemeinschaft*—that is, between

"society" in the sense of an association based on formal relations that serve social functions, and "society" in the sense of a community based on primary relations of immediate contact and belonging. Buber was mainly interested in society in the sense of community—*Gemeinschaft*. As he recognized, the longing for community in modern society is based to a large extend on utopian hopes, since the familiar forms of association in capitalist societies are not based on communal ties. . . . Their discourse with God would guide their spontaneous behavior and lead to an anarchistic society founded on community relationships, which are relationships of dialogue.

Partly because it enhances my own ability to engage in dialogue with lawyers and parties—particularly during sentencing—I prefer to conduct most nonjury work without a robe sitting in the courtroom at a table opposite the lawyers and, where appropriate, their clients, or, more informally, in chairs arranged in an intimate circle around a coffee table in chambers. Nevertheless, as in the case of Buber, it seems likely that the dialogue between any judge and attorneys and litigants is a severely constrained one that has more indicia of communications among equals than reality. On this note, Margalit writes of Buber:

Buber's shift of basic ontology also involves a shift in the way we come to know things. If for Husserl the central sense for constituting objects is vision, while Heidegger perhaps adds the sense of touch, for Buber the main sense is hearing, the sense that is vital for listening to others. Buber's reading of the Bible pays special attention to hearing and listening. Some of Buber's critics felt that he himself was not capable of a real dialogic relationship with others, and that actually he felt at home only with books, while many others have described encounters with Buber in which they noted "what a great listener" he was. My own impression is that Buber had the gestures of a good listener—gestures that are well known to psychiatrists—and include focusing the gaze on the eyes of the other, bending toward him "so that nothing should disturb us," asking questions about details that attest to the complete interest of the questioner in the person being questioned. These can be "tricks of the trade" and not necessarily a relationship of listening with immediacy and absolute mutuality. Perhaps Ben-Gurion was to some extent right in his nasty claim that Buber was capable of a dialogic relationship only with himself.[13]

B. Obligation to Community

However constrained they may be in achieving a sense of equality in dialogue with lawyers and litigants, judges, particularly in mass tort cases, cannot and should not remain neutral and passive in the face of problems implicating the public interest. In mass tort cases, the judge often cannot rely on the litigants to frame the issues appropriately. The judge cannot focus narrowly on the facts before the court, declining to take into account the relationship of those facts to the social realities beyond the courthouse door. The judge cannot depend upon the slow creep of case-by-case adjudication to yield just results and just rules of law.

In this respect the problem is analogous to that of institutional reform litigation. In the Mark Twain Junior High School desegregation cases, my special master and I had to consider neighborhood ethnic relationships, housing, parks, police, transportation, and other problems. We also had to contend with diverse parents groups and federal, state, and city authorities.[14] I have had the same experience in other institutional-reform cases, as have other judges.[15] For example, Judge Leonard B. Sand's tenacious solution to the Yonkers housing discrimination cases, in which he had the full support of the Court of Appeals, stands as a model of public litigation, conducted with sensitivity to the needs of the community.[16]

In a mass tort case, a judge's failure to appreciate the reach and importance of his or her decisions is tantamount to abdication of responsibility.[17] Much as the President steers the ship of state at the head of the executive branch, each federal trial judge, with respect to each case that comes before him or her, stands watch over the judicial branch. The trial judge is in most cases the final arbiter. If the trial judge fails to respond to the needs of the public, the only recourse is to appellate judges who are narrowly confined in matters of fact and who are usually in a less favorable position than the *nisi prius* judge to understand the full scope of a litigation. A rigid and unresponsive judiciary, blind to the needs of various communities and of society at large, is far more likely to cause an erosion of public confidence in legal institutions than a judiciary perceived as overly interested in resolving the problems before it.

In these cases we do not deal with pure economic reasonable person models. We deal with complex sociological, scientific, and psychological problems as well as economics.[18]

Mass tort cases unfortunately do not involve the application of legislative schemes representing careful analysis of the policy problems presented. By their very nature, these cases involve unanticipated problems with wide-ranging social and political ramifications. A judge does not "legislate from the bench"[19] simply because he or she considers the broadest implications of his or her decisions in such a case. Judges not only may take such a view, they must.

Just as the lawyer in the mass tort case should be guided to some extent by the communitarian ethic, so should the judge. For the judge, the task is easier. The judge, unlike the lawyer, does not face the thorny problem of sorting out the interests of some clients from those of others and the lawyer. The judge need be zealous in only one respect: to immerse himself or herself as a diligent student of the case. The judge can strive for an understanding of the needs of the communities, whose members are both inside and outside the courtroom.[20] Because the judge is "impartial" in the sense of lacking any personal stake in a particular outcome, the judge can, through the process of education and evaluation (i.e., judging), become "partial" in favor of the communities' best interests.[21]

Pressures to prevent overly idiosyncratic views by individual judges are substantial. There is, first, the weight of precedent and traditional approaches; second, the advice of attorneys in their briefing and argument; third, the possibility of appellate review; fourth, the criticism of professional and lay journals; and fifth, the pressure of peers.

One danger that every judge must guard against is ego. The sense of power and prestige in supervising a mass tort or public interest case can be heady. The court must control its own sense of importance—sometimes a very difficult chore. Strong attorneys can and should speak up to guard against this danger. Mandamus provides some protection,[22] as do ultimate appeals from final orders. The press and special interest groups can also be helpful in controlling the court. Strong federal judges can do bad as well as good things. They are human.

In the ordinary case the judges' contact with the lawyers, litigants, and institutions involved is relatively brief. As I have reminded those before me on occasion, a judge is no one's "friend" and can be expected to turn suddenly and skewer with a thin smile anyone who moves beyond the line of propriety. When, however, the case drags on for years and requires long-term supervision of institutions, conflicts and partialities have to be particularly guarded against.

I much prefer a clean-cut, self-executing decree to one requiring ongoing supervision. This is partially a judicial view, but also a personal psychological one, because I like to do my very best with a case or problem and then "forget it" and move on. Yet, repeatedly, the needs of the public interest case have frustrated that sense of appropriateness. In the Suffolk Developmental litigation I tried to dismiss the case after finding that the institution was making good faith efforts to comply with my decrees to provide constitutionally required effective treatment to its developmentally disabled clients. The Court of Appeals reversed because the work had not been completed, and I hung on for years, ultimately, having the great satisfaction of seeing all the residents sent to small homes in the community. In Agent Orange I wanted to put the money for the families into the hands of a free-standing foundation, but the Court of Appeals required that I supervise the work. As a result I have had the pleasure of working with dedicated people all over the country helping Vietnam veterans' families. In the Manville asbestos case, much as I try to settle the matter and escape this tar baby, it hangs on. The core sense of being a judge, dispassionate, aloof and apart from it all, and only secondarily a participant in the litigation, is needed to preserve the continuing impartial judicial role in long-term institutional reform and mass torts.

During the course of adminstrating the Agent Orange class assistance program (AOCAP), many lessons were learned about treatment of veterans. Chief among them is that their families—wives and children particularly—need succor, treatment, and assistance at least as much as the veterans with war service. Repeatedly, the many social agencies mobilized by AOCAP to help families of veterans tell the stories of how harsh the effects of the veterans' problems have been on children. They suffer psychologically and physically well into their adulthood as a result of their parents' working out the problems of Vietnam in the privacy of the nuclear family. As its programs winds down, AOCAP has commissioned scores of papers from academics and those with hands-on experience for a national conference to bring those lessons home to Congress, the Executive, and the agencies responsible for veterans affairs. Thus, in addition to the treatises on veterans law and on family entitlements as well as numerous pamphlets and training sessions funded by the programs, AOCAP should leave a legacy both of papers in various journals and volumes on the shelf explaining what needs to be done for families, and of hundreds of experts in the field who know how to do it. Whether this experience is utilized will depend upon veterans organizations and private and governmental agencies. Much that has been said in earlier chapters about communitarian and communicatarian insights in the law applies to veterans affairs. Are such satisfactions in nontraditional out-of-court work forbidden fruits to an Article III judge?

C. COMMUNICATION WITH COMMUNITY

1. EDUCATING THE COURT

How is the judge to know what the communities' needs and wants are? Should the court hold public hearings as does the legislature? In the Mark Twain Junior High School desegregation case, I used a special master to serve as both a bridge and buffer to the many communities, individuals, and government officials affected.[23] I then held a series of public hearings required under Rule 23 of the Federal Rules of Civil Procedure that led to sharpened public awareness.[24] In the *Lora* case, involving allegations that "difficult" students throughout New York City were being warehoused in special schools on a racially segregated basis, I relied on a national panel of educators, as well as public hearings and trips to the schools, before approving development of a curriculum to sensitize all the teachers in the school system to the problems.[25] In the Suffolk County developmentally disabled case, I combined public hearings with many inspection trips to the institutions, conversations with parents, workers, and the disabled, and reports from government agencies and a court-appointed inspector.[26] Such devices can be beneficial in mass torts as a means of connecting the court with the community.

I already have mentioned how a communicatarian ethic might guide a judge in handling matters of secrecy, disclosure, and the public's right to know. It was Justice Brandeis who observed, "Sunlight is said to be the best of disinfectants, electric light the most efficient policeman."[27] Until legislation catches up with our collective conscience, perhaps the judge must use his or her discretionary power to prevent the old secrecy rules from keeping society in the dark. If the plaintiffs' attorney wants to see the documents, but the defense attorney conditions it on a vow of secrecy, the judge is in the best position to see that the public is not left unprotected.

2. LISTENING TO THE COMMUNITY

Open, well-advertised hearings represent the courts' best vehicle for contact. In the Agent Orange case, for example, I held hearings all over the country.[28] I listened to some six hundred people, and I received hundreds of telephone and written communications. I was struck by the deep emotional underpinnings of the litigation. The fact that the science, in my view, did not support a viable cause of action did not warrant ignoring these heartfelt cries for justice. Obviously I was affected by the emotional appeal of veterans who thought themselves abused. Should I have allowed that factor to affect my handling of the litigation? Could I have avoided such an effect?

My contact with those affected in the *Lora* case, the developmentally disabled case, the LILCO case, the prison cases, the school cases, and the DES and asbestos cases were all, I think, helpful in giving me a better understanding of what was at stake. In all those litigations I saw the parties in courthouses or visited them in the field. Yet there are some judges whom I respect who insist that it is a mistake to go beyond the lawyers' courtroom presentations in deciding a case.

A. DIRECT RELATIONSHIP WITH CLAIMANTS

Again I return to the Agent Orange case as an example. In administering the funds available from the settlement, I have tried to take matters of claimant distress into account. For example, the disbursing agency, at my direction, has operated a large bank of toll-free telephones to receive inquiries from veterans and their families. By now over six hundred thousand calls have been answered.[29] The people speaking to the veterans are instructed to try to assist them in obtaining compensation under the scheme set up by the court[30] as well as from the government's Veterans Administration programs. We have also provided an appeal system which has disposed of more than twelve thousand appeals, with decisions briefly stated in plain English and sent to veterans with accompanying explanatory letters and, often, with materials explaining how the veteran can obtain additional help. We have funded a national legal service which has produced explanatory pamphlets and treatises to assist veterans in obtaining help from the court-administered funds and from the VA itself.[31] *The Advocate's Guide to SSI for Children,* for example, financed with Agent Orange funds, has helped obtain large sums for children of Vietnam veterans. A national hot line, administered by a leading academic institution, is used by thousands of veteran families to obtain services from our more than seventy[32] funded programs and other agencies throughout the country. National training conferences sponsored by the Agent Orange Class Assistance Program have helped train people in agencies all over the country to assist Vietnam veteran families. Law students have gone through tens of thousands of court files to find every family that complained to the court about Agent Orange, and we sought to contact each family to see if it needs further help. More than one hundred thousand people have received medical-social services.[33]

The considerable client-court relationship work in Agent Orange has, I think, been fairly successful in meeting the problem. My clerks and the staff who administer these programs sometimes deal, occasionally with no satisfaction for either party, with claimants whose anger and frustration cannot be quenched by a letter. Nevertheless, we have made strides in meeting the communication problem, and I am told that a large part of the veterans community appreciates our efforts.

The system is expensive, but necessary. How it should be improved in future cases, I am not sure. A satisfaction audit by some outside agency would be useful. This would be a good project for a law review or seminar. In Agent Orange and other mass tort cases, a modified technique of ombudspersons serving independently of the court, the compensating agency, or any party or interested attorney might help. Congress, the Federal Judicial Center, or an outside, independently funded organization such as the Rand Institute might do the auditing. Such a survey with recommendations for improvement could also be funded by a charge against the recovery.[34] Ultimately, as indicated in chapter 10, such work should not be left to the courts.

In the Dalkon Shield cases, where many of the claimants proceed pro se, the administering court agency has trained laypeople to work with the claimants and explain procedures. It has produced literature designed to give individual claimants a sense of participation. How well this works, I cannot say from direct observation.

Those affected by DES have achieved some success in forming associations that encourage talk among worried and aggrieved women.[35] The DES victims, independently of their attorneys, have received funds from Congress and have assisted each other in self-help organizations.[36] This success among DES victims—almost all women—may be explained in part by the current phenomenon of middle-class women organizing effectively in consciousness raising and advocacy groups to deal with issues affecting their gender.[37]

The White Lung associations, consisting primarily of blue-collar workers concerned with asbestos-caused diseases, have not, as I understand the matter, received or given much assistance to those injured, although they made their views known to me during the Manville hearings and their insights were helpful. The unions have, I believe, with few exceptions, not made a useful contribution to solving the asbestos problem except insofar as they steered members to individual lawyers favored by union officials. Their major contribution may have been in making their members and their families available to the late Dr. Irving J. Selikoff, whose epidemiological studies at Mount Sinai Hospital in New York are the basis for the most effective plaintiffs' testimony in asbestos cases.

The most spectacular successes politically were those of veterans dealing with Agent Orange and Congress. They were organized, had the political clout, and had the Veterans Administration as an agency designed to help them.[38]

Judges should work with and encourage groups that represent communities whenever possible. Communication between the courts and the community is enhanced where nonlitigant groups take the initiative to educate and speak for the community. The judge should be careful, however, not to mistake those who are vocal for those who need to be heard. The experience with representative groups has varied greatly from case to case, and their agendas must be scrutinized carefully.

As in any experiment in democracy, the judge should be prepared to hear critical and highly abrasive views about judges and lawyers. In the

Agent Orange, LILCO, and Manville cases the public hearings were sometimes more candid than kind to the judge. But such contact with the real world is particularly important for judges. In part because we do not run for office, once we are appointed we tend to grow out of touch with the concerns of average citizens.

B. SUPERVISING ATTORNEY-CLIENT COMMUNICATION

While handling the Manville Trust reorganization, it became clear to me from unsolicited letters from clients that in many instances clients felt abandoned. The Trust does communicate with the relatively small number of pro se claimants to explain the present state of the settlement, but it has thus far felt inhibited about writing to those who are formally represented by attorneys. That some of these attorneys do not keep in touch with their clients is evident from the many settlements that have never been consummated because the attorneys could not find their clients. We need to rethink the rules that prohibit the court or the fund-administering agency from going directly to the client. Explanatory materials jointly produced by the plaintiffs' attorneys and the trust, under the aegis of the court, would be useful. With more than two hundred thousand claims filed against the Manville Trust to date, the issue is not insignificant.

In the proposals made in connection with potential atomic plant explosions by the President's Commission,[39] we deal, as in Bhopal[40] and Chernobyl,[41] with millions of potential claimants. This issue of personal contact between courts and injured persons was not covered in the Commissioner's final report. This omission was understandable since such forms of communication have generally been considered unnecessary under our adversary system. But the traditional adversary system can not be relied upon in mass disasters.

In the *LILCO-Shoreham* case,[42] hundreds of people did not file timely claims despite widespread advertisements. This was a failure of communication. The largest group of those who missed an opportunity to collect from LILCO had left their homes and moved to other states as retirees.[43] I cannot help but think that the lapses here were due in part to the attorneys' and my failure to focus on this problem in time. We might even have paid a bounty to any person who provided the new addresses of any prior LILCO ratepayers.

When the courts deal with so many people, the expense of one-to-one contact can be substantial. Even a single direct mailing, putting aside the cost of production of documents, is great. Yet my talks with communications experts indicate that we can do better.

As a practical matter, of course, getting more people involved in settlement makes a peaceful disposition much more difficult. In the LILCO case, I held a number of hearings throughout the district, both at night and during the day, so that people involved in the Shoreham atomic plant controversy could be heard.[44] As I have already suggested, I took a good deal of oral abuse, which was, perhaps, warranted. The hearings might have been more productive had the attorneys agreed upon a document to explain to those who were to appear what was involved and what the difficulties were. Such a document could have been written by the parties, with the aid of the special master and court, to focus the discussion.

In the DES litigation, with the assistance of the special master, hundreds of cases were settled. After the settlements, as I have noted, I met in chambers with many of the DES claimants and spouses and heard their harrowing stories.[45] The ability to address the court informally, with a reporter present, seemed to provide a kind of catharsis for those who believed themselves harmed by DES.

Some judges think that these practices are dangerous because the judge's emotions may be affected, but I find it easier to understand what is at stake when I can see and hear the real people concerned in their own settings rather than in the artificial courtroom milieu. That the law often requires exchanges with the public, through hearings, public comments, and other means, is evidence of a strong public policy in favor of communication between the judiciary and the public it serves.[46]

The problem of empathy versus impartiality is not an easy one to resolve. Even in a medical model, empathy may be dangerous since subjectivity may interfere with dispassionate analysis and good judgment. The problems may be more difficult in the legal setting. Nevertheless, we must consider parting from a traditional model.

A public debate is not practicable, in the final cutting of a deal. The endgame occurs in small rooms, smoke filled or not, and the results are thereafter ratified publicly. Can the communicatarian ethic and responsibility of the lawyer be met in such circumstances? Perhaps the deal can be struck and then held in abeyance while the claimants, actual and potential, are consulted. The argument against this proposal is that everyone is so eager for a settlement and the clearing of calendars that they will oppose any delay.

My present sense that we must address the matter is confirmed by what is happening, in connection with sentencing, where the courts and the law appear to be going in a direction contrary to the one I propose we consider for mass torts and disasters.[47] The one-to-one relationship of the sentencing judge and the defendant has been largely eroded by mathematical guidelines and statutory mandatory minimums that have had, I believe, a disastrous impact on the soul of the courts and justice.[48] In both mass torts and uniform sentencing we need to treat individuals with their differences because they matter as persons, while not losing the benefits of efficiency.[49]

3. SPEAKING TO THE COMMUNITY

Closely related to questions of how a judge ought to treat secrecy agreements are questions of the extent to which a judge should be permitted or obligated to communicate with the public about matters of public concern.

The Code of Judicial Conduct does not speak directly to this issue. The code admonishes judges not to "make any public comment that might reasonably be expected" to affect the outcome of a proceeding or "impair its fairness."[50] In addition, judges are directed "not to disclose or use, for any purpose unrelated to judicial activities, nonpublic information acquired in a judicial capacity."[51] These provisions appear to leave the matter to the judge's determination. A judge should be careful, in informing the public about what is transpiring within the courthouse, not to impair the freedom of the litigants to pursue their cause.

Our traditional conception of the judge's role does not envision a judge broadcasting the facts of a litigated matter outside the courtroom.[52] Judges traditionally tolerate the presence of the media because of the public's interest in judicial proceedings.[53] They are permitted in limited circumstances to banish the press from the courtroom when considerations of due process override the people's right to know.[54]

Increasingly, however, we recognize the importance of letting the public know what is happening in the courts. The use of television in court, for example, is growing despite some of the dangers.[55] For many years I have favored use of this medium to let the public look into our courtrooms. I would prefer to see it used for the more elevated policy problems such as those before the Supreme Court, but even its trivialization in sensational trials has, I think, led to a better understanding by lay people of how the legal process works.

In a mass tort case, the public's interest in obtaining information can be direct and immediate. Often many of those injured will not be litigants and may not even be aware of their legal rights. The harm may be ongoing, and public awareness may be necessary to prevent further injury. Sometimes the wrongdoing revealed will point to great failures in regulatory oversight or law enforcement that must be addressed promptly by legislative or regulatory agencies to prevent repetition of the disaster. And in still other cases, the lack of adverse proof of causation may have a calming and reassuring effect.

The judge who is sensitive to his or her obligation to the community will not sit passively as new facts of public interest come to light. Simply opening the courthouse doors to all who want to observe proceedings or inspect public documents may not suffice, and the media sometimes cannot be relied upon to translate highly complex legal and scientific matters into laypersons' terms.[56] Sometimes a judge will come across even nonpublic information that might, for compelling reasons, require filing and docketing and thus disclosure.

Judges presiding over mass tort cases must carefully consider the utility and wisdom of communicating with the public. The public hearing as part of a litigation in particular, publicized and conducted within the community or group potentially affected by the harm, can have great value. Ordinarily there will be little the judge can offer in the way of recourse. The most that can be done is to make people aware of the scientific and other relevant data, as well as their legal rights and the limitations on those rights. Even for those who might have no recourse, however, the hearing can offer a kind of catharsis so the community at least understands that the courts are aware of, and listening to, its needs and concerns.

Some few judges have used devices such as press conferences in institutional reform cases. I prefer to rely upon opinions written clearly enough that a reporter can understand them and interpret the matter to the public. Such opinions should be routinely sent to the pressroom. If the court is addressing a professional or scientific group, the judge's speech should also be sent to the pressroom and docketed in any relevant file so the public and parties can ascertain the judge's view. On more general matters of law, speeches and statements to the general press are consistent with the judge's citizenship obligations.[57]

Too often the experience of a community affected by mass harm is an alienating one. An implacable and inscrutable legal system sweeps through the community in the wake of disaster. Some may receive large monetary awards; others may not. Lawyers and judges control the litigation and appear interested in the case only to the point of settlement or verdict. The community is left with the feeling that its voice was never truly heard.[58] The use of friends of the court and the calling by the judge on governmental agencies for input can be helpful in bringing to bear larger community interests.

Judges have relatively little power to ameliorate the actual harm caused by mass torts. Communication between the judge and the community during and after the litigation, however, can go some way toward avoiding some of the secondary harm that can result when a badly damaged community is dealt with insensitively by the legal system.

D. SETTLEMENT AND BEYOND

1. INVOLVEMENT IN SETTLEMENT

Much has been said about the role of the judge in the settlement of mass tort cases,[59] particularly the propriety of "managerial" judging in these cases.[60] It is sufficient for our purposes to observe that the controversy about judicial involvement in settlement, not surprisingly, centers around the tension I have been discussing between the passive and the passionate models of adjudication. In asbestos, Agent Orange, Dalkon Shield, and many other mass tort litigations, judges have found themselves involved in settlement discussions in a manner that would be unusual in an ordinary tort case or commercial dispute. The fact that masses of cases are consolidated rather than bound together through a class action or bankruptcy is, as I have pointed out, of little significance in defining ethical responsibilities of judges and lawyers in mass torts settlements.

Working out a complex settlement may warrant a multiplier for unusual managerial and other skills. Judges who exercise control over fees will be in a position to reward those who best serve the public as well as their clients. The attorney who represents one or a few clients or a boutique firm handling only very strong cases can be left alone to deal with their clients. The attorney with hundreds or thousands of cases may require more supervision.

Involvement of the judge often occurs by force of necessity. The numbers of litigants and claims in these cases and their often overwhelming complexity require that some central authority take control and help guide the litigation. Without such control, progress is sometimes impossible or unnecessarily costly and slow. The court is in a unique position to exercise such power because of its authority to impose scheduling decisions and procedural rulings on the parties. When so many discordant voices are heard and so much money is at stake, a hand with no financial interest in the outcome is necessary to impose order and discipline and avoid chaos.

Few dispute that, at a minimum, a court's strong interest in the efficient and effective management of its docket justifies a more active role in these complex cases.[61] This active role naturally includes acting as a clearinghouse for information and adviser in the course of settlement negotiations.[62] In the case of a class action, the court is required to give ultimate approval to a settlement.[63] The judge in a complex case, the federal courts have long assumed, should encourage the settlement process.[64]

What is far more difficult and controversial is the question of what factors should guide a judge when he or she takes such a role in the settlement of a mass tort case. If a judge is to be at all useful he or she must have some objectives in mind. The goal of "settlement at all costs" is not sufficient. If settlement in virtually any form is a priority, it must be so for some significant reason.

In *Agent Orange*, I was criticized by some for becoming too heavily invested in achieving a settlement.[65] My commitment to settlement, however, stemmed from my underlying objective that the Vietnam veterans not be left without a sense of recourse and that defendants be charged only for harms they might have caused. As a disinterested participant who read all relevant evidence and heard extensive argument from the parties, I arrived at the judgment that the plaintiffs' evidence of general causation was too weak[66] to support a jury verdict in any individual case. Moreover, the government itself resisted every effort to assume any responsibility, by cloaking itself in immunities and by active hostility to the suit in a way that made any political leadership by the President or Congress unlikely. My efforts to guide the parties toward a solution acceptable to all participants did result in the allegedly injured obtaining some sense of relief, while the alleged tortfeasors did not shoulder a burden incommensurate with the harm they may have done by producing a defective product.[67] Of course, I also wanted to relieve the court of a potentially burdensome string of litigations.

The judge can find some guidance for his or her settlement conduct in some aspects of a communitarian ethic. In contrast to the other participants in settlement—the litigants and, more often, the lawyers who represent them—the judge can give voice to the community as a whole. By transcending the narrow interests of the few, the judge can attempt to ensure that the settlement protects both the immediate and long-term interests of the many. A judge can weigh factors that may be of little or no interest to the litigants and their lawyers, such as the protection of those who may be injured in the future,[68] the long-term structural effect of the harm on the community,[69] and the extent to which the poor and minorities may bear a disproportionately heavy burden.[70] A touch of the communicatarian ethic—giving people an opportunity to ventilate their views—may assist in easing pain.

Yet we must bear in mind the need for humility on the part of the court. It often knows little about what goes on outside the courtroom. Its knowledge of the intricacies of the case is limited. Hubris is dangerous. Power tends to corrupt. Even critical counsel, candid law clerks, helpful special masters, and the threat of future critique of legal commentators may not be sufficient checks. The appellate courts' control comes too late and usually is ineffective in mass cases.

I have found that working with other trial judges handling similar cases is helpful in providing a useful sounding board and steadying function.[71] Perhaps this should be a more common practice. Is it ethical? For example, in the asbestos cases judges often consult with each other in coordinating dispositions. The ex parte decisions of cooperating judges on which cases to try or on what a reasonable global settlement should be are critical to litigants, yet secrecy prevails. If such behind-the-scenes manipulation by cooperating judges constitutes a breach of ethical rules, then I and other judges have acted unethically. Should an on-the-record statement of what has occurred not be required? We have cut judges off from consulting with members of faculties. We should not deny them the help of their judicial colleagues, but some limits should be considered.[72]

A judge's refusal to become involved in details of settlement or insistence that only considerations of docket management guide his or her conduct represents, I believe, an abdication of judicial responsibility. It bears mentioning that these mass tort cases have not involved careful legislative consideration and, because of their unanticipated and disastrous nature, are not likely to in the immediate future. The trial judge usually presides over the court of last resort. If he or she is not prepared to assume the heavy responsibility of representing what the court perceives as the voice of the community in the courtroom, no one will.

If the trial judge believes the proposed settlement unfair or unwise in some particulars, he or she should say so either before the settlement is finalized or during the course of settlement hearings while the parties can still negotiate changes. It is wrong to consider the court a slot machine that requires the court simply to say "yes" or "no," with no power to interpret the deal or persuade the parties to modify it.[73] For example, in *Evans v. Jeff D.* the defendants offered plaintiffs all they had sought in injunctive relief provided plaintiffs waived legal fees. Since there was no fund and the clients had little, legal fees should have been provided by defendants. The Supreme Court, over dissents by Justices Brennan, Marshall, and Blackmun, found no ethical conflict. Yet, the trial judge was not bound by technical state rules of ethics in deciding fairness.[74] Legal fees were fair.

I should emphasize the point made when the role of the legislature is discussed below, that the judge's role is a stopgap in the absence of legislative action. Every judge I have discussed this matter with agrees with me that it has been the abdication of legislative responsibility that has forced judges to take an active substantive and procedural role in these matters. We do recognize the dangers in having a nonelected federal judiciary with life tenure creating what is in effect new substantive ad hoc rules.

2. CONTINUING INFLUENCE AFTER SETTLEMENT

An important aspect of the judge's role in the mass tort case is the extent of supervision the court should exercise after settlement.[75] Consider three models. In the Dalkon Shield litigation the court exercises detailed continuing control to assure proper use of a large fund for the benefit of hundreds of thousands of claimants. In the Agent Orange case the court exercises a modest degree of supervision allowing those administering the funds nearly complete discretion, plus reporting, under guidelines set out in the settlement agreement approved by the Court of Appeals. In the DES litigation and most asbestos cases no supervision of postsettlement activities is attempted. Except in the case of the Manville Personal Injury Settlement Trust, there has been little systematic attempt even to control fees in nonclass actions.

Choice of model depends upon the nature of the case as well as the personalities of the judge, special master, and counsel. The Agent Orange case is illustrative. Considerable dialogue took place between the trial and appellate courts through their written opinions. The trial court initially provided for a large portion of the settlement funds to be placed under the care of an independent class assistance foundation to provide services to the veterans and their families.[76] The court established priorities for how the foundation should utilize the funds, such as encouraging birth defect and reproductive problem programs. It also set up a governance structure for the foundation, including a board of directors comprised primarily of veterans and a set of procedures for allocating funds, and it retained the power to intervene and supervise the foundation's operations on behalf of its beneficiaries when necessary.[77]

The Court of Appeals partially reversed this arrangement on the ground that the district court is required in such circumstances to supervise specific programs that will consume settlement proceeds.[78] The Court of Appeals expressed doubt about whether an independent, self-governing foundation would possess the requisite impartiality to allocate settlement funds for the benefit of the class as a whole.[79]

On remand, the trial court convened a Class Assistance Advisory Board, comprised of distinguished Vietnam veterans, to advise the court on the best ways to allocate the funds originally designated for the foundation.[80] The result was a detailed proposal for allocation of the class assistance funds, including such provisions as an information and referral service or "hot line," programs for family- and child-related needs, assistance to homeless veterans, and genetic counseling.[81] This proposal was designed to reach more than a hundred thousand families and to assist thousands of additional veterans through legal services and publications.[82] The court and the advisory board, with the assistance of the special master, set up the detailed financial structure, including accounting and investment banking matters, necessary to administer the class assistance funds through the clerk of the court.[83] While the court signs all contracts and approves all requests for payments, it depends heavily on the director and advisory committee. Direct payments to veterans are made by an insurance company selected by the veterans' committee.

Courts should avoid becoming long-term administrative agencies. The Supreme Court recently has recognized that court supervision of school desegregation eventually must come to a conclusion.[84] In the Agent Orange case I would have preferred an arrangement providing for an independent foundation because it would have meant almost no ongoing court involvement in postlitigation matters. The modified arrangement that followed the Court of Appeals' opinion, however, has functioned effectively without too much meddling by the court. Moreover, it has given me the pleasure of working with many devoted people all over the country who are administering the program and advising and treating veterans and their families.

As a general rule, some court supervision and direction is necessary and desirable, but day-to-day court administration is not. The best administrative schemes are those that strike an appropriate balance by creating entities accountable to (but also independent of) the courts.

3. Postsettlement Trusts and Other Institutions

In the asbestos cases a number of bankruptcies have resulted in independent standing trusts. These trusts and the bankrupt companies they own often are controlled or influenced by one or more plaintiffs' attorneys. If independence from meddling by the court in postsettlement arrangements is important, so too is the need for independence of such entities from the parties.

Whether it consists of a trust, a foundation, or some other type of institution, a vehicle for fund distribution must be absolutely free of insider abuse. Because large sums are involved and fees for various aspects of administration can be substantial, the temptation for insider control of assets for the benefit of cronies is strong. If plaintiffs control the appointment of attorneys, administrators, accountants, and trustees, the entity loses its independence. Such control by those who brought the first major asbestos claims in the Manville bankruptcy is one of the factors that led to the rapid disintegration of the Manville Trust and the need for court intervention to replace management and restructure operations.[85]

The court can establish procedures to ensure that these abuses do not occur. National "headhunters" and committees of plaintiffs and defendants should be used to choose trustees, banks, auditors, attorneys, and administrators. Usually defense counsel, once the case is settled, are perfectly willing to allow plaintiffs' attorneys carte blanche in controlling the settlement funds. This seems to me to be an abdication of responsibility; the court should have their advice on how to distribute funds. Defense counsel have evaluated the worth of claims and can assist in determining how funds should be distributed.

The head of the Agent Orange Class Assistance Program was chosen after a national search for which the fund paid some $25,000. Bids were made by banks and accountants and the main disbursing agency, Aetna Insurance Company. The veterans advisory groups' recommendations were followed. On a pro bono basis, Richard Davis, a former clerk of the trial judge, assisted in choosing banks and accountants on the basis of formal bids. Fees of the special master who helped structure the program and remained as counsel were negotiated down to far below their market value.

Trustees and administrators should be required to produce periodic reports for the court and public, explaining policy, detailing the financial condition of the entity, and justifying all expenses, disbursements, and policy decisions. Such reports should be published so that all can see them.[86] These trusts are quasi-public agencies. The courts must guarantee that they will not be embarrassed by their operations.

The court should retain the power to intervene and replace administrators, trustees, and others if abuses occur. Federal District Judge Robert R. Merhige's removal of three trustees from the Dalkon Shield Claimants' Trust was an example of the proper exercise of such power. The Court of Appeals for the Fourth Circuit approved his decision as within the court's power under Virginia trust law because these trustees were, the court found, responsible for delays that increased administrative costs and had been the source of disharmony and conflict.[87] Much of this conflict reportedly centered on the efforts of these trustees to secure the appointment of their associates among the plaintiffs' bar as lawyers for the trust.[88] In the Manville case, the bankruptcy and district judges who had to intervene to save the trust made their views clearly known that the original trustees and director should resign.

E. Extrajudicial Assistance

When and how can a judge presiding over a mass tort case enlist the help of outside experts,[89] special masters,[90] scientific studies,[91] and the like?[92] Without some assistance in mass tort cases, trial judges cannot competently perform their duties. The need for help stems from both the size and the complexity of these cases. One person cannot manage all the paper and people that are involved in these massive litigations. Judges' legal training usually does not equip them to reach a quick understanding of difficult and disputed questions of science and technology. Yet judges, like litigators, can master technical subjects well enough to handle a specific litigation—even though that understanding may be superficial from a scientist's point of view. At the least, the court should ensure that experts who testify meet minimum standards of credibility.[93]

1. TRADITIONAL VIEW

The traditional model strictly limits the judge's latitude in seeking outside help. The judge, for the most part, is to remain confined to the formal submissions and proof of the parties.[94] The adversary system is founded upon the idea of the judge as tabula rasa. The fairest judge, the model holds, is the one with the least knowledge, the most open mind, and the greatest attentiveness to the evidence and arguments.[95] The Code of Judicial Conduct forbids the judge from receiving communications outside the presence of all parties except for scheduling matters and mediation of settlement.[96]

A recent ruling of the Court of Appeals for the Third Circuit illustrates the seriousness with which a judge's outside contacts can be treated.[97] Judge James McGirr Kelly of the Eastern District of Pennsylvania, while presiding over a national class asbestos matter, attended a conference at which experts discussed the latest scientific discoveries about asbestos.[98] He apparently had forgotten that plaintiffs had funded the conference and that he had approved the use of $50,000 from the settlement fund to pay for it. Viewing this incident in isolation, the appellate panel might reasonably question the judge's impartiality.[99] But when one considers the infinite ways in which judges routinely receive information outside formal judicial processes, disqualification becomes less defensible.[100] When it comes to the commendable and constant process of judges' self-education, it is difficult to separate the permissible from the prejudicial.[101] The best antidote is public knowledge through filing and making available speeches to the press.

As in the case of Judge Sarokin in the tobacco case, I view the disqualification of Judge Kelly as representing questionable policy. If error there was, it was not significant in view of the huge cost of requiring the parties and the courts to educate a new judge to replace these outstanding jurists who had devoted years to understanding the respective complex litigations.

The debate surrounding the use of neutral experts, special masters, and other forms of outside assistance is ongoing.[102] But all reasonable participants in that debate agree that judges alone cannot bear the heavy burdens of controlling mass tort cases. The traditional model in which the passive judge allows the litigants to manage the case through their own motion practice and develop complex factual background through their own experts does not work well in many mass tort cases.

Exercise of central control and effective education of judge and jury are often essential to a just and efficient process. The parties should be informed to the extent possible of what the judge is doing. In the Agent Orange case, for example, I routinely file and docket the studies, reports, and articles I read on the subject.

2. SPECIAL MASTERS

Special masters and other quasi-official personnel are increasingly relied upon in mass torts and other public litigation.[103] This expansion of personnel has had its critics.[104] Yet, if these complex cases remain in the courts it is hard to see how their use can be eliminated.

When special masters are appointed,[105] should the judge be able to speak to them in private, treating them as a kind of ad hoc law clerk? The parties may then use the special master to get to the judge through the back door. Because the use of special masters in mass cases has become so common, we may need to further institutionalize the practice through a code of ethics for special masters.[106] Generally a special master should follow the Code of Judicial Conduct.[107] But special masters, who usually are practicing attorneys, must also be mindful that they are subject in certain capacities to the codes of ethics controlling lawyer conduct.

We need to address problems such as the extent to which the special master should or should not discuss the merits of the case with the judge. The special master's perceived neutrality is essential to his or her success in dealing with all parties. Without some leeway to help the judge see the relative merits of the parties' positions, however, the special master may lose some of his or her value in helping bring about resolution of a case.

Another problem that a special master code of conduct might address is that of the repeat player. The current cadre of special masters is too limited, leading to some potential for conflicts of interest because the same attorneys are involved in these mass cases over and again, often taking different roles from case to case. The special master's past and potential future encounters with the same attorneys may affect his or her actions in the present case. We should try to develop a larger group of dependable special masters, with specialists in various areas, so that judges and parties do not continue to rely on the same people in case after case.[108] Part of such an effort might be to establish rules and funds for the compensation of special masters so that the use of special masters does not depend upon the affluence of the parties.

Given the complexity of mass tort cases, repeated utilization of the relatively few persons with expertise in the area is inevitable. Some litigation over the impartiality of special masters and the propriety of appointments is probably unavoidable. Motions challenging appointments should be made early and be considered waived if they are untimely.[109] Further efficiencies might result from the use of a bidding process for special master appointments, particularly during the remedial phases of a complex litigation when the special master's role can be lengthy and costly.

3. EXPERTS

Even ordinary expert testimony presented to the court and the jury by the parties may be subject to ethical constraints.[110] One of the critical problems in mass torts has been the use of experts testifying to causation based upon highly questionable or incomplete data and analysis.[111] Some experts, such as those in the Bendectin,[112] Agent Orange,[113] and pertussis vaccine[114] cases, are true believers. Others are fairly clearly either incompetent or charlatans.[115]

My own experience in court listening to what surely must have been thousands of experts has been that most are competent and honest. Complaints about their lack of bona fides have been exaggerated.[116] Nevertheless, the question of how to gather scientific data, interpret it, and present it in a timely and useful way is one that vexes both law and science. A broad gray area does exist where skilled persons of good faith can disagree and where it is appropriate for lay triers of fact to reach conclusions.

F. UNIFORMITY OF RULES OF ETHICS

Mass tort cases tend to be national in scope, and attorneys of national prominence handling these cases constitute a national bar. Logically, then, the rules of ethics should also be national in scope and should apply to both state and federal courts in mass torts.[117] It makes little sense for the same lawyers handling large numbers of cases with the same issues in state and federal courthouses across the street from each other to have different ethical rules with respect to such matters as fees, client solicitation,[118] assumption of costs, communication with clients, and the like. The same is true of scattered geographic cases. If they are multidistricted into one court, one rule should apply. The national bar, as well as national technology and defendants, requires a single set of rules for a single mass tort.[119] This is an area given little attention, but one which will grow in importance.

As a concomitant of the ethics question, a single rule of attorney-client privilege or work-product protecting disclosure of documents is needed. When, under *Erie*, the substantive law applied will be state law, Rule 501 suggests that state privilege law be applied. Rule 26 of the Federal Rules of Civil Procedure, by contrast, leads to the conclusion that a single work-product rule can apply. In the actual control of discovery the courts tend to apply a single privilege and work-product rule. In the breast implant litigation, the judge has chosen to apply the least restrictive rule of work-product and privilege. While arguably unauthorized, attorneys recognize that this is the sound approach and they should not object.

G. Summary of Judges' Role

A judge's responsibility in presiding over a mass tort case is an exceptionally heavy one. The judge's obligations, even more than in the ordinary case, run directly to the community outside the courthouse as well as to the parties.[120] The complexity and size of these cases greatly adds to the risk of error. Judges who remain passive and rely solely on the parties to drive the litigation and protect the rights of all those affected will be more likely to fail, I believe, in their duty to society as a whole as well as to the individual parties. Judges should reach out to embrace what competent and neutral help they can secure in the difficult task before them.

A judge whose gaze does not lift from the well of the courtroom and the pages of the lawyer's brief may fail to see the full significance of the case at bar.[121] In mass tort cases the social realities contextual to the details of the litigation bear on the utility of judicial decisions.

This broadening of responsibility has its costs. In place of the relatively hard-edged and tested ethical rules of traditional one-on-one cases, the court has broader and less well-defined responsibilities. One way of clarifying those responsibilities and ethical rules is by engaging in a more open discussion of what is happening in the courts and in the real world of mass torts.

In my survey of some of the ethical dilemmas posed by mass torts, I have suggested that forms of communitarian and communicatarian ethics might help guide lawyer and judge through these largely uncharted waters. Since the law is both eclectic and pragmatic, all the traditional ethical rules and jurisprudential approaches, from Aristotelian to Posnerian, need to be mined for their wisdom and insights.

Many will have different ideas about what sort of ethics should control the conduct of those who participate in mass forms of justice. Most, if not all, I trust, will agree that the old models at least need reconsideration in the area of mass torts.

CHAPTER 6

ETHICS OF PARTIES

Lawyers and judges are not alone in facing ethical dilemmas in mass tort litigations. The corporations that make allegedly harmful products, the scientists who design the products and testify as experts, and the legislators who can control the tort system all have obligations to the community at large. In many cases, they have fallen short of carrying their just burden. Like lawyers and judges, these groups should look toward the community's needs, not simply their own self-interest.

Corporate strategic reactions to avoid payments for mass torts, such as by liquidation, reorganizations, and use of subsidiaries and spin-offs, have not been successful,[1] although bankruptcy has sometimes allowed management to delay payment.[2] In fact, acquisition of companies thought to be stripped of their tort liabilities has proven damaging to some purchasers.[3] The law has not yet clarified the extent to which management can shield assets of a company alleged to be a wrongdoer from those claiming harm in a mass tort.

Attacking the tortfeasor should not, however, be the excuse for attorneys actually taking over and running the defendant after acquiring control through a bankruptcy, class action, or other settlement vehicle. The opportunities for conflicts of interest are too great. The attorney and the attorney's friends in the legal, banking, management, and other fields have too great a temptation to deal with the corpus for their own benefit. They have too many conflicts with their own and future clients. They and the minority shareholders may become involved in disputes over fiduciary responsibilities that distract the attorneys from their main function—representation of their own clients. Attorneys should not run defendant corporations over long periods.

We ought not ignore the sometimes pernicious position of some defendants' executives. The American system sometimes rewards executives with big compensation packages based on current profits rather than on long-term healthy gain. Like politicians, therefore, many try to put off the evil day of paying for mistakes, hoping to avoid addressing the issue on their own watch. The result, as in asbestos litigation, is that the problem festers and builds until it can no longer be controlled. An honest facing-up to the problems of asbestos early in the developing crisis might well have provided a basis for a disposition that avoided the terrible costs that have been and continue to be paid.[4] In newly developing matters such as breast implants and repetitive stress syndrome, perhaps early and responsible management responses will lead to better solutions.

Management has an ethical and economic obligation not to give its attorneys freedom to utilize an unlimited, battle-to-the-death strategy. Our community cannot afford this approach. In the long run it is not even justifiable on a dollar-and-cents basis, and keeping companies out of bankruptcy is important to workers and their communities. Defense counsel and executives of defendant companies have an obligation to work to resolve disputes early so that the defendant and the community can move forward with as little waste in transaction costs as possible.[5]

The available evidence suggests that there may be hope. Alternative dispute resolution, for example, has experienced phenomenal growth and promises to help curtail never-ending litigations. Conversations with counsel from both sides indicate that quietly, behind the scenes, efforts to head off harsh, long-drawn-out litigations are growing in favor.[6] We might even emulate the Japanese executives who apologize to those injured by their companies' failures.

CHAPTER 7

ETHICS OF SCIENTISTS

Scientific experts perform important and sometimes critical functions in the resolution of complex mass tort cases.[1] There are ethical elements that scientists need to address within their own community.[2] First, it is appropriate for responsible national scientific groups such as the American Academy of Science and the Centers for Disease Control as well as a specialist in such fields as statistics to undertake the gathering of scientific data needed in important litigations,[3] preferably to obtain a consensus.[4] Second, there is need for some policing by scientists themselves.[5]

The federal government does try to investigate charges of misconduct in research paid for by the federal government.[6] Perhaps courts should refer some cases of possible scientific fraud in litigation to the Federal Office of Research Integrity, part of the Public Health Service, an arm of the Department of Health and Human Services. Scientists should be expected to meet standards higher than the minimal enforceable by the government.[7] Nevertheless, wide-ranging attacks on the bona fides of many scientists who testify in tort litigation seems overstated and unfair.[8]

In my work on the Panel on Statistical Assessment as Evidence in the Courts of the National Science Foundation, I was impressed by the consensus we reached that scientists' ethical obligations might reduce charlatanism.[9] There are codes of ethics for some scientists,[10] but they do not deal with the role of scientists in the courts. Such standards, along with enforcement by scientific committee review of specific testimony, scientific society discipline, and critical reviews in peer journals, might be useful.[11] They should be available for attacks on the credibility of scientific witnesses by an expansion of rules of evidence, perhaps pursuant to Rules 702 and 703 of the Federal Rules of Evidence.[12] These rules permitting the sword of easy admissibility to be wielded might be turned into a shield of responsible scientific testimony and adequate evaluation of the credibility of professional witnesses.

Part of the law's problem is that we tend to exaggerate the purity of scientists and their ability to provide precise answers when needed. Many scientists themselves are political in the sense that they compete for grants and prestige.[13] Moreover, the degree of mendacity in forcing results and exaggerating support for hypotheses may be more widespread than most of us want to acknowledge.[14] Some skepticism by the legal system is appropriate.

Recently there has been increasing emphasis in the courts on the need for peer review and scientific consensus to protect against bad science.[15] This emphasis overstates the value of much peer review.[16] The matter warrants some attention because it suggests the difficulty of applying any bright line tests for scientific proof in mass tort cases. Judicial discretion helps. But the courts must ultimately depend upon an ethical scientific community as a check against error.

Peer review is of limited utility in eliminating mistakes or even fraud.[17] Graduate students often do the work; confirmation of experiments described is difficult and expensive; general impressions are relied upon; referees may want to enhance or retard careers; different sets of referees may be used after the first set disagrees; the authors may recommend referees; and so on.[18] Given such a dubious process, it is apparent why the courts cannot rely on any single test of admissibility. The editorial process in a good student-run law review seems much more reliable than that of many scientific journals. Unless the scientific establishment can in some way give more assurances to the courts of the value or lack of value of published work, pressures increase to admit everything, leaving it for the jury to make the final determination. A great deal of joint work between the two professions is required.[19] The first step toward a more ethical and satisfactory partnership might well be open acknowledgement of each side's limitations. A series of joint meetings toward that end has been undertaken.[20]

The issues of science in mass cases are too complicated to be solved by rules of ethics alone. Such rules may, however, reduce deliberate and gross distortions for the profit of the expert and those who purchase expert opinions.

Much depends on whether scientific establishments begin to insist on ethical conduct as the minimum norm.[21] In addition to discouraging fringe scientists, increased morale may induce better scientists to come forward.

The court, meanwhile, has an obligation to go beyond the experts proffered by the parties. Where adequate science is not yet available it should encourage research and analysis by independent national groups. It should also utilize its powers to appoint independent experts under Rule 706 of the Federal Rules of Evidence.[22] There are times when it will be appropriate to delay decision or provide for intermediate relief while studies go forward. As in other aspects of mass torts, judges "should engage in the active management of complex science and technology issues throughout the stages of litigation. . . ."[23]

I have suggested that the Carnegie Commission on Science, Technology and Government consider drafting a model contract for experts and attorneys.[24] The expert would then receive some protection against being pressured to shade his or her opinion for venal purposes. Such an agreement would also serve to emphasize to attorneys and scientists that the court expects candor from scientists as well as lawyers.[25] When the court appoints an expert under Rule 706 of the Federal Rules of Evidence, all concerned should expect the highest level of candor and disclosure of adverse information.[26]

The courts have also increasingly become aware of the work of experts on matters of ethics—usually academics. They have become quite important to counsel,[27] particularly as the formerly sharp ethical lines have softened in mass tort and other special kinds of cases. Usually professors in law schools, they are leaders and highly regarded by the profession. The extent to which such ethicists should both comment on the rules and make their services available for a substantial fee requires discussion.[28] Appointment pursuant to Rule 706 by the court may avoid embarrassment to the ethicists and their law schools.[29]

Advising clients not to participate in valid scientific inquiries because such studies may undercut a legal position seems to me both unwise and unethical. The court has the power to supervise such studies through its own experts or special masters. It may order attorneys and parties to cooperate and to desist from interference. A court should not coerce independent eminent scientists, such as the late Dr. Irving Selikoff, to testify if, like he, they prefer to publish their results only in scientific journals.

CHAPTER 8

ETHICS OF LEGISLATURES

Consideration of these ethical questions also raises the possibility of an alternative course. Appropriate guidelines for lawyers' and judges' conduct are not, in fact, the central problem; instead, the roots of the problem lie in the substantive and procedural law itself.[1] The seemingly intractable ethical dilemmas posed by mass tort cases suggest the need to rethink our entire system of compensation and deterrence as well as the law of ethics.

It may be that individual and effective justice cannot be delivered in a mass society by means of traditional courtroom adjudication.[2] Modern problems of harm, from the perspectives of both deterrence and redress, may demand modern systems of substantive and procedural justice that transcend adversarial dispute resolution.[3]

I do not speak primarily of tort reform here.[4] The difficult problems created by mass torts may defy adequate solution by ordinary tinkering with rules of court-administered tort law.[5] I speak of genuine tort alternatives: broad regulatory and compensatory legal frameworks that would dispense with the often wasteful and agonizing process of litigation[6] in favor of quick succor for the injured and clear and direct deterrence of wrongdoing.[7] As indicated in chapter 10, such systems offer the promise of global techniques grounded in sound and carefully considered public policy. They are less likely to overdeter useful conduct on the basis of excessively high estimates of risk.[8] They are more likely to prove more responsive to community needs than our cumbersome, sometimes inaccessible, often inscrutable courts.[9] Increasingly in our democratic society we are using forms of the ombudsperson to intervene between producers or suppliers of services and the consumer.[10]

Such a response to the challenge of individual justice in a mass society must come from legislatures. Yet our legislatures have tended to eschew direct consideration of mass torts except in such narrow areas as black lung disease[11] or childhood vaccines.[12]

These limited measures have only nibbled at the edges of the problem. Congress and the President receive so much in contributions from interested groups that none can be alienated. The result is stasis.

Ultimately legislatures—and particularly Congress—should address the problem in a more systematic way. Despite some serious defects in the past administration of the Social Security Disability System,[13] my impression after deciding many disability appeals is that it does as well as or better than the tort system at much less cost.

Even if a national administrative scheme is not adopted to compensate victims of product or process defects, national tort law is required to govern mass tort cases.[14] Ample authority and justification for such law can be found in the Commerce Clause. Such a law would abolish punitive damages in mass tort cases and impose uniform standards in fields where the federal government has exercised regulatory authority—primarily pharmaceuticals and toxic chemicals. Certification should be obtainable that the protections embodied in federal regulatory law are sufficient, thereby preempting state-based tort actions.[15] A tax on producers such as the one used to pay for the Superfund,[16] with a surcharge for companies liable for excessive claims, could also be considered.

Critics of the present tort system have substantial cause for complaint on the ground that many useful products are not being developed.[17] Uniform federal standards that deal sensibly with public safety issues are required. More rational treatment of risks and costs of protection is possible.

The present system of scattered, uneven compensation and deterrence spread across fifty states, with producers of products sometimes required to comply with fifty different laws and those harmed subject to the vagaries of laws, judges, and juries across the country and between the state and federal systems, is unacceptable. This system advances the goals of compensation and deterrence in a halting and inefficient fashion at best.[18] Our modern, burgeoning nation demands a sensible, national system to deal with its complex health and safety problems. The state-law tort system in mass torts is in many respects an outworn relic. It serves by default because nothing better has been crafted by the legislators.

Just as a broad national consensus has emerged that some form of truly national health care system is required, so too the increasing public frustration with the courts and the tort system suggests a growing impetus for thoroughgoing reform of compensatory and regulatory schemes.[19] Congress should heed this call to action.[20]

The push for procedural reform and innovation must also continue. Legislatures should devise mechanisms allowing transfer of cases broader than the present multidistrict panel system[21] so that one court—state or federal—can try all mass tort related cases together. Such devices should include coordination of bankruptcy proceedings when the chief creditors with respect to a limited fund are actual and potential mass tort claimants. In the asbestos cases it makes no sense to have more than a dozen funds resulting from asbestos-related bankruptcies administered by many different sets of trustees and administrators treating the overlapping claims of the same injured people. Those funds and their distribution should be consolidated and jointly administered.

The obligations of the legislature are another aspect of ethics. Congress should exercise the control and responsibility with which it is endowed by the Constitution. Its enormous power was not meant to be left unused when needed. It should not foist on the courts problems that fall within its own constitutional responsibilities, leaving the courts no choice but to bend the substantive law and procedure in ways that may not have been intended and that may not serve the long-term well-being of the law and the community.

Political gridlock on these problems is understandable but unacceptable. We must keep in mind that among the most important rights in a communitarian-communicative ethic are those guaranteed by the First Amendment, including the right to petition one's government for redress.

Congress and the President are under pressure from powerful contributors—tort lawyers on the one hand and industry on the other. A condition precedent to tort reform may well be campaign financing reform.[22] Perhaps reform will have to await a stronger law limiting contribution-based lobbying by both lawyers and manufacturers.

An ethic committed to guaranteeing the dignity and voice of the individual is not inconsistent with a call for uniform systems of administering justice, such as workers' compensation schemes.[23] Where a national commitment to such resolutions is based upon the decisions of elected representatives, society acknowledges that such a solution is more just than case-by-case adjudications in the courts, with all their shortcomings and limitations. The individual can accept the uniform national solution in the belief that he or she has been heard through the democratic system and the national community as a whole has reached a just compromise.

CHAPTER 9

EQUITABLE POWERS OF COURTS TO ADAPT TO

MODERN MASS TORT REQUIREMENTS[1]

A. INTRODUCTION

The enormous expansion in modern mass tort substantive and procedural law in the United States can only be fully understood in the context of equity and its development. Procedure and substance are so intertwined that they must be considered together to obtain a realistic picture of equity's effect.

Considerations long associated with equity jurisprudence have driven the creative procedural and substantive responses of American courts to the many problems posed by complex multiparty, multi-issue mass tort cases. In recent years it is in toxic tort litigation that we can most clearly see equity at work in "its traditional roles of adjusting legal rules that do not work well, providing a moral force, and shaping new substantive law."[2]

To many, particularly those in other countries, it may seem strange that in the United States we leave it to individual courts to provide essentially ad hoc solutions to modern-day disasters with their national social and economic repercussions. In this country, however, three factors have, by default, left the state and federal courts to their own devices: (1) the lack to date of an effective national administrative regulatory scheme capable of controlling undesirable conduct by manufacturers; (2) the absence of a comprehensive social welfare-medical scheme for compensating victims of mass torts; and (3) the lack of adequate state or federal legislation controlling these cases.

The federal government has not, as it might have, adopted national legislation dealing with the problems[3] except in some narrow areas such as black lung,[4] atomic energy,[5] or vaccines.[6] One report on the vaccine compensation program shows, if it is credited, total compensation costs of 10 percent and attorneys' fees of about 3 percent—a success.[7] By contrast, the huge costs associated with the coal miners' black lung disease legislation have deterred Congress from accepting the costs of even those damages caused by the federal government, such as by a failure to supply masks and adequate ventilation to those workers who built our wartime navy and who now suffer the effects of exposure to asbestos.

While some states have taken relatively minor steps to curtail such litigation,[8] they have not been able to take the effective action required to solve a national, and sometimes international, problem. Proposals for legislative reform of the American Bar Association[9] and American Law Institute[10] are not given much chance of success.

To understand why the United States federal courts and some state courts have felt so free to take action that must be considered radical by judges from other parts of the world, it is necessary to bear in mind that most of these developments have occurred in the half-century since World War II. Buoyed by our participation in the defeat of German armed forces under Hitler and Japanese forces under Hirohito and our enormous economic power, United States judges, in common with the rest of our society, thought their ability to improve the world was almost limitless, and many courts exercised their powers to the fullest. A more becoming modesty is now espoused by the bench and society. That we turned to equity in the judicial arena was partly a result of (1) training in the law schools, where equity was taught as a separate course until the 1950s; (2) a strong tradition of equity as a separate source of judicial power in the federal courts, where a merger of law and equity did not take place until 1938; and (3) the flexibility and effectiveness of the tools of equity in meeting new jurisprudential problems.

Anglo-American equity jurisprudence has historically experienced its most significant growth in periods of great social movement and of changing relationships among people and institutions.[11] American courts in the postwar era responded to social, political, and economic challenges by putting a more humanitarian and democratic face on the old maxim: "Equity will not suffer a wrong to be without a remedy."[12] The federal courts in particular opened their doors to individuals and groups that historically had been disenfranchised and placed beyond the pale of social and economic America, such as black Americans, prison inmates, and the mentally and physically handicapped. Social pressures such as the civil rights movement revealed a need for wholesale structural reforms of institutions and channeled efforts for achieving those reforms through the courts.[13] Congress enormously expanded rights of minorities and the poor, as well as of women and workers generally. The courts in turn discovered new, legally cognizable harms and used their equitable powers to develop the substantive laws and remedies to redress these novel injuries. Other institutions as well as the courts played a large role in this development. This chapter concentrates on the judicial role.[14]

Similarly, the scientific and economic advances of the twentieth century began to be reflected in new technological and legal relationships. Mass production and worldwide distribution of new chemicals and drugs resulted in harms on a comparable scale. Many of the diseases associated with exposure to toxic products were latent illnesses found in the population at large, such as cancers not associated with any particular kind of work or chemical. In such circumstances, establishing causation and identifying the responsible manufacturer or distributor was difficult. Traditional tort doctrines, with their relatively simple models of causation and liability, were ill equipped to address these toxic torts or compensate their victims. In addition to the complex medical and scientific problems of proof associated with toxic torts, the sheer magnitude of mass tort cases rendered traditional bipolar adjudication awkward.

American courts responded by radically departing from the traditional models—at least insofar as they began to apply older equitable forms of aggregation to new categories of private litigants.[15] New judicially created laws were justified in the name of redistributing risk and internalizing costs.[16] Once the province of common law courts and judges, mass tort cases now forced the courts to adopt an equitable posture. Courts of equity traditionally have taken into account the equities—the concrete issues of fact and fairness of the particular situation—in fashioning remedies. In the mass tort context these include (1) fairly and expeditiously compensating numerous victims and (2) deterring wrongful conduct where possible while (3) preventing overdeterrence in mass torts from shutting down industry or removing needed products from the market, (4) keeping the courts from becoming paralyzed by tens or even hundreds of thousands of repetitive personal injury cases, and (5) reducing transactional costs of compensation.

The procedural techniques employed to aggregate and manage these mass disaster cases, such as broad joinder devices and class actions, were developed by equity.[17] Promulgation and adoption of the Federal Rules of Civil Procedure in 1938[18] theoretically merged law and equity in the federal system, which is where most mass tort cases are filed. These rules embodied the philosophical and procedural tenets of equity far more than they did the more rigid common law. After 1938 the flexible techniques that equity once had reserved to protect property holders were to a large extent democratized and made universally applicable to civil actions, whether grounded in constitutional, statutory, or common law.

Were it not for the jury system, protected as it is by the Seventh Amendment to the United States Constitution, the procedural swing to equity would have been even greater. As it is, the growth of deposition practice,[19] summary judgment,[20] and judgment notwithstanding the verdict[21] has tended to attenuate the traditional jury system, characterized by testimony in open court.[22]

On the substantive side, judicially created equitable-legal doctrines enhanced the ability of toxic tort victims to recover for their injuries in the absence of particularized proof of causation and liability. The courts relaxed traditional concepts of fault and causation and expanded the definition of compensable injuries. These innovations, however, are indebted more to a judicial state of mind than to any substantive equitable antecedents. For, despite the fact that equity in post-Medieval England eventually became somewhat incapacitated by precedent, it never lost its aura of gung ho problem solving with the concomitant pragmatic, flexible, and activist view that was embodied in that jurisprudential cast. Even when the chancellors were immobilized by self-imposed restraints they worked in the glow of such maxims as "Equity delights in doing equity." This spiritual reserve remained available to permit judges exercising equitable jurisdiction to create new forms and law to prevent modern injustices.

The expansive procedural devices and innovative substantive doctrines developed to cope with mass toxic torts are currently under attack from a variety of sources. Prominent members of the bench, bar, legal academy, and business community, along with some high-profile government commissions, have charged that increased access to the courts and proplaintiff tort doctrines have failed to solve the problems they were designed to address and have instead resulted in a civil justice system sinking under the weight of mass toxic tort and other product liability cases.[23] These critics also claim that the unintended result has been overdeterrence: soaring jury verdicts and litigation costs that have rendered insurance prohibitively expensive or unavailable at any cost, thereby raising the price of consumer goods, removing needed products from the market, and squelching new development.[24]

As an antidote, these critics propose removing many of these cases from the tort system and instituting an administrative compensation scheme. Failing that, they advocate restrictive interpretations of the federal rules of procedure, designed to limit access to the courts, along with a return to traditional tort doctrines that emphasize fault and curb plaintiffs' recoveries.

These views have enjoyed considerable success. In the federal system, the Supreme Court has exhibited a general desire to restrict the number and types of claims brought in district courts.[25] In the state arena, the mid-1980s witnessed an unprecedented flood of legislative intervention into traditionally common law tort doctrine; the majority of states passed legislation designed to reduce or prevent tort recoveries.

Attacks on the current system are not limited to those who would curb its liberal thrust. The phenomenon of mass tort litigation also has spawned criticism by the plaintiffs' bar, some consumer groups, and a number of prominent law professors who charge that the aggregative devices employed by many courts to consolidate and manage mass tort cases sacrifice individual justice in the name of judicial efficiency and economic expediency.[26] These critics argue that mass dispositions compromise principles of due process and interfere with the plaintiff's property right to control his or her claim.[27] Massing claims, they maintain, distorts the proper attorney-client relationship. Moreover, according to these critics, compelling mass settlements precludes the vindication of individual rights and denies plaintiffs the cathartic effect of telling their stories to a judge and jury. Finally, they warn that mass settlements will undercompensate tort victims and underdeter tortfeasors.

While shedding light on many problems, the arguments of the various critics have serious flaws. I do not believe that the federal and other courts in particular should retreat from their post–World War II role of protecting the injured individual and offering a forum to vindicate economic, political, social, and medical rights. More justice for more people should be our goal—not less justice for ever fewer people. Nevertheless, I cannot agree with those who would have the courts attempt to treat mass tort cases on a one-by-one basis, as though they were two-car accidents.

Mass tort cases have outstripped the ability of the common law, with its relatively rigid adherence to precedent, to fashion remedies that adequately redress the harms of modern technological society. In circumstances where the rules of the common law prove to be too strict and fail to provide adequate remedies, the courts historically have turned to equity.[28]

Balancing the various equities in mass tort litigation inevitably will lead to conflict between the rule of law—that is to say, the "formal and procedural correctness of the means used to reach substantive results"[29]—and justice—by which is meant the intuitive correctness of the substantive end result of the legal system. This conflict is not new. John Locke warned that sometimes "a strict and rigid observation of the laws may do harm."[30] Much of equity jurisprudence, of course, has developed out of this tension between predictability based on rigid rules of the past and flexibility based on present needs of a changing society.

Part B examines a number of procedural devices, along with their equitable antecedents, that are of particular importance in mass tort cases.[31] Their pros and cons are evaluated in light of the equities that must be weighed in all mass tort suits: (1) fair and expeditious compensation at a reasonable transaction cost; (2) avoidance of overdeterrence; and (3) maintenance of a viable court system. Part C surveys some of the substantive legal innovations developed by courts in their attempts to fashion remedies unprovided by the common law and also evaluates them in light of the prevailing equities.[32] Part D reviews some of the aggregated settlements and compensation funds.[33] Part E addresses some of the attacks currently being waged on these procedural and substantive developments.[34] There are a few concluding observations in the final section, Part F.[35]

B. PROCEDURAL TECHNIQUES AND MASS TORTS

1. HISTORY

Any history of the equitable underpinnings of modern-day mass tort law must acknowledge the vast upheaval that accompanied the growth of a global economy. Equity has experienced its greatest growth in times of political, economic, and social change.[36] The increasingly complex worldwide technologies and economies that came to characterize the postwar period proved no exception in this regard.

Tort law too has always been sensitive to changes in modes of production, communications, and marketing. As one prominent torts scholar has observed, social change has driven the "great landmarks of American tort law"—those individual cases that represent radical breaks from the past.[37] The changes wrought by the industrial revolution and subsequent mass production and distribution techniques were reflected in the new meanings given duty of care, reasonableness of an act, and proximate cause.

"[F]rom the beginning, equity's expansiveness led to larger cases . . . than were customary with common law practice."[38] Tort cases, by contrast, were the quintessential example of private law development. Yet, now they began to take on the same expansive character that had marked equitable actions. The response of the courts to toxic torts in particular and mass torts in general—namely, the creation of new tort theories, increases in the size of litigation, enhanced roles for judicial discretion, heavy reliance on documentation, and decreasing dependence on the discretion of the jury—relied heavily on norms and attitudes borrowed from equity.[39]

2. FEDERAL RULES OF CIVIL PROCEDURE AND TRIUMPH OF EQUITY

By the post–World War II period, the procedural techniques that courts would rely on in handling the explosion of mass tort litigation were already largely in place as a result of the 1938 adoption of the Federal Rules of Civil Procedure. Devices that courts of equity had developed to aggregate and manage protracted multiparty litigation were now codified in rules universally applicable to all civil actions.

Blackstone once wrote that the "essential difference" between equity and law lay "in the mode of proof, the mode of trial, and the mode of relief."[40] By the end of the nineteenth century, both England and most states in the United States had moved to eradicate these "essential" differences by adopting one set of procedures—the more flexible ones associated with equity—for both legal and equitable actions. In England, the Judicature Act of 1873 merged law and equity. New York was one of the earliest states to apply equitable procedure to both legal and equitable actions when, in 1849, it partially adopted David Dudley Field's fact-pleading code.[41] The federal courts, however, postponed merging law and equity. Not until 1938, after three decades of efforts by many prominent lawyers and jurists,[42] was this merger accomplished when the Supreme Court promulgated the Federal Rules of Civil Procedure.

The federal rules represented less a merger of equals than the conquest of law by equity. The rules embodied the philosophy and procedures of equity far more than they did those of the common law. The rigid system of writs and technical pleading that had characterized common law practice was rejected in favor of the simplified fact pleading and more flexible procedures of equity.[43] The federal rules actually went well beyond contemporaneous equitable principles. Liberal discovery rules[44] and expansive joinder devices[45] not only permitted the gathering of an entire controversy into one package in a manner that had been unavailable under the rigidities of the common law and various complex state codes of procedures, but also invited into court new kinds of plaintiffs and cases.

The triumph of equity over the common law extended to trial procedures. Historically, trials at common law relied on public, in-court, oral testimony of witnesses familiar with the dispute.[46] There was very limited formal development of evidence prior to trial. Equity, by contrast, traditionally had relied on and required written submissions such as briefs and affidavits, as well as documents produced through discovery.[47]

The merger of law and equity erased this distinction. Today the use of written materials produced through discovery and submitted by the parties is universal. Parties routinely exchange evidence and witness lists, summaries of expected testimony of experts, and other documents. This reliance on documents and "canned" testimony such as written or videotaped depositions[48] is particularly noticeable in mass tort suits where identical testimony by the same relatively small group of experts is presented in case after case. Often that testimony is played to jury after jury on videotape or by reading depositions.

There are other ways in which the "modes of proof and trial," once associated with equity, now dominate our merged systems. For example, we are seeing more and more dispositions on summary judgment in which cases are resolved on the basis of written materials such as experts' reports without submitting the issues to a jury.[49] Dismissals based on "frivolous" pleadings and the imposition of sanctions also have increased. Much of the courts' work now involves the supervision of discovery—so much so that when I was Chief Judge of the Eastern District of New York, I instituted a program of using magistrates to oversee all discovery in civil cases. Once sufficient discovery has taken place, the vast majority of cases in our court settle without trial, frequently without the judges even having been aware that the case was pending.

The domination of equity over law is also illustrated by the frequency and varied circumstances in which courts today turn to equitable remedies. Examples are numerous: injunctions granted under federal environmental statutes regulating pollution and the release of hazardous substances; judicial control of the distribution of limited compensation funds in mass tort cases; and judicial control over attorneys' fees in cases resulting in settlement funds. The equitable nature of these remedies also requires more personal involvement by the judge in enforcing the relief granted. Leaving enforcement to the prevailing party does not always work, and not infrequently court-appointed masters supervise execution of the decree. To the extent that the development and implementation of mass tort compensation funds requires ongoing judicial supervision, the relief in these cases has come to resemble the structural reform cases in which we find court control of prisons, of health care institutions for the mentally retarded, and of schools subject to desegregation orders. All of these developments have pushed the common law trial off center stage and have placed more control over the management of the case and its eventual determination into the hands of judges and magistrate judges.[50]

Were it not for the constitutional grant of a jury trial in suits at common law, the triumph of equity over traditionally common law practice would have gone still further. This Seventh Amendment guarantee is the primary reason why, years after this merger of law and equity, disputes over what belongs to a court of equity and what to law continue to tease us. The Supreme Court continues to require—to determine whether a party to a civil action has a right to a jury trial—that courts embark on a historical inquiry into eighteenth-century English distinctions between law and equity.[51]

With this general overview of the degree to which all procedure now resembles equity procedure, the particular techniques used to aggregate, manage, and dispose of mass torts can be examined.

The traditional aim of equity was "to have in court all persons whose rights or property are involved in any particular litigation and to render a complete decree adjusting all the rights and protecting all the parties against future litigations."[52] There are numerous procedural devices—some codified in the federal rules and others in statutes—that enable claims and parties to be joined. Rule-based aggregative devices include: class actions,[53] consolidation,[54] joinder rules,[55] interpleader,[56] and intervention.[57] Moreover, the use of magistrate judges[58] and special masters[59] has extended the reach of the courts and enhanced their ability to manage complex cases.

Statutory mechanisms allowing aggregation include: statutory interpleader,[60] the bankruptcy code relied on in a number of mass torts, including asbestos, by a growing number of producers,[61] and the multidistrict litigation provision, which permits a national panel of judges to transfer theoretically independent cases to one judge for pretrial discovery, simplification of issues, and settlement.[62]

Courts also have both statutory power under the "change of venue" provision[63] and informal administrative power to assign related cases to one judge in a given district.[64] There also has been some voluntary cooperation between state and federal courts in coordinating control of cases.

Some of the substantive tort law doctrines developed over the past decade by courts to enhance recovery by plaintiffs, such as market share or enterprise liability, also have had the practical effect of aggregating parties—usually plaintiffs, but in many cases defendants.[65]

The ability of groups or other entities such as unions and corporations to bring a lawsuit—or to be sued—and the application of legal doctrines such as collateral estoppel, res judicata, and the law of the case doctrine, all add to the aggregative character of litigation in the United States. So, too, do such standard devices as formal shareholder derivative actions and informal agreements among lawyers specializing in these cases.[66]

All these devices, to varying degrees, have aided in the managing of mass tort litigation. They do not, however, adequately meet the seven criteria that, as I have already suggested in chapter 2, I believe must be satisfied in mass tort cases.[67] Those criteria are: (1) the concentration of decision making in one or a few judges; (2) a single forum responsible for resolving legal and factual issues; (3) a single substantive law; (4) adequate judicial support facilities; (5) reasonable fact-finding procedures, particularly as to scientific issues; (6) a cap on the total cost to defendants such as by limiting punitive damages and allocations for pain and suffering and a method of allocating that cost among multiple defendants; and (7) a single distribution plan with fairly inflexible scheduled payments by injury based on the need of those injured, rather than the social and economic status of plaintiffs, and tailored to the availability of private resources.

The most important modern device for dealing with mass torts is the class action. Use in tort law developed primarily in the 1980s with the Agent Orange litigation. To understand this development, a discussion of the history of class actions is essential.

A. HISTORY OF CLASS ACTION

The modern class action finds its roots as a method for dealing with multiple actions in courts of equity. A bill of peace brought in the early English chancery courts, if granted, enabled a plaintiff to join all defendants and claims in a single forum provided the parties were too numerous for ordinary joinder, shared a common interest in the question to be decided, and if the parties before the court adequately represented absent class members.[68]

There were, however, many significant differences between early group litigation and the modern class action. Perhaps the most important for our purposes is that, unlike its current function of joining diverse parties sharing only a common interest in particular litigation, the numerous parties brought together by Chancery class suits had existed as social groups independently of the litigation, such as tenants on a manor, villagers, or parishioners.[69] For the most part, representation of the class was explicit, with class members electing their representatives and chancellors requiring the consent of the group before an action could be brought.[70] Members of these groups shared permanent bonds of status, as between lord and tenant, or parson and parishioner.[71] These social and economic bonds meant that parties could apply pressure to resolve a dispute aside from litigation and that litigation would not destroy preexisting obligations.[72] Thus, unlike today's mass tort class actions, the early class action did not empower a scattered mass of individuals who did not know each other and had no bonds except those created by a grievance and the group litigation.

Today, the class action actually changes the real power and substantive rights of those whose claims are aggregated. (Other aggregation techniques, such as multidistricting, do the same, but in a more subtle manner; because they are perceived as "neutral" procedural tools, they have not been the object of controversy to the degree that the class action has been.) Both the drafters[73] and the critics of the modern rule perceived this, and it accounts for the political content that underlies some of the attacks made on class actions.[74]

Another important difference between group litigation and the modern class action is that the early cases all involved claims of group status or property disputes, such as the commons privilege of a manor community, rather than individual rights.[75] None of the early cases involved claims for money damages by or against a group (although in some cases, damages were claimed in a second proceeding when an equity decree was disobeyed).[76] The substantive law applied was usually that of local custom, rather than general common law.[77] Chancery acted more like a legislature than a judicial body in that it made rules to govern the prospective legal obligations of the parties, somewhat like declaratory judgments.[78] Furthermore, the "notoriously uncertain and expensive" Chancery enforcement proceedings meant that equity decrees were not enforced in individual cases.[79]

Third, unlike the rarity of defendant classes today, sixteenth- and early-seventeenth-century class actions involved classes of defendants as often as plaintiffs.[80] Group plaintiff suits often faced more obstacles than defendant groups because Chancery suits were prolonged and expensive, the loser faced sanctions of costs and attorneys' fees, and chancellors perceived such suits as harassment of a lord and thus were unlikely to grant a favorable ruling.[81] In addition, the economic, social, and political subordination of tenants and parishioners made them less likely than lords and parsons to consider lawsuits as means of dispute resolution.[82]

The upheavals caused by the transformation of feudal society in the seventeenth century changed the nature of group litigation. The equity courts responded with greater flexibility than did the common law to the needs of new associations of capital and labor. Joint stock companies and "friendly societies" (voluntary trade associations that insured their members against illness and death), whose members were associated not through social bonds, but by membership for limited purposes, required a new rationale for aggregation of parties and issues in the courts.[83] The justification for class actions became one of representation, similar to the new forms of political representation in that it did not require explicit consent, but only a finding of common interest.[84] Eventually legislation recognizing these associations as legal entities entitled to sue and subject to suit was enacted, and group litigation via equity fell into disuse in England.

On this side of the Atlantic, Joseph Story, the most prominent contemporary commentator on equity, described the equitable bill of peace as a device to suppress useless litigation and prevent multiple suits.[85] This description, while ignoring the social and historical context of group litigation, should sound familiar to anyone conversant with the modern-day class action. According to Story, group litigation was allowable (1) where the parties were too numerous to appear before the court; (2) where a question of general interest existed and a few may therefore sue for the benefit of the many; and (3) where parties are members of a voluntary association and may fairly be supposed to represent the whole.[86] Because he viewed the class action as a means of saving judicial time and facilitating disposition of already existing cases, Story advocated liberal use of the device, rejecting adherence to any strict standards that required a preexisting "community of interest."[87]

Over the next century there was a debate over which of two doctrinal approaches constituted an appropriate theory for class actions: the "community of interest" theory, assuming class members shared a common legal right, or the consent theory, which centered on the sharing among many litigants of common questions of law or fact.[88] Story had favored the latter, more liberal theory, but it was the "community of interest" approach that, until recently, was the more generally accepted.

Class suits in the United States came to be allowed in several categories of cases, including suits seeking an injunction against a class of persons jointly causing a nuisance, suits by creditors to enforce a stock assessment against stockholders, taxpayer suits to enjoin a tax, and suits by numerous persons for a single injury.[89] Even where there is nominally only one party in an action, some of the most frequently seen aggregations are, in this country, corporations, unions, and various private associations such as the NAACP and environmental groups.

The equitable bill of peace was not generally available for joining tort suits until the middle of the twentieth century.[90] Personal injury cases were perceived as involving individual wrongs, and litigation in such circumstances was felt to be a personal and individual enterprise.[91] Nonetheless, some prescient contemporaneous critics chafed against this limitation of the bill of peace, arguing that it was a useful method of joining cases and preventing a multiplicity of cases brought at law.

B. CLASS ACTIONS AND MASS TORTS

I. GENERALLY. ▪ Rule 23 of the Federal Rules of Civil Procedure "has been widely regarded as a major achievement of the federal rules."[92] This rule has been the focus of an increasing amount of scholarship, particularly in regard to mass tort litigation.[93]

The modern rule dates from revisions of the class action rule drafted by the standing advisory committee in the early 1960s and promulgated in 1966 by the Supreme Court. The revisions created three types of class actions known as Rule 23(b)(1), (b)(2), and (b)(3) class actions. (The revisions set shareholder derivative actions apart in Rule 23.1 and actions brought by or against members of unincorporated associations in Rule 23.2.) Rules 23(b)(1) and (b)(2) are mandatory class actions that do not allow class members to opt out and bring their own suits.[94] These categories are generally employed where injunctive relief is sought or, in the case of Rule 23(b)(1)(B), where numerous claims are made against "a fund insufficient to satisfy all claims."[95] Attempts to certify Rule 23(b)(1)(B) classes in mass tort litigation have been unsuccessful when there was a failure or inability to prove the existence of a limited fund[96]—and even when a limited fund was shown, some appellate courts and some plaintiff's attorneys favor bankruptcy over the class action.[97]

Where mass torts have been certified as a class it is usually under Rule 23(b)(3) since it permits multiple claims for money damages.[98] Rule 23(b)(3) allows class members to opt out and bring individual claims—a right that not only limits the courts' ability to achieve global solutions, but often imposes significant burdens on class counsel who must provide notice of the class and alternatives to all class members. Another limitation to using this rule to achieve total peace in mass torts is the fact that it is sometimes easy for a plaintiff—and sometimes a defendant—to defeat class certification.

Rule 23 is a useful joinder device, allowing the common claims or defenses of an entire class to be adjudicated with finality in a single proceeding.[99] The Rule has the added advantage of providing representation of the class by one attorney or a small group of attorneys, thus facilitating communication, management, and settlement.

The drafters of the Federal Rules did not foresee that Rule 23 would be useful in the mass tort context. The advisory committee note accompanying the 1966 amendments to Rule 23 specifically admonished against using the class action device in mass tort litigation:

A "mass accident" resulting in injuries to numerous persons is ordinarily not appropriate for a class action because of the likelihood that significant questions, not only of damages but of liability and defenses of liability, would be present, affecting the individuals in different ways. In these circumstances an action conducted nominally as a class action would degenerate in practice into multiple lawsuits separately tried.[100]

As authority for this warning against attempts to use class actions in torts, the note cites an article I wrote as a law professor.[101] As a judge I have been forced to ignore this indiscretion when faced with the practicalities of mass tort litigation. In the earlier 1960s we did not fully understand the implications of mass tort demands on our legal system.

In recent years an increasing number of district courts have been forced to move beyond the advisory committee's notes; they have relied on the language of the rule and the needs of the parties to certify classes in mass torts.[102] Classes have been certified in the Dalkon Shield litigation,[103] in the Agent Orange litigation,[104] and in some asbestos cases.[105]

Faced with innovative district court solutions to seemingly intractable problems, the appellate courts have begun to be slightly more sympathetic to class actions in mass tort cases.[106]

The class action provides advantages and disadvantages when dealing with mass tort cases. In addition to the advantages mentioned above, such as individual or committee representation of large numbers of plaintiffs or defendants, the class action explicitly provides for judicial supervision to ensure some degree of fairness and control over attorneys' fees. As we shall see, with a limited compensation fund, court control over fees and expenses is desirable. With this control the judge can ensure that attorneys charge fees commensurate to the savings that economies of scale of shared discovery, experts, and so on should engender.[107] There is no explicit provision for control of fees in either rule or statutory aggregation procedures.

Opt-out provisions in money damage class actions theoretically reduce the ability of this device to deliver "global peace" in the mass tort context[108]—as does what some perceive (wrongly, in my opinion) to be the inability to join claims filed in state court or to bind future claimants.[109] In fact, very few persons usually opt out of a reasonably run class action since they operate on the "Book of the Month" theory—failure to object because of apathy, or the like, is deemed approval.

The stringent notice provisions often associated with opt-out money damage classes and the ease with which even a small number of plaintiffs or their attorneys can defeat class certification pose additional problems. Moreover, the class action against one or a group of defendants does not provide for the resolution of related matters, such as suits brought against insurers, which sometimes must be disposed of before the mass tort litigation can be "put to rest."[110]

I shall return to class actions in the Agent Orange case a little further on.[111] There I speak of the types of compensation and distribution funds that should be set up in mass tort cases.

II. BANKRUPTCIES ▪ The actuality or imminent probability of bankruptcy has increasingly come to dominate most mass tort, or at least mega–mass tort, litigation. My view is that from the beginning mass torts should be treated similarly to a bankruptcy proceeding. No matter how financially healthy the defendants in these huge cases, the sheer number of present and future victims means that we are ultimately dealing with a limited compensation fund.

The bankruptcies of major defendants have also forced acceptance of class certification of claimants. The Dalkon Shield litigation is particularly instructive in this regard. Attempts on the part of a district court to certify a class prior to the bankruptcy of the manufacturer, A. H. Robins, had failed as a result of opposition from the plaintiffs' bar.[112] In the summer of 1985, Robins, by then defending nearly sixteen thousand suits, instituted bankruptcy proceedings. In doing so, the company effectively achieved its goal of aggregating all the IUD claims in a single forum. By refusing to move on their own for class certification, the plaintiffs' attorneys relinquished some control over events.[113] Defendants have the power to control the use of voluntary bankruptcies. The litigants as creditors also have the power to force a defendant into bankruptcy, although they generally have avoided doing this since the process takes control of the litigation away from them.

Bankruptcy proceedings give the judge considerable equitable powers of supervision. The judge may stay both state and federal actions while bankruptcy proceedings are pending.[114] In the federal courts the district judge has the power to take over the bankruptcy action,[115] as Judge Robert Merhige did in the A. H. Robins Dalkon Shield bankruptcy.[116] State courts also may be able to exercise some power over the compensation funds set up by bankrupt mass tort defendants where the interests of state court plaintiffs are at stake and where the funds are "physically" within the court's jurisdiction. For example, New York state judges may appoint a temporary receiver of property "where there is danger that the property will be removed from the state, or lost, materially injured or destroyed."[117]

C. CONSOLIDATION

Consolidation of claims, like the class action, has its roots in early English courts of law, which developed a method for dealing with a multiplicity of suits arising from the same factual situation. Under a procedure known as "quasi consolidation," a court of law could stay actions pending against a defendant or actions brought by a plaintiff against a group of defendants.[118] The court would then try all common questions of law and fact in a single suit.[119] The effectiveness of quasi consolidation was limited since the suit could bind only those who agreed to be bound.[120] In addition, a common law judge, lacking the broad injunctive powers of the chancery court, could only stay actions pending in his own court.[121]

Before the 1966 revisions of Rule 23 of the Federal Rules of Civil Procedure and the 1968 Multidistrict Litigation Act,[122] there were few instances of compelled consolidation. There are currently two methods to consolidate cases in the federal system: Rule 42 of the Federal Rules of Civil Procedure, which provides for consolidation of related cases in a single jurisdiction, and the Multidistrict Litigation (MDL) statute, which enables consolidation across federal jurisdictional lines for pretrial purposes.

The Multidistrict Act authorizes the Panel on Multidistrict Litigation, which consists of seven judges appointed by the Chief Justice, to consolidate for purposes of pretrial proceedings in a single district court tort claims arising in different federal venues.[123] There is still no formal method of aggregating state and federal cases, although the American Law Institute has proposed a "federal-state intersystem consolidation" statute.[124]

Although the Act only authorizes consolidation for pretrial proceedings, most cases result in settlement before the transferee judge,[125] and in some cases the transferee judge has presided over a mass trial.[126] The panel may order consolidation even over the objections of the parties.[127] There is no right to direct appeal of a decision of the panel; review of a panel's order is available only by extraordinary writ.[128] As Professor Resnik notes in her discussion of MDL:

> After cases have been transferred, subsequently filed cases (called "tag-along actions" that involve "common questions of fact" with cases already transferred) can also be sent to the designated transferee judge. The MDL statute also authorizes the panel to promulgate rules "not inconsistent with Acts of Congress and the Federal Rules of Civil Procedure" and thereby permits nationwide federal procedural rulemaking outside the Rules Enabling Act process.[129]

Unlike class actions, MDL has always permitted mass torts to be aggregated.[130] Professor Resnik finds that, instead of the controversy inspired by Rule 23, drafted only two years earlier, MDL has won almost universal acclaim, particularly from the judiciary. As Judge Stanley Weigel, a member of the MDL panel in 1977, observed: "[t]hrough creative use of their broad powers, transferee judges have developed salutary solutions to many of the staggering problems associated with complicated and intricate multidistrict litigation . . . [thereby] contribut[ing] immeasurably to the public welfare and to the capacity of the federal judiciary to carry its ever increasing burden of litigation."[131] Resnik suggests that in contrast to Rule 23, MDL was mistakenly seen as "merely" procedural—applicable only to pretrial proceedings and as an expediting mechanism for pending cases rather than as a substantive device for enabling new claims—and thus "neutral."[132] MDL thus seemed to present no threat of expanding plaintiffs' rights.

Most of the contemporary suggestions from the American Bar Association, the American Law Institute, and the Federal Courts Study Committee advocate enhancement of the MDL statute to give it more far-reaching effect, or passage of an even more powerful consolidation statute capable of aggregating cases both temporally and geographically across state and federal jurisdictional lines.[133] Most such proposals would place determination of when and what to consolidate under judicial control in the name of judicial economy and rational allocation of judicial business, immunizing these decisions from any requirement of party consensus.[134] The substantive impact of these suggestions is clear, particularly if they would provide for a single choice of substantive law. By contrast, today choice of law in torts is ruled by the states under *Erie R.R. Co. v. Tompkins*.[135]

Currently, consolidation under Rule 42 or the MDL provision, and class actions, fail to offer any solution to the claim that binding or precluding the claims of future plaintiffs violates due process and poses an obstacle to achieving finality and closure in mass tort settlements. The American Law Institute, however, is studying the possibility of structuring a new MDL-type statute that would include provisions for both filing of claims not yet brought and preclusion on notice.[136]

Mass torts subject to consolidation orders have many of the attributes of a class action. In fact, some courts of appeal panels have carried over their hostility to class actions to mere consolidations.[137]

In some aspects consolidation can prove to be an even more powerful tool than class certification. For example, individual claimants whose cases have been consolidated have no right to opt out of consolidations as do claimants in Rule 23(b)(3) class actions, the type of class action most commonly associated with mass torts.

Where there are comparatively few cases relative to the mega–mass torts, such as in DES litigation, consolidation has proven adequate.[138] But, as already indicated, it often does not go far enough. One shortcoming of particular import in mass tort litigation in which the available funds are limited is the lack of any provision for control of attorneys' fees in consolidated actions. In the context of mass torts, where numerous claims are consolidated for trial or settlement, it is undesirable to continue to allow the plaintiffs' bar to receive high contingency fees predicated on the case-by-case trial of claims.[139] Some method of providing fees commensurate with time spent under the American lodestar method,[140] or as a percentage of the common fund settlement, or on the basis of results accomplished or some other method premised on equitable principles,[141] rather than by private contingency fee contract between the attorney and each client, is necessary.[142]

The asbestos litigation provides a good example of consolidation's inadequacies,[143] because some of these cases have been consolidated for pretrial discovery—and in a few instances for trial—in many individual jurisdictions. Asbestos is a mineral with natural heat-resistant and fire-retardant properties. For most of this century it has been used as an insulation product in buildings, water and steam pipes, ships, and many other connections such as brake linings and fire retardant curtains. Several generations of workers, including insulators, pipe fitters, sheet metal workers, and laborers, among others, were heavily exposed to raw asbestos and to asbestos-containing products. As a result, there have been hundreds of thousands of claims, with a rate of about ten thousand new claims filed each year.[144] As indicated in chapter 10, projections indicate that plaintiffs will bring at least ten thousand new cases of asbestos-associated disease or death every year well into the twenty-first century. Under a system of case-by-case resolution, it is estimated that asbestos suits filed in the 1980s in some backlogged federal districts would wait decades before coming to trial.[145] One recent study found that the disposition of all currently pending asbestos personal injury and property damage cases, if handled individually in the normal course of litigation, would require approximately 150 judge years.[146]

Along with a New York state judge, I presided over the pretrial preparation and partial settlement of some 580 consolidated asbestos personal injury and wrongful death cases emanating out of exposure in the New York Navy Shipyard. (The Navy Yard cases do not, of course, represent the total number of asbestos cases currently pending in New York.) Later I tried before a single jury some seventy-five cases and helped settle many more.

These cases were initially consolidated through a series of somewhat novel moves. First, while serving as Chief Judge of the Eastern District, I arranged for the asbestos cases pending in both the Eastern and Southern Districts to be consolidated for pretrial proceedings before Judge Charles P. Sifton in the Eastern District. The state courts in New York City provided for cooperation between Judge Sifton and Justice Helen E. Freedman of the State Supreme Court in New York, to whom all the New York City cases had been assigned. Judges Sifton and Freedman, together with the other judges, particularly Judge Robert W. Sweet, worked closely with each other in jointly handling the state and federal cases. Second, the Navy Yard cases were subsequently administratively assigned to me. Third, I was designated a Southern District judge by the Chief Judge of the Court of Appeals to exercise the power to settle or try the Southern as well as Eastern District Navy Yard cases. Finally, I was assigned by the Chief Judge of the Southern District to handle any Manville Trust problems.[147] The Manville Trust is said to be responsible for some one-third of all asbestos claims nationwide.

Although state and federal courts with mass toxic tort filings have in the past cooperated with each other through shared discovery or the application of stays, there is no formal method of consolidating cases between the two systems. The state judge to whom the New York City asbestos cases had been assigned and the federal trial judges dealt with the problem by appointing the same person, Kenneth Feinberg, as a special master under the Federal Rules and a referee under the local New York procedural code. (He had also served in the Agent Orange case and received a joint federal-state appointment in the DES cases.) Thus, in effect, the state and federal Navy Yard cases were consolidated for purposes of attempting to fashion a global settlement. Judges from the state and federal courts presided together over joint pretrial and trial sessions.[148]

In their modern incarnation, the asbestos personal injury and wrongful death cases have been litigated in the courts for approximately fifteen years.[149] The Manville Corporation, once the nation's largest producer of asbestos-containing insulation products, and a number of other asbestos defendants sought protection in bankruptcy.[150] There are limits to the monies available from insurance funds and the assets of even the largest corporations for compensating victims. If we persist in trying cases on an individual or even small-scale jurisdiction-by-jurisdiction basis, many plaintiffs will die before they are compensated, a great many will wait years, and some may receive nothing as the available monies are dribbled away by earlier awards and transaction costs.[151] Moreover, as one judge has noted, "our attempt to try these virtually identical lawsuits, one-by-one, will bankrupt both the state and federal court systems."[152]

Many believe that the asbestos plaintiffs should have been certified as a class at least for the limited purposes of determining causation, state of the art, and other problems. Some appellate courts, however, have found that there exist "too many disparities among the various plaintiffs for their common concerns to predominate."[153] Not only have asbestos cases generally been perceived as inappropriate for class treatment, but the Multidistrict Litigation Panel repeatedly rejected multidistricting the asbestos litigation until it finally relented in the early 1990s and sent all the federal cases to a single federal judge on the urging of a self-appointed committee of ten federal trial judges.[154] The maturing of this litigation now requires national aggregation.[155] Federal and state trial judges meet separately and together in groups to coordinate their work in asbestos and other mass torts. Responding to this pressure, the MDL panel assigned all the cases to Judge Charles R. Wiener under the title MDL-875-In re Asbestos Products Liability (No. VI) in the spring of 1991.[156]

There are a significant number of issues that are common to all asbestos cases. Questions involving the state of the art and individual defendant culpability—broad terms that encompass information about what the manufacturers and distributors knew, when they knew it, and what they did or did not do as a result—have been largely established over and over again.[157]

In addition, the information on causation is sufficiently developed. Even the usual variables that are presented as too individualistic to allow for aggregative treatment of medical causation—such as smoking habits in lung cancer cases—are amenable to some sort of streamlined determination, perhaps by submission of medical documentation to an independent panel of medical experts appointed by the court pursuant to Federal Rule of Evidence 706.[158]

Other possible approaches are a long-sitting jury which, having been educated on basic issues, could determine damages quickly, or a panel of judges or others who have tried these cases to sit without a jury for quick trials regarding damages. In the Brooklyn Navy Yard cases, one jury sat on over seventy-five cases after being instructed on general medical and legal aspects of the case. Although the trials and deliberations took many months and required hundreds of pages of special findings, it was my impression, as the presiding judge, that the cases were all properly decided with great discrimination and understanding.

The second of these approaches would, of course, require a waiver. Certainly any of these or their like alternatives would be more desirable than the present system of laborious direct examination and cross-examination of thousands of plaintiffs, family members, acquaintances, doctors, and so on to permit a series of lay juries to determine what, if any, percentage of the illness in each plaintiff is attributable to asbestos inhalation. A medical or judicial panel would not need to review thousands or tens of thousands of individual records. They could presumably develop a matrix of values after reviewing a representative sample of medical cases. A long-sitting jury's values would quickly become known so that complete settlements could be expected.

Similarly, the fact that individual exposure and product identification differ from plaintiff to plaintiff should no longer bar class certification. In the New York Navy Yard cases I found that it is possible for a jury to determine with adequate degrees of probability what products were where and when by looking at shipping and stock records as well as the cross-referenced accounts of various workers' identification of particular products. Thus a scale of products and places organized by year can be developed. In fact, however, no such explicit table has been developed in the New York Navy Yard cases, although the verdicts in some one hundred cases would permit such a computation.

While it is certainly easier to develop such a scale when the job site is relatively confined in space, if not time, as in the Navy Yard or a factory, it is not impossible to develop product identification for plaintiffs with other work histories. Plaintiffs' attorneys who computerize cross-referenced lists of witness identification have already accomplished much of the work. Today's sophisticated computer technologies make possible settlements of large numbers of cases while allowing a great deal of individualized variables to be taken into account.[159]

In the DES settlements, Kenneth R. Feinberg and Peter Woodin analyzed settlements of both defendants and plaintiffs in great detail to permit global settlements. This is the way sentence variables were determined under federal guideline sentencing.[160] The state courts, which have been underfunded and which lack institutional access to this kind of technology, are generally unaware of its potential uses. Compensation funds set up in mass tort settlements presumably would be able to take advantage of state-of-the-art technology of this sort.

Of course, many of these complicated scales may turn out to be superfluous. Settlements often involve trade-offs, and, in return for the reduction of costs and attorneys' fees as well as the drawn-out uncertainties of litigation where punitive damages are at stake, defendants interested in global settlement may be willing to forego some of the highly particularized information they would otherwise demand. Putting aside the ethical problems plaintiffs' attorneys face in mass settlements described in chapter 4, my experience has been that global settlements provide for much lower per-capita numbers than do individual cases (perhaps some few attorneys take smaller fees per capita in such multiparty settlements). Furthermore, in the context of a proposed settlement and distribution plan for multiple claimants, in which individual issues of causation in fact and extent of injury are resolved in a claims resolution process, class actions afford a superior mechanism for facilitating relief.[161]

Plaintiffs as a class would benefit from assurances that all claimants, present and future, will receive adequate compensation within a reasonable amount of time. In return, they would forego the possibility that any given individual would receive a windfall verdict by a sympathetic jury. Defendants could probably save money in outlays to claimants as well as in costs of attorneys' fees. The claimant could well get more (especially with attorneys' fees being reduced) and faster relief. The courts could save their energies for other matters of pressing importance—such as the massive influx of drug-related criminal cases.

D. SPECIAL MASTERS

We have already mentioned the role that the special master played in making possible the state-federal consolidation of the New York Navy Yard cases. It is desirable to delve a little deeper into the use that courts faced with mass tort cases have and must make of this officer developed by courts of equity. For even with other aggregation techniques, it is close to impossible for one judge (particularly if he or she hopes to keep up with the rest of the caseload) personally to conduct the necessary fact-finding and negotiations, and then to develop, implement, and oversee a complicated ongoing administrative resolution of a mass tort case. Extending the reach of the court, while at the same time keeping all parties and issues concentrated in one forum, requires help. Fortunately there is a small but growing number of practicing lawyers and law professors who have developed a great deal of expertise in this specialized field.[162]

Federal Rule of Civil Procedure 53 authorizes the reference of a case to a special master only in limited circumstances:

> reference . . . shall be the exception and not the rule. In actions to be tried by a jury, a reference shall be made only when the issues are complicated; in actions to be tried without a jury, save in matters of account and of difficult computation of damages, a reference shall be made only upon a showing that some exceptional condition requires it.[163]

Despite this conservative approach to the use of special masters, in the past twenty years their use has proliferated in a wide variety of situations, only a few of which are expressly contemplated by the Rule. Courts dealing with massive cases have come to view them as indispensable in mass tort cases. In addition, Congress has, in effect, approved an expansion of trial judges' reach through amplifications of personnel by authorizing funds for many magistrate judges and law clerks who often serve some of the same functions as special masters.

In the New York Navy Yard case, in addition to achieving the de facto consolidation of the state and federal cases by virtue of his appointment, the special master-referee was charged with settling the cases. Since arguments among individual defendants over their relative culpability and respective contributions to any settlement routinely disrupt attempts at global settlement, the master devised a plan of blind contribution as one of his approaches. The plaintiffs indicated their evaluation of the aggregate worth of their cases. They were not concerned about the apportionment of that figure between the defendants. Based on the relative amount of each defendant's products placed at the New York Navy Yard, as well as other considerations, the master-referee proposed a figure to each defendant. No defendant knew the amount the master-referee was seeking from any codefendant. By negotiating with each defendant separately, the master-referee attempted to raise an amount as close as possible to the figure put forward by plaintiffs. The special master was able to facilitate one-on-one negotiations between the plaintiffs and individual defendants using the initial blind contribution negotiations as a base from which to work. Eventually, most of the defendants settled with the consolidated group of plaintiffs, and the claimants went to trial against the few holdouts.

Special masters have been used in class actions to aid both in the settlement and then in the design and implementation of compensation funds. Neither the Dalkon Shield nor the Agent Orange settlements could have been created and implemented without the aid of special masters and various other able attorneys or business people brought into the process either at the development or implementation stages. Special settlement masters have proven their utility in complex cases involving large amounts of money, large numbers of plaintiffs and, often, a considerable number of defendants, where parties are faced with the prospect of a protracted litigation of uncertain outcome. These cases are usually of widespread community interest and hence politically sensitive. In these cases, a special master is resorted to out of necessity, because a traditional bipolar litigation would not produce an outcome acceptable to the parties or the community. The defendants or the settlement fund generally provides the source of the special master's fees. In the New York Navy Yard case both defendants and plaintiffs contributed toward the special master's fees since he was helpful to them in organizing the cases to facilitate settlement.

The Agent Orange litigation called for some kind of administrative remedy, but the government's refusal to become involved in the case necessitated the fashioning of a new remedy. The use of special masters to mediate settlement negotiations was a valuable tool. Special masters also have been useful in gathering information in complex mass tort litigation.[164]

In highly volatile, emotion-laden multiparty cases such as the Agent Orange case, the special master serves many purposes. First, he or she is a buffer between the court and the parties. At the same time, he or she also serves as a conduit between the court and the parties and the community at large. Finally, he or she is a mediator, meeting privately with both sides in an effort to bring them together.

In the Agent Orange case, I used three special masters in an effort to achieve a settlement that the government would endorse and play an active role in implementing. One of them had significant contacts in the Democratic Party and Congress, another had similar contacts in the Republican Party and the Executive, while the third was a neutral person who had the strength to oversee difficult negotiations. In the end, the attempt to include the government failed due to its own intransigence and unwillingness to spend any money. As the presiding judge, I was in constant and close contact with all three special masters.

Despite the fact that Rule 53 does not expressly contemplate the use of special masters as we have used them, for example, to mediate settlement negotiations, such uses are within the liberal spirit of the rules and the tradition of equity from which they arose. Courts have come to believe that Rule 53, like the other rules, was intended to be read in an expansive and equitable, not a restrictive mode.

C. Substantive Law

While the equity underpinnings of the federal rules of procedure are widely acknowledged,[165] equity's influence on the development of the substantive law of mass toxic torts has been relatively neglected. There are a number of explanations for this slight. First, there is no substantive equitable action that is clearly the precursor of the modern substantive law of mass torts in the manner that group litigation evolved into the present-day class action and other aggregate techniques. Second, as already mentioned, tort law has always been closely associated with common law modes of trial, and although this type of individual, adversarial process is ill suited to mass torts, it still frames our conception of mass torts. Third, the relief requested in mass tort cases remains the essential legal remedy: money damages.[166] As a result, equity jurisprudence has seemed to most to be irrelevant, if not anathema, to mass tort litigation.

We need to consider revamping the procedures for handling mass torts along equity models of bankruptcy and limited fund mandatory class action proceedings, which give the parties and the judge equitable powers of fashioning innovative remedies. In addition to providing the courts with the procedural tools to effectively aggregate cases, reduce transactional costs, and provide equal payments for similar cases, we must also have one substantive law by which to evaluate all the cases, regardless of the jurisdiction in which they arose. To do otherwise is to ensure that like cases will not be treated equally.

We come to the question then of which substantive law to use and whether to limit the state courts in their historic role developing tort law. In response to modern-day toxic tort and product liability cases the states, in fact, already have begun to create new law to prevent new injustices. As an influential Department of Justice report observed in 1987: "[w]hatever the reasons or justifications for this development, the last two decades have been a period of revolutionary change in tort law with one controlling theme—virtually every judicially created change has operated to expand rather than to limit tort liability."[167] The states, and to a lesser degree the federal courts sitting in their diversity jurisdiction, have presented us with innovations that in their flexibility, creativity, and pragmatism represent the best of equity jurisprudence among which we may choose. It remains for us to amalgamate some of the most useful of these innovations.

Before turning to the substantive law now being applied to toxic tort cases in particular, let us look briefly at some equitable actions that, if not the direct ancestors of modern-day mass tort law, at least offer insights into its development.

Trying to see the equitable action of nuisance as the historical antecedent for the creative substantive doctrines currently utilized in toxic tort cases is tempting, in part because the nuisance action is also associated as the historical antecedent with community protection from the contaminants and hazardous materials that constitute the toxic agents in mass personal injury cases. English courts issued injunctions to abate public nuisances as early as the sixteenth century.[168] Generally, though, both private and public nuisance actions were directed primarily toward protection of property rights and only indirectly—almost inadvertently—to protecting the health of individuals.[169] Any danger posed to individual or public health became one of the equities that judges weighed in the balance along with economic and property rights in determining what, if any, injunctive relief was warranted.

Nonetheless, by forcing judges to grapple with some of the costs and benefits of modern technology, nuisance actions led to some of the most innovative exercises of "equitable discretion and ingenuity in ordering remedies."[170] Some of this ingenuity has carried over to complex toxic tort actions. Recently a number of courts have allowed recovery in toxic tort cases for a diminution in "quality of life" based on a nuisance theory when a number of residents were significantly inconvenienced as a result of the contamination of their water supplies or property.[171] Even where "diminution of quality of life" is not itself an element of damages, nuisance is often one of several theories on which courts have based liability findings in toxic tort actions.[172]

As we have already observed, the strategy employed by some mass tort defendants of seeking corporate reorganization under the bankruptcy laws to shield themselves from further personal injury liability[173] has introduced into the mass tort field corporate-insolvency remedies that developed in the courts of equity.[174] While a discussion of the effects of the reorganizations undertaken by bankrupt mass tort defendants on personal injury claimant-creditor classes is beyond the scope of this book, it bears repeating that the phenomenon of bankrupt tort defendants not only brings all the interested parties together in one forum, but places considerable equitable powers in the judge.[175] Theoretically, it also permits claimants to vote on the bankruptcy plan. The practice is, of course, for the lawyers and large creditors to control negotiations with little input from tort claimants even when they are fairly well organized, as were the Vietnam veterans in Agent Orange.

In the A. H. Robins bankruptcy, the presiding district court judge, Robert Merhige, appointed experts to determine the total value of the Dalkon Shield claims filed against Robins, authorized a court-appointed examiner to find a purchaser for the company, and, after having problems with the initial claimants' committee, discharged them and appointed a new representative committee.[176] Judge Merhige was able to achieve "global peace" in the Dalkon Shield litigation by developing in the same proceedings a method of providing for future and present claimants and resolving the pending litigation between Robins and its insurer, Aetna, as well as the pending litigation between the plaintiff class and Aetna.[177] Neither Rule 23 of the Federal Rules of Civil Procedure nor statutory or rule-based consolidation currently places comparable power in a judge presiding over nonbankruptcy mass tort proceedings.

2. MODERN INNOVATIONS

The primary purpose of mass tort cases has evolved to be compensation of victims,[178] rather than deterrence or punishment of wrongdoers.[179] This is particularly true of mega–mass torts where the assessment of large and multiple punitive damage awards threatens to undermine our ability to adequately compensate all victims. While significant segments of the American public clearly desire to compensate the Agent Orange claimants, DES daughters, Dalkon Shield victims, and sufferers of asbestos-related disease, that desire has failed to coalesce around a national solution. Despite their sympathy for individual Vietnam veterans or asbestos widows, Americans and their representatives have not made compensation of these tort victims a legislative or executive priority. But they do seem to want the courts to do something.

If the courts are to be the instrument of compensation—by choice or default—we cannot hope to apply the usual tort standards of liability and causation. They too would preclude compensation. Let us first examine liability.

A. LIABILITY

Fault—at least in the sense of evil or wrongdoing—has become largely irrelevant in mass toxic tort litigation.[180] The economics of the litigation and the delay involved render this result inevitable. The only real liability issue becomes causation: was this manufacturer's product a substantial cause of this plaintiff's medical problems—however we define them? The issues that the courts and juries are concerned with are not foreseeability and fault, but rather: (1) who should pay for the larger risks of living in a modern industrial-technological society;[181] (2) how large should awards be; (3) who should be compensated; and (4) how should that compensation be distributed.[182]

Removing fault from the equation—at least in its incarnation of negligence—underlies strict liability in fact. To reduce the complexity and the expense of trial in modern product liability cases, courts moved away from requiring proof of negligence and toward the simpler proof of the degree to which a product was defective and therefore unreasonably dangerous. Rather than focusing on the conduct of the manufacturer, strict liability focuses on the product itself.[183] The question most jurors seem to pose to themselves is not what a reasonable person would think of the producer at the time of production, but what a jury thinks of the producer at the time of trial in light of the injury.[184]

In mass tort cases the apportionment of liability is a persistent problem. In the asbestos context the long latency period makes it difficult for plaintiffs to recall exposure incidents or to identify the maker of the product to which they were exposed. A long latency period, combined with a generic drug produced by many companies, also complicates the problem in cases such as DES.

American tort law has a long history, however, of finding ways to allow injured victims to recover fully even when they are not certain who caused their injuries. For instance, under the doctrine of joint and several liability an injured victim who successfully sues at least one of two or more liable defendants may collect the entire award from any one or combination of defendants without having to apportion the harm. This venerable common law doctrine is defended on the principle that it is fairer to make a partially responsible wrongdoer bear the entire cost of a resulting injury than to leave an innocent victim only partially compensated. The rule enables full recovery under two situations: (1) where there is a "concert of action," in which two or more defendants acted together or in accord with a common design, as shown by explicit agreement or implicitly through their conduct; and (2) where wrongdoers did not act together but caused a single, indivisible injury.

Although it has been legislatively curtailed in a majority of states over the past five years,[185] joint and several liability remains crucial to ensuring full recoveries in toxic tort cases brought against many defendants, particularly where some defendants are bankrupt or cannot be located. In the absence of joint and several liability, the plaintiff would have to bear the burden of establishing apportionment to collect from any given defendant, and thus might never receive a full award.

Enterprise and market share liability address situations in which a plaintiff is not only unable to apportion harm, but cannot even identify with a fair degree of probability the manufacturers of the products to which she or he was exposed. These liability theories—which aggregate defendants, rather than plaintiffs—generally are applied to situations in which there is a generic or fungible product, such as DES, which is indistinguishable on the basis of identity of manufacturer. These are cases of indeterminate defendants.

Asbestos has been held to be nonfungible for purposes of liability,[186] but in fact it is largely fungible when asbestos dust from a number of products enters a worker's lungs. The jury must, on slim evidence, decide what proportion of whose product caused the injury.

Under enterprise liability an entire industry is held liable for having acted in concert, for example, in setting an unsafe standard or failing to properly test the generic product.[187] Under a concerted action theory, and where joint and several liability exists, any individual manufacturer in that industry can be held liable for the entire amount of damages.

I first dealt with the problem in the exploding dynamite cap cases in 1972.[188] Highly explosive caps were used to set off dynamite in clearing stumps and rocks on farms and in a variety of building and mining tasks. Many of the caps were left about. Children picked them up, played with them, and were killed or maimed by the hundreds. There was almost no way of telling whose cap it was since the cap had exploded. In a suit brought on the theory that there should have been warnings on the caps, I found enterprise liability—that is, all the six main manufacturers could be jointly liable since they had all helped block corrective warning legislation through their industry association. The question of how to deal with the indeterminate defendant—as well as the indeterminate plaintiff—was discussed at length in the Agent Orange case.[189]

In the landmark case of *Sindell v. Abbott Laboratories*,[190] the California Supreme Court developed market share liability in its current form. Since then it has been adopted in four states,[191] including, most recently, in a slightly modified form, New York.[192] Market share liability was originally applied where concerted action could not be proven. Under a market share theory, even though the plaintiff cannot establish that he or she was exposed to a particular defendant's product, if he or she can join enough defendants to constitute a "substantial share" of the relevant market for a generic product, then he or she may hold each defendant liable for their percentage of that market. Joint and several liability generally does not apply in market share cases.[193]

Although market share theory has not been utilized explicitly in the asbestos cases, the apportionment of culpability determined by juries, in part based on the degree to which workers have been able to identify a given defendant's products and less frequently on business records or reports, amounts in the end to a rough sort of local or regional market share result. If we develop grids on which to apportion damages for large aggregations of classes, the net practical effect will be to incorporate a type of market share liability.[194]

Complex causal issues in toxic-related cases stand "at the frontier of current medical and epidemiological inquiry."[195] The long latency period of many toxic-related diseases and the lack of medical and scientific information on toxins and exposed populations aggravate the problem.[196] In addition, epidemiological data, which is increasingly relied on in toxic tort cases where individual causation is unprovable,[197] may be preliminary or unavailable at the time toxin-exposed victims begin to turn to the courts for redress. Even where available, epidemiological studies, by definition, often do not provide the courts with legally sufficient proof that any given individual's illness was caused by a particular toxic agent. These conditions set the stage for methods of dealing with the indeterminate plaintiff.

The courts have been understandably reluctant to hold that product liability law "preclude[s] recovery until a 'statistically significant' number of people have been injured or until science has had the time and resources to complete sophisticated laboratory studies of the chemical."[198] A number of courts and torts scholars have suggested that as a matter of fairness and equity we should relax the traditional probability standard of 50 percent–plus generally utilized in proving causation. Their suggestions include accepting a broad range of evidence such as animal and in vitro experiments, epidemiological data, and clinical evidence and letting the jury decide on anything from a scintilla of evidence to something less than 50 percent probability.[199] Others advocate shifting the burden of proof and requiring defendants to prove that their product did *not* cause the particular illness.[200] Still others would keep the burden on the plaintiff but require him or her to prove only that there is a "substantial factor of increased risk"—that is, some connection between exposure and injury close enough to warrant liability.[201] Finally, some would dispense with causation altogether[202]—a concept that appears so grossly out of line with traditional notions of fairness as to raise due process constitutional questions. All of these suggestions are motivated by equitable concerns: compensating injured victims and deterring harmful conduct.

A useful suggestion, predicated on proposals of Professor David Rosenberg, would be to discount the damages by the lack of probability that the disease was caused by defendant's product.[203] For example, if there was only a 40 percent probability that plaintiff's cancer was caused by product X and only a 40 percent chance that defendant produced the product X used by the plaintiff, with damages of $100,000 to be allocated for a cancer, the sum awarded plaintiff from the particular defendant would be .40 x .40 x $100,000 = $16,000. Variations on this theme are possible.[204]

Part of the difficulty with this proposal is the unavailability, particularly during the early stages of a massive series of litigations, of reliable scientific material on causation and evidence of fault. To use this system the court would, in most cases, have to delay final decision and obtain the assistance of neutral experts and of governmental or quasi-governmental studies such as those of the Centers for Disease Control or the American Academy of Science. Strong control by the judge to prevent unfounded claims would be essential.

In the Agent Orange case a settlement was fashioned that compensated claimants in the absence of legally sufficient evidence of causation.[205] The case presented a political problem that, while inappropriate for the courts, was clearly going to go begging for a solution in the absence of judicial action. Hovering over the case was the United States government, which refused to take any responsibility. Defendants were happy to pay a substantial sum to avoid the cost of the litigation and the remote possibility that they would be found liable for billions in damages. Plaintiffs were running out of money to conduct the litigation and were convinced that, whatever the jury did, it was improbable that the courts would allow a verdict for the plaintiffs to stand. Ultimately, in fact, the courts ruled that there was no cause of action on the facts or on the law.

C. NEW THEORIES OF COMPENSABLE INJURIES

Other courts have attempted to define new categories of compensable injuries. Accordingly, in addition to recovery for "traditional" noneconomic damages such as pain and suffering and the loss of enjoyment of life—which usually require a physical injury—a growing number of courts have allowed recovery for "injuries" such as: (1) increased risk of disease, (2) fear of disease, (3) medical monitoring, (4) diminution of "quality of life," and (5) immunotoxicity.[206]

These theories are particularly attractive to plaintiffs where there is a limited fund of money and a concern that unless claimants recover now, they will be shut off from any hope of compensation in the future. Immunotoxicity—or chemical AIDS as some members of the plaintiffs' bar and some of the experts they use call it[207]—has been rejected thus far by mainstream science, but the first four have some support in law and science.

Part of the problem is the legal tradition against splitting a cause of action.[208] For example, if there is a small recovery now for fear of cancer, what happens when the feared result actually occurs?[209] Has the cause of action been merged in the prior judgment?[210] Should a separate cause of action arise each time a medically distinct disease manifests itself even when the causal agent remains the same? Should we allow what some courts have considered impermissible "double dipping" in those situations where the latter disease is significantly more serious—and costly—than the former?

Legislatures and courts are considering remedies such as tolling the statutes of limitations or placing such fearful people on a registry with recovery only after the disease is discovered. This model may be used in nondisabling pleural plaque cases in asbestos claims. One possible solution was utilized in the Agent Orange case, where, in effect, a major insurance policy was purchased from an insurance company and certificates issued to claimants. Only on death or disability is there recovery by presenting claims to the insurance facility.

Recovery for increased risk of disease has rarely been allowed by the courts,[211] but where it has, it has been predicated on proving to a reasonable degree of medical probability—that is, a greater than 50 percent chance—that the disease will occur.[212] Allowing recovery in such instances provides compensation for claimants who are forced to file claims before manifestation of a disease as a result of statutes of limitations problems, single disease states,[213] or limited compensation funds. It has the virtue of finality, dealing with potential latent claims in the same time frame in which current claims are addressed.[214]

Disease phobia, or fear of contracting a disease, is essentially a claim for present emotional distress due to the possibility of a future injury. As is true of increased risk actions, the law governing emotional distress claims presently differs from state to state. Most courts require that there be a direct physical injury to sustain a claim for negligent infliction of emotional distress.[215] Just what constitutes sufficient physical manifestation is hotly debated. The courts appear to be split on whether or not a "slight injury" meets the physical manifestation requirement.[216] Some courts have found that the mere fact of exposure to or ingestion of a harmful substance suffices.[217] Others predicate recovery on whether the fear is specifically directed at a particular disease rather than being a generalized and amorphous concern about ill health.[218] In general, recovery can be had only where the fear of disease is "reasonable." This means that it must have an objective basis.[219] Unlike increased risk of disease, a plaintiff claiming a disease phobia generally need not prove that it is more likely than not that he or she will actually contract the disease.[220]

A small minority of courts have even accepted "bystander" cases, allowing family members of a person exposed to toxins to bring emotional distress cases grounded in their observances of the victim's suffering or the fear that the exposed person will contract a disease.[221]

Claims of "immunotoxicity," or "chemically induced immune disregulation," charge "that exposure to a particular chemical or substance compromises a body's normal mechanism for defending itself against virtually any disease, thereby rendering an individual more susceptible to everything from common colds to cancer."[222] The medical and scientific mainstream communities have criticized this theory as being without any immunological or epidemiological basis. Despite this official cynicism, immunotoxicity is sometimes asserted as an independent injury—particularly where increased risk claims are unavailable—and sometimes as a basis for a fear of cancer claim or as a basis for recovering for medical monitoring.[223]

The nuisance-based theory allowing recovery for diminution of "quality of life" has already been touched upon. This element is separate from pain and suffering and appears to have been used on several occasions to compensate residents for the nuisance and inconvenience attendant on being deprived of potable water as a result of the acts of a polluter.[224] As property owners or renters who could not use their regular supply of water, the plaintiffs were obviously inconvenienced and lost part of the value of their property—claims equity would probably have viewed with compassion. This mode of compensation is, it seems, at most indirectly applicable to mass exposure cases. It does have, however, considerable vitality in such cases as those where a toxic dump has depressed the value of surrounding property because people fear for their health if they live in nearby homes. In any event, recovery for such cases should, like that for increased risk, probably be given a lower priority in any mass tort settlement with a limited compensation fund.

Another emerging damages theory—that of providing for the costs of medical monitoring—seems much more promising. The damages associated with medical monitoring or surveillance, unlike increased risk or disease phobia, can be quantified. Costs can be paid as they accrue from an interest-bearing fund, rather than directing defendants to pay out a lump sum for future claimants on assumptions that are highly speculative. This sort of fund addresses, at least in part, the indeterminacy of future damage claims in toxic tort litigation. The costs of surveillance occur over time as people go for checkups designed to provide early diagnosis and treatment should they manifest disease.[225] One valuable benefit of medical monitoring may be the opportunity it presents for sustained studies of exposed populations. As in the case of a pleural plaque asbestos registry, a fund must be available to pay the claimants when they are, in fact, found to have contracted a disease as a result of the exposure in question.

How the substantive law of remedies will settle down is unclear.[226] When asked which of the above should be chosen, it may well be that we will answer "most of the above," depending on the case and circumstances.[227]

D. Settlement Funds and Distribution Plans

1. Generally

Faced with huge numbers of claimants and limited funds, we can no longer afford to grant every toxic tort plaintiff the option of going to trial. Nor can we continue to allow the plaintiffs' attorneys unsupervised control of cases, with the run-up of large expenses for essentially redundant activities and traditional 33 to 50 percent fees under individual contingency fee contracts.[228] We cannot permit the funds of the defendants and their insurers to be spent on legal defense rather than on compensation of victims, particularly in cases such as asbestos where it is fairly clear that insufficient assets are available for future claimants.

If mass tort litigation is allowed to run its course in the tort system the result will be huge discrepancies in the awards received by similarly situated plaintiffs, backlogged courts, lengthy delays in compensation of victims, and enormous transaction costs. The end product will undoubtedly be the bankruptcy of many defendants and the depletion of available insurance and other assets well before all claimants are compensated. There are strong reasons in this situation to treat the entire problem —not just that between an individual defendant and its claimants—as a bankruptcy action or as a Rule 23(b)(1)(B) limited fund class.

In 1985 Judge Robert Parker of the Eastern District of Texas determined that a Rule 23(b)(1)(B) class could not be certified as a result of insufficient evidence of a limited fund.[229] Some nine years later, with the bulk of the insurance coverage disputes between manufacturers and insurers settled, with the industry facing the threat of additional bankruptcies, and with the much-heralded Manville Trust experiencing a severe cash problem, we now have sufficient information about available funds and overwhelming evidence that they are, in the end, too limited to permit unrestrained tort recovery.

Reconceptualizing the problem and aggregating claims generally presupposes a finite pot of money and, as a consequence, the need for a rational system of distribution supervised by one presiding judge, or cooperating judges, assisted by masters using equitable powers to define an appropriate distribution system based on an insurance or matrix scheme. It is possible to provide, in effect, a continuing stream of income from the defendants, dependent in part on how successful in business the defendants will be. Thus, under this sliding scale alternative, the claimants take an equity position in the defendant, somewhat as they might do in a bankruptcy reorganization. A number of federal judges favor just such types of resolutions.[230]

Aggregation of claims works best where there are many beneficiaries but a single recipient through whom the money is channeled. We see this in shareholder-derivative class action suits on behalf of a corporation by its shareholders where there are many who are injured but the award, if the suit is successful, is given to the corporation. Mass tort suits are a good deal more complicated, but one thing we can learn from the shareholder-derivative action is that we need a single entity to collect, invest, and distribute the awards on the basis of preset scales. Discrimination among claimants should be kept as narrow as possible to avoid disputes about variations in compensation.

Without federal legislation too much depends on the views of the individual trial judge—in other words, on the "size of the chancellor's foot."[231] We are beginning to address the problem through pending legislation[232] and American Law Institute and American Bar Association proposals. The report of a Presidential commission on treatment of mass nuclear reactor disasters was also helpful. Meanwhile, until the law settles down, equity will be available with its flexibility to fill the breach. There is no good reason, for example, why the funds available from the asbestos bankruptcies and Rule 23(b)(1)(B) class action settlements should not be jointly administered to benefit all present and future asbestos claimants at a reasonable cost of administration.

2. EXAMPLES OF COMPENSATION FUNDS

Some examples of mass tort resolutions that moved away from the tort system and instead set up administrative, insurance-type installment payment plans supervised by the courts already exist. In these plans matters of equity—namely, the value of removing great burdens on the courts and of achieving closure for the parties and for society—were elevated above the concerns of giving individual due process or of following strict rules of law.

In the Dalkon Shield litigation, some 195,000 claims have been filed since A. H. Robins's bankruptcy resulted in a personal injury compensation trust fund that will eventually total some $2.5 billion. The court appointed five trustees to carry out the functions of the trust. The trustees were responsible for designing and implementing a Claims Resolution Facility pursuant to the guidelines set out in the trust agreement for purposes of resolving the personal injury claims. The trust was funded primarily from the merger of the A. H. Robins Company and another corporation—a merger that undoubtedly would not have occurred had Robins continued to limp forward beset by tens of thousands of tort cases. The Dalkon Shield Trust is to stay in business until the earlier of three dates: (1) the end of the year 2008; (2) the date on which all claims against Robins have been resolved; or (3) the date on which the trustees have put in place irrevocable insurance policies and established claims procedures adequate to discharge all future obligations and expenses. The A. H. Robins Bankruptcy Reorganization Plan establishing this trust not only resolved the litigation against Robins, but—in a move that some have criticized as having disregarded the letter of the Bankruptcy Code[233]—also resolved related litigation brought by claimants against Robins's insurer. Thus a global solution was effected through the bankruptcy action.[234]

The architects of the compensation fund, under Judge Robert Reynold Merhige, Jr., a district judge sitting also as the bankruptcy judge, set up a three-tiered plan:

> The options are designed to encourage the quick resolution of claims, with minimal transaction costs, by establishing procedures for distributing modest awards with very little proof of injury. As the potential size of the award increases, the documentation claimants must submit in support of their claim also increases. The overall objective of the distribution plan is to liquidate claims in an efficient and economical manner, to favor settlement over arbitration and litigation, and to provide compensation to claimants based on "historic" values of Dalkon Shield claims. Any funds remaining in the Claimants Trust after compensatory damage claims are satisfied will be distributed proportionally to the claimants in lieu of punitive damages.[235]

The Agent Orange settlement and distribution plan provides another example of a limited-fund, insurance-type compensation system developed and implemented under the court's ongoing supervision. In the Agent Orange litigation it was the lack of causality that led the court to eschew tortlike treatment. Unlike the Dalkon Shield litigation, which was only aggregated when the defendant voluntarily sought bankruptcy, the Agent Orange litigation was brought as a class action. The court certified a Rule 23(b)(3) opt-out class for the purpose of adjudicating affirmative defenses and general causation.[236] The class potentially included nearly 2.5 million people and consisted of veterans of the United States, Australia, and New Zealand armed forces who served in or near Vietnam from 1961 until 1972 and who claimed that they and their families were injured by exposure to Agent Orange or other phenoxy herbicides.

After the appeals of the settlement were exhausted, the interest earned on the original settlement figure provided about $240 million in the fund. Of the total amount, approximately $170 million was allocated to the Payment Program, $55 million to a Class Assistance Plan, $5 million to Australian and New Zealand Trusts, and $10 million to plaintiffs' lawyers as fees. The Payment Program directly compensates individual veterans or their survivors, while the Class Assistance Plan is designed to fund various organizations that give legal, medical, or other types of aid to the class as a whole, particularly to handicapped children of veterans. The Class Assistance Plan has funded organizations in each of the United States and Puerto Rico, including those that offer substance abuse and psychiatric counseling to veterans and their families, provide legal services, and train severely handicapped children to be as independent as possible. This kind of arrangement would not have been possible under strict tort law. It is an example of a court attempting, with limited resources, to fashion an equitable remedy to a pressing problem.

Like the Dalkon Shield Trust, the Agent Orange Payment Program and Class Assistance Plan are essentially administrative compensation programs designed to continue for some years—in the Agent Orange case, new claims and grant proposals will be accepted until the end of 1994. The Payment Program is administered by the Aetna Insurance Company in Hartford, Connecticut, and the Class Assistance Plan is administered by court-appointed Dennis K. Rhoades, Director, and Michael R. Leaveck, Deputy Director, themselves Vietnam veterans, who have a small staff and whose operations are based in Washington, D.C. In effect they run a foundation for the class. The administration of both arms of the settlement fund is overseen by a special master who reports directly to the court. The programs are periodically audited by certified public accountants, and they submit annual reports to the court. Both programs benefit from the advice of standing advisory committees composed of veterans from around the country.

Eligibility criteria for the Agent Orange Payment Program were established with an eye to compensating the neediest class members quickly. Although beneficiaries need not—and in the court's view could not—show individual causation, they must be totally disabled from a nontraumatic injury, must have served in a branch of the armed forces during the period, and must have been near the locations where records reveal the herbicides had been sprayed. There are additional criteria that give priority to some claimants over others and that authorize payments to survivors of deceased but eligible veterans.

Designing a plan with these criteria that paid out awards in annual installments made it possible to provide some money immediately to claimants, while retaining the ability to compensate future claimants. The settlement plan more closely resembles an insurance plan than a one-time lump-sum tort judgment. It does not, however, differ radically from "structured settlements" often worked out in run-of-the-mill tort cases where annual payments are made to the plaintiff. Some flexibility was achieved in the Agent Orange litigation by allowing a special master for appeals to consider special hardships in departing from the plan's fixed criteria.

In the asbestos litigation it should be possible to aggregate or jointly administer the funds available from various bankruptcies and viable defendants. Such a program, following proposed plans for restructuring the Manville Trust payments, could provide more for claimants.

E. CRITICISM OF EQUITY INITIATIVES

Obviously these equitable procedural and substantive approaches present dangers. What are the proper limits of the judiciary? Does it lose its essential role when it becomes a bureaucratic agency? What are the long- and short-term implications with regard to due process rights and the amount of recovery for tort victims when power is aggregated in the hands of attorneys, special masters, and judges? Who are the people who fill those roles? How should the individual claimant be heard? What is the effect on the resolution of massive societal problems of leaving their solution in the hands of these judicial officers?

In the past decade the equitable developments in American tort law designed to accommodate mass litigation have come under attack. Nearly everyone agrees that there exists a problem of congestion, delay, and expense in the courts—a problem that some perceive as having risen to a crisis and that is undoubtedly contributed to by the surge in drug cases on the criminal side and complex litigation, including mass tort cases, on the civil side.[237]

As a result there has been a backlash on the part of some members of the bench, bar, and legal community as well as in Congress and the state legislatures. Prominent members of the legal and business communities have attacked the "humanitarian" reforms, claiming that their proplaintiff bias has distorted the tort system into a third-party insurance system by turning manufacturers and distributors into de facto insurers of their products regardless of fault,[238] and that the ease with which plaintiffs can win big-money verdicts in products liability cases drives insurance prices up and in some cases renders it unavailable,[239] and discourages industry from developing and marketing vitally needed products.[240] In response, legislators in both Congress and the state legislatures introduced "tort reform" legislation, which was designed to counter some of the innovative theories of causation and liability that made compensation of mass tort victims possible and to circumscribe the amount of money damages available to successful plaintiffs.[241]

In addition to attacking the proplaintiff substantive tort laws of the last two decades, there has also been a more general move to restrict access to the courts, primarily by tightening up the Federal Rules of Civil Procedure[242] and adopting more restrictive notions of who can sue in the federal courts. The influential Federal Courts Study Committee—which was created by Congress and consists of members from the federal executive, legislative, and judicial branches, and representatives from state governments, universities, and private practice—issued a report in which it recommended some severe restrictions on access to the federal courts.[243] Some of our colleagues have shown a greater reluctance in certifying class actions, particularly in civil rights actions.[244]

I cannot agree with either the critics of liberal access or with those who argue that we should return to a traditional fault-based tort regime and dismiss any cases where cause-in-fact cannot be proven by strict tort standards or where specific individual liability cannot be ascertained. The postwar role of the federal courts—particularly when they were exercising their equitable jurisdiction—has been to protect the injured who come before them against those who have caused or are causing unjustified harm.[245] This judicial role is particularly important in the absence of any alternative remedies emanating from the executive or legislative branches.

Bear in mind that we do not yet have, as do other nations, a comprehensive medical-disability system.[246] We still rely heavily on our tort system for remedies granted by other countries through a social welfare network. Personally, I prefer that governmental plan for medical insurance and compensation rather than our own tort system in the United States, but as realists, we deal with the system we have.

There is some merit to the charges that in attempting to do "mass justice" we are destroying individual rights.[247] Critics claim that aggregative procedures sacrifice key values of our justice system: (1) the personal relationship between lawyer and client; (2) the ability of the litigant to control the litigation; (3) the opportunity for a litigant to have a full and fair adjudication of his or her dispute in a court of law before a judge and jury (a concept that encompasses not only notions of fairness but also of catharsis); and (4) the likelihood that mass solutions will leave individual tort claimants with a lower recovery than they might otherwise have obtained.[248]

As pointed out in chapters 3–8, there are undoubtedly ethical and tactical problems presented by aggregation, particularly where relations between clients and attorneys are implicated. For example, in the Agent Orange litigation, some veterans complained that the management committee of plaintiffs' attorneys had not consulted with them and did not reflect their views.

Critics who cite such legitimate and troubling complaints often fail to take into consideration the fact that the individual client's situation is not much different and may be considerably worse in the absence of formal aggregation.[249] A Rand Corporation study found that the type of lawyer-client relationship resulting from the informal aggregative proce-

dures employed by plaintiffs' firms, where there were no formal aggregative procedures such as class actions, were not qualitatively different
from those that resulted from court-imposed formal aggregation.[250] The
study showed that a relatively small number of attorneys represent the
majority of mass tort plaintiffs.[251] Individual plaintiffs' attorneys or firms
have hundreds and sometimes thousands of clients. Moreover, in the
asbestos litigation, the Rand study found that most plaintiffs become
clients through mass, bureaucratic intake procedures, often facilitated
by unions or disease screening programs. Few of these clients reported
having had any individual communication or consultation with their
attorneys. Most felt that they have little or no control over their cases.
Thus the reality is very different from the myth of what happens
between clients and lawyers in the absence of class actions or consolidations. In fact, allowing the court some control over the plaintiff class
may result in a better flow of information between lawyers and clients
since courts can require fuller communication with clients and public
hearings.

Another charge that critics of mass tort litigation have made is that
formal aggregation prevents the injured individuals from telling their
stories.[252] Yet under the traditional tort regime, few cases went to trial.
For example, "[p]rior to the Manville's bankruptcy in 1982, 3.8% of all
asbestos worker injury claims disposed reached a trial verdict."[253] Thus,
very few individual plaintiffs were provided an opportunity under the
traditional case-by-case tort system to "tell their stories" in court.

In the Agent Orange litigation, I held public hearings on the settlement around the country at which numerous class members got the
chance to achieve some sort of catharsis. Was it enough? Probably not.
But it was arguably more than they would have been able to get in a
trial where the Federal Rules of Evidence would likely have prevented
them from placing their Agent Orange–related grievances into the larger grief that formed the tragic legacy of the Vietnam War for many of
these people. In general, settlements made in the context of consolidated actions, where the litigation has many of the characteristics of a class
action, should also be subject to fairness hearings where more plaintiffs
would have a chance to speak to the court than if their cases continued
to be tried under the traditional regime. The Agent Orange court continues to answer scores of letters from veterans each month, and a bank
of sympathetic, trained operators at Aetna has answered hundreds of
thousands of telephone calls.

It is true that some seriously ill plaintiffs would receive less from a
mass settlement fund than they might have, had their case gone to trial.
Others, who get little or nothing under the tort system lottery, would
do better. Overall, the compensation received by similarly situated plaintiffs would cease to vary so wildly. A compensation fund might also

exceed in toto what a series of individual plaintiffs might be awarded in the aggregate and might provide for more expeditious compensation of present plaintiffs as well as safeguarding the rights of future claimants. In addition, aggregative measures such as the class action enable the courts to protect the financial interests of plaintiffs when they diverge from the interests of their attorneys by controlling transaction costs and by reviewing settlements and attorneys' fees.[254] A lower gross award may be at least partially offset by a higher net to the plaintiff. Finally, future claimants who are now unknown can be protected, particularly if epidemiological studies are provided.

F. CONCLUSION

The United States may be the only country where this debate over the right to full-blown individual treatment could be carried on with such vehemence. The contingent fee system, the denial of attorneys' fees to the victor from the loser, and other aspects of our law have helped fuel the legal system. It is very expensive and, as we have seen, somewhat jerry-built. Yet, we have a unique heritage of individualism and a deep libertarian strain that runs through our history. We have a constitutional scheme that elevates the rights of the individual and the protection of private persons and property. We have, by and large, rejected communal solutions to health and welfare problems in favor of individual entrepreneurial response and first-party insurance. We continue to celebrate the nuclear family as the foundation of all values and social stability even as social and economic conditions steadily erode it.[255]

Given these circumstances, our reliance, perhaps our overreliance, on equity is understandable. We have, however, reached a critical period when more stability and predictability through legislation is desirable. As in the past, it is time for equity to retire into the background, to be on call for an emergency in the future when the dust on its ancient trappings will be brushed away and it will assuage us once again with its shining power to meet the new and otherwise unsolvable problems of the moment.

CHAPTER 10

THE FUTURE[1]

Each of the possible systems for dealing with asbestos-related and other toxic substance injuries has some advantages and disadvantages.

The tort system works fairly well in individual cases. To a considerable degree it is independent of political control. It does not work well with mega–mass tort cases. The high transactional costs, the lottery effects, the delays, the lack of assets to cover all future claims, and the haphazard nature of under- and overdeterrence are well known.

What troubles many of us about an administrative remedy to provide individual compensation is that in the absence of a strong independent bar and bench, the system often deteriorates. At first, the system has great promise. Often thereafter, either enough funds are not granted or the system falls under the control of one economic interest or another. We see that repeatedly. Workers' compensation was a splendid idea. But in many jurisdictions the worker obtains such a small award that the courts have been almost forced to find ways to circumvent the workers' compensation laws. In New York, for example, courts permit suits against manufacturers of products which arguably harmed workers. These third parties then turn around and sue the employer.

Any of the systems suggested, including the New Zealand system of no-fault medical and loss of earnings compensation using government funds,[2] or other systems that would treat compensation as a quasi-welfare problem, present difficulties in our complex society. Those problems are revealed when we begin to analyze some of the proposals for an administrative scheme to deal with asbestos-related injuries. The transitional problems are particularly difficult because the present system has been in effect for so long. As Justice Jackson put the matter in *Michaelson v. Unites States*,[3] a case dealing with attacks on a litigant's character,

> We concur in the general opinion of courts, textwriters and the profession that much of this law is archaic, paradoxical and full of compromises and compensations by which an irrational advantage to one side is offset by a poorly reasoned counterprivilege to the other. But

somehow it has proved a workable even if clumsy system when moderated by discretionary controls in the hands of a wise and strong trial court. To pull one misshapen stone out of the grotesque structure is more likely simply to upset its present balance between adverse interests than to establish a rational edifice.[4]

American tort law has worked in strange ways. All kinds of balances have been achieved in a pragmatic way by lawyers, industry, unions, courts, and legislatures. Radical changes now can lead to more injustices and more inequalities.

What should we do about the discrepancies with respect to defendants? Some defendants have put enormous assets into compensation. Some of their insurers have paid large sums on policies. Some defendants have adequate insurance coverage and some have none. How can we treat them equitably?

What should we do about the billions of dollars of assets in the Manville Trust,[5] or the payment facilities that are developing in other bankruptcies? There will be more bankruptcies in the future. Should we take all of that money, all of those assets, and turn them over to this new agency? Professor Lester Brickman's proposal to the Administrative Conference of the United States requires that these Trust funds, which are set aside in chapter 11 bankruptcy proceedings for asbestos-related injury compensation, be absorbed into the proposed administrative program.[6] But what is the effect of that approach on the many people who have relied upon those assets and who have a vested interest in them—for example, the present claimants to the Manville Trust funds. They have a property interest in those huge funds.

From the point of view of the plaintiffs, there are analogous problems. In New York, there are many people who were exposed to asbestos, some as long as forty or forty-five years ago, during World War 2 in the Brooklyn Navy Yard, or in the post–World War period when we were building our huge new electrical generating plants and buildings.[7] For years, plaintiffs could recover nothing because of the way New York's statute of limitations was designed. The statute of limitations ran from the period of exposure rather than from the time the disease was first discovered by a claimant.[8] Recently the statutes were liberalized through legislation; claims that were formerly barred are now permitted.[9] Simultaneously, complex tort reform was taking place in the form of substantive and procedural rules which were adopted by the New York and other legislatures to balance the rights of the parties.[10]

Many asbestos claimants have waited for compensation for many years. How should we treat their claims? Studies undertaken at my direction show that substantial claims will arise into the middle of the twenty-first century for exposure of workers in the 1970s even though installation of new asbestos practically ceased by 1980.

TABLE

PROJECTED MANVILLE TRUST CLAIMS TO YEAR 2049 IN ADDITION TO MORE THAN 200,000 RECEIVED BY 1993			
	ASBESTOS-RELATED CANCER	ASBESTOS-RELATED NON-CANCER	NON ASBESTOS
MEDIAN	52,000	285,000	48,000
LOW	25,000	130,000	21,000
HIGH	209,000	954,000	172,000

SOURCE: PORTION OF TABLE BY RULE 706 PANEL, ROUNDED TO NEAREST THOUSAND

Is it reasonable to treat a person who has waited and suffered all those years in the same way as a new claimant who is just beginning to show signs of disease? Should the law provide that only the new cases will be treated under the compensation schedules that have been proposed, while pending claims should be afforded much more liberal tort recoveries?

As I understand Professor Brickman's proposal, it is to stop all the pending litigation and transfer it to an administrative agency. Someone who sued and recovered a judgment yesterday might get a half-million or a million dollars for an injury. Someone with a similar injury, who may have had a case pending for five, or six, or more years, might get a few thousand dollars from the new agency.

Let us assume a mesothelioma case where, between manifestation and death, there may be a period of just a year or so. In such cases, Professor Brickman's proposal would provide about two years of wages, which is, for many of these cases, a modest sum: perhaps $40,000 or $50,000. A jury award in Brooklyn would be on the order of $1,000,000, with about $600,000 going to the claimant. A tort settlement might net about $400,000 for the claimant. No proposal can be considered without evaluating equities among past, present, and future claimants.

It becomes difficult to shoehorn a new structure into a working tort system. This is particularly true in our country, where we have so many other compensation systems at work. Social Security, government welfare payments, union and other welfare funds, individual insurance, Veterans Administration benefits, and other kinds of benefits all exist simultaneously. How should we fairly handle collateral benefits and problems of overlap? Subtracting such benefits from the administrative compensation scheme would in many instances leave almost nothing for the claimant.

Should we only consider the workers' problems in this new proposed system? The workers, many of whom have suffered and are entitled to benefits, are in some instances better off than other people who are suffering from all kinds of health problems. Should we treat this as a workers' compensation scheme, as Professor Brickman's proposal does, rather than as a welfare benefits problem under Social Security? The latter seems to be a more rational, perhaps more justifiable, system. It covers the many third-party nonworkers who will be affected by asbestos. They include spouses and children who breathed the dust brought home in workers' clothing.

We can deal with the asbestos litigation problem in a more generalized way under a welfare–Social Security system. That is a basic decision.

My own sense of the Social Security disability system is that it works more equitably and better than the tort system. It does not, of course, provide for pain and suffering. Persons who want greater compensation for disabling injuries than Social Security allows can purchase first-party insurance. Expanding Social Security to nonworkers is an action parallel to that of expanding health insurance to all our population. Compensation and deterrence are aspects of social policy and, in the case of mass torts, have very little to do with social responsibility, which is better handled by the criminal law in the most extreme cases of mens rea.[11]

How should an administrative proposal fit into a possible national health plan? Should the scheme be integrated into an overarching system, or will we develop many separate systems and bureaucracies: one for asbestos, one for black lung, one for longshoremen, one for children exposed to vaccines, and so on?

In the cases I have tried I have been struck by the deep grief, the sense of loss, and the feeling of betrayal of the affected families and plaintiffs. There is a sense of injustice at having been let down by society. The government did not protect them. Perhaps the government is doing a better job now of protecting people through OSHA (Office of Safety & Health Administration), the EPA (Environmental Protection Agency), and consumer protection agencies.

During World War II, those responsible for the building of the great vessels that helped us win the war deliberately covered up the dangers of asbestos to the workers in the naval shipyards.[12] They only protected those workers who manifested immediate effects. People who were painting the ship bottoms with toxic paint and were falling ill immediately were taken care of with special masks so that they could get back to their paint brushes and their sprays. But for the men and women who were working with asbestos, who the doctors and manufacturers knew would die, or suspected would die, nothing was done. The government's failures, the whole society's failures, were disgraceful.

We also have to consider that we have an ongoing industrial establishment and society. We cannot destroy all of the affected industries by high compensation and even higher transactional costs. Sometimes the question reduces to this: who is going to own an industry, the injured or the stockholders? But that is not the only consideration. If we destroy the industry the present workers will be unemployed.

How should we pay the cost of past mistakes? One of the problems with the tort system is that it is extremely expensive. The *Findley v. Blinken* Manville Trust decision[13] projected a possible cost of $30 billion or so to pay for present and future asbestos claims unless radical changes were made in methods of disposition. I do not know what the actual cost would be; we know too little about this subject. The ten federal judges (of which I am one) who asked for a radical change and whose efforts have now resulted in consolidation of federal asbestos cases in the Eastern District of Pennsylvania[14] may have caused a substantial change even in the tort approach.

Another problem to consider is the sense of procedural justice of the affected individual.[15] The Rand Institute has done some excellent work in beginning to address this problem.[16] People who have been injured have the sense that they ought to have lawyers who know and care about them individually. The tort system, when it is a one-plaintiff one-defendant system, works well. On a mass basis, it does not work well. If we examine some of the settlements that the plaintiffs' lawyers arranged in *Findley v. Blinken,* we find masses of cases settled at one time. The individual client-attorney relationship is not close—it is often nonexistent. How should we deal with that issue? How should we address a mass societal problem like this one, and give each individual who is hurt a sense that, yes, somebody has heard *me,* somebody has listened to *me,* somebody has tried to compensate *me,* somebody cares about *me.* The tort system, when it works at its best, accomplishes this result. I think other systems can also provide an adequate sense of justice as well as efficiency, but I am not sure how.

We can clear our court calendars. This is the least of our problems. With a few more judges and law clerks we can try or settle the whole New York State asbestos calendar in just a few years. The defendants will not like such dispatch because it increases their cash flow problems. People who have been waiting for compensation for many years, however, may appreciate such timely disposition.

The black lung experience provides a useful comparison. But it is quite different from the asbestos experience for political and other reasons. In the coal cases there was a single union representing most of the affected miners. The workers were people with economic and political power. They were essentially a class with separate problems who had a sense of themselves as members of a group.[17] We do not have that situation in asbestos. We have a large number of unrelated people, from many industries scattered across the country, with different problems.

Even what seems to be a simple issue of the persons who have not experienced very much adverse reaction—for example, persons with pleural plaque—requires more consideration. I have had such cases before me. The injured are terrified. When they get X rays showing that they have asbestos-related plaque, they begin to manifest serious psychological symptoms. They have to pause when walking up stairs. But many of them can do their work, so they would not be compensated under the proposed administrative scheme. I believe them when they testify before me. They are devastated. They cry and appear to be without the ability, really, to think of themselves as men and women with a future. These are the real-life problems we face when considering some of the real people and some of the real-life situations in the courts.

There is a great deal to be said for the scheduling of payments according to the degree of disability—a feature of the proposed administrative scheme.[18] But I have some question about whether it will give many of the people who have been hurt by asbestos a sense that they have been fairly treated. I do not know what the bar is going to be doing about these cases. I am delighted to hear of the responsible attitude that some of the members of the plaintiffs' bar have about deferring less serious cases in global settlement proposals for future claims. Many members of the bar and many claimants do not share that view. The courts have tried to deal with the problem by permitting multiple suits, deferred statutes of limitations, deferred prosecution, and the like.

Every one of the proposed systems has advantages and disadvantages. It may well be that in the area of asbestos, we are going to be left—just because we started down this track—with asbestos claims being handled by the courts, substantially modifying the standard tort approach in a variety of ways, relying in part upon a semijudicial administrative model. That is not wholly desirable. It transforms judges into administrators. As indicated in *In re "Agent Orange" Product Liability Litigation (Ivy v. Diamond Shamrock Chemicals Co.)*,[19] I am administering huge funds, which I should not be, were we limited to classic court traditions.

There are, as demonstrated earlier in this book, ethical problems that need to be faced. The lawyers are handling masses of cases. They sometimes settle five hundred or more cases at a time for a fixed amount of money—say, $5 million for five hundred cases from one defendant.[20] This may be a good figure when you consider all the cases in bulk. But how do you divide it up among the five hundred clients if you are the plaintiffs' lawyer? Some lawyers use the help of a special master to make the allocation. Others deal with the problem in a variety of other ways. Abuses of favoritism are possible. The system, as it works with large masses of cases, does not provide the kind of representation that we envisage when we think of Abraham Lincoln saying to the person coming in off the street, "I'll fight for you, as your lawyer." It is quite different in mass torts.

As tort law is in fact administered in a mass tort case, with many cases in the hands of a few lawyers, we provide a quasi-public, quasi-administrative system.[21] How should we control such a system? As judges, we do not want to become involved in fees and supervision of lawyers. Nor do lawyers want us to supervise them. But fees are a problem we cannot ignore.[22]

Most judges who handle mass tort cases recognize an obligation toward our economy—our productive community. They do not want the fees, the other transactional costs, and huge awards to destroy industries by driving them into bankruptcy.[23]

One of the powerful aspects of our democracy is our strong, independent bar that will tell off the powerful and fight for clients. We do not want to drive our lawyers, either defendants' or plaintiffs', into the ground. But I do not see how we can avoid some limited control of lawyers in mass torts. The expense and the lack of traditional attorney-client relationships mandate some change. Self-regulation is not working well. Fees are often exorbitant.

Yet I am suspicious of administrative systems because of the way they have sometimes been manipulated. I have seen case after case under Social Security in the 1980s where the administration distorted the system to deny people benefits that should not have been denied. I had before me the cases of thousands of schizophrenics who had been arbitrarily put off the compensation rolls. It is the underlying suspicion of government—I say that with great respect for the people who are administering the Black Lung Benefits Act[24] and the Vaccine Act[25]—that gives us pause when we consider an administrative scheme. No matter what the dedication of the administrators, if the money is cut off, if the administration changes or if the administration needs money for other things, the whole system may change radically. At least the tort system in this country, with all its costs and with its lack of coherence, has the advantage of being out in the open and independent of government abuse.[26]

The juries that have tried these cases in my courtroom—more than fifty cases at a time—have done their job extremely well. I think they have achieved results using the tort system that are as consistent as the administrative decisions I have seen in Social Security disability cases. We should not denigrate the jury system as a reason for an administrative scheme.

All of the present and proposed systems can be improved. We can work out hybrids of one kind or another, as we are doing now in the courts. That is what happened in *A. H. Robins Company (Dalkon Shield)*;[27] that is what happened in *Agent Orange;* that is what is beginning to happen in asbestos and breast implant cases.

Until the federal legislature enacts a national tort or administrative scheme the courts can continue to utilize their equitable powers to improve court administration of mass torts. A national disaster court such as was described in chapter 2 would be an interim step utilizing the tort system.[28] So, too, would increased transfer powers and conflicts of laws devices such as those recommended by the American Law Institute.

For future cases such as lead poisoning or an atomic disaster or electromagnetic waves, an administrative scheme worked out now by the legislature would be best, but without legislation the courts will have to continue to find ad hoc solutions.[29] Most desirable would be a uniform social welfare system that would compensate all of the disabled and their families and provide health and loss of income benefits to all who need them, supplemented by first-party, employee, or union insurance.[30] But such a system has its own drawbacks.

One lesson is fairly clear. Deterrence of disasters by tort law or an administrative or welfare compensation scheme is not sufficiently effective in protecting society against the dangers of technology. In place of deterrence through compensation payments we need strict controls and enforcement of safety laws. That aspect of risk assessment and control of risk can be accomplished as readily under an administrative as under a tort scheme.

The many federal regulatory agencies can deter more effectively than a tort system. Particularly in the case of pharmaceuticals and toxic substances with long latency periods before disease is manifested, the costs are paid by insurance companies and the malefactors long after the event. A fine by the appropriate regulatory agency promptly imposed while the responsible management is still in control can be more effective.[31] Fines should be commensurate with the high "value" of a life, estimated by the economist W. Kip Viscusi as $3 to $5 million.[32]

Regulation of safety needs to be enhanced, not reduced as by the disastrous underregulation of the 1980s and before.[33] The relevant governmental agencies are in a much better position to assess risks and to avoid overdeterrence that inhibits necessary research and product development as in children's vaccines or birth control devices.[34]

Where the regulatory agency does not act, qui tam actions, permitting private "whistle blower" suits with the person bringing the suit sharing in the recovery, should be permitted.[35] Frivolous suits can be discouraged by provisions for attorneys' fees and expenses.[36]

Punitive damages would be incorporated in the "fine," thus avoiding the problem of repeated imposition of punitive damages in repeated suits all over the country that overpunish. Such punitive damages and fines should go primarily to the health and welfare programs that are made more expensive by toxic substances. Some substances such as tobacco should pay their share of the huge expenses attributed to smoking by greatly increased taxes. The injury is really to society as a whole.[37]

Regardless of the prospects for legislative reform, lawyers and judges must continue to do their daily work. That labor will include, as it has throughout the history of the law, the critical effort to establish and maintain ethical and professional standards commensurate with the status of lawyers and judges as guardians of a system that defines our society and our relationships to one another. The obligation may well grow weightier as our modern society becomes larger and more complex. But that is no reason to shrink from the task.

The law need not accept any particular philosophical or ethical structure. Its flexibility to meet new conditions must be retained by ethical rules with a capacity to change. It is not wedded to a transcendental scheme. It can appropriately be influenced by the insights of many apparently conflicting schools of thought.[38] Each provides warning signs of dangers as well as illuminating insights.

There are, of course, great dangers in departing from the relatively clear and known constraints of traditional practice. The adversary role of the lawyers and the passive role of the judge (applying fairly well-defined rules of law and procedure) provides powerful boundaries to both discretion and abuse. When these constraints are removed or substantially loosened, they must be replaced by at least some felt sense of appropriateness. Such a sense is still inchoate in the area of mass torts, partly because the problem has been ignored and the reality so far detached from the theory.

Some appellate courts and some academics seem disturbed—understandably—by trial courts' activism in mass torts. But they are not adding to the solution by strictly limiting class actions and consolidations or other procedural devices to hamstring those who must deal with problems in the field and at the trial level. The effect of too conservative a view is to deny effective relief to the parties and the broader communities.

Monstrous mega–mass tort litigations can be tamed. They must be examined with a realistic eye, rather than romantic notions of how the law and lawyers once operated when a tort involved only a private matter of two parties, two lawyers, and a passive court. Ethical and legal norms out of touch with real life lead not to morality, but to hypocrisy, abuse, and waste.[39]

Notes

1. No research has convinced me that the original court decision in Agent Orange would be different today. *See, e.g.,* Keith Schneider, 2 Decades After Toxic Blast in Italy, Several Cancers Show Rise, N.Y. Times, Oct. 26, 1993, at B6 ("Overall the results are reassuring . . . dioxin is not a powerful carcinogen [to human beings]"). Dioxin is quite carcinogenic to some species of rodents; this toxicological effect was largely responsible for the Agent Orange litigations. The explosion in Saveso exposed people to much higher doses of dioxin than did herbicide spraying of troops in Vietnam, except for those who actually sprayed; studies of causation in their cases have so far been largely negative. The studies of birth defects have not demonstrated any causation. It was a great pity that some veterans and their spouses apparently decided not to have children because of fear of Agent Orange–induced defects, despite the clear indication that birth defects for the general population were no different from those where a parent might have been exposed to herbicides in Vietnam. Part of the difficulty in studying the effect of dioxin in Vietnam has been the absence of reliable exposure criteria and information. *See, e.g.,* Michael Gough, Dioxin: Perceptions, Estimates, and Measures, in *Phantom Risk* 241–77 (Kenneth R. Foster, David E. Bernstein, & Peter W. Huber eds., 1993); Wall St. J., Oct. 19, 1993, at A12 (Gulf War and Agent Orange). Analyses of the scientific studies are beyond the scope of this book. I have filed the studies in the Agent Orange litigation folders in the United States District Court for the Eastern District of New York, where they are available for public inspection.

2. Jack B. Weinstein, On the Teaching of Legal Ethics, 72 Colum. L. Rev. 452 (1972).

3. The main lecture was the Second Annual Pope and John Lecture on Professionalism, Northwestern University School of Law, Mar. 18, 1993.

4. Jack B. Weinstein, Individual Justice in Mass Litigation, 88 Nw. U. L. Rev. 901 (1993).

1. *See, e.g.*, Herbert L. Packer, *The Limits of the Criminal Sanction* 292 (1968) ("Assembly-Line Justice").

2. As County Attorney of Nassau County I established with the Office of Economic Opportunity and private funds a legal service for the poor that included social service aid; I was the first Chairman of the Board. This group is now the Nassau-Suffolk Legal Service with a huge budget and caseload. As chief Judge of the Eastern District Federal Court I established a foundation for pro bono cases to pay expenses of attorneys and experts for poor people. Funded at first with my own honoraria, many people have contributed time and money for this project. For my twenty-fifth anniversary as a judge, my law clerks set up a fund to permit legal aid, probation, and the clerk's office to provide emergency funds for poor people before the court. A library fund for jurors in our court in the name of my mother, Bessie Weinstein, was set up with my personal funds. Private philanthropy has a role in the courts.

3. Appellate courts are showing an increased tendency to lean toward defendants in these cases. *See, e.g.*, N.Y. L.J. Dec. 13, 1993, at 1, Deborah Pines, Repetitive Stress Injury Suit Consolidation Vacated ("Continuing a trend of warnings to trial courts against putting efficiency ahead of other concerns in mass-tort litigation, the Second Circuit last week upset the consolidation of some 1,000 repetitive stress injury cases"); Michael Hoenig, Clarification of Warning Law, *id.* at 3 ("warnings [in pharmaceutical cases] may be sufficient as a matter of law" and warrant summary judgment for the defendant).

4. Chief Judge Stephen Breyer has suggested that we are capable "of building an improved, coherent risk-regulating system," adapted for use in the many government agencies that regulate. See Stephen Breyer, *Breaking the Vicious Circle: Toward Effective Risk Management* 8, 60 (1993). Even in its present unsatisfactory state, our bureaucracies do a much better job than our mass tort system in protecting against serious risks to society.

5. The punitive damage system is an awkward and ineffective method of accomplishing extra punishment as deterrence; it is being subjected to constant pressure to reduce its impact. *See, e.g.*, Arvin Maskin & Peter A. Antonucci, *After TXO Production Corp. v. Alliance Resources: A Punitive Damage Primer* (Washington Legal Foundation, 1993); Mack Trucks Inc. v. Conkle, 436 S.E. 2d 635 (1993) (Georgia statute providing that 75 percent of punitive damage awards arising out of product liability cases, less costs and reasonable attorneys' fees, go to state treasury; only one such award may be granted to a product liability defendant).

6. *See, e.g.*, W. Kip Viscusi, *Reforming Products Liability* 10–11, 88, 108 (1993) (computing the value of a human life at some $3,000,000 as reflected in increased wages in risky activities).

7. *See, e.g.,* Michael J. Saks, Do We Really Know Anything About the Behavior of the Tort Litigation System—And Why Not?, 140 U. Pa. L. Rev. 1147 (1992).

8. N.Y. Rev. of Books, Oct. 8, 1992, at 6.

9. 947 F.2d 1201 (5th Cir. 1991).

10. The Communicative Ethics Controversy, afterword by Seyla Benhabib, *Communicative Ethics and Current Controversies in Practical Philosophy* 330 (Seyla Benhabib & Fred Dallmayr eds., 1990).

11. *Id.* at 26.

12. *See, e.g.,* Gary T. Schwartz, The Beginnings and the Possible End of the Rise of Modern American Tort Law, 26 Ga. L. Rev. 601 (1992).

13. *See* Marc Galanter, Bhopals, Past and Present: The Changing Legal Response to Mass Disaster, 10 Windsor Yearbook of Access to Justice, 151, 159 (1991).

14. Gerald M. Stern, *The Buffalo Creek Disaster* (1976).

15. *See* Kai T. Erikson, *Everything in Its Path: The Destruction of Community in the Buffalo Creek Flood* (1976). *See also* the two TV films on the subject.

16. The debate is typified by an article describing the two schools of thought as reflected in trial lawyers' views. *See* Alison Frankel, Et Tu, Stan?, Am. Law., Jan./Feb. 1994, at 68 ("While judges, victims, and some lawyers hail mass torts guru Stanley Chesley as Mr. Fix It, other plaintiffs' lawyers call his quick settlements a stab in the back.") The author writes

> Chesley has a different vision of the tort system than plaintiffs lawyers like Henderson and Schroeter and Baron and Ciresi. They talk about the sanctity of an individual plaintiff's rights, about assessing individual cases. "The tort system is not intended to make sure everyone with [any] injury gets compensated," says Ciresi. "You can't look to the tort system as being able to solve society's ills." In the view of lawyers like these, justice comes case by case.
>
> Chesley, on the other hand, looks through a wide-angle lens, practicing, in the words of Brooklyn federal district court judge . . . Jack Weinstein, "in a much broader framework." His philosophy of mass torts is to supply the most justice to the most people the most quickly.

Id. at 70. I, personally, find much to admire and things to deplore in the work of lawyers on both sides of the issue.

CHAPTER 2

1. This chapter is essentially the author's article, Preliminary Reflections in the Law's Reaction to Disasters, 11 Colum. J. Envtl. L. 1 (1986).

The author is grateful for the assistance of David Brittenham, Columbia J.D. 1984, a former law clerk of the author's, and of Linda Gordon, Columbia University School of Law, Class of 1986, in preparing that article. Permission of the Columbia Journal of Environmental Law to publish is gratefully acknowledged.

2. The Soviet nuclear plant disaster, which increased ambient radiation over a large area, is a dramatic reminder of the potential for catastrophe. Refusal to close the Chernobyl and similar plants in Eastern Europe while they deteriorate and safety violations increase make future disasters of this type increasingly likely. *See* N.Y. Times, Oct. 22, 1993, at A6 (Ukraine to Keep Chernobyl in Operation). *See also, e.g.,* Russia Halts Dumping of Nuclear Wastes in Sea, N.Y. Times, Oct. 22, 1993, at A4. According to one study, dangers exist in part because "dramatic scientific and technological advances" have preceded development of appropriate safety data and techniques. Legislative Drafting Research Fund of Columbia University School of Law, Catastrophic Accidents in Government Programs 1 (1963) [hereinafter cited as Catastrophic Accidents]. Although this study considered only accidents in government programs, the same forces apply in the private sector. Commentators have recognized the increased potential for disaster. *See, e.g.,* C. Perron, *Normal Accidents: Living with High Risk Technologies* (1984); American Bar Association, Special Committee on the Tort Liability System, Towards a Jurisprudence of Injury: The Continuing Creation of a System of Substantive Justice in American Tort Law 11-53–11-63 (1984). Danger may exist where it is least expected—at home or at leisure spots. *Consider* A. Zamm & R. Gannon, *Why Your House May Endanger Your Health* (1980) (discussing the dangers of air pollution in the home); Radioactive Gas Alters Lives of Pennsylvanians, N.Y. Times, Oct. 28, 1985, at A10 (discussing the widespread presence of radioactive gas in homes); Dioxin Detected in Barrels on Upstate Golf Course, N.Y. Times, Feb. 17, 1985, at A48. The Alaska Valdez oil spill with its enormous impact was almost dwarfed by the Amoco Cadiz oil spill in the English Channel, spawning a huge multinational case. *See* MDL 376, *In re* Oil Spill by the "Amoco Cadiz" Off the Coast of France on Mar. 16, 1978 before Judge Charles R. Nagel, Sr. N.D. *See also, e.g.,* N.Y. L.J. Apr. 24, 1989, at 1 (twenty-five class action suits brought in Valdez oil spill cases, with committee organized to coordinate class and other actions). The 1990 Oil Pollution Act created an industry-wide oil spill liability trust fund. Part of the legal problem in Valdez appears to be the government's efforts to treat the natural damage assessment process as confidential. *See* Comprehensive Environmental Response, Compensation and Liability Act 99301(c). In addition to civil litigations, large criminal fines ($125 million) resulted from the Valdez oil spill.

Even more enlightening are some of the predictions of future risk.

The Nuclear Regulatory Commission announced that, mathematically, the odds of a meltdown of a nuclear reactor occurring somewhere in the United States in the next fifty years are 50-50. N.Y. Times, Apr. 17, 1985, at A16. The amount and nature of risk associated with nuclear operations remains uncertain. *See* Scientists Question Studies on Nuclear Accidents, N.Y. Times, Feb. 24, 1985, at L21 (discussing scientific and industry sponsored reports on the radius around nuclear plants for which emergency evacuation plans are necessary); Hiroshima Bomb's Radiation Remains a Scientific Mystery, N.Y. Times, Aug. 5, 1985, at A1 (discussing the difficulties involved in predicting the harm caused by radiation); Examining How Liability Should be Assessed for Damages Caused by Low-Level Radiation Effects Which Appear as Cancer Years after Exposure: Hearings before the Committee on Labor and Human Resources, 98th Cong., 2d Sess. 1 (1984). Incidents in the past indicate that concern about future risks is justified. *See* U.S. Toxic Mishaps in Chemicals Put at 6,928 in 5 Years, N.Y. Times, Oct. 3, 1985, at A1 (summarizing a government report finding that 6,928 accidents involving toxic chemicals occurred in the United States in the last five years resulting in 135 deaths and nearly 1,500 injuries). *See also infra* notes 10–11 and accompanying text.

It should be noted that scientific advances may also lead to prevention or reduction of technologically induced disease. For example, gene research may eventually yield a method for identifying people with abnormally great sensitivity to certain chemicals, enabling sensitive individuals to avoid disease by avoiding exposure.

3. The Bhopal leak incident is an example of a situation in which the harm done and the source of the technology causing it are separated. Union Carbide officials in the United States at one time appeared to have accepted the blame for the leak; according to a news report following a press conference, the president of the chemicals and plastics division said he was "'deeply and personally sorry for the fears and concerns' that the company brought to the community near the . . . plant." N.Y. Times, Aug. 24, 1985, at A1, L29, col. 1 (quoting Robert D. Kennedy). Although Union Carbide has since denied liability for the leak, it remains true that the presence of the plant in India exposed residents in the area. *See* Am. Law., Nov. 1985, at 27 (discussing Union Carbide's denial of liability and claim of sabotage). *But see* N.Y. Times, Oct. 3, 1985, at A20 (report by the Occupational Safety and Health Administration); Carbide Leak Highlights Defects in Systems Handling Toxic Matter, N.Y. Times, Aug. 19, 1985, at A1 (discussing opinions of chemical engineers, consultants, and other experts on causes of the accident).

The case on behalf of those injured was originally brought in the Southern District of New York. Essentially the parameters of the settlement for $500 million were those worked out, with an immediate payment suggested by the trial judge of $5 million to give immediate help to the victims. The case was then transferred to India at the request of the Indian government on the ground that it was a more convenient and appropriate forum. There the case languished. Even though half a billion dollars was available for the victims, they received practically no help. This failure of the political and legal systems would not have been tolerable in the United States with its active tort bar.

The Bhopal incident may have a positive impact by inducing measures to reduce the risks associated with chemical processing. Following the leak, federal officials noted that there were very little data available that could be used to assess risks or to avoid future incidents involving toxic chemical leaks. N.Y. Times, May 20, 1985, at D1. In response, the Environmental Protection Agency (EPA) completed and published a report on production and use of toxic chemicals in the United States. *See* U.S. Names 403 Toxic Chemicals That Pose Risk in Plant Accidents, N.Y. Times, Nov. 18, 1985, at A1. Union Carbide announced at the same time that it had reduced inventories of toxic chemicals by 74 percent. *Id.* at B9. The following day the EPA provided detailed instructions on "how local officials can find highly toxic chemicals in their midst, assess and reduce excessive risks and plan for emergencies." N.Y. Times, Nov. 19, 1985, at B9. Industry interests are for the most part supporting new efforts at risk reduction regulation. *See* Chemical Industry Braces for Tougher Regulation, N.Y. Times, Aug. 15, 1985, at A1; Industry Chiefs Back U.S. Curbs on Polluted Air, N.Y. Times, Mar. 27, 1985, at A1.

Although such efforts will undoubtedly reduce risks in the chemical industry, it is significant that after the Bhopal tragedy, another potentially disastrous leak occurred at a Union Carbide facility in West Virginia. Toxic Cloud Leaks at Carbide Plant in West Virginia, N.Y. Times, Aug. 15, 1985, at A1. It is reasonable to assume that such incidents cannot be completely avoided no matter what precautions are taken. Our legal system must be prepared to handle future disasters of this type.

Partly because of the criticism of the lawyers who flock to disasters to sign up clients, bar associations have begun to develop plans for local disasters. *See* Claudia MacLachalan, Mobile Response to Amtrak Crash, Nat. L.J. Oct. 11, 1993, at 1 (local bar's disaster plan kept lawyers away, but they were criticized for chasing cases anyway). Even Abraham Lincoln was said to have solicited clients outside the courthouse. *See* Bar Groups Battle Increase of "Ambulance Chasers," Register Guard, Eugene, Ore., Oct. 18, 1993, at 6a.

4. For a discussion on human involvement in natural disasters see A. Wikman and L. Timberlake, *Natural Disasters: Acts of God or Acts of Man* (1985); Researchers Predicting Spread of Famine in Africa, N.Y.

Times, Feb. 18, 1985, at A8 (discussing a report concluding that the famine in Ethiopia may in part be caused by the pressure of human activity). It is political rather than economic reasons that produced the famines in Somalia and made sustenance so difficult there and elsewhere.

5. There is a growing collection of legal literature on the litigation of disasters. *See, e.g.,* Peter W. Huber, Safety and the Second Best: The Hazards of Public Risk Management in the Courts, 85 Colum. L. Rev. 277 (1985) (general discussion from the point of view of industry on how mass torts should be dealt with in the legal system); Richard Epstein, The Legal and Insurance Dynamics of Mass Tort Litigation, 13 J. Legal Studies 475 (1984); Francis E. McGovern, Management of Multiparty Toxic Tort Litigation: Case Law and Trends Affecting Case Management, 19 Forum 1 (1983); Note, Class Actions and Mass Toxic Torts, 8 Colum. J. Envtl. L. 269 (1982); *cf.* Abram Chayes, The Role of the Judge in Public Law Litigation, 89 Harv. L. Rev. 1281 (1976). *See also* Victor E. Schwartz, Patric W. Lee, & Kathryn Kelly, *Guide to Multistate Litigation* (1985).

6. The need to reduce the transaction costs attributed to litigation is acute. The cost of asbestos litigation is a well-known example. Letter from William J. Anderson, Director, to The Honorable Daniel K. Inouye and The Honorable Austin J. Murphy (Sept. 19, 1985) (on file in the office of the Columbia Journal of Environmental Law). *See also* J. Kakalik, P. Ebener, W. Felstiner, & M. Shanley, *Costs of Asbestos Litigation* (1983) and J. Kakalik, P. Ebener, W. Felstiner, G. Haggstrom, & M. Shanley, *Variations in Asbestos Litigation Compensation and Expenses* (1984) (both prepared by The Rand Corporation Institute for Civil Justice). Transaction costs in asbestos cases can be measured in the billions.

7. Love Canal residents received compensation for damages that occurred over nine years before. *See* Ex–Love Canal Families Get Payments, N.Y. Times, Feb. 20, 1985, at B1; Settling Some Love Canal Debts, Newsday, Feb. 4, 1985, at 7. In addition, the settlement left uncompensated many who believe they have been injured. Although the government purchased a large amount of property that was within the "disaster area," some residents a few feet from the boundary received no compensation. Forgotten Victims of Love Canal, Newsday, Feb. 28, 1985, at 2. Others were excluded from the personal injury settlement. *Id.* Nevertheless, the extent of the damages, from a scientific point of view, remain problematic. *See also, e.g.,* EPA to Study Safety of an Insecticide, N.Y. Times, Oct. 24, 1993, at A10. (Endasolfan may be linked to some forms of breast cancer; estrogen exposure may be linked to a 50 percent worldwide reduction in sperm count.)

Personal injury suits after a well-known fire disaster took over eight years to settle. After 8 Years, A Complex Case Comes to an End, Nat'l

L.J., Aug. 19, 1985, at 6, col. 1 (settlement of the Beverly Hills Supper Club fire).

In many cases there may be no compensation available for the type of injury alleged by the plaintiff. *See* Note, Tort Law—Emotional Distress and Wrongful Life Claims in DES Litigation: Injury Without Remedy: *Payton v. Abbott Laboratories*, 6 W. New Eng. L. Rev. 1037 (1984).

The Superfund 301(e) Study Group reviewed existing statutory and common law compensation remedies for injuries and damages stemming from hazardous waste. In the course of the study group's evaluation, it noted that:

> [although] the existing legal remedies and actions may be adequate[,] in spite of existing barriers, to deal with small claims . . . [they are] inadequate . . . to deal with the possibility of mass torts, or multiple exposures, and with claims of hundreds of victims, each of whom suffered a few thousand dollars in damages, unless procedures are found, not readily available at present, to join or combine such small claims.

Superfund Section 301(e) Study Group, Report to the Congress on Victim Compensation Pursuant to Section 301(e) of the Comprehensive Environmental Response, Compensation and Liability Act of 1980, Pub. L. No. 96-510, 94 Stat. 2767, at 193 (1982) [hereinafter cited as Study Group Proposal] (all page numbers refer to the numbers at the tops of the pages in the Study Group Proposal).

Other commentators assert that the tort system itself does not provide an adequate remedy. *See* Stephen D. Sugarman, Doing Away with Tort Law, 73 Calif. L. Rev. 558 (1985) ("the straight-forward case against tort law . . . [is] that the costs of the tort system outweigh its benefits"). Consider these points:

> A . . . possible improvement [in the compensation system] would be the establishment of alternatives to the traditional tort remedy. Such alternative remedies should be developed at least for mass-disaster tort situations and should be considered for broader classes of toxic tort situations as well. While proposed alternatives vary widely, four key common threads emerge:
>
> - Eligibility criteria for compensation, including causation requirements, should be relatively unrestrictive.
> - Payment levels to individual plaintiffs should be lower than those under the traditional tort system.
> - Individual claims should be resolved through administrative decision or private settlement mechanisms, without case-by-case adjudication in the courts.
> - Where possible, difficult problems of causation should be avoided.

The Institute for Health Policy Analysis, Georgetown University Medical Center, Causation and Financial Compensation 10 (1986) (Final Report of the Conference Panel: Conference on Causation & Financial Responsibility, Feb. 20–21, 1985). A report by the American Bar Association Special Committee on the Tort Liability System found, however, that the tort system is "vital and responsive" and that "the adversarial process . . . produces a consistently high quality of substantive justice." American Bar Association, *supra* note 2, at 13-1.

8. *See, e.g.,* Garcia v. San Antonio Metropolitan Transit Authority, 469 U.S. 528 (1985). In overruling National League of Cities v. Usery, 426 U.S. 833 (1976), Justice Blackmun attacked the attempt to limit federal action in areas termed to be "traditional governmental functions" of the states, stating that "the fundamental limitation that the constitutional scheme imposes on the Commerce Clause to protect the 'States as States' is one of process rather than one of result." 469 U.S. 528, 554. As long as the "built in restraints that our system provides through state participation in federal governmental action" remain untouched, the power of the federal government to act appears to be limited only by such "process" considerations. *Id.*

9. Procedural changes should be evaluated in light of their ability to satisfy the traditional goal of tort law: "to adjust . . . losses, and to afford compensation for injuries sustained by one person as a result of the conduct of another." W. Prosser & W. Keeton, *Handbook on the Law of Torts* 6 (5th ed. 1984). *See also* Study Group Proposal, *supra* note 7, at 81–109 (discussion of traditional tort doctrines and their applicability to victim compensation).

10. The year 1985 was almost unprecedented in the number of air disasters with fatalities. *Consider, e.g.,* Jetliner Crashes with 524 Aboard in Central Japan, N.Y. Times, Aug. 13, 1985, at A1; 329 Lost on Air India Plane after Crash near Ireland: Bomb is Suspected as Cause, N.Y. Times, June 24, 1985, at A1. Over two thousand people died, and about two hundred thousand people were injured on December 3, 1984, when a cloud of methyl isocyanate gas leaked from a Union Carbide pesticide plant in Bhopal, India. N.Y. Times, Feb. 3, 1985, at A1. Over three hundred people were killed in the Mexico City suburb of Tlalnepantla when a storage area for liquefied gas exploded in flames in a slum area on November 20, 1984. N.Y. Times, Nov. 21, 1984, at A8.

11. On May 28, 1977, the Beverly Hills Supper Club in Southgate, Kentucky, burned, causing 164 deaths. N.Y. Times, July 3, 1977, at A16. On July 17, 1981, two walkways at the Hyatt Regency Hotel in Kansas City, Missouri, collapsed, injuring at least two hundred and causing 113 deaths. N.Y. Times, July 18, 1981, at A1.

12. Dalehite v. United States, 346 U.S. 15 (1953).

13. *See* Catastrophic Accidents, *supra* note 2.

14. *Id.* at 3. In response to the Dalehite decision, Congress enacted the Texas City Disaster Relief Act, Pub. L. No. 84-378, 69 Stat. 707 (1955). The Act provided funds limited to $25,000 per claim. Beginning eight years after the catastrophe occurred, $17 million dollars was eventually paid out. Actual damages were estimated to be between $60 million and "billions" of dollars. Catastrophic Accidents, *supra* note 2, at 4.

15. 42 U.S.C. § 2210(1) (1982 & Supp. I 1983).

16. Air crashes provide examples of effective litigation management. *See, e.g., In re* Air Crash in Bali Indonesia on Apr. 22, 1974, 684 F.2d 1301 (9th Cir. 1982); *In re* Air Crash Disaster at Washington, D.C. on Jan. 13, 1982, 559 F. Supp. 333 (D.D.C. 1983); Schulhof v. Northeast Cellulose, 545 F. Supp. 1200 (D. Mass. 1982).

17. For a discussion of when consolidation for trial of actions for personal injuries, death, or property damages arising out of the same accident is available, see Annot., 68 A.L.R. 2d 1372 (1959). Consolidation is usually permitted when there are different plaintiff parties but common defendants and no party's rights are prejudiced. *Id.* at 1384–85. Consolidation may not always be allowed. *Cf.* Roger H. Trangsrud, Joinder Alternatives in Mass Tort Litigation, 70 Cornell L. Rev. 779 (1985).

For examples of management of mass accidents through class actions, see Hernandez v. Motor Vessel Skyward, 61 F.R.D. 558 (S.D. Fla. 1973), *aff'd mem.,* 507 F.2d 1278 (5th Cir. 1975) (food poisoning); Bentkowski v. Marfuerza Compania Maritima, 70 F.R.D. 401 (E.D. Pa. 1976) (food poisoning); *In re* Gabel, 350 F. Supp. 624 (C.D. Cal. 1972) (airplane crash); American Trading & Prod. Corp. v. Fischbach & Moore, Inc., 47 F.R.D. 155 (N.D. Ill. 1969) (fire).

Although use of the class action device would alleviate many procedural difficulties, it may not always be available. For example, in the Kansas City Skywalk incident, the mandatory class action certified by the lower court was ordered decertified by the appellate court under the Anti-Injunction Act, 28 U.S.C. § 2283 (1982). *In re* Federal Skywalk Cases, 680 F.2d 1175 (8th Cir. 1982), *cert. denied sub nom.* Stover v. Rall, 459 U.S. 988 (1982). Following decertification, however, voluntary classes were certified in state and federal court. *In re* Federal Skywalk Cases, 97 F.R.D. 380 (W.D. Mo. 1983). *But see In re* Asbestos School Litigation, 104 F.R.D. 422 (E.D. Pa. 1984) (class action found appropriate in an asbestos property litigation). *See generally* Comment, Federal Mass Tort Class Actions: A Step Toward Equity and Efficiency, 47 Ala. L. Rev. 1180 (1983); Comment, Class Certification in Mass Accident Cases under Rule 23(b)(1), 96 Harv. L. Rev. 1143 (1983); Note, Class Actions and Mass Toxic Torts, 8 Colum. J. Envtl. L. 269 (1982); Comment, The Use of Class Actions for Mass Accident Litigation, 23 Loy. L. Rev. 383 (1977).

Offensive use of collateral estoppel will be allowed unless the plaintiff asserting the doctrine "could easily have joined in the earlier action" or application of the doctrine "would be unfair to . . . [the] defendant." Parklane Hosiery Co. v. Shore, 439 U.S. 322, 331 (1979). *See also* United States v. United Air Lines, 216 F. Supp. 709 (D. Nev. 1962) (offensive use of collateral estoppel allowed in wrongful death actions following an air disaster), *aff'd sub nom.* United Air Lines v. Weiner, 335 F.2d 379 (9th Cir. 1964), *cert. denied,* 379 U.S. 951 (1964); Stoddard v. Ling-Temco-Vought, Inc., 513 F. Supp. 335 (C.D. Cal. 1981); Maryland v. Capital Air Lines, 267 F. Supp. 298 (D. Md. 1967); Hart v. American Airlines, 61 Misc. 2d 41, 304 N.Y.S.2d 810 (Sup. Ct. 1969); Desmond v. Kramer, 96 N.J. Super. 96, 232 A.2d 470 (Law Div. 1967). *See generally* Douglas J. Gunn, The Offensive Use of Collateral Estoppel in Mass Tort Cases, 52 Miss. L.J. 765 (1982); Note, Erie and the Preclusive Effect of Federal Diversity Judgments, 85 Colum. L. Rev. 1505 (1985).

18. For example, a number of articles have been published on the difficulties that Bhopal plaintiffs faced. *See, e.g.,* A Second Bhopal Disaster, Nat'l L.J., May, 13, 1985, at 13. *See also* Catastrophe at Bhopal: A Challenge to the Law, 3 West's Int'l L. Bull. 7 (1985); Marc S. Galanter, Legal Torpor: Why So Little Has Happened in India after the Bhopal Tragedy, 20 Tex. Int'l L.J. 273 (1985). *See also* discussion *supra* note 7.

19. For a general discussion of thalidomide, see H. Teff & C. Munroe, *Thalidomide: The Legal Aftermath* (1976).

20. *See* Ellis v. International Playtex, 745 F.2d 292 (4th Cir. 1984); Kehm v. Proctor & Gamble, 724 F.2d 613 (8th Cir. 1983); Farnsworth v. Proctor & Gamble, 101 F.R.D. 355 (N.D. Ga. 1984), *aff'd,* 758 F.2d 1545 (11th Cir. 1985); *In re* Rely Tampon Products Liability Litigation, 533 F. Supp. 1346 (J.P.M.D.L. 1982).

21. *See In re* Northern District of California, Dalkon Shield I.U.D. Products Liability Litigation, 693 F.2d 847 (9th Cir. 1982), *cert. denied sub nom.* A. H. Robins Co. v. Abed, 459 U.S. 1171 (1983). *See also* the swine flu cases, *e.g.,* Cardillo v. United States, 622 F. Supp. 1331 (D. Conn. 1984). For a description of how a strong and effective federal judge brought the Dalkon Shield Controversy to an end at reasonable transactional costs, see Ronald J. Bacigal, *May it Please the Court, A Biography of Judge Robert R. Merhige, Jr.* (1992); *but cf.* R. Sobol, *Bending the Law: The Story of the Dalkon Shield Bankruptcy* (1992).

22. Class actions, for example, are often not available in this category. In the *Dalkon Shield* litigation, the trial court certified a mandatory nationwide class. *In re* Northern District of California, Dalkon Shield I.U.D. Products Liability Litigation, 521 F. Supp. 1188, *modified,* 526 F. Supp. 887 (N.D. Cal. 1981). The United States Court of Appeals for the Ninth Circuit reversed the class certification, finding too many factual differences among the parties with respect to injuries and damages.

693 F.2d 847 (9th Cir. 1982), *cert. denied sub nom.* A. H. Robins Co. v. Abed, 459 U.S. 1171 (1983).

23. *See* Allen v. United States, 588 F. Supp. 247 (D. Utah 1984) (awarding recovery to some but not all civilian radiation plaintiffs). *See generally* Daniel Swartzman & Tom Christoffel, *Allen v. The United States of America*: The "Substantial" Connection between Nuclear Fallout and Cancer, 1 Touro L. Rev. 29 (1985).

24. *See* Yandle v. PPG Industries, 65 F.R.D. 566 (E.D. Tex. 1974) (class treatment denied for 135 former employees of an asbestos manufacturer partly because the varying degrees of exposure created difficulties in proving causation). *See also* Reserve Mining v. United States, 498 F.2d 1073 (8th Cir. 1974) (difficulties in determining the threat posed by asbestos led to the staying of an injunction).

Injury claims based on tobacco smoking have also raised difficult causation issues. *See* Pritchard v. Liggett & Meyers Tobacco Co., 370 F.2d 95 (3d Cir. 1966), *cert. denied*, 386 U.S. 1009 (1967); Lartigue v. R. J. Reynolds Tobacco Co., 317 F.2d 19 (5th Cir.), *cert. denied*, 375 U.S. 865 (1963); Is the Tobacco Industry Now Vulnerable to Lawsuits?, Wash. Post, July 28, 1985, at D1; Antismoking Climate Inspires Suits by the Dying, N.Y. Times, Mar. 15, 1985, at B1.

25. The following discussion from a paper prepared by an expert at the Georgetown University–based Institute of Health Policy Analysis illustrates the scientific perspective on causation:

> One can only rarely identify a specific, direct chain of biological events leading from an exposure to a toxic agent to a disease. The scientific concept of "cause" for the diseases associated with toxic torts, therefore, must necessarily be more abstract than one is accustomed to in engineering where "cause and effect" can be determined with relative precision and the chain of events traced directly. Causation is instead a statistical association in which an alteration in the frequency of the putative cause will be accompanied by a change in the frequency of the disease. Because the concept of cause is a statistical association, it is between categories of events and not individual cases.

P. Harter, The Dilemma of Causation in Toxic Torts i-ii (1985) (Institute for Health & Policy Analysis, Monograph No. 1010).

Harter suggests the following criteria for determining causation: (1) strength of association, (2) consistency of association, (3) correct timing, (4) specificity of association, (5) biological gradient, (6) biological plausibility, and (7) prevalence and exposure. *Id.* at ii–iii. *See also* Edwin J. Jacobs, Of Causation in Science and Law: Consequences of the Erosion of Safeguards, 40 Bus. Law. 1229 (1985); Howard Thomas Markey, Science and Law: A Dialogue on Understanding, A.B.A. J., Feb. 1982, at 154. The experience of courts facing difficult science-law questions when reviewing agency decisions are also relevant. *See* Devra L. Davis, The "Shotgun Wedding" of Science and Law: Risk Assessment and Judicial Review, 10 Colum. J. Envtl. L. 67 (1985).

26. *See* David Rosenberg, The Causal Connection in Mass Exposure Cases: A "Public Law" Vision of the Tort System, 97 Harv. L. Rev. 851 (1984); Bert Black & David E. Lilienfeld, Epidemiologic Proof in Toxic Tort Litigation, 52 Fordham L. Rev. 732 (1984); Note, Proving Causation in Toxic Torts Litigation, 11 Hofstra L.J. 1299 (1983). *See also* Final Report of the Royal Commission on the Use and Effects of Chemical Agents on Australian Personnel in Vietnam (July 1985) (nine-volume report finding no causal connection between exposure to Agent Orange and other chemical agents and any medical problems of Australian Vietnam veterans and their families). Subsequent evaluations in the United States were primarily for the purpose of determining whether there was a sufficient possible association between service in Vietnam and certain diseases to warrant Veteran Administration compensation. Wilbur J. Scott, *The Politics of Readjustment, Vietnam Veterans since the War*, chapters 5, Politics 101, and 8, Benefit of the Doubt (1993); Michael Gough, Dioxin: Perceptions, Estimates and Measures, chapter 11 in *Phantom Risk* (Kenneth R. Foster, David E. Bernstein, & Peter W. Huber eds., 1993). They would not have changed the conclusion of the Agent Orange litigation that causation under the tort law had not been shown.

Another commentator has noted that "[e]stablishing that a relationship exists between observed adverse health effects and chemical exposure is somewhat more complex than providing evidence that a future risk of injury/disease is associated with such exposures." J. Highland, Establishing a Relationship between Chemical Exposure and the Future Risk of Disease or Current Health Damage, in 1984 Hofstra Hazardous Waste Litigation Symposium 175.

The need for basic data in the causation area is acute. Once such data have been obtained, we must make certain they are available to those who need it to resolve causation disputes. For an interesting discussion of this topic see Committee on National Statistics, *Sharing Research Data* (1985) (available from National Academy Press), summarized in National Research Council, *News Report*, June 1985, at 15.

27. *See, e.g.,* Bethlehem Mines Corp. v. Massey, 736 F.2d 120 (4th Cir. 1984) (black lung benefits); Rutledge v. Tultex Corat, 308 N.C. 85, 301 S.E.2d 359 (1983) (cotton mill worker); Brawn v. St. Regis Paper, 430 A.2d 843 (Me. 1981) (paper mill, thirty-eight years employment); Swink v. Cone Mills, Inc., 65 N.C. App. 397, 309 S.E.2d 271 (1983) (cotton dust).

See also the discussion of the indeterminate plaintiff problem in one of the Agent Orange opinions. *In re* "Agent Orange" Product Liability

Litigation, 597 F. Supp. 740, 833-37 (E.D.N.Y. 1985).

The majority of the causation problems in this area arise in product liability cases. One commentator has noted that

> [t]hese hard cases [where cause in fact is difficult to prove] frequently involve products alleged to have caused some disease and usually have at least four common characteristics. There is a long latency period, often the better part of a lifetime, before the disease becomes manifest. There are a number of potential causes for the disease. The disease may occur without exposure to the defendant's product. Perhaps because of these first three characteristics, the most troublesome common characteristic of these cases is that there may be a genuine scientific controversy about whether the product in question can cause the disease at all.

Edwin J. Jacobs, Of Causation in Law and Science: Consequences of the Erosion of Safeguards, 40 Bus. Law. 1232 (1985). Jacobs goes on to suggest that causation may be a policy decision best decided in a nonjudicial forum. *Id.* at 1241. *See also* Bert Black & David E. Lilienfeld, Epidemiological Proof in Toxic Torts Litigation, 52 Fordham L. Rev. 732 (1984). This was essentially the ultimate result in the treatment of Agent Orange claims by the Department of Veterans Affairs in the United States.

The fear of electric fields has not yet resulted in a spate of cases because of doubts about general causality. *See* Electric Fields Create Nebulous Peril but Real Fear on L.I., N.Y. Times, Jan. 6, 1994, at B1. There are also problems of indeterminate plaintiffs and defendants. The former cannot be clearly ascertained since the alleged diseases such as leukemia are not signature diseases—that is to say, they exist widely in the population as a result of other causes. The producer of the harm is not clear either even though the greatest fear is of power lines, which are operated by a single known entity. My conversations with scientists suggest that, if there is a danger, local wiring may be much more important than power lines. Electric blankets, electric clocks, and other household devices throw off relatively small electric fields, but are much closer to people when, for example, they sleep a few inches away from an electric clock.

28. For example, in Sindell v. Abbott Laboratories, 26 Cal.3d 588, 607 P.2d 924, *cert. denied,* 449 U.S. 912 (1980), the California Supreme Court shook potential product liability defendants by permitting liability for DES injuries to be assessed on the basis of percentage of market share when the plaintiff was unable to prove which defendant caused the injury complained of. *But see* Murphy v. Squibb, 40 Cal. 3rd 672, 710 P.2d. 247 (Cal. 1985) (refusing to apply *Sindell* to a case

where plaintiff named as a defendant only one manufacturer with a 10 percent share of the market).

For an overview of enterprise liability and other forms of alternative liability, see Study Group Proposal, *supra* note 7, at 53–64. *See also In re* "Agent Orange" Product Liability Litigation, 597 F. Supp. 820–28.

29. Legislation has occasionally allowed injured parties to bypass the litigation process. For example, the Black Lung Benefits Act, 30 U.S.C. §§ 901–62 (1982), provides benefits to miners totally disabled by pneumoconiosis. The program is financed through federal funds, state workers' compensation, and direct payments by mine operators and other sources. *See also* Usery v. Turner Elkhorn Mining Co., 428 U.S. 1 (1975) (upholding the Act against challenges to its retroactive aspects, presumptions and evidentiary rules). *See generally* E. Gellhorn, *The "Black Lung" Act: An Analysis of Legal Issues Raised under the Benefit Program Created by the Federal Coal Mine Health and Safety Act of 1969 as Amended* (1981) (available from the National Judicial Center).

30. Where broad interpretation is allowed, many plaintiff-employees can circumvent workers' compensation limits by bringing a product liability action. *See, e.g.,* Waldrop v. Visitron Corp., 391 So. 2d 1274 (La. Ct. App. 1980); Robards v. Kantzer's Estate, 98 Mich. App. 414, 296 N.W.2d 265 (1980). *See also* Jane F. Lynch, The Clash between Strict Products Liability Doctrine and the Workers' Compensation Exclusivity Rule: The Negligent Employer and the Third-Party Manufacturer, 50 Ins. Couns. J. 35 (1983). An issue then arises whether the product manufacturer may receive contribution from the employer. Some courts have allowed such recovery, raising concerns that workers' compensation may be undermined by allowing indirectly what cannot be accomplished directly. *See, e.g.,* Skinner v. Reed-Prentice Division Package Machinery Co., 70 Ill. 2d 1, 374 N.E.2d 437 (1977), *cert. denied*, 436 U.S. 946 (1978). *See also* Arthur Larson, Third-Party Action over against Workers' Compensation Employer, 1982 Duke L.J. 483; A. Murphy, K. Santagata, & F. Grad, *The Law of Product Liability* 72 (1982).

31. Statutes of limitations for many injuries may begin running when a cause of action "accrues" or when the injury occurs, rather than when the victim discovers or should have discovered the injury. The meaning of "accrual" and "injury" often have been left to the courts, creating a multitude of differing interpretations in the various states. *See* White v. Johns-Manville Corp., 103 Wash. 2d 344, 693 P.2d 687 (1985) (accrual when the act or omission occurs); Steinhardt v. Johns-Manville Corp., 54 N.Y.2d 1008, 430 N.E.2d 1297, 446 N.Y.S.2d 244 (1981), *cert. denied, appeal dismissed sub nom.* Rosenberg v. Johns-Manville Sales Corp., 456 U.S. 967 (1982) (accrual at time of last exposure to asbestos); Garrett v. Raytheon Co., 368 So. 2d 516 (Ala. 1979) (cancer

symptoms appeared in 1975; accrual at time of last exposure to radiation in 1957). For a summary of state statutes of limitations, see Study Group Proposal, *supra* note 7, at 43–45. *See also In re* "Agent Orange" Product Liability Litigation, 597 F. Supp. 799–816; Leonard Finz, Changing the Statute of Limitations—A Case of Simple Justice, N.Y. L.J., Mar. 11, 1985, at 1, col. 3; Annot., 1 A.L.R. 4th 119 (1980 & Supp. 1985) (collected cases on when statute of limitations begins to run as to a cause of action for development of latent industrial or occupational disease); Annot., 91 A.L.R. 3d 991 (1979 & Supp. 1985) (collected cases on running of statute of limitations on product liability claims against manufacturers as affected by plaintiffs' lack of knowledge of defect allegedly causing personal injury or disease).

32. Some states already have coordination statutes. *See, e.g.*, Cal. Civ. Proc. Code §§ 404.1–404.8 (West 1973 & Supp. 1986).

33. *See supra* note 31 and accompanying text.

34. *See* Coburn v. 4-R Corp., 77 F.R.D. 43 (E.D. Ky. 1977) (Beverly Hills Supper Club fire).

35. *See In re* Federal Skywalk Cases, 680 F.2d 1175 (8th Cir.), *cert. denied sub nom.* Stover v. Rau, 459 U.S. 988 (1982) (Kansas City Hyatt Regency Skywalk collapse).

36. *See* ERIA v. Texas Eastern Transmission Corp., 377 F. Supp. 344 (E.D.N.Y. 1974).

37. For a review of the Bendectin litigation, *see, e.g.*, Joseph Sanders, The Bendectin Litigation: A Case Study in the Life Cycle of Mass Torts, 43 Hastings L.J. 301 (1992); Joseph Sanders, *From Science to Evidence: The Testimony on Causation in the Bendectin Case* (1992); Bendectin Battle, Law Scope, May 1985, at 25. *See also, e.g.*, Daubert v. Merrell Dow Pharmaceuticals, Inc. 113 S. Ct. 2786 (1993) (gatekeeping function of trial court in allowing or excluding expert testimony of Bendectin).

Much has been written about the difficulties courts have had with asbestos litigation. *See* National Center for State Courts, Judicial Administration Working Group on Asbestos Litigation (1984) (Final Report With Recommendations); Comment, An Examination of Recurring Issues in Asbestos Litigation, 46 Albany L. Rev. 1307 (1982); Paul Brodeur, Annals of Law—Asbestos, New Yorker, June 10, 17, 24 and July 1, 1985.

The Federal Judicial Center has also focused much attention on asbestos litigation:

Alternatives to trial continue to absorb the attention of federal judges confronted with extremely high caseloads. Nowhere was this more dramatically exhibited than in a Center-sponsored meeting . . . of judges, magistrates, and clerks from districts with a high number of asbestos cases. Obviously, settlement will be a major means of resolving most of these cases; the subject for discussion was how best to achieve that result. The conference heard the proponents of the tried-and-true techniques—reasonable trial dates firmly adhered to and greater participation of the judge in settlement negotiations. The participants also heard testimonials to innovative and promising techniques such as the summary jury trial, a subject covered in a prior Center report. And they heard calls for still more expansive court activity to encourage and facilitate settlement, for example, early advice to parties about the strength and worth of their cases, as well as intelligence systems that would draw on court records to inform parties of the probable discovery costs associated with proceeding to trial.

Federal Judicial Center, Annual Report 1984, at 24–25. *See also* T. Willging, *Asbestos Case Management: Pretrial and Trial Procedures* (1984).

38. *See* Yale Law School Program in Civil Liability, Center for Studies in Law, Economics, and Public Policy, George L. Priest, Lawyers, Liability and Law Reform: Effects on American Economic Growth and Trade Competitiveness (1993), at 48–55 (dismissing cases in which foreign courts refuse to accept United States judgments arising from torts, particularly where punitive damages are awarded).

39. A conference entitled "The Bhopal Disaster—A Challenge to the Law," sponsored by Columbia University's Parker School of Foreign and Comparative Law, addressed the special legal problems created by export of technology and management and the transnational nature of the incident. Colum. L. Sch. News, Mar. 1985, at 1, col. 3. Professor Murphy of the Columbia University School of Law stated that "the real issue in the Bhopal disaster is not whether liability will be established, but rather whether the measure of damages will be made under American or Indian law." *Id*. The Bhopal incident raises diverse issues of conflict of law, jurisdiction, attorneys' ethics, and corporate liability. *Id*. *See also* articles cited *supra* note 18; J. Strock, Coming to Terms with the Compensation Conundrum, A.B.A. J., Sept. 1985, at 68.

40. Although the extent of damage from acid rain remains largely unmeasured, it is generally accepted that it is a widespread problem. According to one study,

Southern California has recently been plagued by acid fogs with pH values as low as 2.2, sufficiently corrosive to sting eyes, nose and throat and to corrode metals. Other communities over widespread areas have experienced similar episodes. In April of 1974 rain with a pH of 2.4, 3,000 times the acidity expected in an average "natural" rainfall, fell on the small hamlet of Pitlochrie, Scotland. That same month, the western coast of Norway suffered through rain with a pH of 2.7, as acidic as vinegar. The most acidic rain ever recorded, 5,000 times more acid than normal, drenched Wheeling, West Virginia, a small town in the Appalachian Mountains of the Eastern United States in the fall of 1978.

G. Wetstone & A. Rosencranz, *Acid Rain in Europe and North America, National Responses to an International Problem* 3 (1983) (citations deleted). Another recent report links acid rain to pollution sources hundreds of miles away, raising serious compensation problems. Distant Pollution Tied to Acid Rain, N.Y. Times, Aug. 23, 1985, at A1. *See also* Marc Pallemaerts, Judicial Recourse Against Foreign Air Polluters: A Case Study of Acid Rain in Europe, 9 Harv. Envtl. L. Rev. 143 (1985); 7 States Sue for Tougher Rules on Acid Rain, N.Y. Times, Aug. 6, 1985, at B11; Quebec Agrees to a Study of Acid Rain Issue, N.Y. Times, Mar. 18, 1985, at A1.

In a report prepared in cooperation with the Canadian special envoy on acid rain, the President's special envoy on acid rain, Drew Lewis, noted that acid rain is currently causing significant ecological and economic damage. The report concludes that the commitment of substantial funds to acid rain research and control technologies is essential to preventing future damage. D. Lewis & W. Davis, Joint Report of the Special Envoys on Acid Rain (Jan. 1986).

Even if acid rain is eliminated in the near future, claims for damage that has already occurred are likely. The legal system must be prepared to handle these claims.

41. Deciding who will speak for a large group of litigants may present a serious problem to the legal decision maker. A flurry of activity surrounded the Indian government's selection of counsel to pursue claims arising out of the Bhopal tragedy. *See* Linda Greenhouse, The Lawyers Chosen by India, N.Y. Times, Mar. 12, 1985, at D1. The district court was obliged to name a three-member plaintiffs' management committee from among a large number of attorneys and several contending factions. *Id.* at D6.

42. *See supra* note 37.

43. Resolution adopted at Midyear Meeting of the Conference of State Chief Justices on Jan. 30, 1992, Jackson, Miss.; Resolution adopted by the Special Committee of Chief Justices, Forty-Fourth Annual Meeting in Lahaina, Maui, Haw., July 23, 1992 (including call for cooperation with federal and state courts on an institutional basis). *See* State Court Mass Tort Litigation Committee, Megatorts: The Lessons of Asbestos Litigation, June 25, 1992 (State Justice Institute) (recommendations for increasing efficiency through active administration by judges, without impairing fairness). This paper mentions favorably the recom-

mendation of the State Judges Asbestos Litigation Committee that, with respect to punitive damages, "federal transferee judges in the multidistrict litigation review the situation with a view toward establishing a national class action where a limited fund exists." *Id.* at 16. Such an action would prevent opt-outs and cover all state and federal cases. *See In re* Joint E. & S. Dists. Asbestos Litig., 134 F.R.D. 32 (E. & S.D.N.Y. 1990) (discussing power of federal court to stay all state and federal actions through device of mandatory class action).

44. *See generally* Francis E. McGovern, The Boundaries of Cooperation among Judges in Mass Tort Litigation (unpublished manuscript 1991).

45. *See* Parties Ordered to Show Cause Why Cases Should Not Be Consolidated, Asbestos Litig. Rep. 22, 391 (Andrews Pub. Feb. 1, 1991).

46. *See In re* Asbestos Prods. Liab. Litig., 771 F. Supp. 415 (Jud. Panel on MDL 1991).

47. Keene Corporation, Annual Report 4 (1992) (listing 17 companies involved in asbestos litigation that reorganized or liquidated under the bankruptcy laws). According to a later article it was Keene itself that was the seventeenth company forced into bankruptcy as a result of asbestos litigation; its settlement of the dispute on a global basis was disrupted when an appellate court dismissed its application for class action status. *See* Andrew Blum, Asbestos Pacts Hit Some Snags, Nat'l L.J. Dec. 20, 1993, at 3.

48. *See, e.g.,* Richard Gotcher, The Never-Ending Mediation Process: Eagle-Pitcher Highlights Chapter 11's Shortcomings, Turnarounds and Workouts, Aug. 15, 1993, at 1 (describing inefficiencies, waste, and delay in bankruptcy proceedings involving asbestos defendants); *Asbestos Verdicts Reached,* Nat'l L.J., Aug. 23, 1993, at 6 ($9.3 million verdict in consolidation of 9,600 suits).

49. The insurance industry is currently struggling with the issue of whether to insure certain activities that may lead to large and unpredictable liability. The uncertainty of what substantive law will apply in a specific case creates uneasiness about insuring those activities, especially when product liability, hazardous waste, or pollution is involved. *See* Insurance Against Pollution Is Cut, N.Y. Times, Mar. 11, 1985, at A1. The article concludes "[m]ost of those interviewed urged that the Federal Government set limits on liability for long-term pollution and reform the personal injury, or tort, legal system that has produced large damage awards." *Id.* at D12. *See also* Liability Insurance Skyrockets, Wash. Post, Aug. 4, 1985, at K1; The Liability Squeeze, Newsday, Jan. 19, 1986, at 5.

The concerns of insurance companies have increased in light of findings of a "duty to defend" in latent injury product liability actions. *Cf.* American Home Products Corp. v. Liberty Mutual Insurance Co., 748 F. 2d 760 (2d Cir. 1984).

The Resource Conservation and Recovery Act, 42 U.S.C. §§ 6901–6987 (1982 & Supp. I 1983), and the Comprehensive Environmental Response, Compensation and Liability Act, 42 U.S.C. §§ 9601–9657 (1982 & Supp. I 1983), both contain liability insurance coverage requirements. Study Group Proposal, *supra* note 7, at 162–72. Imposition of strict liability for injuries on hazardous waste producers would increase their potential liability exposure. According to the Study Group Proposal, continued insurability probably would require tort law reforms through federal legislation. *Id*. at 177. *See* Donald V. Jernberg, Insurance for Environmental & Toxic Risks: A Basic Analysis of the Gap between Liability and Coverage, 34 Fed. of Ins. Couns. Q. 123 (Winter 1984); Richard Epstein, The Legal and Insurance Dynamics of Mass Tort Litigation, 13 J. Legal Studies 475 (1984). The insurance industry in the short haul does not respond directly to changes in tort law. *See* W. Kip Viscusi, *Reforming Products Liability* 192 (1993) ("general failure of insurance pricing to adjust rapidly to the profound economic consequences of changes in the structure of tort law").

One possible solution is for manufacturers to self-insure. *See* Acmat Set to Form Insurance Unit, N.Y. Times, Mar. 16, 1985, at B1.

50. For example, the village of Port Jefferson was forced to eliminate many recreational programs, including ice skating and athletics, after it lost its liability insurance. *See* One Village's Life without Insurance, Newsday, Jan. 19, 1986, at 23. In similar fashion, G. D. Searle & Company recently halted sales of IUDs in the United States. *See* Searle, Assailing Lawsuits, Halts U.S. Sale of Intrauterine Devices, N.Y. Times, Feb. 1, 1986, at A1.

The unavailability of product liability insurance at reasonable rates because of unknown liability can impose high costs on society. Consider the shortage of whooping cough vaccine in late 1984 that arose when one of only two remaining manufacturers withdrew from the market rather than pay "sharply higher rates for liability insurance." *See* Maker of Vaccine Quits Market, N.Y. Times, Dec. 12, 1984, at A21. The shortage has sparked a spirited debate about who should pay for damages. The answer is far from clear. *See* Vaccine Injuries: Who Should Pay?, Nat'l L.J. Apr. 1, 1985, at 1. The controversy resulted in federal protective legislation for the vaccine manufacturers. *Id*. at 27. *See also* U.S. Plan to Curb Damage Claims Aims to Avert Vaccine Shortages, N.Y. Times, Apr. 7, 1985, at A1. When Connaught Laboratories of Swiftwater offered to supply the whooping cough vaccine, it was on the condition that Congress would indemnify it against suits brought on behalf of children who suffer adverse reactions. N.Y. Times, Dec. 20, 1984, at A19. *See also* Institute of Medicine, Division of Health Promotion and Disease Prevention, Vaccine Supply and Innovation 160 (1985) (urging "political decision makers to develop a compensation system for vaccine-related injury" and recommending "that action be taken to reduce the serious deterrents to vaccine manufacturing and innovation that arise from the unpredictable nature of the current liability situation"); Peter W. Huber, Bad Science, Worse Justice, Across the Board, Jan. 1986, at 30, 36 ("Something is dangerously wrong when a company needs legislative protection before it will dare to manufacture a risk-reducing vaccine.").

Other commentators have noted that notwithstanding the benefit society receives from the drug, it is important that those who are injured be compensated. The Cost of Ignoring Vaccine Victims, N.Y. Times, Oct. 15, 1984, at A18.

51. *See* Robert Kasten & Gene Kimmelman, Is It Time for a Uniform Product Liability Law?, A.B.A. J., May 1985, at 38 (a debate between Senator Robert Kasten, who supports uniform product liability legislation, and Gene Kimmelman, the director of a consumer interest group that opposes the legislation); The Time to Stabilize Product Liability is Now, N.Y. Times, Apr. 18, 1985, at A26; Products Liability: The New Morass, N.Y. Times, Mar. 10, 1985, at C1. Expressive of federal concern, for example, is S. 100, 99th Cong., 1st Sess. (1985). This bill and many others like it introduced subsequently would have set uniform procedures, statutes of limitations, and notice requirements and limit available compensation and fee recovery. *Id. See* Senate Comm. on Commerce, Science, and Transportation, Product Liability Act, S. Rep. No. 476, 98th Cong., 2d Sess. (1984), for a committee report analyzing a previous bill. *See also* Michel A. Coccia, Uniform Product Liability Legislation: A Proposed Federal Solution, 1983 Trial Lawyers Guide 236; Michael A. Brown, The Role of Legislation, in Annual Chief Justice Earl Warren Conference on Advocacy Report on Product Safety in America 51 (Roscoe Pound Foundation, 1984).

Achieving this uniformity through changes in rules of choice of law is suggested by the American Law Institute and others. *See, e.g.,* Patrick J. Borchers, The Origins of Diversity Jurisdiction, The Rise of Legal Positivism, and a Brave New World for Erie and Klaxon, 72 Tex. L. Rev. 79, 131 (1993). But conflicts pragmatism leads to a lack of predictability of operative substantive law. *See, e.g.,* Patrick J. Borchers, Conflicts Pragmatism, 56 Alb. L. Rev. 883 (1993).

52. For an analysis of the use of special masters, see Vincent M. Nathan, The Use of Masters in Institutional Reform Litigation, 10 U. Tol. L. Rev. 419 (1979). Doubts about the authority to use such personnel in institutional reform litigation do not apply to their limited use in civil mass tort cases. *See* David I. Levine, The Authority for the Appointment of Remedial Special Masters in Federal Institutional Reform Litigation: The History Reconsidered, 17 U.C. Davis L. Rev. 753 (1984); Fred Strasser, On Orders from the Court, Student Law.,

Jan. 1985, at 24 (discussing the role of special masters in the judicial system).

53. *See, e.g., In re* "Agent Orange" Product Liability Litigation, 611 F. Supp. 1296, 1319 (E.D.N.Y. 1985) (use of clerical staff in assessing attorney fee awards).

54. Rule 702 governs the testimony of experts; Rule 703 governs the bases of an expert's opinion. *See* chapter 7, *infra*, Ethics of Scientists.

55. *See* Daubert v. Merrell Dow Pharmaceutical, Inc., 113 S. Ct. 2786 (1993); Jack B. Weinstein, Improving Expert Testimony, 20 U. Rich. L. Rev. 473 (1986).

56. Statutory limits on the amount of recovery have been generally upheld by the courts. *See* Duke Power Co. v. Carolina Environmental Study Group, 438 U.S. 59 (1978) (upholding the liability limitation of the Price-Anderson Act); Trans World Airlines v. Franklin Mint Corp., 466 U.S. 243 (1984) (upholding the valid application of the Warsaw Convention).

An interesting attempt to limit liability in the air disaster area, the multilateral treaty popularly known as the Warsaw Convention has proved to be somewhat less successful than hoped because of limits on its applicability and the existence of numerous ways in which limits may be circumvented. For example, the Warsaw Convention applies only to a case involving an "accident," a term that the courts have interpreted narrowly. *See* Air France v. Saks, 470 U.S. 392 (1985) (Warsaw Convention does not apply to damage to a passenger's ear occurring during normal flight).

57. *See* Study Group Proposal, *supra* note 7.

58. 42 U.S.C. § 2210 (1982 & Supp. I 1983). Under the Price-Anderson Act, strict liability is applied to injuries stemming from nuclear power production activities. In return for the application of strict liability, liability is capped at a specific level. *Id.* To encourage development of the nuclear industry, the government originally indemnified up to the limit. Now, however, retrospective premiums are assessed against industry participants, eliminating the need for indemnification by 1985. L. Rockett, *Financial Protection Against Nuclear Hazards: Thirty Years of Experience Under the Price-Anderson Act* 19 (1984). Many have attacked the liability limitations of the act in the belief that plaintiffs would recover larger sums through litigation. *See, e.g.,* Tightening Nuclear Liability, N.Y. Times, Jan. 7, 1986, at A21. In a response to these attacks, Professor Arthur Murphy of Columbia Law School noted:

> The belief that the tort system will produce a satisfactory result is, of course, central to this thesis. . . . The unspoken premise is that with-

out Price-Anderson [plaintiffs] would receive full compensation. . . . Their chief response would be a possible action against the utility where the action took place, against a company likely to be bankrupt or close to it because of having lost a major portion of its power production. . . . As has become distressingly clear in recent years, the tort system is not capable of handling mass accidents in a coherent, affordable fashion.

Murphy, Letter to the Editor, N.Y. Times, Jan. 31, 1986, at A30. The important feature is the trade-off between strict liability—and therefore guaranteed compensation—and the liability limitation. *See also* Buffington, The Price-Anderson Act: Underwriting the Ultimate Tort, 87 Dick. L. Rev. 679 (1983).

59. The Wellington proposal was designed to establish a nonjudicial facility to handle asbestos claims more fairly and efficiently and to end litigation between asbestos defendants and their insurers. It was to handle asbestos-related claims on behalf of member insurers and producers. Center for Public Resources, Agreement concerning Asbestos-Related Claims: Highlights (1984) (on file in the office of the Columbia Journal of Environmental Law). It was expected to benefit claimants by providing a central place to file claims without going to court, hence reducing legal costs and speeding up the time process for resolution of claims. Stephen Tarnoff, Asbestos Producers Mulling Agreement, Business Insurance, May 28, 1984, at 12. The facility would only settle claims if all the producers agreed and would not pay punitive damages. *Id.* at 79.

Many plaintiffs' lawyers remained skeptical of the proposal. They planned to "wait and see" if the victims really benefit or if the unified settlement approach gives defendants more leverage. Riley, Plaintiffs' Bar Wary of Asbestos Accord, Nat'l L.J., July 8, 1985, at 3. The Wellington facility was abandoned by defendants after disagreements among them. A smaller group of about twenty defendants now operate a useful cooperative defense group.

60. One interesting proposal was released by Senator John Danforth, then Chairman of the Senate Commerce Committee. In what is labeled a "New Staff Working Draft on Product Liability Reform" (Nov. 27, 1985), Danforth recommended establishing a procedure that makes it easier (and allegedly more efficient) for eligible claimants to recover compensation while simultaneously placing limitations on the nature and amount of the recovery awarded. The Danforth proposal would have created a "no-fault" compensation system for certain products, but such compensation would have been limited to "net economic loss," i.e., medical expenses and lost earnings reduced by claimant compensation recovered from government or employee benefit programs, private

insurance policies and medical plans, or workers' compensation programs. Expedited payment would have been made within sixty days of the filing of a claim.

61. A declaration of bankruptcy can serve to consolidate numerous claims in one forum. *See* Note, Cleaning Up in Bankruptcy: Curbing Abuse of the Federal Bankruptcy Code by Industrial Polluters, 85 Colum. L. Rev. 870 (1985) (suggesting that the bankruptcy code could facilitate settlement of pollution disputes); The Manville Settlement: Pressure, Percolation, Nat'l L.J., Aug. 19, 1985, at 30; 3 Manville Insurers Agree to Pay, Newsday, Feb. 5, 1985, at 37 (Manville Corporation's insurance carrier agreed to pay up to $112 million in asbestos-related health claims). The funds set aside in the Manville Trust proved grossly inadequate. Bankruptcy was also filed in another major product liability case. *See* Robins, in Bankruptcy Filing, Cites Dalkon Shield Claims, N.Y. Times, Aug. 22, 1985, at A1. Plaintiffs are often opposed to consolidation through bankruptcy. *See* Attorneys for Plaintiffs Object to Robins Filing, N.Y. Times, Aug. 23, 1985, at D5 (suggesting that the consolidation of suits in the bankruptcy court would limit the size of the damages that could be recovered).

62. Legislatures have the power to limit compensation by eliminating or restricting traditional damages theories. For example, no-fault insurance schemes that limit or eliminate recovery for pain and suffering have generally been upheld against a variety of challenges. The leading case is Pinnick v. Cleary, 360 Mass. 1, 271 N.E.2d 592 (Mass. 1971). It involved a no-fault scheme that limited recovery for lost wages and eliminated recovery for pain and suffering. The court found the scheme valid despite equal protection and due process challenges because the statute bore a rational relationship to legitimate state objectives and provided an adequate substitute for abrogated rights. *See also* Montgomery v. Daniels, 38 N.Y.2d 41, 340 N.E.2d 444 (1975) (upholding statute that had no recovery for pain and suffering unless expenses are over $500); Bushnell v. Sapp, 194 Colo. 273, 571 P.2d 1100 (1977) (upholding $500 threshold); Chapman v. Dillan, 415 So. 2d 12 (Fla. 1982) (approving the Florida law's threshold).

Some no-fault statutes, however, have been invalidated on equal protection or due process grounds. *See* Kenyon v. Hammer, 142 Ariz. 69, 688 P.2d 961 (1984) (striking down provisions that limited compensable components of pain and suffering as a violation of state's equal protection clause). *But see* Manzanares v. Bell, 214 Kan. 589, 522 P.2d 1291 (1974) (upholding the Kansas no-fault insurance scheme against due process and equal protection challenges despite limitations on pain and suffering recovery). *See generally* J. O'Connell & R. Henderson, *Tort Law, No Fault and Beyond, The Future* (1975).

Malpractice litigation is another example of an area where legislated limits have been upheld. In Fein v. Permanent Medical Group, 38 Cal. 3d 137, 695 P.2d 665, *appeal dismissed,* 474 U.S. 892 (1985), the California Supreme Court upheld against constitutional challenges the statutory limit on recoverable noneconomic damages in medical malpractice actions. New York considered similar limitations. *See* Doctors & Insurers, N.Y. Times, Feb. 28, 1985, at B4. *See also* Hoffman v. United States, 767 F. 2d 1431 (9th Cir. 1985) (upholding California's statutory limit on noneconomic recovery).

Any proposal to limit recovery must be mindful that the amounts awarded may serve a deterrent as well as a compensation purpose. Limiting pain and suffering awards, punitive damages, and excessive awards, however, will probably not have a negative effect in most areas. Consider medical malpractice awards:

> Some few people obtain excessive verdicts. Many more who were wrongfully injured are not aware of their rights or are not getting very much in the way of help from the tort system. . . . Huge lump sum payments are often not a sensible way to ensure that the injured person will receive proper medical and other support during his or her lifetime. . . . Obviously, punitive damages are undesirable. In this field, such awards are wild cards that serve no useful public purpose.

J. Weinstein, Medical Malpractice Cases: A View from the Federal Courthouse, Remarks at the Federation of Jewish Philanthropies Service Corporation Third Annual Conference 5, 13 (Oct. 11, 1985).

63. Some attempts have been made to simplify trials. *See* William Luneburg & Mark A. Nordenberg, Specially Qualified Juries and Expert Nonjury Tribunals: Alternatives for Coping with the Complexities of Modern Civil Litigation, 67 Va. L. Rev. 887 (1981). *See also* procedures discussed *supra* note 17.

64. According to one study of asbestos litigation, plaintiffs on the average receive 32 percent of defendants' (and their insurers') litigation expenses. J. Kakalik, P. Ebener, W. Felstiner, & M. Shanley, *Costs of Asbestos Litigation* 40 (1983). Plaintiffs actually get a smaller percentage of the total expended because most estimates do not take into account court costs, costs of company executive time, and other miscellaneous costs such as insurance premiums used for insurance company overhead costs.

One group of commentators argues that the costs of ordinary litigation are justified, even to defendants, in light of the recoveries that tort plaintiffs can expect. David M. Trubek, Austin Sarat, William L. F. Felstiner, Herbert M. Kritzer, & Joel B. Grossman, The Costs of Ordinary Litigation, 31 UCLA L. Rev. 72 (1983).

65. The multidistrict litigation procedure is pursuant to 28 U.S.C. § 1407 (1982). According to the 1985 Annual Report of the Multidis-

trict Judicial Panel, 14,489 actions have been consolidated for pretrial proceedings pursuant to this procedure since 1968. Annual Report of the Judicial Panel on Multidistrict Litigation 1 (Sept. 1985). The report says that although transfer may increase the workload in some districts, overall "[t]he burden imposed on the courts by the coordination or consolidation of actions for pretrial proceedings under Section 1407 is . . . less than that imposed by separate handling in different districts of a like number of related cases." *Id.* at 17. Subsequent experience has not changed these conclusions.

Courts often recognize the useful role that multidistrict discovery plays. *See, e.g.,* Causey v. Pan Am World Airways, 66 F.R.D. 392 (E.D. Va. 1975) (court denied a class action certification, finding multidistrict litigation treatment would be superior); Yandle v. PPG Indus., 65 F.R.D. 566 (E.D. Tex. 1974) (same).

66. A proposal to expand multidistrict litigation to allow consolidation for trial as well as pretrial was introduced in Congress. *See* H.R. 4159, 98th Cong., 1st Sess. (1983) (introduced by Rep. Kastenmeier). This is essentially the proposal adopted in 1993 by the American Law Institute. Its suggestion includes both state and federal case transfers to one judge.

It should be noted that although under the current multidistrict litigation system cases are consolidated only for pretrial purposes, most cases are never referred back to the courts in which they originated. Instead, they are either settled, or transferred for all purposes, pursuant to the change of venue statute, 28 U.S.C. § 1404 (1982), to the court in which they were consolidated.

67. U.S. Const. art. I, § 8, cl. 3.

68. There have been a number of decisions delineating the breadth of federal commerce power. *See, e.g.,* Garcia v. San Antonio Metropolitan Transit Auth., 469 U.S. 528, *rehearing denied,* 479 U.S. 1049 (1985); Heart of Atlanta Motel, Inc. v. United States, 379 U.S. 241 (1964); Wickard v. Filburn, 317 U.S. 111 (1942).

69. Under existing procedure, if essentially the same action seeking the same relief is going forward in both state and federal court, one action should be stayed or dismissed while the other goes forward. Typically, the federal court exercises jurisdiction over the case. Colorado River Water Conservation District v. United States, 424 U.S. 800, 817 (1976). Only when "exceptional circumstances," as outlined in *Colorado River,* are present is the federal court directed to dismiss its action in favor of the concurrent state proceeding. *See* Telesco v. Telesco Fuel and Masons' Materials, 765 F.2d 356 (2d Cir. 1985) (dismissal of federal action warranted where the federal and state action were essentially the same, the state court had jurisdiction over the case for much longer, and the case was to be decided on state law).

Illustrative of the general rule is *In re* Baldwin-United Corp. (Single Premium Deferred Annuities Ins. Litigation), 770 F.2d 328 (2d Cir. 1985). The district court preliminarily enjoined thirty-one states from bringing suit in state court on behalf of private plaintiffs with state law claims related to federal law claims pending in the Baldwin-United multidistrict securities class action. The lower court invoked the All Writs Act, 28 U.S.C. § 1651 (1982), finding that the injunction was needed to preserve its jurisdiction and to prevent frustration of ongoing settlement negotiations. Baldwin-United, 770 F.2d at 333.

The Second Circuit affirmed, analyzing the All Writs Act issue in light of a similar statute, the Anti-Injunction Act, 28 U.S.C. § 2283 (1982), which prohibits a federal court from enjoining pending state court actions except, *inter alia,* when necessary in aid of its jurisdiction. The Court of Appeals stated that prosecution of parallel, related state court actions "could only serve to frustrate the district court's efforts to craft a settlement in the multidistrict litigation before it" and constituted "a major threat to the federal court's ability to manage and resolve the actions against the remaining defendants." Baldwin-United, 770 F.2d at 337, 338. Thus, so long as a substantial prospect of settlement was present, the injunction was proper. *Id.* at 338. *See also, e.g., In re* Asbestos Cases in the Eastern and Southern Districts of New York, 134 F.R.D. 32 (1990); *In re* Agent Orange, 781 F. Supp. 934 (1992).

Other solutions to the federal-state concurrent jurisdiction problem have been proposed. Many of these proposals, however, seek to limit federal jurisdiction, making consolidation of similar cases for trial more difficult. *See* the discussion of a series of proposed diversity jurisdiction modification bills at 129 Cong. Rec. H26023 (daily ed. July 29, 1983) (Statement of Rep. Kastenmeier).

70. U.S. Const. art. III.

71. *See supra* notes 8, 68–69 and accompanying text.

72. The preemption of state tort law by federal statute is commonplace. *See, e.g.,* Consumer Product Safety Act, 15 U.S.C. §§ 2051(b)(3), 2072 (1982); Civil Rights Act of 1971, 42 U.S.C. § 1983 (1982); Occupational Safety and Health Act, 29 U.S.C. §§ 651–678 (1982). Acts that include compensation schemes also preempt state law. *See, e.g.,* Longshoremen's and Harbor Workers' Compensation Act, 33 U.S.C. § 903 (1982); Price-Anderson Act, 42 U.S.C. § 2210 (1982 & Supp. I 1983); Black Lung Benefits Act, 30 U.S.C. § 955 (1982). Similarly, the Supreme Court has held that state courts have an obligation to enforce federal law even where it conflicts with prevailing state policy. *See* Testa v. Katt, 330 U.S. 386 (1947); Martin H. Redish, Supreme Court Review of State Court "Federal" Decisions: A Study in Interactive Federalism, 19 Ga. L. Rev. 861, 891 (1985).

73. U.S. Const. art. VI.

74. National Center for State Courts, Judicial Administration Working Group on Asbestos Litigation (1984).

75. *Id.* at 5–29.

76. The potential magnitude of this second wave has astounded many commentators. *See* Stephen Tarnoff, The Crisis Grows, Asbestos Property Damage Could Cost Billions of Dollars, Business Insurance, Feb. 18, 1985, at 1; Asbestos Claims Mount, Newsday, Jan. 31, 1985, at 6. *But see* S.C. School District Loses Asbestos Damage Suits, Nat'l L.J., Sept. 2, 1985, at 5 (asbestos defendants successful in second asbestos-contaminated property suit to go to trial; questions raised about the success of future contaminated property claims). *Cf.* Robert D. Land, Danger in the Classroom: Asbestos in Public Schools, 10 Colum. J. Envtl. L. 111 (1985) (indicating that the removal of asbestos is essential to health). Lack of affordable insurance available to companies removing the asbestos compounds the problems.

77. *See* Federal Judicial Center, Annual Report (1984).

78. *See* discussion in Comment, Federal Mass Tort Class Actions: A Step Toward Equity and Efficiency, 47 Alb. L. Rev. 1180 (1983) (concerning the problem of lack of coordination resulting in several ongoing state actions).

79. *See* Jack B. Weinstein, Coordination of State and Federal Judicial Systems, 57 St. John's L. Rev. 1, 10–12 (1982).

80. After all, conflict of laws decisions are made in part based on "the interstate judicial system's interest in obtaining the most efficient resolution of controversies. . . ." World-wide Volkswagen Corp. v. Woodson, 444 U.S. 286, 292 (1980). *Compare* Alfred Hill, The Judicial Function on Choice of Law, 85 Colum. L. Rev. 1585 (1985) *with* Harold L. Korn, The Choice of Law Revolution: A Critique, 83 Colum. L. Rev. 772 (1983).

81. *See, e.g., In re* "Agent Orange" Product Liability Litigation, 580 F. Supp. 690 (E.D.N.Y. 1984) (in a product liability action, federal law or consensus law applied to questions regarding manufacturer's liability, government contract defense, and punitive damages, even though plaintiff had not stated a federal cause of action).

82. The liability of an insurer depends in part on when the court finds the injury actually occurred. If it occurs at exposure to a substance, then an insurer may be liable for all future injuries. If at manifestation, the current insurer may be liable for injuries stemming from past exposures. *Compare* Insurance Co. of North America v. Forty-Eight Insulations, 633 F.2d 1212 (6th Cir. 1980), *cert. denied,* 454 U.S. 1109 (1981) (exposure) *with* Eagle-Pitcher Indus., Inc. v. Liberty Mutual Ins., 682 F.2d 12 (1st Cir. 1982), *cert. denied,* 460 U.S. 1028 (1983) (manifestation).

83. *See, e.g.,* Fla. Stat. Ann. § 25.031 (Harrison 1986). The Florida

certification procedure provides that any federal court may certify questions of state law to the Florida Supreme Court. *Id.* The Florida statute was strongly endorsed by the Supreme Court in Clay v. Sun Insurance Office Ltd., 363 U.S. 207 (1959). The Court noted that "[e]ven without such a facilitating statute we have frequently deemed it appropriate . . . to secure an authoritative state court's determination of an unresolved question of its local law." *Id.* at 210. Such a procedure was used in White v. Johns-Manville Corat, 103 Wash. 2d 344, 693 At2d 687 (1985).

84. Pressure for application of a single substantive law is strong. The Fifth Circuit's refusal to apply federal common law in the asbestos litigation, for example, drew a strong dissent. *See* Jackson v. Johns-Manville Sales Corp., 750 F.2d 1314 (5th Cir. 1985).

85. *See* Senate Commerce Committee, New Staff Working Draft on Product Liability Reform (Nov. 27, 1985). *See also supra* notes 51, 60.

86. Among the groups opposed to the legislation are the ABA, the Association of Trial Lawyers of America, the AFL-CIO, the National Association of Attorneys General, Congress Watch, the Consumer Federation of America, Consumers Union, the National Conference of State Legislatures, the National Governors Association, and the Conference of Chief Justices. Product Liability Bill Fails in Senate Committee, Washington Letter, June 1, 1985, at 1, 4 (published by American Bar Association).

87. An analogy can be drawn between mass tort legislation that would be applicable only under certain circumstances and disaster aid which is available only in certain situations. The Disaster Relief Act of 1974, 42 U.S.C. §§ 5121–5202 (1982), provides relief to mitigate immediate hardships caused by widespread destruction. The aid is available only where the President has declared a federal emergency. *Id.* at § 5141.

88. For a general discussion of this sort of plan, see *In re* "Agent Orange" Product Liability Litigation, 597 F. Supp. 740 (E.D.N.Y. 1984); David Rosenberg, The Causal Connection in Mass Exposure Cases: A "Public Law" Vision of the Tort System, 97 Harv. L. Rev. 851 (1984).

89. Comprehensive Environmental Response, Compensation and Liability Act of 1980, 42 U.S.C. § 9601–9657 (1982 & Supp. I 1983).

90. *See, e.g.,* S. 917, 98th Cong., 1st Sess. (1983) (Victim Compensation and Pollution Liability Act introduced by Senators Stafford and Randolf); S. 945 and 946, 98th Cong., 1st Sess. (1983) (Environmental Poisoning Compensation Act introduced by Senators Mitchell and Randolf); H.R. 2482, 98th Cong., 1st Sess. (1983) (Toxic Victim Compensation Act introduced by Rep. LaFalce); H.R. 2582, 98th Cong., 1st Sess. (1983) (Hazardous Substance Victim Compensation Act of 1983 introduced by Rep. Markey); H.R. 2330, 98th Cong., 1st Sess. (1983)

(Toxic Victim Compensation Act introduced by Rep. LaFalce). None of these bills was enacted.

During the reauthorization of the Comprehensive Response, Compensation and Liability Act (CERCLA), 42 U.S.C. § 9601 (1982), an amendment authored by Senator Mitchell was considered that would have created a five-year, five-state demonstration Victim Compensation Program. Office of United States Senator George J. Mitchell, Press Release (May 1, 1985) (on file in the office of the Columbia Journal of Environmental Law). A Senate Committee report noted that such a program would assure that when CERCLA is next considered "Congress will have information required to make reasoned judgments on the issue of victim compensation." Sen. Comm. on Environment and Public Works, Superfund Amendments of 1984, S. Doc. No. 631, 98th Cong., 2d Sess. 31 (1984). The proposal was eventually defeated in the Senate by a vote of 49 to 45. Senate Passes Superfund, Sierra Club National News Report, Oct. 11, 1985, at 1.

For an overview of hazardous waste victim compensation proposals see Note, Developments in Victim Compensation Legislation: A Look Beyond the Superfund Act of 1980, 10 Colum. J. Envtl. L. 271 (1985). Most of these proposals have not received wide acceptance, indicating that it is unlikely such a plan will become a reality in the near future. *Id.* at 293.

For a similar plan aimed at compensation of radiation victims see Radiation Cancer Compensation Act of 1983, S. 921, 98th Cong., 1st Sess., *reprinted* in 129 Cong. Rec. S3918 (daily ed. Mar. 24, 1983) (introduced by Sen. Hatch).

91. *In re* Bendectin Products Liability Litigation, 749 F.2d 300 (6th Cir. 1984).

92. *See, e.g., In re* "Agent Orange" Product Liability Litigation, 100 F.R.D. 718, 725–29 (E.D.N.Y. 1983), *mandamus denied*, 725 F.2d 858 (2d Cir.), *cert. denied*, 465 U.S. 1067 (1984); *cf. In re* Asbestos School Litigation, 104 F.R.D. 422 (E.D. Pa. 1984) (discussion of punitive damages in class actions); *In re* Asbestos Litigation in Eastern and Southern Districts of New York, 129 B.R. 710 (1991).

93. *See supra* notes 88–90 and accompanying text (discussion of victim compensation plans).

94. State jurisdictions are split on whether a multistate class will be certified in state court. *Compare* Phillips Petroleum Co. v. Shutts, 105 S. Ct. 2965 (1985) (Kansas courts could obtain jurisdiction through a class action over nonresidents, but Full Faith and Credit Clause prohibited application of Kansas law to all transactions), and Miner v. Gillette, 87 Ill. 2d 7, 428 N.E.2d 478 (1981), *cert. dismissed*, 459 U.S. 86 (1982) (upholding certification of out-of-state class members), *with* Klemow v. Time, Inc., 466 Pa. 189, 352 A.2d 12, *cert. denied*, 429 U.S. 828

(1976) (certification of class denied) and Feldman v. Bates Mfg., 143 N.J. Super. 84, 362 A.2d 1177 (1976) (reversing order of certification).

95. 472 U.S. 797 (1985).

96. For example, service of process under the Federal Interpleader Act, 28 U.S.C. § 2361 (1982), is nationwide, providing a party who may be subjected to multiple liability with a remedy in the federal courts which would be unavailable in any state court.

In a recent Rhode Island case involving federal environmental statutes, nationwide service of process was denied. See Violet v. Picillo, 613 F. Supp. 1563 (D.R.I. 1985). The court noted that although nationwide service of process might further the goals of the Comprehensive Environmental Response, Compensation, and Liability Act, such extended service should be approved by a legislative, not a judicial, decision. *Id.* at 1573.

97. U.S. Const. art. III.

98. *See supra* note 41. *See* chapter 4, *infra,* Ethics of Lawyers.

99. *Id.* Attorneys' fees have raised a number of questions. *See, e.g., In re* "Agent Orange" Product Liability Litigation, 611 F. Supp. 1396 (E.D.N.Y. 1985); 611 F. Supp. 1452 (E.D.N.Y. 1985). It seems that adequate but not exorbitant fees are essential to induce competent lawyers to take cases with merit, but how this is to be accomplished given the risks and uncertainties is not clear. A speech on malpractice litigation by the author noted:

> At the high end of the scale, attorneys' fees in some cases are much too large. The transactional costs in this type of litigation are too great. The Greater New York Hospital Association estimates that only 20 percent of the amounts spent on malpractice is retained by the injured person. While the Association is an interested party, this estimate is not substantially out of line with those resulting from studies in other tort fields.

J. Weinstein, *supra* note 62, at 6.

100. Voluntary cooperation of this sort occurred in the litigation involving MER/29, a drug marketed between 1956 and 1962 for use in lowering cholesterol levels. A correlation between cataract development and use of the drug was found. Over 1,500 civil suits were filed against manufacturers of the drug. A voluntary group was formed by plaintiffs' attorneys to serve as a clearinghouse for the litigation. Over 288 member lawyers or law firms paid between $100 and $300 for assistance from the group which concentrated mainly on managing the discovery process. *See* Paul D. Rheingold, The MER/29 Story—An Instance of Successful Mass Disaster Litigation, 56 Calif. L. Rev. 116 (1968).

Other examples of voluntary coordination include the formation of the Dalkon Shield Group in 1974, the DES cases, and the actions against Chevrolet for motor mount failure. *See* Paul D. Rheingold, Mass Disaster Litigation and the Use of Plaintiffs' Groups, Litigation, Spring 1977, at 18.

One attorney active in mass tort litigation noted that "it is necessary in almost all cases against large corporate defendants, such as the chemical and drug manufacturers, to put together a syndicate of lawyers from different firms around the country in order to come up with the money necessary to perform the massive amount of discovery vital to winning a case." Annual Meeting of Association of Trial Lawyers of America, 54 U.S.L.W. 2094–95 (Aug. 13, 1985). The need for such cooperation is apparent in light of the complexity of many of these cases. *See* Megatrials, Nat'l L.J., Mar. 25, 1985, at 1.

101. *See supra* note 59 (discussion of the Wellington asbestos proposal).

102. The Center for Public Resources in New York (CPR) initiated efforts to develop pragmatic methods for reducing the social and economic costs of corporate legal and regulatory disputes. It publishes a manual presenting papers on corporate dispute resolution issues. Of particular interest is a paper on disputes involving science and technology. *See, e.g.*, Stephen B. Goldberg, Eric D. Green, & Frank E. A. Sander, *Dispute Resolution* (1985).

Courts are now becoming active in alternative dispute resolution:

> Under rule 53 of the Federal Rules of Civil Procedure, courts are authorized to appoint special masters "to secure the just, speedy, and inexpensive determination of every action." Traditionally, special masters have been used as fact finders, charged with conducting hearings and making findings of fact in complex, fact-intensive litigation. More recently, Rule 53 has been used as authority for the appointment of settlement masters to help mediate between the parties in complex, multi-party disputes. Settlement masters are effective for the same reasons that traditional mediators are effective. The difference is that through the use of Rule 53, the court can greatly assist the parties in mediation.
>
> . . .
>
> Some court-administered Alternative Dispute Resolution mechanisms should be organized on a district-wide level. Among these is court-annexed arbitration. Several federal courts have adopted local rules providing for mandatory, non-binding arbitration. A pilot program—one of ten in the Federal courts—is due to start operating soon in the Eastern District. Money to finance it is being made available by the Administrative Office because the Chief Justice is particularly interested in encouraging this practice. Under the program, all

cases involving claims for money damages only in an amount of $50,000 or less will be referred to a panel of three arbitrators. Any party dissatisfied with the arbitrators' decision will have the right to demand a trial de novo. At the trial de novo, evidence concerning the conduct or conclusion of the arbitration proceeding will be inadmissible. The court-annexed arbitration program is being tried in the Eastern District [of New York] because it appears to have worked well elsewhere. Similar programs in other Federal District courts— particularly the Eastern District of Pennsylvania—have reduced the number of cases going to trial by as much as 50%.

J. Weinstein, Warning: Alternative Dispute Resolution May Be Dangerous, 12 Litigation 5 (1986). The United States District Court for the Eastern District of New York now has a pamphlet outlining its many ADR procedures.

103. *See* Representatives for Future Claimants Approved, Legal Times, Mar. 4, 1985, at 10 (discussing appointment of a representative for future asbestos claimants in Johns-Manville's bankruptcy proceeding).

104. For example, in Haygood v. Olin, Doc. No. 83-5021, a special master assisted in the handling of a massive toxic tort case based upon DDT exposure in Alabama. Fred Strasser, On Orders from the Court, Student Lawyer, Jan. 1985, at 27. The special master designed a case-management system for discovery involving over nine thousand plaintiffs. Of the plan one defense counsel noted:

> Without the master's plan the extensive discovery in the case might have been impossible. . . . The court might not have permitted taking 9000 plaintiff's depositions. Even had the court been willing to go along with such a massive project, the cost would have been prohibitive.

Id. *See also* articles cited, *supra* note 52.

105. A special master prepared an extensive settlement proposal in the Agent Orange litigation. *See* Report of the Special Master Pertaining to the Disposition of the Settlement Fund, *In re* Agent Orange Products Liability Litigation, 580 F. Supp. at 690.

106. One example of the use of an expert by a judge was United States District Judge Merhige's retention of a financial expert to help him determine whether to certify a class action in the Dalkon Shield litigation. Judge Plans to Hire Expert in Robins Case, Wash. Post, Aug. 12, 1985, at Bus. 3; Michael Hoenig, Drawing the Line on Expert Opinions, N.Y. L.J., May 22, 1985, at 1.

As the author has noted elsewhere:

> Courts have been reluctant to invoke use of their power to appoint neutral experts, but such experts can be indispensable in ensuring

proper disposition of complex cases requiring expert testimony on technical issues. In particular, neutral experts can be helpful in cases involving complex statistical evidence. Courts often have difficulty determining which side's experts to believe because judges are not sufficiently familiar with proper statistical technique to be able to identify improprieties. A neutral expert can analyze each side's statistical evidence and then explain to the judge or jury the strengths and weaknesses of each party's statistical case. Besides helping to ensure a more just outcome, neutral experts indirectly help encourage settlements. Litigants with weak cases will be less likely to go to trial in hopes of fooling the finder of fact with an impressive but specious statistical display when they know that a neutral expert will be there to demonstrate the flimsiness of their claims.

J. Weinstein, *supra* note 102. *See also* chapter 7, *infra*, Ethics of Scientists.

We will need to reevaluate the use of independent scientific experts, perhaps drawing on the German model. Some commentators have suggested expanding the use of experts to assist judges, particularly in the area of review of agency decisions. For example, one proposal would create a group of technical experts who would review and summarize technical data in the record and serve as an intermediary between judges and other technical experts. Sheldon L. Trubatch, Informed Judicial Decisionmaking: A Suggestion for a Judicial Office for Understanding Science and Technology, 10 Colum. J. Envtl. L. 255 (1985).

Some of the work of the National Research Council, such as that of the Panel on Statistical Assessments as Evidence in the Courts, may also be helpful. *See* Draft Recommendations of the Panel on Statistical Assessments as Evidence in the Courts (May 1985) (on file in the office of the Columbia Journal of Environmental Law).

107. For example, Workers' Compensation and Black Lung Compensation.

108. *See supra* note 30.

109. A Department of Labor Report on Occupational Diseases addresses the adequacy-of-compensation issue:

- A general measure of the adequacy of compensation for occupational disease victims can be ascertained by examining the extent to which lost earnings are replaced. Such data show that public and private income support programs replace about forty percent of the wages lost by individuals who are severely disabled from an occupational disease, compared with a sixty percent replacement rate for occupational injury victims. The major source of extra income support received by occupational injury victims is workers' compensation.

- The major sources of income support for those severely disabled from an occupational disease are: social security (fifty-three percent), pensions (twenty-one percent), veterans benefits (seventeen percent), welfare (sixteen percent), workers' compensation (five percent), and private insurance (one percent).

- Not all of those severely disabled from an occupational disease receive income support, while some receive support from more than one program. Among those severely disabled from an occupational disease, one out of every four receive no income support payments. One in every three receive multiple benefits.

United States Department of Labor, An Interim Report to Congress on Occupational Diseases 2–3 (1980).

110. Black Lung Benefits Act, 30 U.S.C. § 901 (1982). *See supra* note 29.

111. *See* Lewis H. Klar, New Zealand's Accident Compensation Scheme: A Tort Lawyer's Perspective, 33 Toronto L.J. 80, 81 (1983).

The act prohibits suits in New Zealand for personal injury or death by accident in New Zealand, replacing tort law compensation with "a compulsory, universal social insurance program." *Id.* at 81, 85.

112. *See* Asbestos Workers' Recovery Act, H.R. 5966, 98th Cong., 2d Sess. (introduced in Congress June 28, 1984, to provide prompt, exclusive, and equitable compensation, as a substitute for inadequate tort remedies for disabilities or death resulting from occupational exposure to asbestos). *See also* S. 2708, 98th Cong., 2d Sess. (introduced May 23, 1984, by Senators Percy, Pell, and Inouye). *See also* the victim compensation proposals cited, *supra* note 90.

113. *See* Study Group Proposal, *supra* note 7, at 196.

In broad outline, the Study Group recommends a two-tier system of remedies. The first tier, which is expected to be the part of the system most heavily relied on by persons injured by exposures, will provide an administrative compensation scheme without showing of fault. The administrative compensation scheme would be established by federal legislation, but would be operated largely by the states pursuant to federal law. . . . The second tier would keep the existing system of tort law in several states, with some recommendations for procedural and other improvements.

Id. at 197.

114. Other commentators are critical of the Study Group Proposal. *See e.g.*, Theodore L. Garrette, Compensating Victims of Toxic Sub-

stances; Issues Concerning Proposed Federal Legislation, 13 Envtl. L. Rep. (Envtl. L. Inst.) 10,172 (1984).

115. *But see* Toxic Waste Termed Far Greater than U.S. Estimates, N.Y. Times, Mar. 10, 1985, at A1 (indicating that the EPA may have severely underestimated the number of national priority hazardous waste sites).

116. *See* articles cited, *supra* note 49. *See also* Harvey L. Pitt & Karl Groskaufmanis, Staving Off Punitive Disaster, Nat'l L. J., Dec. 6, 1993, at 18; Victor Schwartz & Mark Behrens, The American Law Institute's Reporter's Study on Enterprise Responsibility for Personal Injury: A Timely Call for Punitive Damage Reform, 30 San Diego L. Rev. 263 (1993).

117. *But see* James Granelli, The Attack on Joint and Several Liability, A.B.A. J., July 1985, at 61 (discussing how allowing contribution may lead to the deep pocket paying a disproportionate share of the recovery).

118. Duke Power Co. v. Carolina Envtl Study Group, 438 U.S. 59 (1978); *see supra* note 62 (no-fault compensation discussion).

119. The constitutionality of workers' compensation schemes has been upheld under both the federal and state constitutions. For example, in Booth Fisheries Co. v. Industrial Comm'n of Wisconsin, 271 U.S. 208 (1926), the Wisconsin Workman's Compensation Act was upheld despite the claim that application of strict liability denied due process to employers. Similar issues of constitutionality have been raised concerning automobile accident no-fault compensation plans.

120. Final Report of Micronesian Claims Commission, Part II at 79 (1976).

121. *Id.* at 86.

122. *See* Jamison M. Selby & David P. Stewart, The Practical and Legal Aspects of Arbitrating Claims before the Iran-United States Claims Tribunal, 18 Int'l Law. 211 (1984).

123. The Tris statute gives the United States Claims Court jurisdiction to "hear, determine and render judgment upon any claims for losses sustained by a producer, manufacturer, distributor, or retailer of children's sleepwear" when the losses were caused by use of Tris to comply with federal law. The act requires proof of proper disposal of treated fabric and specifically rejects the use of class actions before the court. *See* United States Court of Claims, Jurisdiction—Tris Sleepwear, Pub. L. No. 97-395, 96 Stat. 2001-4 (1982).

124. The 1969 International Convention on Civil Liability for Oil Pollution, *done* Nov. 29, 1969, 9 I.L.M. 45 (1970), which the United States has yet to ratify, sets maximum liability limits and places all liability for oil pollution damage on the ship owner. Because this convention did not provide for complete compensation, the International Conven-

tion on the Establishment of an International Fund for Compensation for Oil Pollution Damages, *done* Dec. 18, 1969, 11 I.L.M. 284 (1972), was created to fill in the gaps in the 1969 convention. The fund was established through contributions assessed on contracting states receiving oil at ports.

The United States has signed a claims settlement agreement with the parties involved in the 1979 Sedco oil well blowout and spill in the Gulf of Mexico. *See* IXTOC Agreement between Sedco and the United States, 22 I.L.M. 580 (1983).

125. The Convention on Third Party Liability in the Field of Nuclear Energy (Paris Convention), signed July 29, 1960, has operated the channeling concept [for liability] at an international level successfully for almost a quarter of a century. This system . . . [involved] . . . (1) strict but exclusive liability, (2) limitation of liability, (3) compulsory financial security, and (4) a government-financed excess liability fund.

Study Group Proposal, *supra* note 7, at 263.

126. Litigation has at times been successful in resolving international disputes. *See* United States v. Canada, 3 R. Int'l Arb. Awards 1911 (1941) (Trail Smelter). This case arose out of damage done to United States crops, pasture lands, trees, agricultural interests, and livestock by fumes from a privately owned smelting plant in British Columbia. The claim was submitted to an arbitral tribunal that existed under a 1935 convention between the United States and Canada. The tribunal held that the case involved a controversy between two governments, assumed jurisdiction, awarded damages of $78,000 to the United States, and prescribed a detailed permanent regime for the smelter which included maximum permissible levels of pollution.

For the most part, however, efforts to determine international liability have been futile. *See* G. Wetstone & A. Rosencranz, *Acid Rain in Europe and North America, National Responses to an International Problem,* 156–63 (1983); J. Carroll, *Environmental Diplomacy* (1983) (examining Canadian–United States transboundary environmental relations). *But see* New York v. Thomas, 613 F. Supp. 1472 (D.D.C. 1985) (granting summary judgment to plaintiffs in a suit by northeastern states to compel the EPA to comply with Clean Air Act by requiring midwestern states to abate transnational boundary pollution of eastern Canada).

127. *See* G. Wetstone & A. Rosencranz, *supra* note 126, for a discussion of international efforts in the area of acid rain.

The available mechanisms offer no effective recourse for nations seeking redress for transboundary pollution problems. Domestic suits are too limited in their scope. Diplomatic channels are, in general, not adequate to promote the changes in national energy and environmental policies which may be necessary to avoid widespread environmental damage. The international legal structure offers useful principles of environmental responsibility, but they are neither sufficiently defined nor sufficiently enforceable to support effective application to specific controversies. Finally, the international Clean Air Act provisions in the United States and Canada, while admirable in their intent, are too generally formulated and too vulnerable to domestic political pressures to yield the changes in national policy needed to address transboundary pollution problems.

Id. at 162. *See also* Office of Technology Assessment, U.S. Congress, Acid Rain and Transported Air Pollutants: Implications for Public Policy 300–311 (1984).

128. ECE Convention of 1979 on Long Term Transboundary Pollution, T.I.A.S. No. 10591, 18 I.L.M. 1442 (1979). The agreement was signed by all thirty-four members of the UN Economic Commission for Europe (ECE) and came into force in February 1983. Signatories to the 1979 Convention—most European countries and the United States and Canada—have agreed to "endeavor to limit and, as far as possible, gradually reduce and prevent air pollution including long-range transboundary air pollution using the best technology 'economically feasible.'" F. Grad, *Treatise on Environmental Law* § 13.03[4][b] (1983).

129. The United States has pledged itself to cooperate in this area. *See* 28 U.S.C. § 1782(a) (1982), which authorizes judicial assistance to foreign tribunals:

Section 1782 reflects Congress' determination to broaden the scope of international judicial assistance afforded by the federal courts. The legislative history stresses international cooperation—having the U.S. adjust its procedures to those of sister nations, thereby providing equitable and efficacious procedures for the benefit of tribunals and litigants involved in cases with international aspects.

53 U.S.L.W. 2410 (Feb. 26, 1985).

Commentators have noted that, because of intracountry boundaries, the problems of transboundary liability may go beyond the difficulties of gaining the agreement of individual countries. In Canada, for example, provincial jurisdiction may play an important role. *See* The American Assembly and Counsel on Foreign Relations, Canada and the United States: Enduring Friendship, Persistent Stress 42 (1985).

This problem is not relevant in the United States because treaties are traditionally supreme over state law. In Missouri v. Holland, 252 U.S. 416 (1920), the Supreme Court upheld the Migratory Bird Treaty Act of July 3, 1918, 40 Stat. 755, against a challenge that it unconstitution-ally interfered with the rights reserved to the States by the Tenth Amendment. The Migratory Bird Treaty, signed by the United States and Canada, specified hunting seasons as well as other protectionist measures. These are matters usually thought to be within the power of the states. In response to the challenge, the Court noted:

> Here a national interest of very nearly the first magnitude is involved. It can be protected only by national action in concert with that of another power. The subject matter is only transitorily within the State and has no permanent habitat therein. . . . We see nothing in the constitution that compels the Government to sit by. . . . It is not sufficient to rely upon the states. The reliance is in vain, and were it otherwise, the question is whether the United States is forbidden to act. We are of the opinion that the treaty and statute must be upheld.

Id. at 435. Despite attempts to overturn this decision by constitutional amendment in the 1950s, this reasoning is still authoritative. This would seem to indicate that the federal government will be able to bind the states to the terms of any treaty dealing with transboundary pollu-tion.

130. 42 U.S.C. § 2210(e) (1982). *See* L. Rockett, *Financial Protec-tion against Nuclear Hazards: Thirty Years of Experience under the Price-Anderson Act* 14 (1984).

131. 42 U.S.C. § 2210(f) (1982 & Supp. I 1983).

132. *Id.* at § 2210(o).

133. *See* European Countries Adopt Product Liability Directive, Business Insurance, Aug. 5, 1985. The main purpose of this directive was to harmonize product liability laws between members of the Euro-pean Economic Community. The directive uniformly imposes strict lia-bility but leaves to the individual member countries the decisions regarding the state-of-the-art defense and caps on compensation. As the Community has become more integrated, more sophisticated provisions have been developed.

134. L. Rockett, *Financial Protection against Nuclear Hazards: Thirty Years of Experience under the Price-Anderson Act* (1984).

135. Study Group Proposal, *supra* note 7, at 4.

136. *Id.* at 178–254.

137. Emergency Price Control Act of 1942, Pub. L. No. 77-421, 56 Stat. 23 (1942).

138. 15 U.S.C. § 3416(c) (1982). The court was granted *exclusive* jurisdiction over controversies arising under the emergency provisions of the Natural Gas Policy Act of 1978. 15 U.S.C. § 717(u) (1982). It was staffed by convening a panel from among twenty-nine available fed-

eral judges. The Temporary Court of Appeals was originally established by the Economic Stabilization Act of 1970 and had jurisdiction over price control disputes. *See* 12 U.S.C.A. § 1904, notes (1982).

The United States Foreign Intelligence Surveillance Court is another example of a specialized court. The court is composed of seven federal district court judges from different judicial circuits, designated by the Chief Justice of the United States for a term of seven years. Foreign Intelligence Surveillance Act, 50 U.S.C. § 1803(a) (1982). Individual judges sit approximately every six months. *Id. See also* Alan N. Kornblum & Lubomyr M. Jachnycky, America's Secret Court: Listening in on Espionage and Terrorism, The Judges Journal, Summer 1985, at 14, 16. The court must authorize all electronic surveillance of foreign powers and agents of foreign powers for foreign intelligence purposes. *Id.*

The Act establishes a court of review consisting of three circuit court judges, similarly designated by the Chief Justice for staggered seven-year terms, who sit to hear appeals from the lower court. *Id.*

A proposal for another specialized court, the Environmental Court, was rejected. Section 9 of the Federal Water Pollution Control Act of 1972 directs the President of the United States through the Attorney General to consider the feasibility of an environmental court. Pub. L. No. 92-500, 86 Stat. 816 (1972). The court would have had jurisdiction over any suit that involved a claim under one of a number of designated environmental statutes. The Attorney General chose not to recommend formation of such a court, citing the potential problems of maintaining its caseload, determining jurisdiction, and perhaps additional delay. *See* Scott C. Whitney, The Case for Creating a Special Environmental Court System—A Further Comment, 15 Wm. & Mary L. Rev. 33 (1973); Comment, The Environmental Court Proposal: Requiem, Analysis, and Counter Proposal, 123 U. Penn. L. Rev. 676 (1975). Whether these problems would have been significant is open to question. Benefits would include the consolidation of judicial energy and expertise. In addition, some consolidation of cases would probably have taken place under the system.

139. *See* Letter from the Honorable Howard T. Markey, Chief Judge, United States Court of Appeals for the Federal Circuit (Mar. 7, 1985) (in 1985, of twenty-seven law clerks, sixteen had scientific or technical undergraduate degrees) (on file at the Columbia Journal of Environmental Law).

140. *See supra* note 61.

141. *See supra* note 50.

142. In the Oraflex controversy, debate centered around the light punishment given to the parties responsible for withholding information on the danger of the drug from the public. Newsday, Sept. 9, 1985, at 52, col. 1 (Eli Lilly & Co. fined a "mere" $25,000 for not reporting

foreign deaths from the arthritis drug Oraflex while simultaneously seeking federal approval for this arthritis medicine; "The [Justice] department's easy treatment of Lilly trivializes the offense"); Official Says He Barred More Prosecutions at Lilly, N.Y. Times, Sept. 12, 1985, at A23 (Deputy Attorney General overruled staff lawyers' recommendation to prosecute federally three Eli Lilly & Co. officials for failing to disclose Oraflex-related deaths and ailments). Other Lilly officials who were prosecuted pleaded guilty. N.Y. Times, Aug. 22, 1985, at A16.

143. Study Group Proposal, *supra* note 7, at 255–267.

144. *See supra* text accompanying notes 63–140.

145. Intercircuit judicial assignments are common. Between February 1 and August 15, 1985, the Chief Justice approved forty-seven assignments of thirty-eight judges. Report of the Judicial Conference Committee on Intercircuit Assignments 1 (Sept. 1985) (available in the office of the Columbia Journal of Environmental Law). *See* Note, Considerations Relating to the Enactment of Venue Schemes as Applied to Specialty Courts, 93 Colum. L. Rev. 1738 (1993).

146. The Bar Harbor Resolution is a series of proposals adopted by the Committee on Court Administration "for the purpose of assuring that cases likely to be protracted, difficult, or unusual are not allowed to pend for periods more lengthy than that required for so-called routine cases." Annual report of the Director of the Administrative Office of the United States Courts 70–71 (1972) (Report of the Proceedings of the Judicial Conference of the United States, Washington, D.C., Mar. 15 and 16, 1971, and Oct. 28 and 29, 1971).

147. The Price-Anderson Act triggering system may provide a useful analogy. The system is activated when the Nuclear Regulatory Commission (NRC) determines that a nuclear incident is an "extraordinary nuclear occurrence" (ENO). According to NRC regulations, the ENO determination is a two-part test. The first threshold is met when a discharge or disposal constitutes a "substantial amount of source, special nuclear or by-product material, or has caused substantial radiation levels offsite." 10 C.F.R. § 140.81(b)(1) (1985). The second part of the test requires a determination that "there have in fact been or will probably be substantial damages to persons offsite or property offsite." 10 C.F.R. § 140.81(b)(2) (1985).

The first threshold—presence of radioactivity—is met when there is a perturbation of the environment clearly above that which could be anticipated from normal activities. The second threshold—injury or damage—is met when:

(1) The Commission finds that such event has resulted in the death or hospitalization, within 30 days of the event, of five or more people located offsite showing objective clinical evidence of physical injury

from exposure to the radioactive, toxic, explosive, or other hazardous properties of source, special nuclear, or byproduct material,
    or
(2) The Commission finds that $2.5 million or more damage offsite has been or will probably be sustained by any one person, or $5 million or more of such damage in the aggregate has been or will probably be sustained, as the result of such event; or $5,000 or more of such damage will probably be sustained by each of fifty or more persons, provided that $1 million or more of such damage in the aggregate has been or will probably be sustained, as the result of such event.

U.S. Nuclear Regulatory Commission, The Price-Anderson Act—The Third Decade E-3 (1983) (Report to Congress).

Such specific criteria are required because there must be no doubt about when the strict liability provisions of the Act apply. The same certainty would be required of the National Disaster Court.

148. *See* discussion *supra* note 65.

149. *In re* Asbestos Insulation Material Products Liability Litigation, 431 F. Supp. 906, 909 (J.P.M.D.L. 1977) (denying multidistrict treatment of asbestos suits).

150. *See supra* note 147.

151. *See supra* note 87.

152. In response to the Three Mile Island nuclear plant accident, representatives of the nuclear insurance industry arrived on March 29, 1979, to ascertain the necessity of an emergency claims office. When the Governor of Pennsylvania advised certain persons to evacuate the area, the insurance companies paid the living expenses of people who complied. A total of $1,217,000 in evacuation claims was paid to some 3,170 claimants. In addition, $92,000 in lost wage claims was paid. U.S. Nuclear Regulatory Commission, The Price-Anderson Act—The Third Decade A-7. *See also* L. Rockett, *Financial Protection against Nuclear Hazards: Thirty Years of Experience under the Price-Anderson Act* 28 (1984).

153. *See supra* notes 56–60. The movement to put a cap on punitive damage awards has already begun. *See* Montana Puts Cap on Punitive Damage Awards, Nat'l L.J., Apr. 22, 1985, at 7, col. 1; Punitive Award Rejected in Market Share Case, Nat'l L.J., May 27, 1985, at 6, col. 1. Commentators have discussed the problems created by large punitive damage awards. Irene A. Sullivan, Multiple Punitive Damage Awards in Huge Cases Pose Risks, Nat'l L.J., Jan. 3, 1985, at 11, col. 1.

The Supreme Court, however, limited federal preemption of punitive damage awards under state law. In Silkwood v. Kerr-McGee Corp., 464 U.S. 38 (1984), the Supreme Court reversed a lower court denial of punitive damages, finding that the Price-Anderson Act did not preempt such an award. In light of Silkwood, the preemption of state law punitive damages provisions must be express.

154. *Cf.* Jack B. Weinstein, Coordination of State and Federal Judicial Systems, 57 St. John's L. Rev. 1, 1–29 (1982).

155. Some attempts along this line have already been made; however, many commentators believe that so far these transboundary efforts have not been successful. *See, e.g.,* G. Wetstone & A. Rosencranz, *Acid Rain in Europe and North America, National Responses to an International Problem* 123–30 (1983). Other commentators are more encouraging:

> The United States could deal differently with some of the possible problems by international agreement, depending on the nations involved. Nations receiving dangerous weapons from the United States Government should assume the risks of having them, and the agreements of transfer should expressly preclude claims against contractors, just as they already preclude claims against the United States Government. The NATO nations might extend the Status of Forces Agreement to apply to accidents caused by weapons of NATO members that are not presently covered by the agreement; it would be appropriate to apply the loss-sharing principles embodied in the agreement, or perhaps to extend them to distribute among all NATO members the financial burden of catastrophic losses from accidents caused by NATO military activities. Bilateral agreements on the NATO model might similarly be extended to apply to accidents not now covered by them.

Catastrophic Accidents, *supra* note 2, at 21.

Other types of agreements may also be possible, at least with some other nations not sharing common military activities or purposes. Such agreements might express the existence of an American obligation to make some compensation for accidents as well as the principle that both the United States and the nation affected by catastrophe would participate in the determination of claims.

One model of successful transnational dispute resolution is the International Center for Settlement of Investment Disputes (ICSID). This organization exists pursuant to a convention between the members of the International Bank For Reconstruction and Development. Convention on the Settlement of Investment Disputes Between States and Nationals of Other States, Oct. 14, 1966, 17 U.S.T. 1270, T.I.A.S. No. 6090, 575 U.N.T.S. 159. The Convention sets procedures for arbitration and conciliation of international disputes concerning investments.

An international consulting engineering association is working with international dispute resolution groups to limit future litigation over contract disputes. Kristensen, The Contribution Lawyers Make, Int'l Consulting Engineer 2 (1983).

156. *See* Dames & Moore v. Regan, 453 U.S. 654 (1981) (upholding the settlement of the Iranian claims).

157. *See, e.g.,* Michie v. Great Lakes Steel Division Nat'l Steel Corp., 495 F.2d 213 (6th Cir. 1974), *cert. denied,* 419 U.S. 997 (Canadian citizens' action against United States polluters); United States v. Hooker Chem. & Plastics Corp., 776 F.2d 410 (2d Cir. 1985) (Canada awarded no relief but allowed to intervene in a nuisance action against a chemical company).

158. New Bhopal Law May Affect Future Role of U.S. Lawyers, Nat'l L.J., Mar. 11, 1985, at 4, col. 3.

The law directs the central government to frame a "scheme" for registering claims and collecting and disbursing compensation for victims. It also includes the power to settle and to represent individuals with suits filed. *Id.*

159. G. Wetstone & A. Rosencranz, *Acid Rain in Europe and North America, National Responses to an International Problem,* 45–162 (1983). Wetstone and Rosencranz noted in part that:

> [courts] are of far less utility in the context of efforts to prevent the large-scale environmental effects associated with overall transboundary pollution flow, especially where remedial actions would require significant changes in national air pollution policies.

Id. at 160.

CHAPTER 3

1. I am grateful for the assistance of my former law clerks Samuel W. Buell and Laraine Pacheco for their assistance on this chapter and chapters 4–8. These materials were printed in an abbreviated form in the Northwest University Law Review, 88 Nw. U. L. Rev. 469 (1994). Permission to reprint was granted by the Law Review. Commentaries on these article were: Geoffrey C. Hazard, Jr., Reflections on Judge Weinstein's Ethical Dilemmas in Mass Tort Litigation, 88 Nw. U. L. Rev. 569 (1994); Linda S. Mullenix, Mass Tort as Public Law Litigation: Paradigm Misplaced, 88 Nw. U. L. Rev. 579 (1994); Thomas W. Henderson & Tybe A. Brett, A Trial Lawyer's Commentary on One Jurist's Musing of the Legal Occult: A Response to Judge Weinstein, 88 Nw. U. L. Rev. 592 (1994).

2. The American Law Institute's ongoing project on "The Law Governing Lawyers," for example, has dealt with the single-party model and generally has not addressed problems raised by mass cases. *See generally* American Law Institute, Restatement of the Law Governing Lawyers,

Tentative Drafts Nos. 1–5 (1989–1992).

3. One commentator has stated the problem as follows:

> When the rules governing the professional conduct of attorneys were first given shape in the late nineteenth and early twentieth centuries, an important assumption as to the nature of law practice animated their structure. Specifically, the lawyer-client relationship was envisioned almost exclusively in terms of a simple, elegant paradigm that centered on a one-to-one personal relation between the layman and the professional.

Vincent Robert Johnson, Ethical Limitations on Creative Financing of Mass Tort Class Actions, 54 Brook. L. Rev. 539, 539–40 (1988); *see also* Lawrence J. Fox, Litigation in 2050: A Backward-Forward, Topsy-Turvy Look at Dispute Resolutions, 60 Fordham L. Rev. 297 (1991) (contrasting practice of law in 1932 with that of today).

4. David Rosenberg, The Causal Connection in Mass Exposure Cases: A "Public Law" Vision of the Tort System, 97 Harv. L. Rev. 849 (1984) (advocating public law approach by courts to deal with mass tort cases by combining aggregative procedural devices and an active supervising court role).

5. *The World Almanac and Book of Facts* 386 (Mark S. Hoffman ed., 1993).

6. *Id.* at 387 (as of 1990, with large numbers of illegal immigrants uncounted).

7. 5 *The Collected Works of Abraham Lincoln* 537 (Roy P. Basler ed., 1953); *see also* Garry Wills, *Lincoln at Gettysburg: The Words that Remade America* (1992) (historical meaning of Gettysburg address).

8. Thom Loverro, Wash. Times, Oct. 5, 1993, at B7. Baltimore Orioles purchased by Peter M. Angelos, Esq., from profits litigating thousands of asbestos lawsuits obtained from union connections.

9. *See* Jody Brennan, "He's One Of Us," Forbes, Aug. 16, 1993, at 84 (describing "entrepreneurial" lawyer who has over ten thousand clients).

10. *See* Letter to Counsel for Asbestos Personal Injury Plaintiffs from Stephen M. Snyder, Aug. 25, 1993.

11. *See In re* Joint E. & S. Dists. Asbestos Litig., 129 B.R. 710, 771–73 (E. & S.D.N.Y. 1991) (discussing representative of future claimants in Manville case), *vacated,* 982 F.2d 721 (2d Cir. 1992), *modified,* 993 F.2d 7 (2d Cir. 1993); Memorandum and Order and Preliminary Injunction, *In re* Joint E. & S. Dists. Asbestos Litig., No. CV 93-2129 (E. & S.D.N.Y. July 1, 1993) (appointing representative of subclass of future claimants in limited fund class action encompassing claims against Keene Corporation); *see also In re* "Agent Orange" Prod. Liab. Litig., 781 F. Supp. 902 (E.D.N.Y. 1991), *aff'd,* 996 F. 2d 1425 (2d Cir. 1993) (approval of class action which would have encompassed

over a million veterans, binding even those who were not aware that they had been injured or were members of the class), *cert. denied sub nom.* Ivy v. Diamond Shamrock Chemicals, 114 S. Ct. 1125 (1994).

12. *See* Hilary Putnam, The Permanence of William James, Bull. of the Amer. Academy of Arts & Sci. 17, 30 (Dec. 1992) ("For James, as for Socrates, the central philosophical question was *how to live.*") (emphasis in original). *Cf.* David Lyons, *Moral Aspects of Legal Theory* (1993).

13. Some of my colleagues on the bench and in academia as well as many outstanding members of the plaintiffs' and defense bar have considered these questions with me in private conversations. These discussions proved invaluable in stimulating my thoughts. In interviewing the following people for this study it was agreed that they would not be quoted by name; summaries of the interviews or correspondence with the names redacted have been sent to the Northwestern University Law Review for filing. The persons interviewed were:

Plaintiffs' attorneys: Thomas W. Henderson, Stanley Levy, Eugene Locks, Paul D. Rheingold, Sol Schreiber, Sybil Shainwald, David S. Shrager, Robert B. Steinberg, and Melvyn Weiss.

Defendants' attorneys: John D. Aldock, Sheila L. Birnbaum, Marc S. Klein, and Roger E. Podesta.

Academics: Margaret A. Berger, Daniel J. Capra, John C. Coffee, Jr., Margaret Farrell, Monroe H. Freedman, Mark Peterson, Judith Resnik, Aaron Twerski, and Georgene M. Vairo.

Judges: Justice Helen E. Freedman, Chief Judge Stanley H. Fuld, Judge Eugene H. Nickerson, and Judge Charles P. Sifton. I had many informal conversations with other judges.

Special masters: Kenneth R. Feinberg and Francis E. McGovern.

Scientists: Various members of panels I sat on for the American Academy of Science seminars and Carnegie Foundation Commission on Science, Technology, and Government were interviewed informally.

14. It can be argued that the growth of a powerful plaintiffs' bar together with post–New Deal legislation constituted a major swing toward consumers' rights after a move favoring producers in the mid-nineteenth century. *See, e.g.,* Morton J. Horwitz, *The Transformation of American Law, 1780–1860,* at 253–54, 266 (1977). Horwitz explains:

> By the middle of the nineteenth century the legal system had been reshaped to the advantage of men of commerce and industry at the expense of farmers, workers, consumers, and other less powerful groups within society. . . . [There was a] subjection of an already internally eroded tradition of substantive justice to an increasingly formal set of legal rules, which were themselves now stridently justified as having nothing to do with morality.

Stuart M. Speiser, in *Lawsuit* (1980), attributes the present high-flying status of the plaintiff tort lawyer to the following developments:

1. The right to *jury trial* in most civil cases.
2. The *contingent fee* (a percentage of the money the client receives upon winning the case, and no fee at all if the case is lost).
3. The *entrepreneur-lawyer* (an advocate who carries a client on his shoulders by providing and financing services that most individual clients cannot afford—services which can put an average individual on an equal litigation footing with a corporate giant).

Largely because of these three developments—which we might call the trinity of torts—our civil courts today are open to almost anyone who has a legitimate grievance. But that has not always been so. We started out with a civil legal system that was useful only to the rich and powerful—a copy of the harsh eighteenth-century English system.

Id. at 120 (emphasis in original).

The pendulum began to swing somewhat toward the producers again in the 1980s in the Reagan and Bush administrations and in the curbing of the "excesses" of tort law. *See, e.g.,* Michael J. Saks, Do We Really Know Anything about the Behavior of the Tort Litigations System—And Why Not?, 140 U. Pa. L. Rev. 1147, 1157 ff. (1992); *see also* Jack B. Weinstein, After 50 Years of the Federal Rules of Civil Procedure: Are the Barriers to Justice Being Raised?, 137 U. Pa. L. Rev. 1901 (1989); Jack B. Weinstein, Procedural Reform as a Surrogate for Substantive Law Revision, 59 Brook. L. Rev. (forthcoming 1994).

There are, of course, minor social perturbations, as witness the increasing use of fines, forfeitures, and the criminal law to enforce environmental law against producers. *See generally* Donald J. Rebovich, *Dangerous Ground: The World of Hazardous Waste Crime* (1992); Thomas C. Green & James L. Connaughton, Defending Charges of Environmental Crime—The Growth Industry of the 90's, The Champion, Apr. 1992, at 14. The Superfund technique utilizes a strict-liability tort-administrative approach to cleanup designed to protect the public. Its transactional costs are high and its deterrent effect unproven. *See, e.g.,* Jan Paul Acton & Lloyd S. Dixon, *Superfund and Transaction Costs* (Rand Institute 1992).

15. The American Law Institute's ongoing project on "The Law Governing Lawyers," for example, has dealt with the single-party model and generally has not addressed problems raised by mass cases. *See generally* Restatement of the Law Governing Lawyers (Am. Law. Inst. Tentative Draft Nos. 1-5, 1989-1992).

16. *See* Abram Chayes, The Role of the Judge in Public Law Litigation, 89 Harv. L. Rev. 1281 (1976) (describing modern phenomenon of "public law" litigation); *see also* Abram Chayes, Foreword: Public

Law Litigation and the Burger Court, 96 Harv. L. Rev. 4 (1982).

17. *See generally* Kenneth R. Feinberg & Jack B. Weinstein, *Cases and Materials on Mass Torts* (Temp. ed., 1993).

18. *See, e.g.,* Ryan v. Dow Chemical Co., 618 F. Supp. 623 (E.D.N.Y. 1985) (approving $180 million settlement involving Vietnam veterans who came into contact with herbicide Agent Orange); *see also* Ryan v. Dow Chemical Co., 781 F. Supp. 902, 904–07 (E.D.N.Y. 1992) (providing citations and summaries for all Agent Orange opinions), *aff'd*, 996 F. 2d 1425 (2d Cir. 1993), *cert. denied sub nom.* Ivy v. Diamond Shamrock Chemicals Co., 114 S. Ct. 1125.

19. *See, e.g., In re* Joint E. & S. Dists. Asbestos Litig., 129 B.R. 710 (E. & S.D.N.Y. 1991), *vacated and remanded*, 982 F.2d 721 (2d Cir. 1992), *modified on rehearing*, 993 F.2d 7 (2d Cir. 1993).

20. *See, e.g.,* Ashley v. Abbott Labs., 789 F. Supp. 552 (E.D.N.Y. 1992) (finding personal jurisdiction in New York over DES manufacturer that was not present in New York and did not sell DES there), *appeal dismissed*, 7 F.3d 20 (2d Cir. 1993).

Mass torts are not limited to these few examples. *See, e.g.,* Watson v. Shell Oil Co., 979 F.2d 1014 (5th Cir. 1992) (seeking $32 billion in damages stemming from explosion in oil refinery for a plaintiffs' class comprised of over 18,000 members), *rehearing granted*, 990 F.2d 805 (5th Cir. 1993).

21. *See* Hart v. Community School Bd. of Educ., 383 F. Supp. 769 (E.D.N.Y. 1974), *aff'd*, 512 F.2d 37 (2d Cir. 1975).

22. *See* Society for Good Will to Retarded Children, Inc. v. Cuomo, 572 F. Supp. 1300 (E.D.N.Y. 1983) (ordering corrective measures at state institution for mentally retarded children to remedy violations of constitutional rights), *vacated*, 737 F.2d 1239 (2d Cir. 1984).

23. *See, e.g.,* Order, Manicone v. Cleary, No. 74 C 575 (E.D.N.Y. Dec. 12, 1977) (prisoners' access to telephones); United States v. Kahane, 396 F. Supp. 687 (E.D.N.Y. 1975) (government refused to permit defendant to obtain food meeting dietary requirements); Wilson v. Beame, 380 F. Supp. 1232 (E.D.N.Y. 1974) (tolerance for Muslim prisoners).

24. *See* David Luban, *Lawyers and Justice: An Ethical Study* 342 (1988) (comparing the conflict among groups represented in school cases and the Agent Orange case).

25. *Cf.* A. Morgan Cloud III, Introduction: Compassion and Judging, Conference of Association of American Law Schools: Panel on Compassion and Judging, 22 Ariz. St. L.J. 13, 16 (1990) ("Whatever principled theories we adopt concerning the nature of law, in some situations almost all of us prefer—no, even expect—a judge to exercise compassion, even if that requires that she create an escape route from the literal language of the law."); John T. Noonan, Jr., Heritage of

Tension, Conference of Association of American Law Schools: Panel on Compassion and Judging, 22 Ariz. St. L.J. 39, 42 (1990) ("I think empathy is an important quality of a judge which will lead to a better rule."); and Mary M. Schroeder, Compassion on Appeal, Conference of Association of American Law Schools: Panel on Compassion and Judging, 22 Ariz. St. L.J. 45, 46 (1990) ("justice with compassion is a legitimate, even necessary end for judges to strive to achieve, if the law is to serve human needs, as I believe it should.").

26. *See* Jack B. Weinstein, The Effect of Austerity on Institutional Litigation, 6 Law and Hum. Beh. 145 (1982).

27. One noted scholar disagrees with my view, taking the position that the community in mass torts is usually limited to those injured and their attorneys. He writes,

> the community in most mass tort litigations is among those persons who are or might be parties to the litigation (plaintiffs, victims who might become plaintiffs, future victims, defendants, potential defendants). This community among participants arises from the interdependency of values among individual mass tort claims. Because a large plaintiff verdict increases the value of all other claims and defeat reduces all other values, every plaintiff (or potential plaintiff) has an interest in the outcome of every other case. (And enormous stakes rest on the outcome of one or a few cases. . . .)

Letter from Mark A. Peterson, Rand Institute for Civil Justice, to author, Apr. 30, 1993, at 2.

28. *See generally* Robert A. Bohrer, Fear and Trembling in the Twentieth Century: Technological Risk, Uncertainty and Emotional Distress, 1984 Wis. L. Rev. 83 (1984) (discussing feasibility of compensation for severe emotional trauma and psychic injuries that many who have been exposed to toxic substances experience during the long latency periods awaiting the manifestation of physical symptoms); *see also* Complex Statutory Scheme Creates Heartache and Heartbreak for Radiation Claimants, Veterans Advocate, Apr. 1993, at 1 ("Veterans' sufferings from the cancers and other diseases caused by exposure to ionizing radiation (usually radiation from a nuclear explosion) are only increased by the complex interplay of statutes, regulations, and directives governing service-connected composition benefits for diseases caused by radiation exposure—an interplay that leads to the denial of many claims for those benefits by the U.S. Department of Veterans Affairs.").

29. *See, e.g.,* Stanley Pierce & Charlotte A. Biblow, Electromagnetic Fields Attract Lawsuits, Nat'l L.J., Feb. 8, 1993, at 20 (despite lack of scientific studies of causation, lawsuits for harm from electromagnetic field radiation are being brought and the issue might become "the

asbestos of the 90s"); Cellular Phone Scare Discounted, N.Y. Times, Feb. 2, 1993, at C1 (reporting "public panic that cellular telephones may cause brain cancer"); Health Claims Cause Turmoil in the Cellular-Phone Market, N.Y. Times, Jan. 30, 1993, at A1 (reporting dumping of cellular-phone stocks by investors when a man stated on a television talk show that his wife's use of a cellular telephone led to her brain cancer); Paul Brodeur, The Cancer at Slater School, New Yorker, Dec. 7, 1992, at 86 (reporting concerns about high incidence of cancer at California school, and others, located near high-voltage transmission lines); Victoria Slind-Flor, Fertile Fields of Litigation, Nat'l L.J., Apr. 26, 1993, at 1 (a coalition of plaintiffs' firms and scientific experts are espousing previously untested theories of cancer causation associated with proximity to high-voltage power lines); Day v. NLO, Inc., 814 F. Supp. 646 (S.D. Ohio 1993) (for example, including claims for emotional distress, of increasing number of litigations involving nuclear plants and their possible health effects on surrounding communities); Flats Yields No Easy Answers, Denver Post, Oct. 4, 1992, at C1 (Rocky Flats atomic plant); Nuclear Weapon Plants Face Lawsuits around the Country, N.Y. Times, Aug. 8, 1990, at A15; Weapons Plant Pressed for Accounting on Toll on Environment and Health, N.Y. Times, Feb. 15, 1990, at B15.

30. *See, e.g.,* Gary D. Brewer, Lecture, Environment, Economy and Ethics (Feb. 19, 1993) (Ethics and Science Lecture Series, School of Natural Resources, Univ. of Mich.). Brewer writes:

> Determining what risks are real is itself a matter left wide open to human interpretation. Those with presumed special insight or knowledge, such as a scientist or responsible decision maker, are often tempted to dismiss frightened and angry citizens as being "misinformed" or "overly emotional." Such dismissal by those in authority usually only makes a difficult situation worse as it is virtually "guaranteed to raise the level of hostility between community members and agency representatives and ultimately to stand in the way of a successful resolution of the problem."

Id. at 3 (citation omitted). Brewer quoted the great naturalist Aldo Leopold as saying:

> All ethics . . . rest upon a single premise: that the individual is a member of a community of interdependent parts. His instincts prompt him to compete for his place in that community, but his ethics prompt him also to cooperate (perhaps in order that there may be a place to compete for).

Id. at 8 (quoting Aldo Leopold, *A Sand County Almanac and Sketches Here and There* 203–4 (1949)); *see also* B. J. Hance et al., Improving

Dialogue with Communities: A Risk Communication Manual for Government (N.J. Dep't of Envt'l Prot. 1988); Paul Slovic et al., Perceived Risk, Trust and the Politics of Nuclear Waste, 254 Science 1603 (1992).

31. One defense attorney, after a jury awarded more than $5.1 million in damages to twelve plaintiffs in the trial involving the San Juan DuPont Plaza Hotel fire, praised the system for "accomodat[ing] the most complex and enormous kinds of litigation if managed efficiently by the courts." That trial had utilized satellite-transmitted testimony. The jury was seated for fifteen months, unable to take notes, yet carefully differentiated among damage awards. Marcia Coyle, Both Sides Are Claiming Victory; DuPont Fire Litigation, Nat'l L.J., Oct. 15, 1990, at 3.

The complex nature of a mass tort trial is exemplified by the case involving the Stringfellow dump site in California.

> The trial is being held in a former assembly room for jurors, the only space large enough to accommodate all that the trial will entail: more than 30 lawyers and 24 jurors, including 12 alternates; 300,000 pages of court records, and 13,000 defense exhibits and 3,600 plaintiffs' exhibits, mostly scientific data, diagrams and soil samples, all of them to be displayed on 18 computer-linked video screens that have been placed throughout the room. Plaintiffs and defendants jointly spent $150,000 to equip the room with the electronics.

Largest-Ever Toxic Waste Suit Opens in California, N.Y. Times, Feb. 5, 1993, at B16.

32. Research has revealed that the success of aggregating mass tort cases depends heavily on the personalities of the participants as well as on the procedures used. Rand Institute for Civil Justice, Annual Report 48 (1993). That includes the flexibility of the appellate courts. See Malcolm v. Nat'l Gypsum Co., 995 F.2d 346 (2d Cir. 1993) (disapproving consolidation in powerhouse cases, but approving it in Brooklyn Navy Yard cases). The reversal in the powerhouse cases seems ill advised.

"One" judge can include a number of judges cooperating closely. In the asbestos cases, for example, I worked with Justice Helen E. Freedman of the New York Supreme Court, Judge Charles P. Sifton of the Eastern District of New York, Judge Robert W. Sweet of the Southern District of New York, and Special Master Kenneth E. Feinberg—jointly serving both the state and federal judges involved—in disposing of thousands of asbestos cases. In the asbestos cases multidistricted to Judge Charles R. Weiner, Special Master Professor Stephen Burbank assisted the court, and a critical asbestos class action was transferred by Judge Weiner to another judge of the Eastern District of Pennsylvania. See Orders, Carlough v. Amchem Prods., Inc., C.A. No. 93-215 (E.D.

Pa. June 29, 1993; Apr. 15, 1993). In the DES cases I participated in similar state-federal cooperative arrangements.

The Federal Judicial Center held a National Conference on State-Federal Judicial Relationships in April 1992 that brought together state and federal judges, administrators, and others to consider fundamental issues of intersystem coordination. *See* Special State-Federal Issue: A Distillation of Ideas from the National Conference on State-Federal Judicial Relationships, F.J.C. Directions 5 (Federal Judicial Center August 1993); *see also* Jack B. Weinstein, Coordination of State and Federal Judicial Systems, 57 St. John's L. Rev. 1 (Fall 1982).

An indirect form of "consolidation" before one judge can take place where all but the first action is stayed. *See, e.g.,* Northwest Airlines, Inc. v. American Airlines, Inc., 989 F.2d 1002 (8th Cir. 1993).

33. *See* Jack B. Weinstein & Eileen B. Hershenov, The Effect of Equity on Mass Tort Law, 1991 U. Ill. L. Rev. 269 (1991) (treating many of these issues), printed as speech by Jack B. Weinstein in *Equity and Contemporary Legal Developments* (Stephen Goldstein ed., 1992) (First Int'l Conf. on Equity, Hebrew Univ. of Jerusalem, 1990).

34. *See* American Law Institute, Complex Litigation Project (Tent. Draft No. 3, Mar. 31, 1992). As one example of the widespread criticism of the ALI proposal for consolidation of state and federal cases and use of a single substantive law, *see, e.g.,* Joan Steinman, Reverse Removal (1993) (unpublished article on file). Professor Steinman in her comprehensive paper stresses litigant autonomy.

35. *See* American Law Institute, Project: Compensation and Liability for Product and Process Injuries (1991).

36. ABA Commission on Mass Torts, American Bar Association, *Report No. 126 to the ABA House of Delegates* (Aug. 1989).

37. For a summary of the different procedural devices available, *see* Cutler v. The 65 Security Plan, 831 F. Supp. 1008 (E.D.N.Y. 1993).

38. Judicial Conference Ad Hoc Comm. on Asbestos Litig., Report to the Chief Justice of the United States and Members of the Judicial Conference of the United States (1991).

39. *See* Sandra Mazer Moss, State-Federal Interstate Cooperation, Case Management Techniques Move Complex Litigation, Hasten Disposition of Asbestos, Other Cases, State-Federal Judicial Observer 3 (Apr. 1993) (describing how Philadelphia County courts have eliminated their asbestos backlog by working with federal courts to "share ideas, coordinate strategies, combine joint settlement packages, promulgate similar rules and present a united front to the asbestos bar nationwide").

40. *See* American Law Institute, Complex Litigation Project, Tent. Draft No. 1 (Apr. 14, 1989), Tent. Draft No. 2 (Apr. 6, 1990), Tent. Draft No. 3 (Mar. 6, 1992). This comprehensive scheme would provide for transfers of both federal and state cases to one court, either federal

or state, for both pretrial and trial purposes. In addition to political problems, the proposal founders on the problem of applying one law given that under the *Erie* doctrine state substantive laws may have to apply. *See* American Law Institute, Complex Litigation Project, Reporter's Preliminary Memorandum on Choice of Law in Complex Actions (Apr. 6, 1990).

Granting power to one court to supersede the substantive laws controlling liability and remedies of all the states will not, except in the most unusual situations, be acceptable to the bar. The only politically practical way of providing a single law consistently is through federal legislative action. *See* Colloquy, An Administrative Alternative to Tort Litigation to Resolve Asbestos Claims, 13 Cardozo L. Rev. 1817 (1992). Substantial theoretical studies have provided a good start toward a national law. *See, e.g.,* American Law Institute, Reporter's Study, Enterprise Responsibility for Personal Injury (Vols. 1 and 2, 1991); Tort Law and the Public Interest: Competition, Innovation, and Consumer Welfare (Peter H. Schuck ed., 1991) (Report of the American Assembly, Columbia Univ. and the Tort and Insurance Practice Section of the American Bar Association); Michael J. Saks, Do We Really Know Anything About the Behavior of the Tort Litigation System—And Why Not?, 140 U. Pa. L. Rev. 1147 (1992); *Causation and Financial Compensation* (Lawrence B. Kovey ed., 1985) (Institute for Health Policy Analysis, Georgetown Univ. Medical Center); ABA Commission on Mass Tort, Report to the House of Delegates (1990); Mark A. Peterson & Molly Selvin, *Resolution of Mass Torts: Towards a Framework for Evaluation of Aggregative Procedures* (Rand Institute 1988); Peter W. Huber, Safety and the Second Best: The Hazards of Public Risk Management in the Courts, 85 Colum. L. Rev. 277 (1985); Symposium, Mass Tort Reform, 27 Gonzaga L. Rev. 147 (1992); *see also* Andrew Blum, Schwartz on Torts, Nat'l L.J., July, 1993, at 1 (describing efforts to pass federal products liability legislation).

41. *See In re* Silicone Gel Breast Implants Prods. Liab. Litig., 793 F. Supp. 1098 (J.P.M.L. 1992). Some states have also moved in the direction of consolidating state-court breast implant cases. *See* Daniel Wise, Joinder of Breast Implant Suits Seen, N.Y. L.J., Mar. 15, 1993, at 1 (reporting likelihood of consolidation of three thousand cases in New York state courts, similar orders in California and Oklahoma, and city-wide consolidations in Dallas, Houston, and Detroit). Nevertheless, the breast implant litigation still threatens to spawn asbestos-sized problems. *See* Andrew Blum, Implant Makers, Insurers Feud, Nat'l L.J., Aug. 23, 1993, at 3.

42. *See* Revised Case Management Order, *In re* Silicone Gel Breast Implants Prod. Liab. Litig., 793 F. Supp. 1098 (N.D. Ala. 1992) (Pointer, J.); *see also* Computer to Courts' Rescue, Hous. Chron., Nov. 14,

1992, at 37; High-Tech Pain Reliever for Huge Legal Headache; Cutting the Paper; Computer CDs Should Speed Up Implant Lawsuit, Hous. Chron., Oct. 28, 1992 Business, at 1; Decision Time Near for Implant Suits, N.Y. Times, Sept. 2, 1992, at C12; Alison Frankel, Implant Litigation: Heavy Politics, Lingering Questions, Am. Law., Sept. 1992, at 90.

43. The availability of increasingly specialized research materials for mass cases is an indication of the level of sophistication of the mass tort bar. Andrews Publications, for example, now offers specialized weekly or monthly litigation reports in the areas of asbestos, asbestos property damage, breast implants, repetitive stress injuries, hazardous waste, DES, electromagnetic fields, and tobacco, among others. Widely publicized seminars conducted by experienced attorneys and members of the medical profession form an important part of the plaintiffs' attorneys' networking strategy. *See, e.g.,* Nat'l L.J., Mar. 15, 1993, at 39 (announcing second annual symposium on Breast Implant Litigation). In New York, about two dozen plaintiffs' firms have formed the New York State Breast Implant Litigation Group. *See* Daniel Wise, Joinder of Breast Implant Suits Seen, N.Y. L.J., Mar. 15, 1993, at 1; *cf. In re* Two Appeals Arising out of the San Juan DuPont Plaza Hotel Fire Litigation, 994 F.2d 956, 965 (1st Cr. 1993) ("In this multidistrict litigation, involving upward of 2,000 parties and raising a googol of issues, Judge Acosta's power to mandate contributions to, *inter alia,* a central discovery depository can scarcely be doubted.").

44. Fed. R. Cr. P. 23 (class actions).

45. *See* Working Draft of Proposed Amendments to the Federal Rules of Civil Procedure and Federal Rules of Evidence, Mar. 1991 (considered by the Advisory Committee on Civil Rules, but not adopted); Peter Greenberger, Plans for Class-Action Reform, Nat'l L. J., Jul. 8, 1985, at 32.

46. *See, e.g., In re* "Agent Orange" Prod. Liab. Litig., 100 F.R.D. 734 (E.D.N.Y. 1983) (providing for notice to class relying on press).

47. *See, e.g.,* Bruce H. Nielson, Was the 1966 Advisory Committee Right?: Suggested Revisions of Rule 23 to Allow More Frequent Use of Class Actions in Mass Tort Litigation, 25 Harv. J. on Legis. 461 (1988).

48. The drafters of the 1908 ABA Canons of Ethics relied upon the writings of George Sharswood in An Essay on Professional Ethics, 32 A.B.A. Rep. 1 (5th ed. 1907), first published as A Compend of Lectures on the Aims and Duties of the Profession of Law, Delivered before the Law Class of the University of Pennsylvania (1854).

49. Vincent Robert Johnson, Ethical Limitations on Creative Financing of Mass Tort Class Actions, 54 Brook. L. Rev. 539, 542 (1988).

50. *See* American Law Institute, Restatement of the Law Governing Lawyers, Tent. Draft Nos. 1–5 (various dates to 1992).

There is one notable exception. Currently the Committee on Professional Responsibility of the Association of the Bar of the City of New York is studying the applicability of the traditional rules of ethics in the context of class action litigation. *See* Committee of Professional Responsibility, Ass'n of the Bar of the City of New York, Final Report, Financial Arrangements in Class Actions, and the Code of Professional Responsibility (1992). The committee acknowledges that "the needs of the class action—particularly as to funding and other financial arrangements—[are] in conflict with the Code." *Id*. at 2–3. The Report includes a compendium of court decisions that have attempted to resolve this conflict.

The American Bar Association had taken another step toward developing ethical rules for modern litigation. In its first formal opinion dealing with mass torts, it characterizes as an "impermissible restriction on the right to practice" any global settlement that restricts a plaintiff's attorney's ability to represent additional present or future clients against that defendant. ABA Comm. on Ethics and Professional Responsibility, Formal Op. 371 (Draft, 1993).

51. A recent New York State Bar Ethics Opinion points out how unrealistic the rule regarding multiple representation of clients with differing interests is in a mass tort context. *See* State Bar Ethics Opinion 639, *reprinted in* N.Y. L.J., Mar. 3, 1993, at 2. Concurring with ethics opinions from two other states, the Opinion forbids a lawyer from representing all plaintiffs, for example, in a automobile accident case, "where the assets are not sufficient for the full satisfaction of all potential claims and a recovery by one claimant would reduce the assets available for the satisfaction of the other claims." In such a situation the attorney must decline employment or consider obtaining consent after full disclosure. Consent is possible only if the respective interests differ only as to lack of sufficient assets. Where one client's damages vastly exceed the other's, multiple representation is also improper. The opinion concludes with the following caution:

> In the settlement context, [the ethics rules] prohibit a lawyer from making an aggregate settlement of claims of multiple clients unless each consents after being advised of *(1) the existence and nature of all claims involved, (2) the total amount of the settlement, and (3) the participation of each person in the settlement*. . . . A multiple representation that appeared appropriate at the outset may nevertheless require the lawyer to withdraw representing either client if the circumstances—such as the aggregate settlement proposal—place the clients in an irreconcilable conflict.

Id. (emphasis added). Can such guidance really be applied to mass torts? Is each attorney to rush to the courthouse to get the limited fund? Is this equitable to those who would get nothing even though their claim was as valid as those would get paid? A limited fund class action under Rule 23(b)(1)(B) of the Federal Rules of Civil Procedure would be much more sensible if many claimants were involved.

52. Academics' criticism of judicial activism, while probably a minority position, has been strongly articulated. *See, e.g.,* Judith Resnik, Managerial Judges, 96 Harv. L. Rev. 374 (1982); Judith Resnik, Failing Faith: Adjudicatory Procedures in Decline, 53 U. Chi. L. Rev. 494 (1986); E. Donald Elliott, Managerial Judging and the Evolution of Procedure, 53 U. Chi. L. Rev. 306 (1986); Owen M. Fiss, Against Settlement, 93 Yale L.J. 1073 (1984); Peter H. Schuck, *Agent Orange on Trial* (1986). Some authors blame excessive activism by judges, legislators, and lawyers for expensive, unnecessary, and dangerous removals of asbestos from buildings. *See, e.g.,* Michael J. Bennett, *The Asbestos Racket: An Environmental Parable* (1991). Others contrast the effect of lack of activism on injustices as in the delayed British reaction to problems involving thalidomide. The Sunday Times of London Insight Team, *Suffer the Children: The Story of Thalidomide* (1979).

Judges generally have taken a favorable view of activism in complex cases. *See, e.g.,* Manual for Complex Litigation Second § 20.1 (1985) (judicial supervision); Robert Peckham, The Federal Judge as Case Manager, 69 Calif. L. Rev. 770 (1981); William Schwarzer, Managing Civil Litigation: The Trial Judge's Role, 61 Judicature 400 (1978); Manual for Litigation Management and Cost and Delay Reduction (Fed. Jud. Center 1992).

53. *See* Civil Justice Reform Act of 1990, Pub. L. Nos. 101-650, 104 Stat. 5089.

54. *See, e.g.,* Stephen Gillers & Roy D. Simon, *Regulation of Lawyers: Statutes and Standards* (1991) (collecting applicable law).

55. *See* Jack B. Weinstein, On the Teaching of Legal Ethics, 72 Colum. L. Rev. 452 (1972). For an integration of these subjects in a teaching tool *see* Jack B. Weinstein, *The Law Reacts to a Nuclear Explosion in Brooklyn and Love Triumphs* (1990).

56. The *Oxford English Dictionary* defines ethics as both "[t]he science of morals; the department of study concerned with the principles of human duty" and "[t]he rules of conduct recognized in certain associations or departments of human life."

57. *See, e.g.,* Monroe H. Freedman, *Understanding Lawyers' Ethics* 13–42 (1990).

58. *See* Village Bd. of the Village of Fayetteville v. Jarrold, 423 N.E.2d 385, 387 (1981) (clarifying rules governing granting of variances to "ensure that actions of zoning officials do not impair or subvert the public interest").

59. It is an anomaly, if Professor Unger is correct, that before law

was needed there had to be a breakdown of the strongest sense of community oneness. *See* Robert M. Unger, *Law in Modern Society* (1976). He writes:

> From the standpoint of consciousness, the disintegration of community means the development of a situation in which one feels increasingly able to question the rightness of accepted practices as well as to violate them. Only then do explicit and formulated rules become possible and necessary. Positive law remains superfluous as long as there is a closely held communion of reciprocal expectations, based on a shared view of right and wrong.

Id. at 61.

60. *See* Geoffrey C. Hazard, Jr., *Communitarian Ethics and Legal Justification*, 59 Colo. L. Rev. 721, 736–39 (1988) ("In real life, even in very simple societies, an individual stands in multiple relationships in multiple contexts, moving among them in continuous transition.").

61. *See, e.g.*, Philip Selznick, The Idea of a Communitarian Morality, 75 Cal. L. Rev. 445, 460 (1987) (basing decisions on individual preference would be incomplete; to get beyond individual preference, one should "take seriously the shared beliefs we hold regarding what is good for a community or institution"); Joel F. Handler, *Dependent People, the State, and the Modern/Postmodern Search for the Dialogic Community*, 35 U.C.L.A. L. Rev. 999 (1988) (examining dialogic community in three empirical settings (informed consent in medical ethics, special education for community and poor, and community care for the frail, elderly poor) and concluding that an efficient dialogic community will not fully emerge in these situations and those that are similar because of autonomy and power lacking in the class of people being helped; this uneven balance of power results in the sector of the community being helped not having their needs addressed through active dialogue).

62. There is an increasing trend to require businesses to pay for possible damage to the community. *See, e.g.*, Comprehensive Agreement between the City of Berkeley and Miles Inc. for the Miles Inc. Long-Range Development Program (1992). This agreement deals with zoning and "not-in-my-backyard" objections by providing many community programs such as housing, child care, worker training, and the like.

63. For a recent collection of writings on communicative ethics, see generally Seyla Benhabib & Fred Dallmayr, *The Communicative Ethics Controversy* (1990). Passages of particular relevance to communicatarian ethics within the judicial system can be found in Fred Dallmayr, Introduction, *id.* at 1, 6–10, 17; Karl-Otto Apel, Is the Ethics of the Ideal Communication Community a Utopia?, *id.* at 23, 50–52; Jurgen Habermas, Discourse Ethics: Notes on a Program of Philosophical Justification, *id.* at 60, 63, 72, 103–5; Albrecht Wellmer, Practical Philoso-

phy and the Theory of Society, *id*. at 293, 297, 303, 311–12; Seyla Benhabib, Afterword: Communicative Ethics and Contemporary Controversies in Practical Philosophy, *id*. at 330, 332–34, 349–50, 358–61; *see also* Seyla Benhabib, *Critique, Norm and Utopia: A Study of the Foundations of Critical Theory* 279 (1986).

64. *See* John Stuart Mill, *On Liberty* 32 (R. McCallum ed., 1947 [1859]) ("Nor is it enough that he should hear the arguments of adversaries from his own teachers, presented as they state them, and accompanied by what they offer as refutations. That is not the way to do justice to the arguments, or bring them into real contact with his own mind. He must be able to hear from persons who actually believe them; who defend them in earnest, and do their very utmost for them.") (quoted in Red Lion Broadcasting Co., Inc. v. FCC, 395 U.S. 367, 392, n.18 (1969)); *see also* Alan Ryan, Invasion of the Mind Snatchers (review of David Bromwich, *Politics by Other Means: Higher Education and Group Thinking*), N.Y. Rev. of Books 13, 15 (Feb. 11, 1993) ("Mill's Essay *On Liberty* . . . is in its entirety an argument for keeping up controversy for the sake of intellectual vigor, boldness, and vividness. 'Antagonism of opinion' was Mill's recipe for a lively democratic culture."); *cf*. Abrams v. United States, 250 U.S. 616, 630 (1919) (Holmes, J., dissenting) ("[T]he best test of truth is the power of the thought to get itself accepted in the competition of the market. . . .").

65. We often overestimate the satisfaction of clients with communications with their lawyers even in simple cases. Laypersons' frustration is one of the reasons for the bar's poor image. See Alan Levine, Communicating with Your Client, N.Y. State Bar News, Sept. 1993, at 5, listing the following common complaints of clients: they take me for granted, they don't understand me, they are condescending, they tell me what they think I want to hear, they tell me what to do, they cannot be found or reached, and they speak in legalese.

66. *See* Jurgen Habermas, Discourse Ethics: Notes on Philosophical Justification, in *The Communicative Ethics Controversy* 60 (Seyla Benhabib & Fred Dallmayr eds., 1990). In describing communicative decisionmaking, the author argues:

[T]he categorical imperative needs to be reformulated as follows:

Rather than ascribing as valid to all others any maxim that I can will to be a universal law, I must submit my maxim to all others for purposes of discursively testing its claim to universality. The emphasis shifts from what each can will without contradiction to be a general law, to what all can will in agreement to be a universal norm.

This version of the universality principle does in fact entail the idea of a cooperative process of argumentation.

Id. at 72 (quoting Thomas McCarthy, *The Critical Theory of Jurgen Habermas* 326 (1978)).

67. The observations of one commentator on the role of sympathy in the law are apt:

> Lon Fuller identifies participation as the crux of the adjudicatory system. The system brings parties face-to-face with the judge and invites judge and party to engage in a sympathetic exchange. Even complex class action litigation preserves adjudication's sympathetic structure by clustering multiple interests under the banner of a 'party representative' and avoiding the cacophony of voices that would obstruct more direct interpersonal conduct.

Note, Sympathy as Legal Structure, 105 Harv. L. Rev. 1961, 1969 (1992) (*citing* Lon L. Fuller, The Forms and Limits of Adjudication, 92 Harv. L. Rev. 353, 369 (1978)). Sympathy and participation, two pillars of our system of justice, must not be lost in the rush to deal efficiently with mass tort cases:

> On the process side, there are dignity considerations for individual litigants: parties should have an opportunity to tell their stories and should be treated humanely. The community has an interest in assuring that disputes are resolved in a just way. Participation educates citizens about law and societal problems, and empowers them to help govern.

Stephen N. Subrin, The Empirical Challenge to Procedure Based in Equity: How Can Equity Procedure Be Made More Equitable?, in *Equity and Contemporary Legal Developments* 761, 771–72 (Stephen Goldstein ed., 1992).

68. *See, e.g.,* Symposium, Improving Communication in the Courtroom, 68 Ind. L.J. 1033 (1993).

69. 33 A.B.A. Rep. 574, 571 (1908)

70. *See* Russell G. Pearce, Rediscovering the Republican Origins of the Legal Ethics Codes, 1992 Geo. J. Leg. Eth. 241, 250. Professor Pearce believes that Sharswood's vision survives in the current version of the ethics code and that lawyers have broad freedom to exercise discretion in client representation. *Id.* at 274. He states:

> The realization that the codes permit a non-adversarial ethic leads to a . . . challenge to critics of the adversarial system. Most of them argue that lawyers' actions under the existing codes are often immoral. Analysis of Sharswood's republican vision reminds us, however, that ethical schemes providing lawyers with broad discretion rely on an assumption that lawyers are capable of, and will tend toward, moral conduct. Therefore, if, as the modern critics assert, lawyers who cur-

rently have discretion do not exercise it appropriately, the critics need
to explain how lawyers could be made to act more virtuously in the
future.

Id. at 281 (footnotes omitted). He concludes with this comment:

Sharswood leaves us with one final challenge. By his republican
approach to lawyers' ethics, he asserts in effect that legal ethics standards in large part define the nature of our society. This claim is stun-
ning, especially at a time when the reputation of lawyers is so low. If,
upon assessing Sharswood's assertion, we find that it has any merit,
we will have to remake the field of legal ethics.

Id. at 282 (footnotes omitted).
    71. *Id.* at 258.
    72. *Id.*
    73. *See generally* Gerald M. Stern, *The Buffalo Creek Disaster* (1976);
Kai T. Erickson, *Everything in its Path: Destruction of Community in
the Buffalo Creek Flood* (1976).
    74. As one observer reminds us:

[What] happened on Buffalo Creek . . . can serve as a reminder that
the preservation (or restoration) of communal forms of life must
become a lasting concern, not only for those charged with healing
the wounds of acute disaster, but for those charged with planning a
truly human future.

Kai T. Erikson, *Everything in Its Path: Destruction of Community in the
Buffalo Creek Flood* 259 (1976).
    75. *See In re* Joint E. & S. Dists. Asbestos Litig., 129 B.R. 710,
737–39 (E. & S.D.N.Y. 1991) (history of failure to take elementary
precautions long after dangers were known), *vacated on other grounds,*
982 F.2d 721 (2d Cir. 1992), *modified on rehearing,* 993 F.2d 7 (2d
Cir. 1993).
    76. *See, e.g.,* N.Y. Times, Mar. 8, 1993, at A9 (full page advertise-
ment listing scores of telephone lines and agencies available in central
locations for help); N.Y. Daily News, Mar. 11, 1993, at 22 (same);
Newsday, Mar. 10, 1993, at 31 (Gov. Cuomo presenting checks for
business loans within days of explosion); David Henry, State Touts
Help for Trade Center Jobless, Newsday, Mar. 12, 1993, at 43 (unemployment programs available to cushion financial pain of explosion).
    77. New York Telephone advertisements made clear what communi-
cations facilities were being made available. *See, e.g.,* N.Y. Post, Mar. 10,
1993, at 15 (World Trade Center Crisis Update #6, Business Anything
but Usual); *see also* N.Y. Times, Mar. 12, 1993, at B5 ("Port Authority
of New York and New Jersey approved a $15 million aid package for

more than 300 corporations . . . giving them . . . rent rebates, free parking . . . and other benefits."); PA Tells Tenants: We Care, Newsday, Mar. 12, 1993, at 37 (economic stimulus plan approved by Port Authority).

78. *See* For Blast Survivors, Shock Waves of Stress, N.Y. Times, Mar. 10, 1993, at A1 (outlining medical help available).

79. *See* Pamphlet, Dispute Resolution Procedures in the Eastern District of New York (available from Clerk of the Court, E.D.N.Y.).

80. *See In re* Joint E. & S. Dists. Asbestos Litig., 129 F.R.D. 434 (E. & S.D.N.Y. & N.Y. Sup. Ct. 1990) (joint order by state and federal judge appointing single settlement master for all federal and state cases).

81. Note, however, that the average settlement in the MGM Grand Hotel fire for breathing smoke, walking down stairs, and fear was in the tens of thousands of dollars. The Exxon Valdez oil spill is, perhaps, an even better example of the need for a communitarian approach since so many jobs and national environmental values were affected.

82. *See* Jack B. Weinstein, Preliminary Reflections on Managing Disasters, 11 Colum. J. Envt'l L. 1 (1985) (emergency services); Jack B. Weinstein, *The Law Reacts to a Nuclear Explosion in Brooklyn and Love Triumphs* (1990).

83. *See* Report to the Congress from the Presidential Commission on Catastrophic Nuclear Accidents (2 vols., Aug. 1990).

84. Jack B. Weinstein & Eileen B. Hershenov, The Effect of Equity on Mass Tort Law, 1991 Ill. L. Rev. 269. See Chapter 9, *infra,* Equitable Powers of Courts.

85. The continued effects of the 1989 oil spill in Alaska, for example, illustrate the need to fashion settlements and resolutions that take account of the full scope of the community's needs. *See, e.g.,* Harm from Alaska Spill Goes On, Scientists Say, N.Y. Times, Feb. 6, 1993, at A6 (continuing effects of spill on Alaskan environment); Studies Show Exxon Spill Hurt People as Well as Wildlife, Feb. 6, 1993, Reuters News Service, *available in* LEXIS, Nexis Library, Reuters File (describing social disruptions and psychological stress in surrounding communities caused by spill, cleanup, litigation, and aftermath).

86. *See* David Sive, Standing Debate Continues at High Court, Nat'l L.J., Apr. 5, 1993, at 20; *see also* Lujan v. Defenders of Wildlife, 112 S. Ct. 2130, 2145 (1992) (Scalia, J.) (plurality opinion) ("'The province of the court' [according to *Marbury*] 'is, solely, to decide the rights of individuals.' Vindicating the *public* interest (including the public interest in government observance of the Constitution and the laws) is the function of Congress and the Chief Executive.") (quoting Marbury v. Madison, 5 U.S. (1 Cranch) 137, 170 (1803)).

87. *Cf.* Lucie White, Mobilization on the Margins of the Lawsuit: Making Space for Clients to Speak, 16 N.Y.U. Rev. L. & Soc. Change 535 (1987–1988) (arguing that "welfare litigators" should craft litiga-

tion into an opportunity for education and mobilization of poor communities as well as a weapon for coercion); Paul R. Tremblay, Toward a Community-Based Ethic for Legal Services Practice, 37 U.C.L.A. L. Rev. 1101, 1112 (1990) (arguing that legal services lawyers, faced with scarcity of time and funds, should allocate their resources by applying a "community-based ethic" by which the lawyer would evaluate "competing client demands" with "norms reflecting community interests and needs"); Derrick A. Bell, Jr., Serving Two Masters: Integration Ideals and Client Interests in School Desegregation Litigation, 85 Yale L.J. 471 (1976) (discussing problems of school desegregation litigators, in cases involving large communities and extending over decades, in identifying client desires and suggesting that these litigators sometimes lose touch with their clients' needs).

88. *Cf.* Marion Smiley, *Moral Responsibility and the Boundaries of Community: Power and Accountability from a Pragmatic Point of View* 196 (1992). Smiley writes:

[E]ven if the boundaries of a particular community are tied up with both individual interests and the assertion of power, the valuation of community per se is independent of them and must be taken into consideration as such. The other is that although we ourselves may not be willing to accept as legitimate the value of retaining communal boundaries, we nevertheless have to face the fact that we often incorporate our sense of these boundaries into both our configuration of social roles and our expectation of particular individuals.

Id.; cf. Thomas L. Shaffer, *Faith and the Professions* 28 (1987) (professionals act ethically in a community, not alone); *id.* at 228 (it is the community that teaches the lawyer how to be a friend).

89. In the Talmud, Hillel says:

Do not withdraw from the community.
Put no trust in thyself until the day of thy death.
Do not judge thy comrade until thou hast stood in his place.

Judah Goldin, *The Living Talmud: The Wisdom of the Fathers and Its Classical Commentaries* 86 (1957).

90. *Cf.* Many Patients Unhappy with H.M.O.'s, N.Y. Times, Aug. 18, 1993, at A10 (medical director of one community health plan states that large organizations can become impersonal and doctors must be trained to produce "satisfaction for patients").

91. The following reading of Kant supports this observation:

Kant's Categorical Imperative . . . can be read as saying that each person is entitled on an equal basis to be both the subject and object of all moral discourse. Another analysis is that the Categorical Imperative is a desacrilized version of the Golden Rule, i.e., Do Unto Others as Ye Would Have Them Do Unto You.

Geoffrey C. Hazard, Communitarian Ethics and Legal Justification, 59 U. Colo. L. Rev. 721, 726 (1988). John Rawls's "veil of ignorance" construct in *A Theory of Justice* (1971) can also be viewed as a variant of the Golden Rule. *See also* Lesley Arthur Mulholland, *Kant's System of Rights* 397 (1990) (Kant supplies a stronger ground for the basic assumption of Rawls that "*all* human beings are persons (have the innate right).") (emphasis in original); Stuart Hampshire, Liberalism: The New Twist, N.Y. Rev. of Books, Aug. 12, 1993, at 43 (discussing Rawls's theories and reviewing his new collection of essays, John Rawls, *Political Liberalism* (1993)). The increasing interest in Kant in the law schools as a foundation for liberal concepts of individual rights is reflected in the Symposium on Kantian Legal Theory, 87 Colum. L. Rev. 421 (1987).

The hazards of ignoring human dignity and empathy with the other are emphasized by Hannah Arendt, who looked into the fires that destroyed so many when abstract ideology was cut loose from respect for the other as for ourselves. *See, e.g.*, Hannah Arendt, *Antisemitism* in Part One, *The Origins of Totalitarianism* (1967); *Imperialism* in Part Two, *id.* (1968); *Totalitarianism* in Part Three, *id.* (1968); *see also* Ronald Bernier, *Political Judgment* 109 (1983).

92. For an extensive discussion of compensation distribution schemes, see Symposium, Claims Resolution Facilities and the Mass Settlement of Mass Torts, 53 Law & Contemp. Probs. 1 (1990).

93. *See, e.g.*, Rivka Horowitz, *Buber's Way to "I and Thou"* (1988).

94. An example of someone prevailing in this lottery is the jury verdict of $105.2 million against General Motors for an accident caused by a defective fuel-tank design. *See* G.M. Is Held Liable Over Fuel Tanks in Pickup Trucks, N.Y. Times, Feb. 5, 1993, at A1. The available empirical material, however, indicates that most negligently inflicted injuries go undercompensated or uncompensated.

95. *Cf.* David A. J. Richards, *The Moral Criticism of Law* 5 (1977) ("Serious moral thought about Social Questions of any complexity obviously requires close attention to matters of empirical fact."). John T. Noonan, Jr., in his charming book *Persons and Masks of the Law* (1976) points out the cruelty in the famous *Palsgraf* case when the detailed facts were ignored in favor of high abstractions. *Id.* at 111. The jury, not Cardozo, had it right. Why a poor and guileless seamstress taking her child to the beach on the railroad should be denied compensation when a public utility's scale fell on her while she was waiting for the train is hard to understand. She not only had her verdict taken from her, but she was charged with costs on appeal that constituted a large part of her annual income.

96. Harry W. Jones, Legal Realism and Natural Law, in *The Nature of Law* 261-62 (M.P. Golding ed., 1966).

97. *See generally* Stephen N. Subrin, The Empirical Challenge to Procedure Based in Equity: How Can Equity Procedure Be Made More Equitable, in *Equity and Contemporary Legal Developments* 761 (Stephen Goldstein ed., 1992) (discussing tension between rules and equity).

98. *See* Aaron Kirschenbaum, *Equity in Jewish Law: Halakhic Perspectives in Law* 40 (1991) ("[Too] rigorous an adherence to the formal *din Torah,* biblical law, is a violation of Biblical law itself."); Aaron Kirschenbaum, *Equity in Jewish Law: Beyond Equity,* lxiii (1991) ("[B]oth formalism [and] flexibility have legitimate roles to play in the history of the law . . . and are indispensable components of the civil law of Halakhah").

99. Accommodation of the individual lies at the heart of equity. Aristotle defined equity as a "rectification of law where law is defective because of its generality." Kirschenbaum, *supra* at note 98. Equity does not, in Aristotle's view, nullify the law. *Id.* at xxxv. Equity "refines" the law, "brings it closer to perfection," and "motivates the authoritative interpreters of the law to seek out its spirit." *Id.; see also* Aaron Kirschenbaum, *Equity in Jewish Law—Halakhic Perspectives in Law: Formalism and Flexibility in Jewish Civil Law* 21 (1991) ("According to the Rabbis, legal formalism has been one of the plagues of mankind from its inception. The dispute between Cain and Abel was engendered by each one's insistence upon his legal rights.").

100. *See In re* Joint E. & S. Dists. Asbestos Litig., 129 B.R. 710, 767–70 (E. & S.D.N.Y. 1991) (describing settlement in Manville case).

101. Alasdair MacIntyre has defined communitarianism as follows:

> What I am . . . is in key part what I inherit, a specific past that is present to some degree in my present. I find myself a part of a history and . . . one of the bearers of a tradition.

Alasdair MacIntyre, *After Virtue* 206 (1981). This version of communitarianism has also been stated as involving "common interest as a basis for deciding what norms shall prevail, participation as the medium of decision, recognition of the wholeness and historicity of normative choices." Geoffrey C. Hazard, Communitarian Ethics and Legal Justification, 59 U. Colo. L. Rev. 721, 733 (1988).

102. Arthur Schlesinger, Jr., The Radical (review of George F. Kennan, *Around the Cragged Hill: A Personal and Political Philosophy*), N.Y. Rev. of Books, Feb. 11, 1993, at 3.

1. *See* ABA Model Rules of Professional Conduct, Rule 1.7, comment 1 ("Loyalty is an essential element in the lawyer's relationship to a client.").

2. The duty of undivided loyalty has been described as follows:

> The ideal of the Code [governing lawyers] is that the lawyer's principal duty (or set of duties) runs hard and straight to the client. To be sure, other duties exist, for example, duties to the court and sometimes, in limited ways, to third parties, but the present focus is on the *basic* duty of the American lawyer to the client.

Kenneth L. Penegar, The Five Pillars of Professionalism, 49 U. Pitt. L. Rev. 307, 322–23 (1988) (emphasis in original).

3. *See* David Luban, *Lawyers and Justice: An Ethical Study* 50–103 (1988) (describing nature of adversary system and examining a variety of theoretical justifications for dispute resolution by adversarial proceeding).

4. *See, e.g.*, Colin Croft, Reconceptualizing American Professionalism: A Proposal for Deliberative Moral Community, 67 N.Y.U. L. Rev. 1256 (1972) (collecting authorities).

5. ABA Model Rules of Professional Conduct, Preamble, ¶ 7.

6. ABA Model Rules of Professional Conduct, Rule 1.1 ("A lawyer shall provide competent representation to a client. Competent representation requires the legal knowledge, skill, thoroughness, and preparation reasonably necessary for the representation."), 1.3 ("A lawyer shall act with reasonable diligence and promptness in representing a client.").

7. *See* ABA Model Rules of Professional Conduct, Rules 1.7, 1.8, 1.9.

8. ABA Model Rules of Professional Conduct, Rules 1.1, 1.3.

9. ABA Model Rules of Professional Conduct, Rule 1.2(a).

10. *Id.*

11. *See* Georgene M. Vairo, The Dalkon Shield Claimants Trust: Paradigm Lost (or Found)?, 61 Fordham L. Rev. 617, 619 & n.9 (1992) (nine lawyers or law firms represent more than ten thousand Dalkon Shield claimants; articles indicate some lawyers are representing thousands of claimants); Deborah R. Hensler, Symposium: Conflict of Laws and Complex Litigation Issues in Mass Tort Litigation: Resolving Mass Torts: Myths and Realities, 1989 U. Ill. L. Rev. 89, 96 (1989) (two attorneys briefly represented nine hundred Dalkon Shield clients).

12. One attorney I interviewed noted that a few plaintiffs' lawyers have become so experienced in handling mass cases that it was "developing into a cottage industry."

13. *See* ABA Model Rules of Conduct, Rule 1.3, comment 1 ("A lawyer's work load should be controlled so that each matter can be handled adequately.").

14. *See, e.g.*, Jane Bryant Quinn, Getting Fraud Refunds, Wash. Post,

Aug. 5, 1990, at H11 (extremely complicated for investors to find out if they are eligible to share in disgorgement plans).

15. *See* Airlines, Orlando Sent., Oct. 24, 1991, at C1 (federal judge "studying ways to notify passengers" about antitrust class action that might provide them with refunds); How to Claim Your Share of the Airline Fare Settlements, Phoenix Gaz., Mar. 29, 1993, at D6.

16. Expansion of clinical work in the law schools is a means of emphasizing the humane aspects of the relationship between attorney and client.

17. One commentator has suggested, in the class action context, that a requirement that lawyers record contacts with class members might foster communication:

> [A]symmetries between class interests and preferences will often force counsel to function more as a Burkean trustee than instructed delegate. Even so, it should be possible to recast that trusteeship role to encompass more explicit fiduciary obligations to dissenting con-stituencies. Requiring attorneys to record contacts with the class and perceptions of conflict would, if nothing else, narrow their capacity for self-delusion about whose views they were or were not represent-ing. Explicit professional obligations, even those unlikely to trigger any formal sanction, often affect behavioral norms simply by sensitiz-ing individuals to the full implications of their conduct.

Deborah L. Rhode, Class Conflicts in Class Actions, 34 Stan. L. Rev. 1183, 1258 (1982).

18. Even in formal class actions one could argue that some form of effective communication with all class members should be required. *See* Michael D. Ricciuti, Equity and Accountability in the Reform of Settle-ment Procedures in Mass Tort Cases: The Ethical Duty to Consult, 1 Geo. J. Legal Ethics 817 (1988) (arguing for a form of consultation require-ment in settling class actions).

19. A lawyer involved in a major toxic spill litigation provided me with examples of newsletters that the Plaintiff's Steering Committee sent to thousands of clients, updating them on the progress of the liti-gation. The lawyer was able to keep in close touch with the relatively small committee.

20. This attorney mails a detailed letter to all of her clients every sev-eral months updating them on recent developments in DES litigation in New York. These letters also encourage the clients to contact the office with questions at any time.

21. Some attorneys might view newsletters produced by distribution trusts against whom they are litigating as mere "propaganda," but such newsletters generally contain useful and important information. *See, e.g.,* Manville Personal Injury Settlement Trust Newsletter, June 30,

1992 (including information about timing and procedure for paying claims); Letter from Michael M. Sheppard, Exec. Dir., Dalkon Shield Claimants Trust to author, Oct. 1, 1992 (discussing newsletter regularly produced by Dalkon Shield Trust and enclosing examples). However, one highly respected plaintiffs' attorney in private conversations has criticized certain newsletters as "biased and misleading."

22. *See* ABA Model Rules of Professional Conduct, Rule 4.2.

23. *See* Letter from Patricia G. Houser, Exec. Dir., Manville Personal Injury Settlement Trust, to Robert C. Heinemann, Clerk, United States District Court, E.D.N.Y., Aug. 18, 1992 (expressing concern that attorneys who represent claimants against Manville Trust are not communicating fully with the clients; suggesting possibility of court approval for direct communication between the Trust and represented claimants).

In a significant step in the right direction, one well-respected plaintiffs' firm has, after consulting with an academic expert on legal ethics, entered into detailed retainer agreements in a complex mass environmental case that requires extensive consultation. Methods of communication and use of lay representatives chosen by clients are specified in writing.

More typical is the situation represented by the following colloquy in Findley v. Falise, No. 90-3973 (E.D.N.Y.), Dec. 17, 1993. The attorneys represented clients whose positions were in conflict because if the earlier claims were paid in full, there would be nothing for the later claimants, whom they also represented (at 15–17):

THE COURT: Are they aware of the fact [that] you are now making this presentation which will have a great impact, I would suppose, on their recovery?

MR. HENDERSON: No, I haven't informed the two or three hundred people that Mr. Pile represents that we are here today—

THE COURT: Has Mr. Angelos told the 11 thousand, probably ten thousand, in this category, or more, of the nature of these presentations and what the effect may be on whether they receive anything and when—

MR. HOGAN: I can't speak for individuals—representation to individual clients. There are instructions to tell people the status of the Johns Manville trust people earlier in line of rights under the plan they may not enjoy, but how people take that and exactly how individual clients are communicated to I can't represent to the Court.

When I speak personally to a client which is frequently, I tell them these particular items. We are involved in this litigation and that is how we are progressing.

I can tell the Court we don't have much by way of instructions from clients that we are doing wrong.

THE COURT: Are you affirmatively going out to communicate with each of the clients rather than just respond[ing] when they make inquiry?

MR. HOGAN: As times comes up. I have not personally called individual clients. To my knowledge, I don't know of any letter we sent out explaining the exact maneuvers. Perhaps we should.

I have . . . particularly difficulty with the entire process in that it is difficult to explain that this procedure might in some respects be deemed to put us at odds with our client.

THE COURT: What?

MR. HOGAN: This procedure may be deemed by the Court to put us at odds with our client. If we have conflicts with—

THE COURT: I don't deem anything. I am asking you whether you've considered fully your obligations under the rules of ethics and whether you have taken it up with your clients.

The answer I guess is you are not sure whether you have.

MR. HOGAN: Because I have not spoken with every client, Your Honor.

THE COURT: Has Mr. Angelos taken it up with his 11 thousand clients?

MR. HOGAN: I don't believe he has because that would be my job.

24. *Cf.* ABA Model Rules of Professional Conduct, Rule 1.4, comment 1 ("The client should have sufficient information to participate intelligently in decisions concerning the objectives of the representation and the means by which they are to be pursued, to the extent the client is willing and able to do so.").

25. *See, e.g.,* Tom R. Tyler, The Role of Perceived Injustice in Defendants' Evaluations of Their Courtroom Experience, 18 Law & Soc. Rev. 51 (1984) (study of litigant perceptions in traffic court suggesting, contrary to conventional wisdom, that perceived procedural fairness may be as or more important to litigant support for the system than favorable outcomes).

26. *See* Monroe H. Freedman, *Understanding Lawyers' Ethics* 39–41 (1990) (studies suggest that perceptions of fairness may be higher where litigants participate in adversary proceedings); Deborah R. Hensler, Symposium: Conflict of Laws and Complex Litigation Issues in Mass Tort Litigation: Resolving Mass Toxic Torts: Myths and Realities, 1989 U. Ill. L. Rev. 89, 98-99 (1989) (reporting Rand study indicating that, compared to litigants whose cases were arbitrated or settled, litigants whose cases went to trial had as high or higher levels of perceived control, participation, and comprehension).

27. In disciplining an attorney, the Nevada Supreme Court stated:

It cannot be overemphasized that communication . . . is, in many respects, at the center of all services. The failure to communicate creates the impression of a "neglectful" attorney and leads to client discontent even if the case is competently and expeditiously handled. This, in turn, brings disrepute upon the attorney and the legal profession as a whole.

State Bar v. Schreiber, 653 P.2d 151 (Nev. 1982).

28. *See* Tom R. Tyler, The Role of Perceived Injustice in Defendants' Evaluations of Their Courtroom Experience, 18 Law & Soc. Rev. 51 (1984) ("Political and legal theorists have generally agreed that government authorities can only function effectively when citizens support them enough to comply willingly with their directives.").

29. *See* Albrecht Wellmer, Practical Philosophy and the Theory of Society, in *The Communicative Ethics Controversy* 293, 303 (Seyla Benhabib & Fred Dallmayr eds., 1990) ("In terms of [the discursive] principle, institutions and power become *legitimate* only if their claim to recognition can be grounded in an unconstrained consensus reached by means of domination-free discourse.") (emphasis in original).

30. *See* Marcia Coyle & Claudia MacLachlan, Getting Victimized by the Legal System, Nat'l L.J., Sept. 21, 1992, at S8.

31. *See* Getting Victimized by the Legal System, Nat'l L.J., Sept. 21, 1992, at S8.

32. *See, e.g., In re* Joint E. & S. Dist. Asbestos Litig. (Keene Corporation), 14 F.3d 726 (2d Cir. 1993); *In re* Joint E. & S. Dists. Asbestos Litig., 982 F.2d 721 (2d Cir. 1992), *modified on rehearing,* 993 F.2d 7 (2d Cir. 1993).

33. *See* Edward A. Adams, Bankruptcy Fees Here Are the Highest in Nation, N.Y. L.J., June 3, 24, 1993, at 1.

34. Measures can be taken to maintain confidentiality even in large meetings. Rules that would maintain that such meetings violate established norms of lawyer-client confidences would be ill advised and would only further frustrate lawyer-client communication.

35. Many small law firms are "affiliated with" these national leaders. *See, e.g.,* Mealey's Litig. Rpts., Asbestos, Aug. 20, 1993, at 1 (some seventy firms).

36. *See* John Flynn Romey, Discovery Expedited in Breast Implant Cases, Chi. Daily L. Bull., Sept. 23, 1992, at 1.

37. The Agent Orange Class Assistance Program (AOCAP) has utilized electronic mail (E-mail) as an inexpensive method of communication since the establishment of its offices in April 1989. The E-mail system, called VETnet, is a subsystem of the Telenet E-mail system owned by U.S. Sprint.

VETnet enables subscribers to communicate through any computer equipped with a modem with any other subscriber who has similar equipment or a fax machine. Messages sent through VETnet are stored in an "electronic mailbox" in a mainframe computer which can only be accessed by the owner of that particular mailbox.

VETnet has evolved into the primary means of communication within the AOCAP network. The system is regularly used to transmit announcements of systemwide interest, and AOCAP grantees use the system to transmit their quarterly program reports.

VETnet has played a crucial role in the operation of the AOCAP initiative to contact and provide services to the original claimants in the Agent Orange Settlement. These claimants, who submitted claims on behalf of their children in 1984, are contacted by the National Information System (NIS) and asked to call its toll-free number. After an assessment by NIS, veterans are referred to the nearest community AOCAP project that can help them. NIS staff then uses VETnet to notify that particular AOCAP project of the referral and to transmit the client assessment and any relevant "casenotes."

In addition to being able to communicate more inexpensively than by phone or fax, VETnet allows AOCAP to send messages to any number of subscriber mailboxes simultaneously. Messages can be sent with a return "receipt" so the sender can verify that the message was received. VETnet also lets the sender transmit messages at his or her convenience, rather than only when the receiving party is available.

38. *See* Charles Boisseau, High-Tech Pain Reliever for Huge Legal Headache; Cutting the Paper; Computer CDs Should Speed Up Implant Lawsuit, Houston Chron., Oct. 28, 1992, Business, at 1.

39. *Cf.* Turning the Desktop PC into a Talk Radio Medium, N.Y. Times, Mar. 4, 1993, at A1 (discussing "radio talk show" to be "broadcast" on computer network linking ten million scientists, academics, engineers, and high-tech executives).

40. *See In re* School Asbestos Litig., 977 F.2d 764 (3rd Cir. 1992) (criticizing judge for attending a conference financed by plaintiffs' attorneys).

41. Fourth Annual Report of the Special Master on the Distribution of the Agent Orange Settlement Fund, Sept. 30, 1992.

42. *Id.*

43. *See, e.g.*, The Veterans Self-Help Guide on Agent Orange, Nov. 1991 (containing basic overview and history of the Agent Orange problem with information on how to obtain benefits and get help); New Alliances for Vietnam Veterans and Their Families: Resource Guide (1992) (describing eight national support projects).

44. *Cf.* United States v. Mosquera, 813 F. Supp. 962 (E.D.N.Y. 1992) (appointing coordinating counsel in large multilingual, multide-

fendant case with many thousands of documents, parties' documents paid for by government, in essence permitting court to take over traditional function in managing documents in their own cases).

45. *See e.g.,* United States v. Kras, 409 U.S. 434 (1973) (requiring payment of filing fee by indigents to obtain bankruptcy relief).

46. These "focus groups" are widely used in the advertising industry.

47. *See* ABA Model Rules of Professional Conduct, Rules 1.7, 1.8, 1.9 (conflicts of interest); *see also* American Law Institute, Restatement of the Law Governing Lawyers, Tent. Draft No. 4, chapter 8 (1991) (conflicts of interest).

48. Differences in interests had been observed in class actions before the age of mass torts. *See, e.g.,* Stephen Ellman, Client-Centeredness Multiplied: Individual Autonomy and Collective Mobilization in Public Interest Lawyers' Representation of Groups, 78 Va. L. Rev. 1103 (1992); John C. Coffee, Jr., Regulation of Entrepreneurial Litigation: Balancing Fairness and Efficiency in the Large Class Action, 54 U. Chi. L. Rev. 877 (1987); Brian J. Waid, Ethical Problems of the Class Action Practitioner: Continued Neglect by the Drafters of the Model Rules of Professional Conduct, 27 Loy. L. Rev. 1047 (1981); Symposium, Developments in the Law—Class Actions, 89 Harv. L. Rev. 1318 (1976).

49. *See* Michael D. Ricciuti, Equity and Accountability in the Reform of Settlement Procedures in Mass Tort Cases: The Ethical Duty to Consult, 1 Geo. J. Legal Ethics 817 (1988) (proposing a form of "communication" between class attorneys and class members in order to minimize conflict). The author defines the problem as follows:

> [T]here is no definable client who can exercise the same level of restraint upon attorney conduct that exists in [a] one-to-one case, nor is the attorney bound to as explicit a set of ethical guidelines as exist in the one-to-one suit. These factors, coupled with the difficulties in judicial supervision of class attorney conduct, may allow the class attorney to use the class device only as a means of generating fees, where "the attorney for the plaintiff is the dominus litus and the plaintiff only a key to the courthouse door disposable once entry has been effected. . . ."

Id. at 842 (quoting Saylor v. Linsley, 456 F.2d 896, 900 (2d Cir. 1972); *see also* Manual for Complex Litigation Second § 30.41 (1985) ("As a practical matter, the dynamics of class action settlement may lead the negotiating parties—even those with the best of intentions—to regard the interests of the class members too lightly.").

50. *See* John J. Donohue III, The Effects of Fee Shifting on the Settlement Rate: Theoretical Observations on Costs, Conflicts, and Contingency Fees, 54 Law & Contemp. Probs. 195, 211 (1991).

51. In general, my view is that civil suits should not be used to punish, but to correct and compensate for past errors. The criminal law serves better for punitive purposes. This is one of the reasons I oppose punitive damages in cases in which they punish over and over again without regard to fault or rehabilitation.

52. *See* ABA Model Rules of Professional Conduct, Rule 1.5(c). The Committee on Professional Responsibility of the Association of the Bar of the City of New York recently undertook a study of regulations governing contingency fees and alternative contingent fee arrangements. *See* The Regulation of Contingent Fees, Including Alternative Contingent Fee Arrangements, Record of the Assoc. of the Bar of the City of N.Y. 637 (1990).

53. Stuart M. Speiser identifies the "entrepreneur-lawyer" as one of three features unique to American tort litigation. Stuart M. Speiser, *Lawsuit* 119–20 (1980).

54. *See* Nancy Morawetz, Bargaining, Class Representation, and Fairness, 54 Ohio St. L. J. 1, 4 n.10 (1993) (noting that "commentators and the courts have expressed concern about lawyers placing their own economic interest in a large and certain fee award over the interests of the class"; collecting literature on the problem); *cf.* Franks v. Kroger Co., 649 F.2d 1216, 1224–26 (6th Cir. 1981) (reversing settlement in civil rights class action that provided for $10,000 and a promotion for one named plaintiff, $500 for another named plaintiff, $47,000 in attorneys' fees for class counsel, and only an individual claims procedure but no recovery for other class members, on grounds that class members would have been as well or better off bringing their own claims), *on rehearing,* 670 P.2d 71 (6th Cir. 1982) (vacating prior opinion and reinstating settlement).

55. For an analysis of the ethical dilemma of the class action lawyer and discussion of several proposed norms that might guide the lawyer's decisionmaking, see Nancy Morawetz, Bargaining, Class Representation, and Fairness, 54 Ohio St. L. J. 1 (1993).

56. *In re* Joint E. & S. Dist. Asbestos Litig. (Johns-Manville Corporation), 982 F.2d 721 (2d Cir. 1992), *modified on rehearing,* 993 F.2d 7 (2d Cir. 1993); *see also* Note, 58 Brook L. Rev., 553, 626 (1992) (criticizing Second Circuit opinion for requiring so many subclasses).

57. *See* Michael D. Ricciuti, Equity and Accountability in the Reform of Settlement Procedures in Mass Tort Cases: The Ethical Duty to Consult, 1 Geo. J. Legal Ethics 817, 829 (1988) ("In practical terms, the lack of guidance in the ethical framework provides class attorneys with almost unfettered control over the action.").

58. *See* note 56, *supra;* Note, *In re* Eastern and Southern Districts Asbestos Litigation: Bankrupt and Backlogged—A Proposal for the

Use of Federal Common Law in Mass Tort Class Actions, 58 Brook. L. Rev. 553, 626 (1992).

59. *See* Stalled Tobacco Suit Is Revived by Ruling, N.Y. Times, Feb. 1, 1993, at B5. A new powerful consortium of twenty-six major law firms will now finance class and other actions. Andrew Blum, Tobacco Fight Grows Hotter, Nat. L.J., Apr. 18, 1994, at A6

60. *See, e.g.,* Cullen v. New York State Civil Serv. Comm'n, 566 F.2d 846, 848 (2d Cir. 1977) (in class action brought on behalf of county employees alleging coerced political contributions, trial judge's decision to replace inexperienced proposed class counsel with more experienced civil rights litigator upheld on grounds that ruling was not appealable and the "court's selection of counsel for the absent class should be guided by the best interests of those members, not the entrepreneurial initiative of the named plaintiffs' counsel").

61. *See* David Luban, *Lawyers and Justice: An Ethical Study* 341-57 (1988) (discussing problem of intraclass conflicts); Nancy Morawetz, Bargaining, Class Representation, and Fairness, 54 Ohio St. L. J. 1 (1993) (examining dilemma facing class action attorney in discerning desires and best interests of class as a whole).

62. *See* Fed. R. Civ. P. 23(c)(4); *In re* Joint E. & S. Dists. Asbestos Litig., 982 F.2d 721, 739 (2d Cir. 1992), *modified on rehearing,* 993 F.2d 7 (2d Cir. 1993).

63. *In re.* Joint E. and S. Dists. Asbestos Litig., 982 F.2d 721, 725 (2d Cir. 1992), *modified on rehearing,* 993 F.2d 7 (2d Cir. 1993) (in concluding that the judgment approving the settlement must be vacated, the court wrote, "to the extent that the judgment rests on diversity jurisdiction, the use of a mandatory non-opt-out class action without proper subclasses violates the requirements of Rule 23 of the Federal Rules of Civil Procedure").

64. In the breast implant litigation two local attorneys were appointed as liaison counsel in part apparently because they did not represent a substantial group of clients and had no connection with any of the attorneys seeking control. *See* Alison Frankel, Implant Litigation: Heavy Politics, Lingering Questions, Am. Law., Sept. 1992, at 90 (describing the seventeen lawyers Judge Pointer appointed to the steering committee as "five class action supporters, seven class action opponents, and five lawyers who had not aligned themselves with [either] faction").

65. A recent ethics opinion issued by the American Bar Association expressed serious concerns about conflicts among present clients in mass representation, particularly with respect to the creation of "deferred docket registries" for less serious asbestos-related diseases. *See* ABA Committee on Ethics and Professional Responsibility, Formal Opinion 93-371 (Apr. 16, 1993). The opinion quotes the Comment to

Model Rule 1.7(b), which states, "An impermissible conflict may exist by reason of . . . the fact that there are substantially different possibilities of settlement of the claims of liabilities in question. Yet deferred docket registries are widely used for claimants with pleural plaque in asbestos cases if a disability due to asbestos disclosure is potential."

66. Deborah R. Hensler et al., Asbestos in the Courts: The Challenge of Mass Toxic Torts 96–97 (Rand Institute, 1985).

67. *See* Law Firm of Shea & Gardner, Washington, D.C., Executive Summary: CCR Class Action Settlement (Feb. 2, 1993); *see also* Don J. DeBenedictis, Model for Asbestos Settlements, A.B.A. J., Apr. 1993, at 22 (describing agreement by companies to pay one hundred thousand asbestos plaintiffs more than $1 billion over ten years).

68. This problem is a version of the following familiar political dilemma: "How can presently existing people commit their descendants to political decisions without knowing what they want?" David Luban, *Lawyers and Justice: An Ethical Study* 347, 347–51 (1988) (discussing problem of future claimants in class action context). In most mass tort cases to date, much as in our dealings with the federal budget deficit, the rights of future claimants have been determined not by an attempt to discern what they want, but rather by default: by not accounting for the rights of future claimants we, in practical effect, destroy those rights.

69. The issue also sometimes arises in cases not involving limited funds. *See, e.g.,* David Lauter, Bendectin Pact Creating Furor, Nat'l L.J., July 30, 1984, at 1 (reporting proposed Bendectin settlement involving Merrell Dow setting aside funds for future claims).

The many unanswered questions that arise when massive enterprise liability and uncertain future claims collide with the bankruptcy code are discussed in Mark J. Roe, Bankruptcy and Mass Tort, 84 Colum. L. Rev. 846 (1984). The author advocates early reorganization when future claims are large relative to overall firm value. To do otherwise, he claims, might result in operational collapse, seriously impairing the value of future claims. *See also* Frederick M. Baron, An Asbestos Settlement with a Hidden Agenda, Wall St. J., May 6, 1993, at A11 (criticizing a class action settlement that permitted a solvent firm to bind all future claimants as allowing the corporation to obtain a bankruptcy result without filing for bankruptcy).

70. *See, e.g., In re* Joint E. & S. Dists. Asbestos Litig., 133 F.R.D. 425 (E. & S.D.N.Y. 1990) (denying motion to disqualify representative of future claimants on ground that he represented present claimants); Locks v. United States Trustee, No. 93-410, 1993 U.S. Dist. LEXIS 10408 at 34 (W.D. Pa. July 19, 1993) (motion by attorney to be appointed legal representative of postpetition and future asbestos disease creditors in H. K. Porter bankruptcy denied due to relationship of lawyer to prepetition claimants).

71. Much of the debate over the asbestos settlement in Philadelphia involving the Center for Claims Resolution (CCR), which represents a group of asbestos defendants, has focused on the settlement's effect on the rights of future claimants. *See, e.g.,* Opposition Swells to Asbestos Settlement, Nat'l L.J., Feb. 1, 1993, at 6; Weiner Grants Class Certification in CCR Futures Deal, 8 Mealey's Litig. Rpts., Asbestos 6 (Feb. 5, 1993); Long-Awaited Futures Class Action and Settlement Filed, Asbestos Litig. Rptr. (Andrews), Jan. 22, 1993, at 26,772; New Plaintiffs' Organization Opposes Class Settlement of Future Claims, Asbestos Litig. Rptr. (Andrews), Nov. 6, 1992, at 26,316. Objectors to the proposed settlement have claimed that it violates ethical rules because class counsel purport to represent both present and future claimants. *See* Preliminary Fairness Hearings in Carlough Slated for Aug. 23, 8 Mealey's Litig. Rpts., Asbestos 4 (Aug. 20, 1993).

Other asbestos litigation frequently has involved the problem of future claimants. *See, e.g., In re* Joint E. & S. Dists. Asbestos Litig., 129 B.R. 710, 783-84 (E. & S.D.N.Y. 1991) (describing input of representative of future claimants in settlement of class action), *vacated,* 982 F.2d 721 (2d Cir. 1992), *modified on rehearing,* 993 F.2d 7 (2d Cir. 1993); National Gypsum Judge Indicates Confirmation Imminent, 8 Mealey's Litig. Rpts., Asbestos 3 (Feb. 5, 1993) (bankruptcy court enjoined current claimants from proceeding against bankrupt's successor but refused to enjoin future claimants); Bankruptcy and District Courts Rule on 'Futures' Representation in H. K. Porter, 8 Mealey's Litig. Rpts., Asbestos 8 (Aug. 6, 1993) ("The proposed reorganization plan for H. K. Porter Company Inc. is not confirmable because it fails to provide for asbestos claimants who will manifest injuries prior to final distribution of the estate"); Stacy Adler, Raymark Asbestos Claims Combined into Class Action, Bus. Ins., June 20, 1988, at 2 (asbestos class action suit against Raymark Industries included future claims); *see generally* Guerry R. Thornton, Jr., A Debtor Can Halt the Onslaught of Pending Cases, New Actions, Nat'l L.J., Jan. 9, 1989, at 18 (discussing use of bankruptcy laws in tort cases to resolve future claims).

72. In one global settlement a large group of law firms agreed to "recommend the terms of this Agreement to all Future Claimants and to use its best efforts to have such Claimants' Claims fully resolved and disposed of pursuant to the terms of this Agreement," Mealey's Litig. Rpts., Asbestos 4, Aug. 20, 1993.

73. *See In re* Joint E. & S. Dists. Asbestos Litig., 129 B.R. 710, 783–84 (E. & S.D.N.Y. 1991), *vacated,* 982 F.2d 721 (2d Cir. 1992), *modified on rehearing,* 993 F.2d 7 (2d Cir. 1993).

74. *See Id.* at 926–31 (interim report of court-appointed expert regarding process of estimating future claims); *see also In re* Joint E. & S. Dists. Asbestos Litig., 982 F.2d 721 (2d Cir. 1992) (affirming appoint-

ment of Rule 706 expert), *modified on rehearing,* 993 F.2d 7 (2d Cir. 1993).

75. One early estimate of the minimum number of future suits in asbestos litigation was thirty thousand. Alexander Walker et al., Projections of Asbestos-Related Disease 1980–2009, 25 J. Occupational Med. 409 (1983). A "sensitivity analysis" of Walker's work suggests that Walker substantially underestimated the uncertainty of his projections. *See* Joel E. Cohen et al., An Analysis of Alexander M. Walker's "Projections of Asbestos-Related Disease 1980–2009" (August 1984) (unpublished manuscript); *see also* Michael A. Stoto, The Accuracy of Population Projections, 78 J. Am. Stat. Ass'n 13 (1983) (concluding that the more complex the projection technique, the greater the error in prediction). My own best estimate at the moment of future claims is somewhere between three hundred and six hundred thousand claims into the mid-twenty-first century.

The reliability of long-term forecasting in the social sciences has been debated since the first computer studies predicted a global population collapse in the twenty-first century. *See* D. H. Meadows et al., *The Limits to Growth* (1972) (study produced for the Club of Rome); Gerald O. Barney, *The Global 2000 Report to the President Entering the 21st Century* (1980). These studies were criticized on the grounds that critical corrective factors had been omitted or underestimated. *See, e.g.,* Julian L. Simon & Herman Kahn, *The Resourceful Earth: A Response to Global 2000* (1984). The overpopulation debate remains subject to widely differing analyses.

The new science of chaos theory addresses the problem of accuracy in long-term predictions. *See generally* I. Peterson, *The Mathematical Tourist* 144–49 (1988). While many complex systems are amenable to accurate prediction, a "chaotic" system is not, even though it may be governed by simple, deterministic (nonrandom) rules which are fully understood. Prediction fails in a chaotic system because the governing rules rapidly compound unavoidable small errors until they dominate the system.

The best-known example of chaos relates to weather prediction, where the sensitivity of the governing rules has been termed the "butterfly effect." *See* Edward Lorenz, Predictability: Does the Flap of a Butterfly's Wings in Brazil Set Off a Tornado in Texas?, Address to the Annual Meeting of the American Association for the Advancement of Science, Washington, D.C. (Dec. 29, 1979). If a computer were programmed with the billions of equations that govern the weather, but a single flap of a butterfly's wings was not accounted for, predictions of global weather patterns a few days later might be completely unreliable. The weather equations might rapidly magnify the minute initial error until it dominated our prediction.

Prediction of future claimants in any given mass tort litigation does not necessarily constitute a chaotic system. Chaos theory suggests, however, that we should not place great confidence in our ability to predict the future. This is especially true in the social sciences, where our understanding of the governing principles is limited.

76. The plaintiffs' bar recognizes the dilemma and is seeking estimates in a number of different trusts and proposed settlements. Letter from Mark Peterson, Rand Institute for Civil Justice, to author, Apr. 30, 1993, at 7.

77. *See* Peter H. Schuck, The Worst Should Go First: Deferral Registries in Asbestos Litigation, 15 Harv. J.L. & Pub. Pol'y 541 (1992) (describing phenomenon of pleural registries and examining possible legal bases for their creation); *see also In re* Asbestos II, 142 F.R.D. 152 (N.D. Ill. 1992) (establishing deferral registry); Burns v. Celotex Corp., 587 N.E.2d 1092 (Ill. App. Ct. 1992) (order establishing deferred docket registry held nonappealable); *In re* Asbestos Cases, 586 N.E.2d 521 (Ill. App. Ct. 1991) (same).

78. *See* Stipulation Regarding Voluntary Dismissal of Cases upon Certain Conditions, *In re* Mass. Asbestos Litig., M.D.L. Nos. 1–5 (D. Mass., Nov. 7, 1985) (agreement to voluntarily dismiss certain cases on condition that statute of limitations be tolled).

79. *See* Letter from Law Firm of Shea & Gardner, Washington, D.C., to The Honorable Charles R. Weiner, United States District Judge, Eastern District of Pennsylvania, Jan. 4, 1993 (describing deferred docket registries in detail and stating that "across-the-board judicial creation of deferral dockets for claimants who have been exposed to asbestos but who presently have no asbestos-related impairment is extremely important to the effective national management of asbestos litigation").

80. *See* ABA Model Rules of Professional Conduct, Rule 1.6 ("A lawyer shall not reveal information relating to representation of a client unless the client consents after consultation"); *see also* American Law Institute, Restatement of the Law Governing Lawyers, Tent. Draft Nos. 2–3, chapter 5 (1991) (confidentiality responsibilities of lawyers).

81. For example, the claims by the government that lawyers have an obligation to inform regulators about the delicts of their clients. Almost all cases have been settled, leaving this critical question unresolved by the courts. Amy Stevens, S & L Lawsuits Fail to Answer Questions of Ethical Standards, Wall St. J., Oct. 29, 1993, at B6. *But cf.* Marianne Lavelle, High Court to Decide Whether S & L Lawyers Have Duty to Disclose, Nat'l L. J., Dec. 13, 1993, at 7 (O'Melveny & Myers v. FDIC, suit by receiver of bank against former attorneys for bank).

82. *See* Daniel Wise, Abrams Advocates Government Access to Court-Sealed Files; Responsibility for Safety Cited, N.Y. L.J., Apr. 12,

1991, at 1 (describing New York Attorney General's efforts to enact legislation to give government agencies access to materials shielded from the public by court orders).

83. Secrecy is also an issue when alternative dispute resolution is employed. There is difficulty, for example, in ensuring the confidentiality of the proceeding after its conclusion when the "minitrial" (a dry run before an impartial person or jury with evidence submitted in a summary form) is utilized. Unlike settlement offers, which are traditionally entitled to protection from discovery, it is unsettled whether minitrial statements or opinions of neutral advisers are afforded the same protections. *Compare* Grumman Aerospace Corp. v. Titanium Corp. of Am., 91 F.R.D. 84 (E.D.N.Y. 1981) (requiring report prepared by neutral adviser to be produced) *with* Cincinnati Gas & Elec. Co. v. General Elec. Co., 117 F.R.D. 597 (S.D. Ohio 1987), *aff'd,* 854 F.2d 900 (6th Cir. 1988), *cert. denied,* 489 U.S. 1033 (1989) (upholding confidentiality of a summary jury trial. *See generally* Joseph T. McLaughlin, Alternative Dispute Resolution, ALI-ABA Course of Study, Trial Evidence, Civil Practice, and Effective Litigation Techniques in the Federal Courts 355, 377–78, Feb. 25–27, 1993.

84. Judgments, too, are routinely sealed. *See* Alan Cooper, FDA Liable for Polio Vaccine, Nat'l L.J., Feb. 8, 1993, at 3 (describing how "substantial" judgments—possibly in excess of $20 million—were settled in the cases of men who had contracted polio after their children had taken oral vaccine).

85. An analogous desire for secrecy arises in the context of suits against the military or defense contractors. The desire for secrecy in this context is sometimes driven by national security concerns, as well as the more traditional worries about negative publicity and exposure to additional lawsuits. The Air Force and other military services have established procedures under which they prepare a special litigation report routinely made available to the public. In this way, the military is able to exercise some control over the flow of information from the outset of the case. *See* Stuart M. Speiser, *Lawsuit* 341 (1980) (such reports usually contain "enough information to determine the cause of the accident, and . . . [include] photographs of failed parts which may form the basis for product liability claims."); *see also* Nat'l L.J., May 3, 1993, at 6 (claims of workers based on exposure to exotic chemicals in producing stealth bomber).

86. *See* Teresa M. Hendricks & Joseph W. Moch, Protective Orders Assault Consumers, Nat'l L.J., Feb. 8, 1993, at 15 (accusing corporate defendants of "shuffl[ing], hid[ing] or destroy[ing]" relevant documents and characterizing Federal Rule of Civil Procedure 26(c) as "the silencer on the smoking gun—keeping all evidence of dangerous products secret for good cause"); *see also* Stuart Mieher, Westinghouse

Lawyer Urged in '88 That Toxic-Safety Records Be Destroyed, Wall St. J., Feb. 26, 1993, at A4 (describing an "entry-level attorney'[s]" memo suggesting that plant safety audits be destroyed because they revealed that the company knew of hazards from toxic substances but failed to take corrective measures); Janice Toran, Secrecy Orders and Government Litigants: "A Northwest Passage around the Freedom of Information Act," 27 Ga. L. Rev. 121 (1992) (discussing how the Freedom of Information Act is evaded through secrecy orders).

87. This approach can backfire, however. For example, Pfizer, Inc., the pharmaceutical company, has been accused of "implement[ing] . . . a decade[-long] strategy of relying on high-priced lawyers and lobbyists to avoid a full-scale public debate over its production of defective heart valves." Greg Rushford, Pfizer's Telltale Heart Valve: Secrecy Strategy in Tatters as Questions Mount, Legal Times, Feb. 26, 1990, at 1. Despite Pfizer's strategy of settling suits and keeping documents secret, aggressive plaintiffs' lawyers have been able to "piece together a record of Pfizer's conduct." *Id.*

88. Breast implant litigation overcame prior secrecy agreements with big verdicts. In an early case, a jury awarded plaintiff $25 million, including $20 million in punitive damages. The verdict gave plaintiff's attorney considerable leverage in negotiating settlements in 250 other cases. *See* Amy Singer, Look over Here, Am. Law., Mar. 1993, at 86–88.

89. A recent appellate court decision held that even the bringing of a subsequent qui tam action will not permit the revelation of previously sealed documents. United States *ex rel.* Kreindler & Kreindler v. United Technologies Corp., 985 F.2d 1148 (2d Cir.), *cert. denied*, 113 S. Ct. 2962 (1993). Kreindler (a law firm) had entered into a settlement and secrecy agreement in a previous action against the defendant corporation. The court ruled that in the qui tam action filed under the False Claims Act, 31 U.S.C. § 3729 (1988), the firm was prohibited from disclosing information contained in the sealed documents despite the public interest in knowing about the safety of the helicopters involved. *See also* Smith v. MCI Telecommunications Corp., 1993 U.S. Dist. LEXIS 6114 (D. Kan. Apr. 28, 1993) (First Amendment bars court-imposed confidentiality order after settlement agreement where confidentiality was not negotiated as part of settlement).

90. *In re* "Agent Orange" Prod. Liab. Litig., 104 F.R.D. 559 (E.D.N.Y. 1985), *aff'd*, 821 F.2d 139 (2d Cir. 1987) (adopting magistrate judge's opinion modifying protective orders issued in pretrial phase of the litigation ordering that (1) class members were entitled to disclosure of materials shielded by protective order in the absence of good cause; (2) manufacturer must show need for confidentiality to maintain protective order; and (3) confidential medical records and

trade secrets in possession of EPA would not be disclosed. For a detailed recounting of the discovery order, see Shira A. Scheindlin, Discovering the Discoverable: A Bird's Eye View of Discovery in a Complex Multi-District Class Action Litigation, 52 Brook. L. Rev. 397 (1986).

91. In May 1990 a subcommittee of the Senate Judiciary Committee examining court secrecy as it affected victims' rights and public policy interests heard poignant testimony from a man who stated, "I believe that secrecy killed my wife." She had died from a defective heart valve. He later learned that even before his wife had her heart valve implanted, dozens of other valves had malfunctioned. Several lawsuits had been filed, but the settlements were conditioned on secrecy. Abraham Fuchsberg, The Blindfold of Justice, N.Y. L.J., Oct. 4, 1990, at 2.

92. One judge who did consider the public interest demonstrated that even the secrecy of the grand jury may have to yield to the public's need to know. Judge Sherman G. Finesilver ordered the United States government to redact a grand jury report on environmental crimes at the Rocky Flats nuclear weapons plant. Although Judge Finesilver declined to accede to media requests that he unseal the report, he cited the public interest in ensuring the region's environmental safety as a compelling reason to create a new version of the report for public release. Judge Aims to Release a Version of Jurors' Report on Bomb Plant, N.Y. Times, Dec. 5, 1992, at A9.

93. There are times when secrecy may serve a higher goal. For example, a pharmaceutical company has no duty to disclose the names of health care providers reporting adverse reactions in patients because the information is available from the FDA, albeit with patients' and physicians' names redacted. Eli Lilly & Co. v. Marshall, 850 S.W.2d 155 (Tex. 1993). Requiring disclosure, the court reasoned, would jeopardize the voluntary reporting system. Id. at 160.

94. Part of the problem associated with ensuring consumer health and safety stems from the fact that federal regulation is on a patchwork basis with no clear indication of preemption. See Toy Manufacturers of America v. Blumenthal, 986 F.2d 615 (2d Cir. 1993) (state law regulating hazardous toys not preempted by Consumer Product Safety Commission); Burke v. Dow Chem. Co. et al., 797 F. Supp. 1128 (E.D.N.Y. 1992) (in product liability action on behalf of brain-damaged child injured by mother's exposure to insecticide, mislabeling claims were preempted by FIFRA but other claims were not).

95. Note, Timothy D. Zick, Reporting Substantial Product Safety Hazards under the Consumer Product Safety Act: The Products Liability Interface, 80 Geo. L.J. 387, 389 n.9 (1991).

96. Id. at 390.

97. 15 U.S.C. § 2084 (West Supp. 1991).

98. See Timothy D. Zick, Reporting Substantial Product Safety Haz-

ards under the Consumer Product Safety Act, 80 Geo. L.J. 387, 399 (1991).

99. Unsafe Toys: Weak Government Regulation Cited in Report on Toy Injury Hazards, BNA, Daily Report for Executives, Nov. 26, 1992, at A1. The report criticizes the CPSC for failing to take aggressive steps to prevent dangerous toys from getting into the hands of consumers. While at least one-sixth of the toys sampled are so unsafe as to warrant recall, the Commission only tests 1 percent of the toys on the market. *Id*. In the preceding year (1990), 164,000 children were involved in toy-related injuries. *Id.; see* Carl Tobias, Consumer Agency Falling Down on Job, Legal Times, Mar. 20, 1989, at 19.

100. Unsafe Toys: Weak Government Regulation Cited in Report on Toy Injury Hazards, BNA, Daily Report for Executives, Nov. 26, 1992, at A1.

101. *See* Labor Union Says OSHA Failing to Protect Workers, Christ. Sci. Mon., Apr. 29, 1992, at 3.

102. *See, e.g.,* Big OSHA Fines Often Cut Down to a Pittance, Houst. Chron., Apr. 2, 1992, at A1 (describing how a $6.4 million fine lodged against Phillips Petroleum Co. was reduced to $4 million and serious charges were dropped even though OSHA found close to six hundred violations after an explosion killed twenty-three in a chemical plant); *see also* OSHA Accused of "Pitifully Weak" Enforcement of Job Safety Rules, L.A. Times, Sept. 2, 1988, at D1.

103. Susan D. Carle, Note, A Hazardous Mix: Discretion to Disclose and Incentives to Suppress under OSHA's Hazard Communication Standard, 97 Yale L.J. 581, 581–82 (1988).

104. *Id*. "OSHA's effectiveness ha[s] been undermined by budget cuts, shortages of inspectors, lax enforcement practices and egregious lags in creating standards for hazardous substances." Ronald E. Roel, Are Cuts Crippling a Watchdog?: OSHA, under Attack from Labor, Vehemently Denies Its Record as Injuries Rise and Inspections Lapse, Newsday, May 8, 1988, at 66.

105. *See, e.g.,* Two Studies Link Breast Implants and Antibodies, N.Y. Times, Mar. 20, 1993, at A8; The FDA and the Implant Mess, Chi. Trib., Feb. 29, 1992, at 20. Plaintiffs have had great difficulty securing information about breast implants from the Dow Corning Corporation. After hiring former attorney general Griffin Bell to help with the legal and public relations controversy surrounding the implants, Dow Corning refused to release the investigative report claiming it was privileged. Plaintiffs' attorneys disagreed. Andrew Blum, Bid Made for Implant Papers, Nat'l L.J., Feb. 1, 1993, at 3.

106. Gina Kolata, FDA Critics Doubt Agency Has Power to Protect the Public, Houst. Chron., Jan 26, 1992, at A2. The same problems are associated with the FDA's handling of the sleeping pill Halcion which

has been linked to psychotic behavior. "It shouldn't take a court case and the subpoena power of the criminal justice system to learn all there is to know about a drug's safety." Editorial, The Halcion File, Wash. Post, May 21, 1992, at A24; *see also* Andrew Blum, UpJohn Spars on Halcion Papers, Nat'l L.J., Oct. 26, 1992, at 3 (describing the company's battle to keep from public view documents used before juries in two cases).

The FDA has also been severely criticized for its failure to monitor the Shiley heart valve which is allegedly responsible for the deaths of some two hundred patients. *See* Report Attacks Sale of Faulty Heart Valves, L.A. Times, Feb. 26, 1990, at A3.

Perhaps we should not be surprised by the FDA's failures. A congressional report released in 1991 painted a grim picture of the agency with its crumbling buildings, inadequate staff, lack of funds and weak leadership. *See* Report Outlines Serious Weakness in FDA, USA Today, May 15, 1992, at 5D.

107. In response to criticism of its effectiveness in monitoring the safety of medical products that are permitted to enter consumer market, the FDA is calling for tighter scientific controls of clinical trials run by producers of medical devices. The FDA Commissioner cites the agency's experience with breast implants and intrauterine devices as pointing to questions about the efficacy of FDA evaluation procedures. *See* FDA to Toughen Testing of Devices, N.Y. Times, Mar. 5, 1993, at A18.

108. The FDA itself apparently doubts that it can adequately protect the public given the fact that it lacks subpoena power and is constantly stymied by secrecy orders that keep information out of its reach. *See* Questions Raised on Ability of FDA, N.Y. Times, Jan. 26, 1992, at A1 (describing how the FDA relies on manufacturers' test results and lacks the subpoena power to obtain documents that are available only to trial lawyers, leaving the agency with no means to discover fraud or misrepresentation of data provided by companies). The article also describes the FDA's frustration with the companies' ability to obtain secrecy orders that routinely keep information about the safety of drugs and devices out of their reach.

109. This effort is spearheaded by the Association of Trial Lawyers of America. Not surprisingly, some defense lawyers have characterized these efforts as "purely self-serving." Robert N. Weiner, The Case for Protective Orders, Manhattan Law., Nov. 1991, at 42. The author criticizes the one-sided nature of these rules and cautions that defendants might respond by either vigorously resisting discovery or settling early and paying more money. Either response, he warns, will result in increased consumer prices. The author also contends that plaintiffs rely solely on anecdotal evidence in urging these revisions. The Federal Courts Study Committee, he notes, "examined the issue of confiden-

tiality in the federal judiciary and found no basis for concern nor any reason to limit the court's discretion." *Id.* at 43.

110. A contrary point of view is espoused in Arthur R. Miller, Confidentiality, Protective Orders, and Public Access to the Courts, 105 Harv. L. Rev. 427 (1991). Professor Miller argues against reforms proposed to create a presumption of public access to discovery on several grounds. First, he suggests that curtailment of judicial discretion or restrictions on protective orders would decrease cooperation between litigants and lead to abuses. *Id.* at 463. Second, he argues that significant privacy and property rights would be jeopardized should reforms be adopted. *Id.* at 464–77. Finally, Professor Miller claims that there is an exaggerated concern over secrecy problems in our judicial system since "the number of cases that could contain information that has any bearing on public health or safety is minuscule compared to the corpus of litigation in this country." *Id.* at 477. He asserts that courts already possess the authority to protect public health and safety and that judges routinely use their discretion to do so. *Id.* at 478–79.

111. Plaintiffs' attorneys are not the only ones who are lobbying for legislation that will be favorable to them in a trial setting. The Texas Legislature, which adopted a strong antisecrecy rule, recently approved two reforms that will have the effect of limiting jury awards. The state is known as a proplaintiff forum. One law will create exemptions from product defect lawsuits for certain industries, including alcohol and tobacco. The other will require plaintiffs to offer proof that a manufacturer ignored a safer, more cost-effective alternative before they can prevail on a product defect claim. *See* Texas Legislature Approves Two Bills That Are Meant To Limit Jury Awards, Wall St. J., Feb. 25, 1993, at B3.

112. *See* Federal Arbitration Act, 9 U.S.C. §§ 1-14, 201–208 (1988).

113. *See* David Luban, *Lawyers and Justice: An Ethical Study* 206–34 (1988) (arguing for an ethical obligation of corporate counsel to reveal smoking-gun documents where public health and safety is threatened); United States *ex rel.* Kreindler & Kreindler v. United Technologies Corp., 985 F.2d 1148 (2d Cir. 1993) (denying qui tam action by attorneys).

114. Fla. Stat. Ann. Ch. 69.081 (West Supp. 1993): Sunshine in Litigation Act.

115. Tex. R. Civ. P. 76(a). *See generally* Michael J. Mucchetti, Public Access to Public Courts: Discouraging Secrecy in the Public Interest, 69 Tex. L. Rev. 643 (1991). The author, a Texas Supreme Court Justice, describes the genesis of Rule 76(a) and explains its provisions in detail.

116. A Texas appeals court recently reversed the lower court's disclosure order in Ford Motor Co. v. Benson, 846 S.W.2d 487 4 (Tex. Ct. App. 1993). In construing Rule 76(a) and its interface with Rule 166.5(c) which authorizes a trial court to issue a protective order, the

court ruled that Rule 76(a) applies only to "court records." The records involved in the case were not court records, rendering Rule 76(a) inapplicable. The court remanded for the trial court to make the requisite determination of whether there was "good cause" to protect the documents under Rule 166.5(c). *See* Texas Court Deals Loss to Foes of Secrecy, Nat'l L.J., Jan. 25, 1993, at 6.

One public-minded Texas judge, presiding over an asbestos suit, ignored a protective order on certain documents issued by another court. The appellate court found the judge's act improper and an abuse of discretion. Keene Corp. v. Caldwell, 840 S.W.2d 715 (Tex. Ct. App. 1992).

117. *See generally* Product Safety and Liability Reporter, BNA, Protective Orders: 50 State Survey (Special Report) Nov. 27, 1992; Richard A. Rosen & Karen E. Steinberg, New Developments in State Protective Order Legislation and Procedural Rules, ALI-ABA Course of Study, Trial Evidence, Civil Practice, and Effective Litigation Techniques in the Federal Courts 337, Feb. 25–27, 1993. *See also* Andrew Blum, Protective Order Battle Continues, Nat'l L.J., Jan. 11, 1993, at 3 (discussing plaintiffs' bar's continuing efforts to expand antisecrecy legislation and counterefforts of defense bar).

A brief historical overview of the practice of sealing records with commentary on the newly proposed statutes is found in John S. Kiernan & Shlomo Huttler, More Public Access to Discovery Documents?, Litig., Fall 1991, at 19. The authors offer tips for attorneys seeking to maintain confidentiality. *Id.* at 59. They conclude that despite the efforts to change the balance between confidentiality and disclosure, "[t]he inertia and desire for private resolution that have led to protective orders and sealing orders in the past are likely to survive the new wave of demands for increasing access." *Id.*

118. A bill introduced in the Senate by Herb Kohl (D-Wis.) would make information gathered in the course of civil litigation presumptively available to the public, unless particularized findings of fact by the judge showed that confidentiality of the information would not restrict the disclosure of information that is needed for the protection of public health and safety. The bill would also prohibit agreements between the parties that forbid disclosure of information to federal and state regulators. *See* Congressional and Administrative Highlights, 16 Federal Case News 33 (West Aug. 20, 1993), S. 1404, 103d Cong. 1st Sess. (1993), 139 Cong. Rec. S10, 854–57 (daily ed. Aug. 6, 1993) (text of bill).

Proposed changes in the federal discovery rules requiring early revelation without request may increase public disclosure. *See* Griffin B. Bell et al., Automatic Disclosure in Discovery—The Rush to Reform, 27 Ga. L. Rev. 1 (1992) (criticizing proposed amendment to Rule 26 to require mandatory disclosure before discovery practice as likely to result in inefficiency, delay, and conflict with attorneys' ethical obligations); *compare*

George F. Hritz, Plan Will Increase Cost, Delay Outcomes, N.Y. L.J., Apr. 13, 1993, at 3 (criticizing experimental mandatory disclosure rules in the Eastern District of New York) *with* Charles P. Sifton, Experiment a Bold and Thoughtful Step, N.Y. L.J., Apr. 13, 1993, at 3 (defending E.D.N.Y. experiment).

119. *See* Bill Ainsworth, Business Lobbying to Kill Secret Settlements Bill, Recorder, May 15, 1991, at 1.

120. *Id.*

121. *Cf.* Andrew Blum, Westinghouse Loses on Papers: Asbestos Memos at Issue, Nat'l L.J., Mar. 22, 1993, at 1 (reporting orders of three separate courts in asbestos litigation denying Westinghouse's claim of privilege for internal memorandum that discussed possibility of document destruction program).

122. *But cf.* Alan B. Morrison, Protective Orders, Plaintiffs, Defendants and Public Interest in Disclosure: Where Does the Balance Lie?, 24 U. Rich. L. Rev. 109 (1989). The author identifies the conflicting interests affected by the failure to disclose and the defendant's rationale for limiting disclosure. He argues for a general rule that the particular lawsuit be the primary focus of the litigation rules. *Id.* at 121. Any significant change in the current system of protective orders would, he argues, result in chaos. *Id.* at 122. Limited exceptions to the rule should be created, he suggests, to allow plaintiffs to share information with other plaintiffs and to allow regulatory and legislative bodies, such as the FDA, to obtain the information while the suit is pending. *Id.* at 122–24.

123. Erie R.R. Co. v. Tompkins, 304 U.S. 64 (1938).

124. The use of confidential settlements has apparently been on the rise since 1986. *See* Bob Gibbons, Secrecy Versus Safety, A.B.A. J., Dec. 1991, at 74 (citing examples of "the threat posed by secrecy" and arguing for a strong presumption of openness of court records).

125. Negotiations between counsel for each side should be encouraged. Here secrecy is necessary. In many mass cases scores of attorneys may be consulting by phone and in face-to-face national meetings. Without such national meetings no agreement could have been reached among the majority of counsel in the Manville Trust reorganization case.

The same kind of negotiations should be encouraged by counsel for the defendants. In fact, highly useful joint defendant facilities such as the original asbestos claims facility, Wellington, and its successor, the Center for Claims Resolution, involved in recent settlements would not be possible without such free negotiations. Whatever antitrust objections may exist should be deemed waived, if necessary through court protective orders.

The utility of secrecy in negotiations was, in effect, recognized by Congress when it adopted Rule 408 of the Federal Rules of Evidence. It provides: "Evidence of conduct or statements made in compromise negotiations is . . . not admissible." Such material should also be considered work-product under the Federal Rules of Civil Procedure.

126. *See* Defense Ordered to Release Some Settlement Documents, 1 Mealey's Litig. Repts., Breast Implants at 1 (Aug. 12, 1993) (The judge required the release of all settlement amounts under $10,000 unless precluded by a protective order, stating "If we do not have the amount, we are not able to get into the determination of whether there is a course of conduct that needs to be brought to the attention of this court.")

127. The tension between the Model Rules of Professional Conduct and the attorney's concern for the interests of third parties when engaging in confidential settlements is discussed in Laleh Ispahani, Note, The Soul of Discretion: The Use and Abuse of Confidential Settlements, 6 Geo. J. Legal Ethics, 111 (1992). The author argues that attorneys should have an ethical duty not to enter into such settlements where public health and safety concerns are at stake. Such a rule, she argues, would have little effect on the number of settlements concluded since settlements are so favorable to all parties and the system as a whole. *Id.* at 131.

128. *See* Jill E. Fisch, Captive Courts: The Destruction of Judicial Decision by Agreement of the Parties, 1993 N.Y.U. Envtl L.J. (forthcoming [1994]); Transcript of Symposium Discussion, *id.* (comments of Jack B. Weinstein on suppression of opinions).

129. *See* note 128.

130. *See, e.g.,* Armster v. United States Dist. Ct., 792 F.2d 1423 (9th Cir. 1986) (refusing to withdraw an opinion declaring suspension of jury trials unconstitutional because matter might arise again).

131. *See* Professor Says Disappearing Decisions Threaten Integrity of Judicial Process, Toxics Law Rptr., Mar. 17, 1993, at 1210–11 (including author's response that withdrawing opinions is acceptable where no overriding matter of public importance is at stake).

132. Bear in mind too that the vast bulk of opinions by many judges are oral. Whether to recast them for publication in a computer service like LEXIS or Westlaw, to send them for limited printing in a specialized collection, or to print in the national reporter system may be affected by the wishes of the parties. *See* Transcript of Symposium Discussion, Secrecy in Environmental Law, 1993 N.Y.U. Envtl L.J. (forthcoming [1994]) (comments of Jack B. Weinstein on suppression of opinions).

133. *See* ABA Model Rules of Professional Conduct, Rule 5.6(b). According to one commentator, a settlement offer "more generous than [the attorney's] wildest dreams" conditioned on that attorney's not representing other clients against the same defendant is "absolutely" unethical. Joanne Pitulla, Co-opting the Competition: Beware of Unethical

Restrictions in Settlement Agreements, A.B.A. J., Aug. 1992, at 101. "Buying off the most experienced plaintiff's [sic] lawyers clearly deprives the public of topflight representation." *Id.*

134. *See* The Committee on Professional Responsibility, The Attorney's Duties to Report the Misconduct of Other Attorneys and to Report Fraud on a Tribunal, 47 The Record 905 (Assoc. of the Bar of the City of N.Y. 1992).

135. The history of this disaster as described below is set forth in Marc Galanter, Bhopals, Past and Present: The Changing Legal Response to Mass Disaster, 10 Windsor Yearbook of Access to Justice 151, 157–60 (1990).

136. *Id*. at 160.

137. *Id*. at 166.

138. In the asbestos context, defendants and a number of plaintiffs' counsel have struck different, but arguably related, private agreements. Under these agreements plaintiffs' attorneys agree to place future non-malignant claims on pleural registries in exchange for a favorable settlement. See Memorandum Opinion and Order of Judge Weiner, Carlough v. Amchem Prods., Inc., C.A. No. 93-215, at 6 (E.D. Pa. Apr. 15, 1993). Similarly, in other agreements, plaintiffs' counsel agree not to file or refer any future claims against the defendant unless and until that claim meets certain medical criteria. These agreements have the effect of deferring the filing of claims by those potential asbestos claimants whose injury, if any, is not sufficient to warrant compensation at this time, especially given the thousands of meritorious claims already burdening the defendants and the court system. The agreements are accompanied by a tolling of any statute of limitation that might otherwise force the claimant to file a lawsuit promptly after the first indication of radiological markings.

Given the limited and specialized nature of these agreements, and the purpose they serve, they arguably do not raise the ethical concerns presented by the "buyout" arrangements discussed above. An ethicist and a state judge have found no ethical problem in this approach. *See* Asbestos Litig. Rptr. (Andrews), July 2, 1993, at 27, 829–30. Since the issue is before the court, I take no position on this particular settlement or class action.

139. *See* ABA Model Rules of Professional Conduct, Rule 1.8(g) ("A lawyer who represents two or more clients shall not participate in making an aggregate settlement of the claims of or against the clients . . . unless each client consents after consultation, including disclosure of the existence and nature of all the claims or pleas involved and of the participation of each person in the settlement.").

140. Theoretically, each client has the option of rejecting his share of a settlement. A majority vote on a settlement is not permitted. *See*

Hayes v. Eagle-Picher Indus., 513 F.2d 892, 894 (10th Cir. 1975); *see also* Ellen Relkin, Practical Aspects of Settling Toxic Tort Cases, 5 Toxics L. Rptr. 894-95 (BNA). 891, 894–95 (Dec. 12, 1990). In practice the attorney almost always can make a global settlement and convince the clients to accept it.

141. One defense attorney I interviewed did not fault plaintiffs' attorneys for taking all available cases because ordinarily each plaintiff recovers something in large settlements.

142. Lester Brickman, Michael J. Horowitz, & Jeffry O'Connell, A Procedure to Enforce Ethical Standards and More Promptly Compensate Personal Injury Claimants Represented by Contingent Fee Counsel (1993).

143. *See* letter from Mark A. Peterson to author, Apr. 30, 1993, at 8 (describing work of Judge Parker in Jenkins v. Cimino). The issue created some tension between the court and the plaintiffs' bar when I insisted on fee caps in payments by the Manville Trust.

144. After a substantial number of cases have been tried in any geographic area, lawyers believe they can assign values to individual cases based on probable recoveries. These numbers are discounted when there are large blocks of settlements. In theory, payments to individuals are based on a pro rata share of these projections. *See* letter from Mark A. Peterson to author, Apr. 30, 1993, at 8 (values based on statistical samples can be quite useful, a technique tried by both Judge Robert Parker and Judge Thomas Lambros).

145. This scheme is outlined in Glen O. Robinson & Kenneth S. Abraham, Collective Justice in Tort Law, 78 Va. L. Rev. 1481, 1490–96 (1992). It is similar in some ways to an approach used by Judge Robert Parker in Cimino v. Raymark Industries, 751 F. Supp. 649, 653 (E.D. Tex. 1990), in which the court conducted special trials of representative claims to determine a set of model valuations for claims by class of injuries and other relevant criteria.

146. If more than 5 percent of plaintiffs reject the settlement it can be aborted.

147. One such arrangement, in which thirteen of eighteen plaintiffs voted to accept a settlement, was accepted by a trial court but reversed on appeal. Hayes v. Eagle-Picher Indus., 513 F.2d 892 (10th Cir. 1975). The appellate court stated:

> An agreement such as the present one which allows a case to be settled contrary to the wishes of the client and without his approving of the terms of the settlement is opposed to the basic fundamentals of the attorney-client relationship. Inasmuch as the attorney is merely an agent for the client in negotiation and settlement, the approval of the client is an all important essential to a settlement which is to be

binding, and if this approval is not present the court is placed in a most unfavorable position in enforcing it.

Id. at 894.

148. One experienced practitioner has described the importance of financing as follows:

> At Columbia Law School, I got the impression that litigation was a quest for the Holy Grail of truth. Nobody told me that it was also a financial contest, and that in order to succeed, either you or your client must have the economic staying power to weather the stormy seas of litigation. Since the average plaintiff in a tort case does not have the money or the staying power to enter the arena against a giant opponent, it is the entrepreneur-lawyer who must supply these requisites, and must furnish the services of an organization for which the plaintiffs themselves could not afford to pay.

Stuart M. Speiser, *Lawsuit* 560 (1980).

149. Filing costs and clerk's fee in the lower court came to $142. Dr. Hammond [an expert witness] charged $125. Mrs. Palsgraf made $416 a year. At the time of trial, she had not yet paid Dr. Parshall's [her doctor] bill of $70, now three years due. It is improbable to the point of implausibility that she would have the cash on hand to pay the court and Dr. Hammond a total of $267.

John T. Noonan, Jr., *Persons and Masks of the Law* 125 (1976).

150. The tobacco cases provide a good example of how the costs of litigation can cause plaintiffs or their attorneys to give up. Not all courts, however, will allow attorneys to abandon cases simply on financial grounds.

The Cipollone family and its attorneys were permitted to drop their suit because the litigation was "too expensive." *See* Cigarette Suit Dropped, A.B.A. J., Feb. 1993, at 30; Cipollone Family Drops Landmark Cigarette Suit: Decision Is Major Victory for Tobacco Firms, Wash. Post, Nov. 6, 1992, at B1.

The attorneys in the *Haines* case attempted to withdraw because the litigation "ha[d] become an unreasonable financial burden." *See* Haines v. Liggett Group, Inc., 814 F. Supp. 414, 418 (D.N.J. 1993). After nearly nine years of litigating eight cases, sometimes in conjunction with two other law firms, the plaintiff's attorneys had expended more than $500,000 in out-of-pocket costs and more than $5 million in lawyer and paralegal time. *Id.* To gauge its expenses in *Haines,* the firm relied heavily on its experience in *Cipollone,* which cost more than $500,000 in out-of-pocket expenses and $2 million to try. *Id.* The attorneys urged the court to allow them to withdraw because "it has become apparent that the amount of recovery against the tobacco industry is not likely to exceed these costs." *Id.* at 419. The firm also argued that, from a public policy standpoint, the benefits derived from its considerable work on the cigarette cases, such as the revelations about the tobacco industry's practices, would remain unaffected if it were permitted to withdraw. *Id.* at 420.

The court denied the motion. It rejected any argument that the firm's expenses in other litigations should affect its position as representative of this particular plaintiff, or that the firm's experiences in *Cipollone* should serve as a financial barometer for *Haines*. To the contrary, the court reasoned that the work in *Cipollone* had provided much of the groundwork for *Haines* and might result in more focused discovery, narrower issues, and fewer expenses. *Id.* at 424.

Also influential in the court's decision was that withdrawal would impair the plaintiff's ability to remain in the action. *Id.* at 425. Even if plaintiff could find substitute counsel, the complexity of the case and the firm's wealth of experience in tobacco litigation raised serious questions as to whether a transition between lawyers could be effected without prejudicing the plaintiff. *Id.* The firm was ethically obligated to protect its client's interests. *Id.* at 426.

Despite plaintiff's counsel's contention that the public interest is not served by continuing lawsuits that are not viable, the court properly recognized the strong public interest in continuing the case. *Id.* at 426 n.9.

151. See Jack B. Weinstein, Comments on Syndicating Litigation and Mass Torts, Speech at Annual Meeting of the ABA, Aug. 8, 1993 (unpublished).

152. The order "establishes a plaintiffs' litigation expense fund to reimburse attorneys for costs incurred for the 'common benefit.' MDL liaison counsel will open an interest bearing account and designate an escrow agent to handle incoming funds and disbursements." Defense Ordered to Release Some Settlement Documents, 1 Mealey's Litig. Repts. 19, at 4 (Aug. 12, 1993).

153. This procedure is set forth in *In re* "Agent Orange" Prod. Liab. Litigation, 611 F. Supp. 1396 (E.D.N.Y. 1985), *aff'd in part, rev'd in part*, 818 F.2d 179 (2d Cir. 1987); *see* Vincent Robert Johnson, Ethical Limitations on Creative Financing of Mass Tort Class Actions, 54 Brook. L. Rev. 539, 545–88 (1988) (comprehensive analysis of the fee arrangement and its treatment by the courts).

154. This same idea was expressed by a number of the attorneys I interviewed.

155. *In re* "Agent Orange" Prod. Liab. Litig., 818 F.2d 216, 222 (2d Cir. 1987).

156. *See* Vincent Robert Johnson, Ethical Limitations on Creative Financing of Mass Tort Class Actions, 54 Brook. L. Rev. 539, 553

(1988) ("In declaring the [*Agent Orange* fees] agreement invalid, the [Second Circuit] held, in effect, that the defendants had failed to demonstrate that the issue of class action financing required special ethical treatment: everyday 'Euclidian' rules applied.").

157. The auction model is described in detail in Jonathan R. Macey & Geoffrey P. Miller, The Plaintiffs' Attorney's Role in Class Action and Derivative Litigation: Economic Analysis and Recommendations for Reform, 58 U. Chi. L. Rev. 1, 105–16 (1991).

158. *See, e.g.,* Donald F. Tucker & Mark G. Kaylian, Investing in Justice, The Brief, Spring 1992, at 26; Jack B. Weinstein, Comments on Syndicating Litigation and Mass Torts, Speech at Annual Meeting of the ABA, Aug. 8, 1993 (unpublished).

159. Professor John O. Coffee, Jr., in a letter to the author dated August 12, 1993, makes the following criticism of the auction approach to the lowest bidding lawyer:

> There are two distinct problems [to the auction approach] here: First, it discourages pre-filing research and investigation. Would you as a profit-maximizing attorney investigate a claim (for example, by reviewing carefully the medical literature on some toxic tort) if the case, once filed by you, could be given to a higher bidder (who could by reading your papers effectively appropriate your research)? To use a humble analogy, the lawyer who initially investigates a new field (i.e., a new toxic tort) is much like a prospector for gold. The problem is that once he stakes out his claim, he can be divested by late-arriving claim-jumpers who invested nothing in research and who (partially as a result) can afford to out bid him. This is why we have patent and copyright laws to protect other forms of intellectual property. Second, even if auctions are accepted in principle, there is no consensus on what constitutes the best bid. Should it be the lowest hourly rate, the lowest percentage of the recovery or a fee that is based on an increasing percentage of the recovery? That is, a plaintiff's attorney who bids that it will take 10% of the recovery or one who agrees to take a $100 hourly fee. Here, our ability to rank the bids requires agreement on the criteria. Perhaps, the Federal Judicial Center could do this. Finally, there is a basic problem of asymmetric information, which I think undercuts the auction approach. If the defendant (or its allies) can bid, they may even arrange to be sued in order to get a general release cheap.

160. *See* Lester Brickman, Contingent Fees without Contingencies: Hamlet without the Prince of Denmark?, 37 UCLA L. Rev. 29 (1989). The Brickman fee analysis has been questioned. *See* Letter from Mark A. Peterson to author, Apr. 30, 1993, at 8–9.

161. *See* Jack B. Weinstein, Recovery of Attorneys' Fees, Speech at

Annual Meeting of the ABA Litigation Section, Aug. 11, 1993 (unpublished).

162. Answers of Lester Brickman to Written Questions Proposed by the Subcommittee on Intellectual Property and Judicial Administration of the House Judiciary Committee, Nov. 8, 1992, at 1.

Professor Brickman's extensive research on contingent fees is found at Lester Brickman, Contingent Fees without Contingencies: Hamlet without the Prince of Denmark, 37 UCLA L. Rev. 29 (1989) (discussing the legitimacy of contingent attorneys' fees).

163. Answers of Lester Brickman to Written Questions Proposed by the Subcommittee on Intellectual Property and Judicial Administration of the House Judiciary Committee, Nov. 8, 1992, at 1.

164. *Id*. at 2.

165. *Id*. at 3.

166. *Id*. at 3–13. *See also* Michael J. Saks, Do We Really Know Anything about the Behavior of the Tort Litigation System—And Why Not?, 140 U. Pa. L. Rev. 1147, 1192 (1992) (mass tort cases often begin as expensive-to-litigate, complex cases in which lawyers rightfully demand higher rates of return, but later become routine and easily replicated, more like automobile negligence cases).

167. The commerce in asbestos claims is extensive. Because of the social policy implications, the facts should be brought into the public view. The only way this can be done is by judges ordering plaintiffs' lawyers to disclose all relevant retainer and fee sharing agreements and to enter that into the record. However, I have yet to see such an order.

Letter from Professor Lester Brickman to The Honorable John F. Grady, United States District Judge, Northern District of Illinois, Sept. 3, 1991.

168. *See* Mealey's Litig. Rpts., Asbestos, Mar. 19, 1993, at 4–5; Asbestos Litig. Rptr., Feb. 5, 1993, at 26,883.

169. *See, e.g.*, Geoffrey C. Hazard, Jr., *Ethics in the Practice of Law* 99 (1978).

170. *See, e.g.*, Charles W. Wolfram, *Modern Legal Ethics* 498–99 (1986); F. B. MacKinnon, *Contingent Fees for Legal Services* 160–68 (1964).

171. See proposals for control advocated by Lester Brickman, Michael Horowitz, & Jeffrey O'Connell, in A Proposal to Align the Contingency Fee System with Its Policy Roots and Ethical Mandates (Manhattan Institute, 1994).

172. *See* Jack B. Weinstein, Recovery of Attorneys' Fees, Speech at the Annual Meeting of the ABA Litigation Section, Aug. 11, 1993 (unpublished).

173. Consider the recent ruling by Judge Alfred Lechner, Jr., in the

District of New Jersey, prohibiting a noted law firm from withdrawing from tobacco litigation. Haines v. Liggett Group, Inc. et al., 814 F. Supp. 414 (D.N.J. 1993). The firm urged the court to view the case "in the context of the past ten years of litigation which [had] demonstrated that the costs of litigating against the tobacco industry are far greater than anyone could have reasonably expected at the time the contingency contract was signed." *Id.* at 418. Three firms that had originally agreed to jointly litigate cigarette-related health claims had already expended approximately $6.2 million. *Id.* The plaintiff characterized the law firm's motion for leave to withdraw as "a perfect example of the success of defendant's strategy" in that "after ten years not one of the tobacco cases . . . had been resolved." *Id.* at 421 n.14.

That was not a mischaracterization of defendant's strategy. As defense counsel stated: "To paraphrase General Patton, the way we won those cases was not by spending all of [the company's] money, but by making that other son of a bitch spend all of his." *Id.* at 21 (citing memorandum from defense counsel).

In refusing to allow the firm to withdraw, the court noted that the plaintiff would not be able to find replacement counsel. *Id.* at 425. It therefore rejected reliance on *In re* "Agent Orange" Prod. Liab. Litigation, 571 F. Supp. 481 (E.D.N.Y. 1983) (permitting withdrawal of plaintiffs' attorneys who were unable to meet the burdens of the litigation) because in that case replacement counsel was available and the class action nature of the case lacked the private client-attorney relationship element present in *Haines. Haines,* 814 F. Supp. at 425 n.27; *see also* Stalled Tobacco Suit Is Revived by Ruling, N.Y. Times, Feb. 1, 1993, at B5; *see also* Andrew Blum, Will Next Round of Smoking Challenges Be Worth Pursuing?, Nat'l L.J., Jun. 27, 1988, at 3 (noting that plaintiffs' attorneys might be discouraged from representing future clients against cigarette companies given that more than $2 million in costs resulted in an award of only $400,000).

174. Lester Brickman, Michael J. Horowitz, & Jeffrey O'Connell, *Rethinking Contingency Fees* (1994). Professor Brickman has studied fees extensively. Professor O'Connell was largely responsible for substantial changes in auto accident compensation plans. Their proposal was designed for run-of-the-mill cases which can be disposed of promptly. Changes to permit use in mass tort cases are possible, but they would probably require court intervention.

175. *Id.* at 27–28.

176. Yale Law School Program in Civil Liability, Center for Studies in Law, Economics and Policy, Daniel L. Rubinfeld and Suzanne Scotchmer, Contingent Fees for Attorneys: An Economic Analysis, Working Paper No. 157, at 19 (1992) ("Our conclusions suggest that attempts to cap contingent fees could lead to a reduction in the number of low

quality cases filed as well as the number of cases taken by high quality attorneys. This is likely to reduce the overall level of deterrence.").

177. One attorney I interviewed noted that the imprimatur of the court on attorneys' fees is essential to prevent malpractice liability.

178. *See* Georgene M. Vairo, The Dalkon Shield Claimants Trust: Paradigm Lost (or Found)?, 61 Fordham L. Rev. 617, 621 (1992) (asking whether courts should treat mass representation in large consolidations similarly to class action representation in order to protect due process interests).

179. In securities class action litigation, attorneys have made it a practice to challenge fees, settlements, and adequacy of representation (receiving part of the savings, if any, as a fee). This practice has not, thus far, been followed in mass torts, another reason for court intervention.

180. *See, e.g.,* Andrew Blum, GM Settlement Praised, Opposed, Nat'l L.J., Aug. 2. 1993, at 3 (in settlement involving pickup truck fuel tanks, attorneys received millions in fees while plaintiffs received $1,000 rebates on purchase of a new truck and old trucks remained on the road); GM Switched Strategy to Get Pickup Accord, Wall St. J., July 21, 1993, at B1 (same).

181. *See* John C. Coffee, Jr., Claims Made Settlements: An Ethical Critique, N.Y. L.J., July 15, 1993, at 1 (such arrangements threaten to generate conflicts between interests of lawyer and client).

182. *In re* Oracle Sec. Litig., 131 F.R.D. 688, 693 (N.D. Cal. 1990).

183. *Id.*

184. Beverly C. Moore, Jr., Going Once, Going Twice: Bidding for Work, Legal Times, Dec. 17, 1990, at 27.

185. *Id.*

186. *Id.*

187. *Id.*

188. *In re* San Juan DuPont Plaza Hotel Fire Litig., 982 F.2d 603 (1st Cir. 1992) (vacating fee award), *appeal after remand,* 994 F.2d 956 (1st Cir. 1993); *cf.* City of Burlington v. Dague, 112 S. Ct. 2638 (1992). The primary phase of the *DuPont* litigation, involving some 200 defendants and 2,337 plaintiffs, culminated in a settlement yielding a common fund of $220 million. 982 F.2d at 606. A battle over attorneys' fees followed between those attorneys who represented individual plaintiffs and those who guided the litigation as members of the plaintiffs' steering committee. The trial judge, who had initially indicated that a contingency fee approach would be used (awarding the steering committee members around 10 percent of the total recovery), decided to apply a lodestar approach that would result in more money for the steering committee members. *In re* San Juan DuPont Plaza Fire Litig., 768 F. Supp. 912 (D.P.R. 1991), *vacated after remand,* 982 F.2d 603

(1st Cir. 1992), *appeal after remand*, 944 F.2d 956 (1st Cir. 1993). The individually retained attorneys appealed that decision, arguing that their important services to individual clients were greatly undervalued.

The Court of Appeals vacated the fee scheme on the ground that the procedures utilized in conducting hearings violated due process. 982 F.2d 603 (1st Cir. 1992). The court found that the individually retained plaintiff's attorneys (IRPAs) were "hogtied" at the fee-determination hearings—their role was limited to that of spectators, with no opportunity to present their side of the controversy. 982 F.2d 613. The court cautioned:

> [W]hen a judge constructs a process for setting fees, the process must contain at least the procedural minima that the Due Process Clause requires; and, moreover, those procedures must apply in a fair and evenhanded manner to the parties in interest, without preferring one group of disputants over another. In this instance, we cannot see how a court could fairly adjudicate this dispute unless it afforded the IRPAs a viable means (comparable to the means afforded the PSC [Plaintiffs Steering Committee]) of describing their contribution with the PSC's contribution, and questioning the PSC members regarding their work.

Id. at 614. The plaintiffs' attorneys in this case are still engaged in "full-scale battle" over fees, with allegations of questionable billing and expenses. *See* Andrew Blum, DuPont Lawyers Battle on Fees, Nat'l L.J., July 5, 1993, at 3.

189. *See* Jack B. Weinstein, Comments on Syndicating Litigation and Mass Torts, Speech at the Annual Meeting of the ABA, Aug. 8, 1993 (unpublished).

190. *But see* Donald Tucker and Mark G. Kaylian, The Syndication of Commercial Claims (Aug. 14, 1991); David A. Gauntlett, *The Syndication of Commercial Claims: A Contrary View* (1991); Edward S. Wright, *Investment in Litigation from the Plaintiffs' Perspective* (1991); Richard Lieb, Vulture, Beware: Risks of Purchasing Claims Against a Chapter 11 Debtor, 48 Bus. Law. 915 (1993); Susan Lorde Martin, Syndicating Lawsuits: Illegal Champerty or New Business Opportunity?, 30 Am. Bus. L.J. 485 (1992); Daniel C. Cox, Comment, Law Syndication: An Investment Opportunity in Legal Grievances, 36 St. Louis U. L.J. 153 (1990).

191. *See* Michael E. Tigar, 2020 Vision: A Bifocal View, 74 Judicature 89, 92 (Aug.–Sept. 1990) ("I have been studying complex lawsuits. I find—and I concede that the evidence is so far anecdotal—that lawyers are convincing sophisticated consumers of legal services such as corporate and public parties that the right amount of discovery and motions practice is what the client can afford, and not what the case inherently requires.").

192. *See* ABA Model Rules of Professional Conduct, Rules 3.1, comment 1 ("The advocate has a duty to use legal procedure for the fullest benefit of the client's cause, but also a duty not to abuse legal procedure."), and 3.2 ("A lawyer shall make reasonable efforts to expedite litigation consistent with the interests of the client.").

193. In addition, the technical revolution may enable defense attorneys to pool their resources and reduce costs. *See* Database Linking Law Firms and Clients May Slash Fees, Wall St. J., Feb. 26, 1993, at B2 (describing how a program called Counsel Connect will enable corporate law departments to have access to an on-line network to share legal research with large law firms to enable them to decide, if necessary, which law firm has the "most impressive database material" on specific topics should outside counsel need to be retained).

194. For example, the same morning a massive explosion ripped through a Shell Oil refinery in Norco, Louisiana, a federal class action suit was filed. *See* Watson v. Shell Oil Co., 979 F.2d 1014, 1017 (5th Cir. 1992), *rehearing en banc granted,* 990 F.2d 805 (5th Cir. 1993).

195. *See, e.g.,* N.Y. Daily News, Aug. 10, 1993, at 22 (full page advertisement placed by plaintiffs' attorney soliciting breast implant cases).

196. *See* John C. Coffee, Rescuing the Private Attorney General: Why the Model of the Lawyer as Bounty Hunter Is Not Working, 42 Md. L. Rev. 215, 248–52 (1983) (describing dynamic of struggle for lead counsel positions).

197. *See* Thomas M. Burton & Junda Woo, Lawyers Contest Implant Class Action Suit, Wall St. J., Mar. 16, 1992, at B5 ("A rancorous squabble has erupted among plaintiffs' lawyers in breast implant cases over how—and in what courts—the hundreds of complex federal liability suits should be tried.").

198. *See* John C. Coffee, Rescuing the Private Attorney General: Why the Model of the Lawyer as Bounty Hunter Is Not Working, 42 Md. L. Rev. 215, 249 (1983) ("[C]urrent practices, as sanctioned by the *Manual for Complex Litigation,* encourage the large class action to be organized through a log-rolling political coalition, in which implicit vote-buying and other tactics reminiscent of Tammany Hall politics have become commonplace.").

199. *See id.* at 249–52 (describing vote-buying process), 259-62 (describing vote-buying in *Fine Paper* antitrust litigation).

200. *See* Terry Carter, Asbestos Lawsuits Grind to Halt, Nat'l L.J., Jan. 1, 1989, at 3.

201. *Id.*

202. I was struck by the vehemence of many of those I interviewed about the role of defense counsel in "churning of work" and "perpetuating litigation," particularly in bankruptcy cases. Judges and corporate executives are at fault when this occurs.

203. One matter that has troubled some defense counsel is that they need admission to many state and federal bars to handle national litigation. In a mass tort, pro hoc vice admission to all state and federal bars should be assumed. When local counsel is retained it should be at the option of the litigant for tactical reasons.

Judge Pointer eliminated this problem in the breast implant multidistrict litigation in Alabama by issuing the following order:

> *Admission of Counsel.* Attorneys admitted to practice and in good standing in any United States District Court are hereby permitted to appear pro hoc vice in this litigation without need for any other motion, order, or payment of fee. Association of local counsel is not required.

In re Silicone Gel Breast Implants Prods. Liab. Litig., No. CV 92-P-10000-S (N.D. Ala. Sept. 15, 1992).

An additional problem stems from the conflicts among the state ethics codes that often present a dilemma for an attorney. One sensible approach has been suggested by the ABA Standing Committee on Ethics and Professionalism. *See* Randall Samborn, Streamlined Ethics Rule Proposed, Nat'l L.J., May 24, 1993, at 3 (proposing that attorneys in litigation, no matter where admitted, be subject only to the rules of the tribunal).

204. Letter from now Special Master Deborah E. Greenspan to author, Apr. 4, 1993.

205. *See* Fourth Annual Report, Agent Orange Class Assistance Program, Sept. 30, 1992; New Alliances for Vietnam Veterans and Their Families: Resource Guide (Agent Orange Class Assistance Program, 1992).

206. Fourth Annual Report, *supra* note 205 at 1; *see also In re* "Agent Orange" Prod. Liab. Litig., 996 F.2d 1425 (1993). The production of a series of treatises and pamphlets and instructional meetings financed by Agent Orange litigation funds all over the country have leveraged the funds into benefits to the veterans community worth additional hundreds of millions of dollars.

207. *See, e.g.,* Gideon v. Wainwright, 372 U.S. 335 (1963) (indigent criminal defendant has fundamental right to assistance of counsel).

208. In point of fact, it is unlikely that total defensible fees would be lower under a community-centered resolution of a mass tort.

209. *See, e.g.,* Laura Parker, Air Crash Lawsuits: A Clash of Customs: East Does Not Meet West on Large Liability Awards, Wash. Post, Mar. 20, 1987, at F1 (describing the Japanese "custom and societal practice" of apologizing after crash of a jumbo jet).

210. *Cf.* Randall Sanborn, Anti-Lawyer Attitude Up, Nat'l L.J., Aug. 9, 1993, at 1 (reporting poll results supporting "the widely held perception that resentment of lawyers—ranging from lawyer bashing jokes to

outright vilification—is running at a fever pitch.").

1. 28 U.S.C. § 455. Forthcoming articles of the author based on lectures at the University of Arizona in November 1993, at the University of Dayton in April 1994, and at the New York County Lawyers Association in March 1994 deal with other aspects of ethics and the limits on judges acquiring knowledge.

2. *See, e.g.,* Martin Marcus, Above the Fray or into the Breach: The Judge's Role in New York's Adversarial System of Criminal Justice, 57 Brook. L. Rev. 1193, 1193 (1992) (in the adversarial model exemplified by the American and British systems, "the judge is a neutral and detached magistrate whose function is to mediate and resolve the opposing parties' inevitable conflicts."). *Cf.* Barry R. Schaller, State Judges Now Need Managerial Know How, Nat'l L.J., Nov. 1, 1993, at 5. ("[T]he managerial judge should take the initiative to create a litigation environment conducive to mutual problem-solving and, in addition, should be willing to adopt non-traditional solutions to problems, including methods used in other fields such as management and negotiation").

3. Model Code of Judicial Conduct Canon 3E(1) (1990); *see also* 28 U.S.C. § 455(a) (emphasis added).

4. Haines v. Liggett Group, Inc., 975 F.2d 81 (3d Cir. 1992).

5. Haines v. Liggett Group, Inc., 140 F.R.D. 681, 683 (D.N.J.), *vacated,* 975 F.2d 81 (3rd Cir. 1992).

6. *Cf.* Statement of Judge Miles Lord (Feb. 29, 1984), reprinted in The National Women's Health Network, The Dalkon Shield 19–23 (1986) (lambasting officers of the A. H. Robins Company for their "monstrous mischief" after noting "that I am specifically directing and limiting my remarks to that which I have learned and observed in these consolidated cases before me"). Judge Lord's lengthy rebuke of these corporate officers was later expunged from the record in the Dalkon Shield litigation. *See* Andrew Blum, Out of Bounds? Critics on Judge Sarokin, Nat'l L.J., Sept. 28, 1992, at 3 (Robins brought disciplinary action, and remarks were stricken).

7. For a more thorough explication of the author's views on judicial recusal, see Panel Discussion, Disqualification of Judges (The Sarokin Matter): Is It a Threat to Judicial Independence? (Remarks of Jack B. Weinstein), 58 Brook. L. Rev. 1 (1993).

8. See John T. Noonan, Jr., and Kenneth I. Winston, *The Responsible Judge: Readings in Judicial Ethics,* 19 (1993) quoting Alfred Denning, *The Closing Chapter* (1983): "she does better without a bandage round her eyes. She should be blind indeed to favour or prejudice, but clear to

see which way lies the truth: and the less dust there is about the better."

9. We sometimes forget the simple admonition that "[o]ne must always remember that the judge is a person. . . . The classic error is to mistake the body within the black robe for an automaton who will respond predictably to any stimulation." Bertram Harnett, *Law, Lawyers and Laymen* 259 (1984).

10. *In re* "Agent Orange" Prod. Liab. Litig., 996 F.2d 1425, 1438–39 (2d Cir. 1993).

11. *See, e.g.*, Bilello v. Abbott Labs., 825 F. Supp. 475 (E.D.N.Y. 1993) (refusal to recuse because of having listened to injured claimants tell of their illnesses and problems); *In re* "Agent Orange" Prod. Liab. Litig., 597 F. Supp. 740, 764–75, 858–61 (E.D.N.Y. 1984) (fairness opinion based on information gathered at public hearings finding settlement reasonable and in parties' as well as public's interest), *aff'd* 818 F.2d 145 (2d Cir. 1987), *cert. denied,* 484 U.S. 1004 (1988).

12. Avishai Margalit, Prophets with Honor, N.Y. Review, Nov. 4, 1993, at 66, 70 (discussing the work of Professor Yeshayahur Leibowitz and Martin Buber in connection with recent studies).

13. *Id.* at 71.

14. Hart v. Community Sch. Bd. of Brooklyn, N.Y. Sch. Dist. #21, 383 F. Supp. 699, 706–26, 747–52, 756–58 (E.D.N.Y. 1974), *aff'd,* 512 F.2d 37 (2d Cir. 1975). *See also* Curtis J. Berger, Away from the Court House and into the Field: The Odyssey of a Special Master, 78 Colum. L. Rev. 707 (1978) (author's account of his experience acting as special master in *Hart*); *Cf.* David I. Levine, The Modification of Equitable Degrees in Institutional Reform Litigation: A Commentary on the Supreme Court's Adoption of the Second Circuit's Flexible Test, 58 Brook. L. Rev. 1239 (1993).

15. *See, e.g.*, Knight v. State, 787 F. Supp. 1030 (N.D. Ala. 1991) (action brought by United States to desegregate colleges and universities in Alabama), *rev'd and vacated in part,* F.3d 1534 (11th Cir. 1994); Armour v. Ohio, 775 F. Supp. 1044 (N.D. Ohio 1991) (constitutional challenge to recent state legislative reapportionment brought by black voters); Ayers v. Allain, 674 F. Supp. 1523 (N.D. Miss. 1987) (action against various state officials alleging constitutional and civil rights violations from racially dual system of higher public education), *rev'd,* 893 F.2d 732 (5th Cir. 1990), *aff'd en banc,* 914 F.2d 676 (5th Cir. 1990), *vacated sub nom.,* United States v. Fordice, 112 S. Ct. 2727 (1992).

16. *See* United States v. Yonkers Bd. of Educ., 624 F. Supp. 1276 (S.D.N.Y. 1985), *aff'd,* 837 F.2d 1181 (2d Cir. 1987), *cert. denied,* 486 U.S. 1005 (1988).

17. Paraphrasing Immanuel Kant, a judge or lawyer "shows moral worth, not in doing good from inclination, but in doing it for the sake of duty. It is the motive of duty, not the motive of inclination, that

gives moral worth to an action." H. J. Paton, *The Moral Law: Kant's Groundwork of the Metaphysic of Morals* 19 (1948).

The proposition is wrong when duty is construed, as in the case of someone like Adolf Eichmann, to require repugnant action. Hannah Arendt, *Eichmann in Jerusalem: A Report on the Banality of Evil* (1964) (distortion of Kant's philosophy because Eichmann thought he had to apply the "law" rigidly without mercy and without considering whether monstrous edicts could be characterized as "law"). It is a useful guide, however, in the area of practical ethical choices for judges and lawyers because it limits personal idiosyncratic views, forcing the court into the law's mainstream. Kant's categorical imperative ("act only on the maxim through which you can at the same time will that it should become a universal law," Paton, *supra,* seeking an abstract rule for all people at all times, to be followed for its own sake, *id.* at 22–23) is beyond jurists. We can, however, eschew the impulsive while seeking the prudential without sacrificing the moral, to the extent that we know it. Dialogue on the subject of what is ethical, what we ought to do, should at least narrow the range of the acceptable and avoid the hypocrisy of espousing a rule while ignoring it as impractical under the circumstances. It will at least force us not to ignore the "ought" questions.

18. *See* Hart v. Community Sch. Bd. of Brooklyn, N.Y. Sch. Dist. #21, 383 F. Supp. at 709-10. *See also* Sally Engle Merry, The Culture of Judging, 90 Colum. L. Rev. 3211 (1990) (reviewing Lawrence Rosen, *The Anthropology of Justice: Law as Culture in Islamic Society* (1989)); Sanford Levinson, Strolling Down the Path of the Law (And toward Critical Legal Studies?): The Jurisprudence of Richard Posner, 91 Colum. L. Rev. 1221 (1991) (reviewing Richard Posner, *The Problems of Jurisprudence* (1990)).

19. The increasing use of this term has been unfortunate and unhelpful, glossing over meaningful discussion of judging. *See, e.g.,* Dole Wary That Abortion May Color Court Selection, N.Y. Times, July 23, 1990, at A8 (quoting President Bush as saying, "I've always said I want somebody who will be [on the Supreme Court] not to legislate from the bench but to faithfully interpret the Constitution.").

20. The need for such communication has been identified in constitutional cases with respect to the Supreme Court:

> To avoid straying too far from public opinion, the Court must enter into an exchange with the body politic. For all the advantages they gain from being insulated from the body politic, however, courts suffer from the absence of a medium of exchange with the people. Courts cannot send out questionnaires. . . .
>
> [C]ourts do not talk easily with other branches or with the public. And so there is a need for alternate ways to raise storm warnings

when trouble is afoot, ways to express—both from the perspective of courts identifying rights, and from the perspective of defendants against whom the rights will be enforced—the level of importance or difficulty accompanying the declaration of rights. There must be other means of dialogue. *That* is what enforcement or remedies is all about.

Barry Friedman, When Rights Encounter Reality: Enforcing Federal Remedies, 65 S. Cal. L. Rev. 735, 779–80 (1992).

21. *See In re* "Agent Orange" Prod. Liab. Litig., 996 F.2d 1425 (2d Cir. 1993).

22. *See* Fed. R. App. P. 21.

23. *See* Hart v. Community Sch. Bd. of Brooklyn, N.Y. Sch. Dist. #21, 383 F. Supp. 699, 764–67 (E.D.N.Y. 1974), *aff'd,* 512 F.2d 37 (2d Cir. 1975).

24. *See, e.g.,* Curtis J. Berger, Away from the Courthouse and Into the Field: The Odyssey of a Special Master, 78 Colum. L. Rev. 707, 710, 730–33 (1978).

25. *See* Lora v. Board of Educ. of N.Y., 456 F. Supp. 1211, 1294–95 (E.D.N.Y. 1978), *vacated,* 623 F.2d 248 (2d Cir. 1980).

26. *See* Society for Good Will to Retarded Children, Inc. v. Cuomo, 572 F. Supp. 1300, 1303 (E.D.N.Y. 1983), *vacated,* 737 F.2d 1239 (2d Cir. 1984).

27. Louis D. Brandeis, *Other People's Money and How the Bankers Use It* 92 (1st ed. 1914).

28. *See In re* "Agent Orange" Prod. Liab. Litig., 597 F. Supp. 740, 764–75, 858–61 (E.D.N.Y. 1984) (fairness opinion based on information gathered at public hearings finding settlement reasonable and in the parties' as well as the public's interest), *aff'd,* 818 F.2d 145 (2d Cir. 1987), *cert. denied,* 484 U.S. 1004 (1988); John Riley, Is It Fair? Lawyers, Vets Offer Divergent Views at Hearings on Agent Orange Accord, Nat'l L.J., Aug. 27, 1987, at 1; *see also* Peter H. Schuck, *Agent Orange on Trial: Mass Toxic Disasters in the Courts* 173–78 (1986).

29. Report of Deborah Greenspan, Special Master, Dec. 1992, on File Agent Orange Case, E.D.N.Y., with prior and subsequent reports.

30. As of Sept. 30, 1992, the fund had awarded approximately $146 million to almost thirty-one thousand individual veterans and survivors. Fourth Annual Report of the Special Master on the Distribution of the Agent Orange Settlement Fund 4, Sept. 30, 1992. As of April 1993, the Agent Orange Veteran Payment Program had paid out more than $150 million in direct cash benefits. *Id.* The Program was paying on over five hundred claims per month during 1993. Letter from Special Master Deborah Greenspan to author, Apr. 2, 1993.

31. As of September 1992 more than forty thousand claims had been

filed by veterans on behalf of themselves and their families. Letter from Gerson M. Ratner, Director of Litigation, National Veterans Legal Service Project, to author, Nov. 24, 1992. *See* Michael E. Wildhaber et al., *Veterans Benefits Manual,* Vols. 1 and 2 (1991) (a comprehensive guide, funded by Agent Orange settlement funds, designed to assist advocates in representing veterans and their dependents).

32. As of March 1993. Other programs have used up their funding so that the number fluctuates slightly. More than 181 grants worth approximately $33.2 million have been awarded to seventy-two projects providing services to an estimated 101,000 class members in forty-eight states. Fourth Annual Report of the Special Master on the Distribution of the Agent Orange Settlement Fund 21–22 (Sept. 30, 1992).

33. *See* Agent Orange Class Assistance Program, Fourth Annual Report (Sept. 30, 1992) (as of 1992, over $33 million in grants had been awarded, and over one hundred thousand veterans and family members had been served by social services programs receiving grants).

34. Our academics and ethicists seem to prefer library research to field research. This preference is understandable since field work is so time consuming and expensive, but lack of it may lead to academic commentary having little relation to the real world. Should law professors have ethical obligations to resist becoming insulated and detached from the day-to-day realities of litigation and to produce work that can be better utilized by the public and the courts?

35. One such group is the DES Cancer Network, established in 1982 for women with clear cell cancer caused by in utero exposure to DES. The network provides both medical and legal information and facilitates peer support. Yearly meetings provide an opportunity for DES cancer survivors to meet and learn more about DES issues. The organization also publishes a newsletter several times a year devoted to medical and research news and member letters. Letter from Margaret Lee Braun, Director DES Cancer Network, to Eileen Hershenov, Esq., Dec. 1, 1992.

36. The efforts of the DES Cancer Network, in cooperation with another DES advocacy group, resulted in the enactment of the DES Education and Research Amendment, 42 U.S.C. § 281a *et seq.* (Supp. IV 1992). The law establishes programs for research, training and dissemination of health information associated with exposure to DES.

37. *See* New Studies on Breast Cancer Sought by D'Amato and Women, N.Y. Times, Jan. 8, 1993, at B5 (describing how the Long Island Breast Cancer Coalition, dismayed by a federal study that found no correlation between environmental factors and the high rate of breast cancer on Long Island, was "taking matters into [its] own hands" and organizing a study of its own).

Noted plaintiffs' attorney Sybil Shainwald feels the activities of women's groups were crucial in communicating to women the dangers of the

Dalkon Shield intrauterine device, that the defendant, A. H. Robins, was on the verge of bankruptcy, and that there was a deadline for filing claims. Elizabeth Newman and Laura Fry, The Dalkon Shield and Women's Litigation 32 (undated) (unpublished manuscript on file with the Northwestern Law Review).

38. Wilbur J. Scott, *The Politics of Readjustment: Vietnam Veterans since the War,* chapter 5, Politics 101, and chapter 8, Benefit of the Doubt (1993).

39. *See* Price-Anderson Act, 42 U.S.C. §2210(1) (1988) (establishing President's Commission on Catastrophic Nuclear Accidents to study and recommend "means of fully compensating victims of a catastrophic nuclear accident" when aggregate claims exceed the $7 billion liability limitation of the Act); *see also* Presidential Commission on Catastrophic Nuclear Accidents, Report to the Congress, vol. 1, 5–11 (Aug. 1990).

40. The system India devised to deal with the Bhopal disaster was praised as efficient way to deal with a "problem of mass proportions." *See* Bano Bi v. Union Carbide Chemical, 984 F.2d 582, 586 (2d Cir. 1993) (affirming the lower court's refusal to grant Indian citizens access to United States courts, and recognizing the Bhopal Act's grant of exclusive standing to the Indian government to represent disaster victims, because to do otherwise would frustrate India's efforts), *cert. denied,* 114 S. Ct. 179 (1993).

> [India] decided in an act passed by its democratic parliament to represent exclusively all the victims in a suit against Union Carbide and to use the money it received in settlement of that suit to fund a plan, framed pursuant to the Bhopal Act, to process the claims of all the victims.

Id. at 586; *see also In re* Union Carbide Corp. Gas Plant Disaster at Bhopal, India, 634 F. Supp. 842 (S.D.N.Y. 1986), *aff'd in part and modified in part,* 809 F.2d 195 (2d Cir. 1987), *cert. denied,* 484 U.S. 871 (1987). In practice, the Indian system has been much too slow in getting the money and resources to the victims of the disaster. *See* Settlement Slow in India Gas Disaster Claims, N.Y. Times, Mar. 25, 1993, at A6 (in the year since the program began disbursements, only seven hundred people have received only about $2 million of the $700 million fund).

41. *See, e.g.,* Soviet Nuclear Accident Sends Radioactive Cloud over Europe: Tass Says Mishap near Kiev Caused Unspecified Casualties, Wash. Post, Apr. 29, 1986, at A1.

42. County of Suffolk v. Long Island Lighting Co., 710 F. Supp. 1387 (E.D.N.Y. 1989), *modified,* 710 F. Supp. 1487 (E.D.N.Y. 1989).

43. Those still living in the LILCO service areas received automatic refunds via reductions in present bills.

44. County of Suffolk v. Long Island Lighting Co., 710 F. Supp. 1424, 1428 (E.D.N.Y. 1989), *modified,* 710 F. Supp. 1487 (E.D.N.Y. 1989) (order to hold and notify public of hearings on the proposed settlement and fairness opinion based on information gathered at public hearings finding proposed settlement reasonable).

45. *See* Bilello v. Abbott Labs., 825 F. Supp. 475 (E.D.N.Y. 1993) (denying defendant's disqualification motion based on court's expressed compassion for DES victims who recounted their experiences in chambers).

46. *See, e.g.,* Marine Sanctuaries Act, *codified in relevant part at* 16 U.S.C. § 1434 (1988); Federal Aid Highways Act, *codified in relevant part at* 23 U.S.C. § 128(a) (1988); Surface Mining Control Act, *codified in relevant part at* 30 U.S.C. § 1263 (1988); Clean Water Act of 1977, *codified in relevant part at* 33 U.S.C. §§ 1317(b)(1), 1341(a)(1) (1988); Atomic Energy Act, *codified in relevant part at* 42 U.S.C. § 2021(o)(3)(A) (1988); Environmental Policy Act, *codified in relevant part at* 42 U.S.C. § 4332(2)(c) (1988); Clean Air Act Amendment of 1977, *codified in relevant part at* 42 U.S.C. § 7607(h) (Supp. III 1991); Comprehensive Environmental Response, Compensation, and Liability Act, *codified in relevant part at* 42 U.S.C. § 9617 (1988).

47. *See* Sentencing Reform Act of 1984, Pub. L. No. 98-473, 98 Stat. 1987 (1984) (codified as amended at 18 U.S.C. §§ 3553–3559, 3561–3566, 3571–3574, 3581–3586 (1988) and 28 U.S.C. §§ 991–998 (1988); *see also* United States Sentencing Commission, Guidelines Manual (Nov. 1992).

48. For the author's writings on current sentencing practices, in addition to published opinions, see Jack B. Weinstein, A Trial Judge's Second Impression of the Federal Sentencing Guidelines, 66 S. Cal. L. Rev. 357 (1993); A Trial Judge's First Impression of the Federal Sentencing Guidelines, 52 Alb. L. Rev. 1 (1987); A Trial Judge's Reflections on Departures from the Federal Sentencing Guidelines, 5 Fed. Sent. Rep. 6 (July–Aug. 1992); Prison Need Not Be Mandatory, Judges' Journal 16 (Winter 1989).

49. *See* United States v. Rogers, 972 F.2d 489, 494 (2d Cir. 1992) ("In the tangled wake of the Sentencing Guidelines, there is a danger that district judges will conclude in frustration" that "the traditional role of a district judge in bringing compassion and common sense to the sentencing process . . . has been eradicated."); Steve Y. Koh, Reestablishing the Federal Judge's Role in Sentencing, 101 Yale L.J. 1109, 1134 n.158 (1992) (describing current "spiritlessness" of sentencing).

50. Model Code of Judicial Conduct, Canon 3B(9).

51. *Id.,* Canon 3B(11).

52. *But see* Jack B. Weinstein & Diane Zimmerman, Let the People Observe Their Courts, 61 Judicature 156 (1977) (supporting greater

use of TV, particularly in the appellate courts, including the Supreme Court of the United States).

53. *See* Press-Enterprise Co. v. Superior Court, 464 U.S. 501, 508 (1984) ("The value of openness lies in the fact that people not actually attending trials can have confidence that standards of fairness are being observed; the sure knowledge that *anyone* is free to attend gives assurance that established procedures are being followed and that deviations will be known").

54. *Id.* at 510 ("The presumption of openness may be overcome only by an overriding interest based on findings that closure is essential to preserve higher values and is narrowly tailored to serve that interest.").

55. The combination of irresponsible journalism, a plaintiffs' bar geared up and capable of advertising for clients, available capital, know-how to take advantage of any mass tort opportunity, and inadequate scientific knowledge has presented a difficult challenge to fair adjudication. *See* Litigation Journalism Is a Scourge, N.Y. Times, Feb. 15, 1992, at A15. ("[T]he role of the courts is being pre-empted and their procedures undermined as more cases are tried in the public arena long before official hearings take place.") The author refers to graphic media coverage of, for example, a death allegedly attributable to the cellular phone scare on a segment of "Larry King Live." (Ironically, a suggestion by a Veterans Administration clerk on television started the Agent Orange case.) *But see* Chandler v. Florida, 449 U.S. 560, 574–75 (1981) ("An absolute constitutional ban on broadcast coverage of trials cannot be justified simply because there is a danger that, in some cases, prejudicial broadcast accounts of pretrial and trial events may impair the ability of jurors to decide the issue of guilt or innocence uninfluenced by extraneous matter").

56. The press owes a responsibility to study the matter and try to educate. Sometimes quick and "cheap shot" sensationalism, particularly about product and other dangers, rather than responsible reporting confuses the issue. I note, however, that press coverage of cases I have tried has been almost uniformly responsible and useful.

57. *See, e.g.,* Communities Control Better than Courts, Newsday, July 6, 1993, at 61 (limits of criminal law in controlling society); Drugs, Crime and Punishment, N.Y. Times, July 8, 1993, at A19 (drug laws require public debate).

58. *See* Jurgen Habermas, Discourse Ethics: Notes on Philosophical Justification in *The Communicative Ethics Controversy* 60, 70 (Seyla Benhabib & Fred Dallmayr eds., 1990) ("[T]he impartiality of judgment is expressed in a principle that constrains *all* concerned to adopt the perspective of *all others* in the balancing of interests.").

59. *See, e.g.,* Ronald J. Bacigal, *The Limits of Litigation: The Dalkon Shield Controversy* (1990); Peter H. Schuck, *Agent Orange on Trial:*

Mass Toxic Disasters in the Courts (1987).

60. *See, e.g.,* Peter H. Schuck, The Role of Judges in Settling Complex Cases: The Agent Orange Example, 53 U. Chi. L. Rev. 337 (1986); Judith Resnik, Managerial Judges, 96 Harv. L. Rev. 374 (1982).

61. *See* Manual for Complex Litigation, Second § 20.1 (1985).

62. *Id.* § 23.1.

63. *See* Fed. R. Civ. P. 23(e).

64. *See* Manual for Complex Litigation, Second § 23.1 (1985).

65. *See, e.g.,* Peter H. Schuck, *Agent Orange on Trial: Mass Toxic Disasters in the Courts* 163 (1987) ("A well-meaning but overzealous judge may occasionally go too far and 'coerce' settlement, and Weinstein himself has been accused of this.").

66. *See* Dorothy J. Howell, *Scientific Literacy and Environmental Policy: The Missing Prerequisite for Sound Decision Making* 33 (1992). The author observes that the absence of scientific answers in Agent Orange led to studies that are "scientific scam[s], perpetrated solely for political reasons." *Id.* at 35.

67. *See* Wilbur J. Scott, *The Politics of Readjustment: Vietnam Veterans since the War,* chapter 7, Better Settled Than Tried, at 163 ff. (1993).

68. *See text supra,* chapter 4 (discussing problem of potential future claimants); *see also In re* Joint E. & S. Dists. Asbestos Litig., 129 B.R. 710, 763 (E. & S.D.N.Y. 1991) (discussing the use of court-appointed expert to review projections of future claims against the Manville Trust in order to create a realistic payment plan), *vacated and remanded,* 982 F.2d 721 (2d Cir. 1992), *modified on rehearing,* 993 F.2d 7 (2d Cir. 1993).

69. *See text supra,* chapters 1 and 2 (discussing shortcomings in Buffalo Creek case).

70. *See* Naikang Tsao, Note, Ameliorating Environmental Racism: A Citizen's Guide to Combatting the Discriminatory Siting of Toxic Waste Dumps, 67 N.Y.U. L. Rev. 366, 366 (1992) (noting that 40 percent of the total landfill capacity in the United States is located in areas where the population is predominantly African-American or Hispanic); Pollution-Weary Minorities Try Civil Rights Tack, N.Y. Times, Jan. 11, 1993, at A1 (reporting grass-roots organizing by minorities to combat disproportionate burden of environmental harm); Special Investigation, Unequal Protection: The Racial Divide in Environmental Law, Nat'l L.J., Sept. 21, 1992 (special section) (reporting disproportionate burden of environmental harm on minority communities); Marianne Lavelle, Environmental Racism Targeted, Nat'l L.J., Mar. 1, 1993, at 3 (reporting scheduling of congressional hearings to investigate discrimination against minorities with respect to environmental dangers).

71. *See, e.g.,* Judges Organization Broadens Its Mission, Asbestos Litig. Rptr. (Andrews) 26,709 (Jan. 8, 1993) (describing Mass Torts

Litigation Committee, an organization of state judges formed to discuss mass tort cases and promote cooperation among state judges and between state and federal courts); Letter from Chief Judge Thomas D. Lambros to Chief Judge Charles R. Wolle, Jan. 6, 1993 (arguing for active role of federal judiciary in Mass Tort Litigation Committee to promote cooperation of state and federal judges); *see also* William W. Schwarzer et al., Judicial Federalism in Action: Coordination of Litigation in State and Federal Courts, 78 Va. L. Rev. 1689 (1992) (describing instances of extraordinary cooperation between state and federal courts in mass tort cases); *cf.* ABA Model Code of Judicial Conduct Canon 3B7(b) (1990) (judge may obtain advice of a disinterested party on the law).

72. A public interest organization recently released a report severely criticizing the practice of judges attending educational seminars on issues such as law and economics funded by corporations and others. *See* Alliance for Justice, Justice for Sale: Shortchanging the Public Interest for Private Gain (1993). So long as the matter is public and the seminar run by an organization such as a law school or bar association with well-recognized, responsible lecturers, the criticism seems unfounded. It might be better, however, if the judicial budget paid the expenses of the judge in attending.

73. *Cf.* Evans v. Jeff D., 475 U.S. 717 (1986) (court may reject proposal and postpone trial to see if a different settlement can be achieved), *rehearing denied,* 476 U.S. 1179 (1986). *But cf. In re* Joint E & S. Dists. Asbestos Litig., 982 F.2d 721, 731, 740 (2d Cir. 1992) (opinion may not modify terms of settlement).

74. Several states make it unethical to ask plaintiffs to waive fees as part of a settlement. David Austern, Legal and Judicial Ethics and the Supreme Court, 22 Trial 22 (July 1986).

75. It has been suggested that judges are too concerned about consolidation and settlement and should focus instead on what happens after the case is settled and the lawyers attempt to collect their fees. Christopher P. Lu, Note, Procedural Solutions to the Attorney's Fee Problem in Complex Litigation, 26 U. Rich. L. Rev. 41 (1991) (advocating innovation by the courts to prevent fee abuses including the use of magistrates and special masters to oversee the fee process, pretrial conferences to set ground rules for attorneys fees, requiring submission of contemporaneous time records, and making interim fee awards).

76. *In re* "Agent Orange" Prod. Liability Litig., 611 F. Supp. 1396, 1431–43 (E.D.N.Y. 1985), *aff'd in part, rev'd in part,* 818 F.2d 179 (2d Cir. 1987).

77. *Id.*

78. *In re* "Agent Orange" Prod. Liab. Litig., 818 F.2d 179, 185–86 (2d Cir. 1987), *cert. denied,* 487 U.S. 1234 (1988).

79. *Id.*

80. *In re* "Agent Orange" Prod. Liab. Litig., 689 F. Supp. 1250, 1254–57 (E.D.N.Y. 1988).

81. *Id.* at 1270–75.

82. Supported by AOCAP funding, the National Veterans Legal Services Project has made available to both veterans and advocates a wide range of specialized and highly useful resource material. *See, e.g., Veterans Benefits Manual: An Advocate's Guide to Representing Veterans and Their Dependents* (2 vols. 1991); *Agent Orange Self-Help Guide* (1991); *Veterans Family Benefits Self-Help Guide* (1992); *VA Education Benefits Self-Help Guide* (1991); *VA Health Care Self-Help Guide* (1992); *Discharge Upgrading Self-Help Guide* (1990); *The Veterans Advocate* (issued monthly).

83. *In re* "Agent Orange" Prod. Liab. Litig., 689 F. Supp. 1250, 1275–80 (E.D.N.Y. 1988).

84. *See* Freeman v. Pitts, 112 S. Ct. 1430 (1992) (although temporary supervision of school system may have lasted for decades, ultimate objective remains to return school district to control of local authorities); Board of Educ. of Oklahoma v. Dowell, 498 U.S. 237, 241 (1991) (desegregation injunctions are not intended to operate in perpetuity).

85. *See In re* Joint E. & S. Dists. Asbestos Litig., 129 B.R. 710, 905–06 (E. & S.D.N.Y. 1991), *vacated*, 982 F.2d 721 (2d Cir. 1992), *modified on rehearing*, 993 F.2d 7 (2d Cir. 1993).

86. Trustees who serve in these unique institutions face their own ethical difficulties. One of the Dalkon Shield trustees has raised some of the questions:

> How can trustees, who are charged to act as fiduciaries, do so knowing that at least some subset of claimants will become adversaries? Do Trustees owe a higher duty to some claimants than others? For example, the [Dalkon Shield] Plan provides for Late Claimants to receive payments if money is left over after all timely claimants are paid. Do Trustees owe a higher duty to timely claimants?

Georgene M. Vairo, The Dalkon Shield Claimants Trust: Paradigm Lost (or Found)?, 61 Fordham L. Rev. 617, 621 (1992) (citations omitted).

87. *In re* A. H. Robins Co., 880 F.2d 779, 786–88 (4th Cir. 1989).

88. *Id.* at 787–88. Some trust mechanisms have functioned very well. The Dalkon Shield Claimants Trust has been, on the whole, a success. The history of the Dalkon Shield litigation and the formation of the Trust is set out in detail in Georgene M. Vairo, The Dalkon Shield Claimants Trust: Paradigm Lost (or Found)?, 61 Fordham L. Rev. 617, 624–37 (1992). The Trust's decisionmaking is driven by three overriding principles: (1) treat all claimants fairly and equally, always

focusing on the best interests of claimants collectively instead of on the interest of a particular claimant or group of claimants; (2) preserve the funds available to claimants with valid claims by keeping administrative expenses at a minimum; and (3) prefer settlement and prompt payment of claims over arbitration and litigation. *Id.* at 637–39.

The Trust also communicates with claimants through "plain English" newsletters and by employing "Personal Contacts" assigned to claimants whom the claimant can call for information. *Id.* at 640–41; *see also* Letter from Marietta S. Robinson to author, Aug. 4, 1992 (explaining Personal Contact program and enclosing training materials and rigorous examination administered to those seeking to serve as Personal Contacts). There is some evidence, unfortunately, that claimants represented by attorneys may be receiving less information than those who deal directly with the Trust. The Trust also has a commendable program under which claimants seeking help with in vitro fertilization or reconstructive surgery can obtain a portion of their award up front upon showing likelihood of recovery. The payment need not be reimbursed if the claimant does not ultimately recover from the Trust.

89. Rule 706(a) of the Federal Rules of Evidence states:

> The court may *on its own motion* or on the motion of any party enter an order to show cause why expert witnesses should not be appointed, and may request the parties to submit nominations. The court may appoint any expert witnesses agreed upon by the parties, and *may appoint witnesses of its own selection.* (emphasis added)

See also In re Joint E. & S. Dists. Asbestos Litig., 982 F.2d 721 (2d Cir. 1992) (affirming district court's appointment of expert witnesses who would testify on the expected number of future claimants against the Manville Trust), *modifed on rehearing,* 993 F.2d 7 (2d Cir. 1993); Manual for Complex Litigation, Second § 21.51 (1985) (discussing practical considerations of court appointment of experts); *In re* Swine Flu Immunization Prods. Liab. Litig., 495 F. Supp. 1185 (W.D. Okla.), *aff'd,* 707 F.2d 1141 (10th Cir. 1980) (panels of medical experts appointed to assist in resolving complex issues arising from the National Swine Flu Immunization); Harold Leventhal, Environmental Decisionmaking and the Role of the Courts, 122 U. Pa. L. Rev. 509, 546–54 (1974) (discussing how outside scientific experts can aid the courts).

It has been proposed that "science courts" adjudicate technologically complex issues. *See* Arthur Kantrowitz, Proposal for an Institution for Scientific Judgment, 153 Science 763 (1967), *reprinted in* 113 Cong. Rec. 15,256 (1967); John W. Wesley, Note, Scientific Evidence and the Question of Judicial Capacity, 25 Wm. & Mary L. Rev. 675 (1984) (discussing the science court and other methods of utilizing scientists).

Such "courts" can serve an advisory function, but final adjudication in a non-ADR setting should be by a court or a court and jury, better able to apply the nonscientific criteria almost always implicated.

90. Rule 53(b) of the Federal Rules of Civil Procedure authorizes reference to a special master in limited circumstances:

> A reference to a master shall be the exception and not the rule. In actions to be tried by a jury, a reference shall be made only when the issues are complicated; in actions to be tried without a jury, save in matters of account and of difficult computation of damages, a reference shall be made only upon a showing that some exceptional condition requires it.

Fed. R. Cir. P.53(b). *See, e.g., In re* New York City Asbestos Litig., 129 F.R.D. 434 (S. & E.D.N.Y. & N.Y. Sup. Ct. 1990) (joint federal-state appointment of Kenneth R. Feinberg, Esq., as Settlement Master-Referee in asbestos litigation); *see also* Jack B. Weinstein & Eileen B. Hershenov, The Effect of Equity on Mass Tort Law, 1991 U. Ill. L. Rev. 269, 300–302 (1991) (arguing that special masters are indispensable in mass tort cases); Francis E. McGovern, Resolving Mature Mass Tort Litigation, 69 B.U. L. Rev. 659, 669–71 (1989) (concerning the utility of special masters in gathering information in complex mass tort litigation); Jack B. Weinstein & Jonathan B. Wiener, Of Sailing Ships and Seeking Facts: Brief Reflections on Magistrates and the Federal Rules of Civil Procedure, 62 St. John's L. Rev. 429 (1988).

91. Rule 201(b) of the Federal Rules of Evidence states in relevant part:

> A judicially noticed fact must be one not subject to reasonable dispute in that it is either (1) generally known within the territorial jurisdiction of the trial court or (2) capable of accurate and ready determination by resort to sources whose accuracy cannot be reasonably determined.

Fed. R. Evid. 201(b). *See, e.g.,* Browning-Ferris Indus. v. Muszynski, 899 F.2d 151, 161 (2d Cir. 1990) (appellate court may take judicial notice of the existence of a body of scientific literature).

Rule 803(8)(C) of the Federal Rules of Evidence states that "in civil actions, factual findings resulting from an investigation made pursuant to authority granted by law, unless the sources of information or other circumstances indicate lack of trustworthiness [are not excluded by the hearsay rule]." *See, e.g.,* Kehm v. Proctor & Gamble Co., 580 F. Supp. 890 (N.D. Iowa 1982) (epidemiological study on toxic shock syndrome conducted by the Center for Disease Control was properly admitted under one or more of the hearsay exceptions), *aff'd,* 724 F.2d 613 (8th Cir. 1983); *In re* "Agent Orange" Prod. Liab. Litig., 611 F. Supp. 1223,

1240 (E.D.N.Y. 1985) (scientific studies conducted by various government agencies were admissible under Rule 803(8)(C) where plaintiffs failed to meet their burden of showing that the studies were untrustworthy), *aff'd*, 818 F.2d 187 (2d Cir. 1987), *cert. denied*, 487 U.S. 1234 (1988).

92. Rule 39(c) of the Federal Rules of Civil Procedure states in part that "in all actions not triable of right by a jury the court, upon motion or of its own initiative may try any issue with an advisory jury." *See generally* Charles A. Wright & Arthur R. Miller, *Federal Practice and Procedure* § 2335 (1971). If a case involves complex scientific evidence, the advisory jury might consist of scientists from appropriate fields, in which case the jury would resemble a "science court." John W. Wesley, Note, Scientific Evidence and the Question of Judicial Capacity, 25 Wm. & Mary L. Rev. 675 (1984).

It has been proposed that judges should receive scientific training, either generally, or for particular cases. *See, e.g.*, Vuyanich v. Republic Nat'l Bank, 521 F. Supp. 656 (N.D. Tex. 1981) (trial judge did extensive reading and permitted a lecture by an expert to help him comprehend statistical data) *vacated on other grounds*, 723 F.2d 1195 (5th Cir. 1984), *cert. denied*, 469 U.S. 1073 (1984); William A. Thomas, A Report from the Workshop on Cross-Education of Lawyers & Scientists, 19 Jurimetrics J. 92 (1978) (report from the National Conference of Lawyers & Scientists recommending cross training of the two disciplines). *Contra* David L. Bazelon, *Coping with Technology Through the Legal Process*, 62 Cornell L. Rev. 817, 822–23 (1977) (arguing that judges should not scrutinize technical merits of decisions, but should ensure that the decision-making process is thorough and rational).

93. *See* Daubert v. Merrell Dow Pharmaceuticals, Inc., 113 S. Ct. 2786 (1993). *See* Jack B. Weinstein, First Reaction of a Trial Judge to the Supreme Court's *Daubert* Opinion, Speech to the ABA at Annual Meeting, Aug. 9, 1993 (unpublished) (stresses need for ethical relations between science and law).

94. Canon 3 of the Model Code of Judicial Conduct for United States Judges states in part that:

> A judge shall accord to every person who has a legal interest in a proceeding, or that person's lawyer, the right to be heard according to law. A judge shall not initiate, permit, or consider ex parte communications or consider other communications made to the judge outside the presence of the parties. . . .

Articles by the author on the subject of the related problems of "How a Judge May Learn and What a Judge May Say and Do" are forthcoming in Judicature, Arizona Law Review, and Dayton Law Review.

95. *See* 28 U.S.C. § 453 (1988) (oath of justices and judges to act impartially); 28 U.S.C. § 455(b)(1) (Supp. 1993) (judge should recuse

him- or herself where he or she has personal knowledge of disputed evidentiary facts); *see also* John Leubsdorf, Theories of Judging and Judge Disqualification, 62 N.Y.U. L. Rev. 237 (1987) (discussing what constitutes impartiality); Note, Disqualification of Judges and Justices in the Federal Courts, 86 Harv. L. Rev. 736, 757–59 (1973) (discussing predispositions that might affect a judge's approach to a case).

In Laird v. Tatum, 409 U.S. 824, 835 (1971), respondents moved that Justice Rehnquist recuse himself because he had once testified on behalf of the Department of Justice on an issue raised in their action. Justice Rehnquist noted that a Justice's mind cannot be "a complete tabula rasa," and if it were it "would be evidence of a lack of qualification, not lack of bias." Chief Justice Hughes also chose to sit in West Coast Hotel Co. v. Parrish, 300 U.S. 379 (1937), despite having written a book addressing the issue raised in the case.

96. *Contrast* Model Code of Judicial Conduct Canon 3B(7) (judge may obtain advice of expert on law only upon notice to parties and provision of an opportunity to be heard) *with* Joe S. Cecil & Thomas E. Willging, Defining a Role for Court-Appointed Experts, FJC Directions 6, 13 (Fed. Jud. Center, Aug. 1992) (in interviews with judges, about one-quarter indicated they communicated with court-appointed expert on technical matters outside presence of parties).

97. *In re* School Asbestos Litig., 977 F.2d 764 (3d Cir. 1992), *amended,* 24 Fed. R. Serv. 3d (Callaghan) 39 (3rd Cir. 1992).

98. In the breast implant cases, the attorneys for plaintiffs and defendants voluntarily provided a fund of $50,000 used to pay expenses of state trial judges who travel to meetings with the federal judge assigned to the case in order to coordinate state and federal discovery and pretrial control; the federal judge uses federal government sources of funds for his own expenses. Oral statement of Judge Samuel C. Pointer, Jr., at the 26th Transferee Judges Conference, Palm Beach, Fla., Oct. 6, 1993. Coordinating state and federal cases is vital, but judges' expenses should not, if at all possible, be paid for by litigants.

The asbestos conference attended by Judge Kelly was also attended by state judges; the state judges' expenses were paid for by state funds. Conversation of author with Justice Helen E. Freedman, Oct. 11, 1994. *But cf. In re* School Asbestos Litig. 977 F.2d 764, 770 (3d Cir. 1992) (allegations that judge had some of his own expenses at conference paid for out of funds controlled by litigants). Expenses of state judges in connection with the State Court Mass Tort Litigation Committee have been paid by the National Center for State Courts and the State Justice Institute, with federal monies. Conversation with Justice Freedman, *supra.*

Early in the Manville Trust litigations, state judges attended conferences paid for out of Trust funds expended through the National Judicial College, Reno, Nev. *Id*. This was at a time when the Trust was not involved with the litigation.

It would be useful to add a line to the federal budget for expenses of state and federal judges coordinating the administration of cases in a few selected mass torts. A similar line in the budget of the Federal Judicial Center to increase the Center's ability to encourage the education of federal judges and a limited number of state judges cooperating in national complex litigation would also be helpful. The Center already has an extensive general training program for federal judges.

99. *See* Model Code of Judicial Conduct Canon 3E(1) (1990) (judge shall disqualify him- or herself in proceeding in which impartiality might reasonably be questioned); 28 U.S.C. § 455(a) (Supp. 1993) (same).

100. *See* Jack B. Weinstein, Panel Discussion, Disqualification of Judges (The Sarokin Matter): Is It a Threat to Judicial Independence?, 58 Brook. L. Rev. 1 (1993).

101. One of the judges I interviewed emphasized that the public nature of mass tort cases effectively results in all information being public. There is little, if any, information that the judge is not exposed to in some way.

102. *See generally* James S. DeGraw, Note, Rule 53, Inherent Powers and Institutional Reform: The Lack of Limits on Special Masters, 66 N.Y.U. L. Rev. 800 (1991) (arguing that the discretionary powers granted to masters create great potential for abuse); Linda J. Silberman, Judicial Adjuncts Revisited: The Proliferation of Ad Hoc Procedure, 137 U. Pa. L. Rev. 2131, 2132 (1989) (arguing that delegations of authority to masters and magistrates has replaced a precise code of procedure with one that is "customized" for each case); Jack B. Weinstein & Jonathan Wiener, Of Sailing Ships and Seeking Facts: Brief Reflections on Magistrates and the Federal Rules of Civil Procedure, 62 St. John's L. Rev. 429 (1988); Charles A. Wright & Arthur R. Miller, *Federal Practice and Procedure* § 3934, at 229 (1977) (discussing the overuse of special masters under Rule 53).

In United States v. United Shoe Mach. Corp., 110 F. Supp. 295 (D. Mass. 1953), *aff'd*, 347 U.S. 521 (1954), Judge Wyzanski appointed the distinguished economist Carl Kaysen as his law clerk during the year he was considering the antitrust action. Judge Wyzanski later conceded that it was inadvisable to select a clerk with knowledge of the subject matter that was superior to his own.

103. Special masters are subject to most judicial ethical provisions while they are serving. See Code of Conduct for United States Judges, Compliance with the Code of Conduct, B. Judge Pro Tempore, 830 F. Supp. 193, 208 (1993) (approved by Sept. 22, 1992, Session of United States Judicial Conference).

104. *See, e.g.*, Linda Silberman, Judicial Adjuncts Revisited: The

Proliferation of Ad Hoc Procedure, 137 U. Pa. L. Rev. 2131, 2141 ff. (1989); Edward V. DiLello, Note, Fighting Fire with Firefighters: A Proposal for Expert Judges at the Trial Level, 93 Colum. L. Rev. 473, 486–89 (1993) (noting the problems associated with increasing use of special masters, including possible bias, invalid delegation, procedural inconsistency, delay, vagueness as to legal status of fact-finding, and lack of accumulated expertise); *cf.* Joel Seligman, The Disinterested Person: An Alternative Approach to Shareholder Derivative Litigation, 36 U. Mich. L. Sch. L.Q. 28 (1993).

105. It is important to note that the court's power to appoint a special master is not unrestricted. *See, e.g.,* Prudential Ins. Co. of Amer. v. U.S. Gypsum Co., 991 F.2d 1080 (3d Cir. 1993) (vacating appointment of special master where "exceptional circumstances" standard not satisfied).

106. *Cf.* James S. DeGraw, Note, Rule 53, Inherent Powers, and Institutional Reform: The Lack of Limits on Special Masters, 66 N.Y.U. L. Rev. 800, 836–49 (1991) (arguing for a rule of civil procedure governing activities of special masters that would be more restrictive than current Rule 53). The appropriate answer to ethical problems posed by the increasing use of special masters is not to inhibit their useful functions by restricting their authority and powers, but to adopt ethical guidelines governing their relationship with the judge and parties.

107. *See In re* Joint E. & S. Dists. Asbestos Litig., 737 F. Supp. 735, 739 (E. & S.D.N.Y. & N.Y. Sup. Ct. 1990) ("In general a special master or referee should be considered a judge for purposes of judicial ethics rules."). *See* Margaret G. Ferrell, Federal Judicial Center, Special Masters: Defining the Role of Special Masters Appointed Under Federal Rule of Civil Procedure 53(b), Federal Judicial Center, draft copy (1993), chapter 7, Ethical Restraints on Masters.

108. For nearly two decades, District Judge Robert Zampano of the District of Connecticut has used the special master approach in what has been characterized as a hybrid system of minitrial and neutral fact finder. He currently utilizes twelve lawyers from various fields of expertise in teams of two, as well as professors and businesspersons, to help resolve the enormous volume of discovery and pretrial motions. These pretrial sessions often result in settlements. *See* Joseph T. McLaughlin, Alternative Dispute Resolution, ALI-ABA Course of Study, Trial Evidence, Civil Practice, and Effective Litigation Techniques in the Federal Courts 16–17, Feb. 25–27, 1993.

109. *See In re* Joint E. & S. Dists. Asbestos Litig., 737 F. Supp. 735, 744–46 (E. & S.D.N.Y. & N.Y. Sup. Ct. 1990) (challenge to impartiality of special master not timely since party bringing motion knew of relevant facts at time of appointment and failed to object).

110. One expert witness broker promises, "If the first doctor we refer doesn't agree with your legal theory, we will provide you with the name of a second prospective expert." David Bernstein, Out of the Frying Pan and into the Fire: The Expert Witness Problem in Toxic Tort Litigation, 10 Rev. Litig. 117, 120 (1990); *see also* Steven M. Schatz & Jeremy G. Epstein, Ethical Considerations in the Use of Experts, PLI Order No. H4-5042 (1988) (discussing contingency fees for expert witnesses under ABA Model Code of Professional Responsibility).

Expert witnesses who are engineers are subject to the Codes of Ethics of their professional societies, such as the American Society of Mechanical Engineers (ASME). Such codes contain provisions such as "[A member] shall hold paramount the safety, health and welfare of the public in the performance of their professional duties." In practice, professional societies do not sanction their members for giving testimony of dubious scientific merit, and sanctions cannot exceed the loss of membership in the organization.

111. A recent example of the critical importance of unsettled scientific analysis in establishing causation in mass tort cases is the emerging litigation involving electromagnetic field radiation emitted by power lines. *See* Electromagnetic Fields Attract Lawsuits, Nat'l L.J., Feb. 8, 1993, at 20.

112. *See, e.g.*, Lynch v. Merrell-Nat'l Labs., Inc., 830 F.2d 1190 (1st Cir. 1987) (criticism of selected epidemiological studies by Shanna Helen Swan was not published and could not show causation); Will v. Richardson-Merrell, Inc., 647 F. Supp. 544 (S.D. Ga. 1986) (plastic surgeon's testimony concerning effects of Bendectin was properly excluded where he admitted he was not an expert and had no knowledge of studies that had been conducted on the drug).

113. *In re* "Agent Orange" Prod. Liab. Litig., 611 F. Supp. 1223, 1283 (E.D.N.Y. 1985), *aff'd*, 818 F.2d 187 (2d Cir. 1987) (no facts rationally supporting the opinion of Dr. Carnow), *cert. denied*, 487 U.S. 1234 (1988).

114. Jones v. Lederle Labs., 785 F. Supp. 1123, 1127 (E.D.N.Y. 1992) (plaintiffs' experts Drs. Geier and Charash "misdescribed the historical facts"), *aff'd*, 982 F.2d 63 (2d Cir. 1992). The pertussis cases arose after the publication of a cautiously worded study suggesting that while the vaccine saved thousands of lives, it might cause twenty-five cases per year of serious brain damage. Alan R. Hinman & Jeffrey P. Koplan, Pertussis and Pertussis Vaccine: Reanalysis of Benefits, Risks and Costs, 2151 J. A.M.A. 3109, 3112 (1984).

115. *See, e.g., In re* "Agent Orange" Prod. Liab. Litig., 611 F. Supp. 1223, 1246 (E.D.N.Y. 1985), *aff'd*, 818 F.2d 187 (2d Cir. 1987) (rejecting Dr. Singer's affidavit because "no reputable physician relies

on hearsay checklists by litigants to reach a conclusion with respect to the cause of their afflictions"), *cert. denied,* 487 U.S. 1234 (1988); Richardson v. Richardson-Merrell, Inc., 857 F.2d 823 (D.C. Cir. 1988) (plaintiff's witness, Dr. Alan Done, had not performed his own studies, but testified in contradiction to the findings of researchers who had studied and published in the twenty-odd years since the investigation of Bendectin began), *cert. denied,* 993 U.S. 882 (1989); *In re* Swine Flu Immunization Prod. Liab. Lit., 508 F. Supp. 897 (D. Colo. 1981), *aff'd sub nom.* Lima v. United States, 708 F.2d 502 (10th Cir. 1983) (plaintiff's experts rejected as speculative and not supported by the medical literature); DeLuca v. Merrell Dow Pharmaceuticals, 791 F. Supp. 1042 (D.N.J. 1992) (after remand, expert's lack of qualifications and sloppy testimony devastatingly exposed), *aff'd,* 6 F.3d 778 (3d Cir. 1993).

116. *Compare* Peter W. Huber, *Galileo's Revenge: Junk Science in the Courtroom* (1991) *with* Jack B. Weinstein, Rule 702 of the Federal Rules of Evidence Is Sound; It Should Not Be Amended, 138 F.R.D. 631 (1991).

117. *See* David B. Isbell & Arvid E. Roach, One Court, One Rule on Ethics, Nat'l L.J., Aug. 9, 1993 (discussing problem of lawyer faced with conflicting ethical duties). In Haines v. Liggett Group, Inc., 814 F. Supp. 414 (D.N.J. 1993), despite the fact that the tobacco litigation was national in nature, the court applied the New Jersey ethical rules in determining plaintiff's attorneys' withdrawal motion. *Cf. In re* "Agent Orange" Prod. Liab. Litig., 800 F.2d 14, 18–20 (2d Cir. 1986) (ethical rules established outside class action context should not be applied "mechanically" to problems that arise in class action settlements); Lawyer's Duty of Disclosure: Hearing on S.485 before the Subcommittee on Criminal Law of the Senate Committee on the Judiciary, 98th Cong., 1st Sess. 39 (1983) (statement of Monroe H. Freedman, Professor of Law, Hofstra University) ("[I]t is urgent that the Congress assume responsibility for a comprehensive code of ethical conduct for lawyers practicing before Federal courts and agencies."); County of Suffolk v. Long Island Lighting Co., 710 F. Supp. 1407, 1413 (E.D.N.Y. 1989) (applying federal ethical standards to lawyers in a Rule 23 class action), *aff'd,* 907 F.2d 1295 (2d Cir. 1990).

118. Ethics professor Monroe Freedman criticizes the profession's attempt to "burnish its image" by proposing a new ethical rule, inspired by events surrounding the fire at the DuPont Plaza Hotel in Puerto Rico and the disaster in Bhopal, that would prohibit trial lawyers from going to the scene of a disaster "without an invitation." Monroe Freedman, Ambulance-Chasing in the Public Interest, Legal Times, July 16, 1990, at 20. As Professor Freedman notes:

These rules of etiquette might enhance the appearance of gentility sought by some lawyers, but in the real world, disaster victims and their families are often not in a position to issue "invitations." And unless they are solicited by lawyers, victims of neglect, who may not even know they have rights, may never get relief.

Id.

Freedman is highly critical of newspaper stories that portray the "ugly lawyer" who rushes to the scene of an accident. These stories, he points out, fail to reveal that often it is only the lawyers who remain to serve the poor and uneducated. "[S]ome of the best lawyers in the world travel thousands of miles to offer their services to impoverished people, and instead of celebrating that fact, there are those who bemoan it." *Id.* Solicitation, the author argues, may be the only way to fulfill the ethical obligation to make legal counsel available to the poor.

The extent to which plaintiffs' lawyers are organized is perhaps epitomized by efforts made by an advertising agency soliciting attorneys for breast implant newspaper and television advertisements. The company, appropriately called "Rainmaker Marketing," will customize a series of television and newspaper ads for $5,000. As one attorney who agreed to be quoted in the ad commented, "The first time Rainmaker placed the newspaper ads, we signed 32 cases and received 30 referrals from other attorneys." *See* Breast Implant TV and Newspaper Ads, Nat'l L.J., Feb. 15, 1993 at 6.

A recent decision of a Florida district court held that the Florida bar's thirty-day ban on personal injury and wrongful death litigation targeted direct mail lawyer advertising violated the First Amendment. McHenry v. The Florida Bar, 808 F. Supp. 1543 (M.D. Fla. 1992). The court found that the Florida rule would "substantially impair and impede the availability of truthful and relevant information that can make a positive contribution to consumers in need of such legal services." *Id.* at 1548.

But cf. Lawrence A. Dubin, Ethics, Nat'l L.J., May 11, 1992, at 15 (describing how two New Jersey lawyers were reprimanded for soliciting the parents of a Syracuse University student, the day after his remains were identified in the debris of Pan Am Flight 103). The attorneys had made false and misleading statements about fees and had overstated their qualifications. *Id.* at 17. The New Jersey Supreme Court refused to "view the practice of law as akin to the sale of aluminum siding." *In re* Anis, 599 A.2d 1265, 1269 (N.J. 1992), *cert. denied*, 112 S. Ct. 2303 (1992). The court noted that "[t]he familiar spectacle of lawyers and their agents preying on the victims of disaster has occasioned revulsion and prompted calls for reform." *Id.* at 1266.

119. The question of whether federally employed attorneys are sub-

ject to state ethics rules was recently answered in the negative by a federal judge in Washington, D.C. District Judge Norma Holloway Johnson enjoined the New Mexico Supreme Court Disciplinary Board from calling an Assistant U.S. Attorney to a hearing to discuss his having accepted telephone calls from a represented defendant. For a history of the case *see* Cris Carmody, U.S. Judge's Opinion: Justice Dept. Rules Trump State Ethics, Nat'l L.J., Mar. 1, 1993, at 7. *See also* County of Suffolk v. Long Island Lighting Co., 710 F. Supp. 1407, 1414–15 (E.D.N.Y. 1989) (under Supremacy Clause, Federal Rule of Civil Procedure 23, permitting attorneys to advance costs of litigation in class action, trumps New York State ethics rule prohibiting attorney from doing so without getting assurance of reimbursement), *aff'd,* 907 F.2d 1295 (2d Cir. 1990). Additional cases treating the relationship of state ethics rules to class actions are chronicled in Final Report, Financial Arrangements in Class Actions, and the Code of Professional Responsibility, Committee on Professional Responsibility, Ass'n of the Bar of the City of N.Y., Dec. 1992.

120. *Cf. In re* Folding Carton Antitrust Litig., 744 F.2d 1252 (7th Cir. 1984) (reversing trial judge's decision to designate surplus recovery in antitrust case to fund "Antitrust Development and Research Foundation" to promote the study of complex litigation and antitrust law and ruling that, by statute, surplus escheats to United States), *cert. dismissed,* 471 U.S. 1113 (1985); Richard L. Marcus & Edward F. Sherman, *Complex Litigation: Cases and Materials on Advanced Civil Procedure* 382 (1985) ("[S]ome class members entitled to compensation may fail to contact the court or file for their share. As a result, there may be a surplus left after all class members' claims have been satisfied. The courts have differed on proper disposition of the surplus, although generally approving exercise of *cy pres* authority over the funds."); *see also* United States v. Reserve Mining Co., 56 F.R.D. 408 (D. Minn. 1972) (ruling in pre-EPA litigation over discharges into Lake Superior that granted fifteen applications for intervention, including application of environmental groups on ground that community could have voice in litigation through them).

121. *See* Michael Polanyi, *The Study of Man* 91 (1959). Polyani writes:

> A correct judicial decision is an action that can be explained by its reasons, but it is also the action of the judge as a creature of flesh and blood. Insofar as the judge is acting in the service of justice, his mind and body function subsidiarily to the process of justice.

Id.

1. *See, e.g.,* Mark J. Roe, Corporate Strategic Reaction to Mass Tort, 72 Va. L. Rev. 1, 59 (1986). The author suggests that corporations may strategically avoid mass tort liability by manipulating the firm's operations to avoid payment. Strategies include quick liquidation and limiting liability to subsidiaries to separate risks. Despite obstacles to such maneuvers, the author identifies three plausible options for firms: strategic liquidation, slowly running down the firm's assets, and mass tort bankruptcy liquidation.

2. *See, e.g.,* Mark J. Roe, Bankruptcy and Mass Torts, 84 Colum. L. Rev. 846 (1984) (discussing problem of giving future claimants power to initiate reorganization and to protect them in view of uncertainty of amount of future claims and suggesting amending bankruptcy law to address problem directly).

3. *See, e.g.,* Claudia MacLachlan, Asbestos Claims Hang over One of the '80s' Big Buyouts, Nat'l L.J., Mar. 29, 1993, at 1; *see also* Keene Corporation, Annual Report (1992) (reporting development and status of asbestos litigation against Keene Corporation due to its acquisition in 1968 of Baldwin-Ehret-Hill, a manufacturer of acoustic ceilings and insulation).

4. *Cf.* ABA Model Rules of Professional Conduct, Rule 2.1 (1993) ("In representing a client, a lawyer shall exercise independent professional judgment and render candid advice. In rendering advice, a lawyer may refer not only to law but to other considerations such as moral, economic, social and political factors, that may be relevant to a client's situation.").

5. The responsibilities of the corporation also should be determined with reference to the community as well as to shareholders. *See* Robert N. Bellah, *The Good Society* 11 (1991) ("The corporation is a central institution in American life . . . [and as] an institution it is a particular historical pattern of rights and duties, of powers and responsibilities, that make it a major force in our lives."); *see also* Lyman Johnson, *Individual and Collective Sovereignty in the Corporate Enterprise* (book Review), 92 Colum. L. Rev. 2215 (1992) (arguing for a broader theoretical framework for corporate law, including but extending beyond economic analysis).

Some corporations are wisely becoming actively involved in a form of alternative dispute resolution by developing ombudsman programs. The ombudsman's role, which is currently used primarily in employer-employee disputes, is to work out solutions to prevent simple disagreements from evolving into disputes. *See* Joseph T. McLaughlin, Alternative Dispute Resolution, ALI-ABA Course of Study, Trial Evidence, Civil Practice, and Effective Litigation Techniques in the Federal Courts 24, Feb. 25-27, 1993.

The alternative to reducing transaction costs is bankruptcy of large parts of the insurance industry. *See* John H. Snyder, Environmental/

Asbestos Liability Exposures: A P/C Industry Black Hole, Best Week, Mar. 28, 1994, P/clb (payments and reserves will reach $40 billion or more); with plaintiff fees and disbursements at about 37 percent and defense litigation costs at 39 percent, plus costs of courts and executives, some 20 percent of the dollar spent goes to claimants. Letter from Mark Peterson to author dated April 19, 1994.

6. *See, e.g.,* Richard L. Marcus & Edward F. Sherman, *Complex Litigation* 983 (2d ed. 1992) (chapter on alternatives to litigation); Center for Public Management, *Corporate Dispute Management* (1984); Am. Bar Assoc., Litigation Section, *Emerging ADR Issues in State and Federal Courts* (Frank E. A. Sander ed., 1991); Joseph T. McLaughlin, Alternate Dispute Resolution in *ALI/ABA Evidence, Civil Practice and Litigation Techniques* 385 (Sol Schreiber ed., 1993).

CHAPTER 7

1. *See* Jack B. Weinstein & Robert Kushen, Scientific Evidence in Complex Litigation, presented at ALI-ABA Course of Study: Trial Evidence, Civil Practice and Effective Litigation Techniques in Federal and State Courts (July 24–26, 1991); *see also* Joan M. Cheever & Joanne Naiman, The View from the Jury Box, Nat'l L.J., Feb. 22, 1993, at S2 (in poll, 89 percent of jurors responded that they found paid experts believable). To take just one example, even today it remains unclear how sound or necessary is removal of asbestos from most buildings, as a matter of good science and practical risk evaluation. *See* Lee S. Siegel, Note, As the Asbestos Crumbles: A Look at New Evidentiary Issues in Asbestos-Related Property Damage Litigations, 20 Hofstra L. Rev. 1139 (1992).

2. *See, e.g.,* Robert Rosenthal & Peter David Blanck, Science and Ethics in Conducting, Analyzing, and Reporting Social Science Research: Implications for Social Scientists, Judges and Lawyers, 68 Ind. L.J. 1209 (1993).

3. Extensive research was funded by the federal government in connection with the Agent Orange case. *See, e.g.,* National Academy of Engineering, Keeping Pace with Science and Engineering, Case Studies In Environmental Regulation; James A. Moore, Kenneth D. Kimbrough, & Michael Gough, The Dioxin TCDD: A Selective Study of Science and Policy Interaction, at 221 (Myron F. Uman ed., 1993); Phantom Risk, Dioxin: Perceptions, Estimates, and Measures, chapter 11 by Michael Gough (Kenneth R. Foster, David E. Bernstein, & Peter W. Huber eds., 1993); The DES Cancer Network, DES Bill (DES Education and Research Bill, signed October 1992).

4. *See generally* J. B. Cordaro & Annette Dickinson, *Consensus: The Holy Grail or the Cheshire Cat?*, 41 Food Drug Cosm. L.J. 85 (1986);

William A. Thomas, Some Observations by a Scientist, 115 F.R.D. 142 (1987); Mark McCormick, Scientific Evidence: Defining a New Approach to Admissibility, 67 Iowa L. Rev. 879 (1982); Paul C. Gianelli, The Admissibility of Novel Scientific Evidence: Frye v. United States, a Half-Century Later, 80 Colum. L. Rev. 1197 (1980) (discussing procedural safeguards and a special burden of proof that might reduce the misuse of unreliable novel scientific evidence). *Cf., e.g.,* National Science Foundation, Compensation of Victims of Toxic Pollution—Assessing the Scientific Knowledge Base, Research Rep. 83-6 (Mar. 1983); Kenneth R. Foster, David E. Bernstein, and Peter W. Huber, *Phantom Risk, Scientific Inference and the Law* (1993) (various authors; sponsorship by the Manhattan Risk Institute). As the Supreme Court noted in Daubert v. Merrell Dow Pharmaceuticals, Inc., 113 S. Ct. 2786 (1993), the law will continue to rely on judgment of the judges as scientific gatekeepers to the courts.

5. The views in this section are treated in more detail in Jack B. Weinstein, First Reaction of a Trial Judge to the Supreme Court's Daubert Opinion, Speech at the Annual Meeting of the ABA, Aug. 9, 1993 (unpublished). *See generally* Robert Bell, *Impure Science: Fraud, Compromise and Political Influence in Scientific Research* (1992) (discussing how funding pressures encourage fraudulent science); William Broad & Nicholas Wade, *Betrayers of the Truth* (1982) (discussing the long history of fraud in science); Scientific Fraud and Misconduct and the Federal Response: Hearing before the Human Resources and Intergovernmental Relations Subcommittee on Governmental Operations, 100th Cong., 2d Sess. 108 (1988) (concerning the frequency of fraud and the infrequency of reported fraud).

6. Science and Law Clash over Fraud-Case Appeals, N.Y. Times, Nov. 8, 1993, at B10.

7. The need for higher standards of due process may require dropping of charges for what many scientists might believe to be at least shoddy work. *See, e.g.,* United States Drops Misconduct Case against an AIDS Researcher, N.Y. Times, Nov. 13, 1993 (failure to credit other scientists with assistance in project and failure to cooperate promptly with these testing hypothesis plus possibly contaminating strains of virus). *See generally* David J. Miller & Michael Hensen, *Research Fraud in the Behavioral and Biomedical Sciences* (1992); Her Study Shattered the Myth That Fraud in Science Is a Rarity, N.Y. Times, Nov. 23, 1993, at 6.

8. *See, e.g.,* Kenneth J. Chesebro, Galileo's Retort: Peter Huber's Junk Scholarship, 42 Am. U. L. Rev. 1637 (1993), criticizing in great detail and persuasively, Peter W. Huber, *Galileo's Revenge: Junk Science in the Courtroom* (1991). The Huber book was sponsored by the Manhattan Institute, whose funding and bias is described at great length by

Chesebro. *See, e.g.,* 42 Am. U. L. Rev. text at n.325 and ff. A subsequent book sponsored by the Manhattan Institute, *Phantom Risk, Scientific Inference and the Law* (Kenneth R. Foster, David E. Bernstein, & Peter W. Huber eds., 1993), appears to be more balanced, but should be read carefully in view of the fact that it was "Published for the Manhattan Institute by the MIT Press." See back of title page. *See also, e.g.,* Jeff L. Lewin, Calibresi's Revenge, Junk Science in the Work of Peter Huber, 21 Hofstra L. Rev. 183 (1992) (book review).

9. *See The Evolving Role of Statistical Assessment as Evidence in the Courts* 11, 162, 167, 234 (Stephen E. Feinberg ed., 1988).

Professional licensing requirements are silent on the issue of an engineer's affirmative duty to come forward with knowledge of design or other defects. Professional licensing is a state matter. In New York, the relevant law for all licensed professions is found in N.Y. Educ. Law §§ 6500-6512 (McKinney 1990). While various types of misconduct are described, there is no provision dealing with knowledge of health and safety hazards relevant to mass torts. The law specific to engineers is found in N.Y. Education Law §§ 7200–09 (Engineering and Land Surveying). As one engineer advised:

> We must tell what we know [of unsafe practices], first through administrative channels, but when these fail, through whatever avenues we can find. Many claim that it is disloyal to protest. Sometimes the penalty—disapproval, loss of status, even vilification—can be severe. Today we need more critical pronouncement and published declarations by engineers in high professional responsibilities. In some instances, such criticism must be severe if we are properly to serve mankind and preserve our freedom. Hence it is of the utmost importance that we maintain our freedom of communication in the engineering profession and to the public.

As recounted by Allan J. McDonald, Engineering Ethics and the Challenger Accident, Address to Brigham Young University, Dec. 4, 1986, at 10.

10. *See, e.g.,* Codes of The American Institute of Chemical Engineers (AIChE), The Institute of Electrical and Electronics Engineers (IEEE), The American Society of Mechanical Engineers (ASME), and The American Society of Civil Engineers (ASCE). These codes have some differences, but all begin with the statement that in performing their professional duties, engineers must safeguard the "safety, health, and welfare" of the public. The similarity of the codes apparently arises from an umbrella document, "The Fundamental Principles of the Code of Ethics of Engineers," produced by the Accreditation Board for Engineering and Technology, Inc. (ABET), which accredits many undergraduate

and graduate engineering programs. Some societies, such as IEEE, have simply approved the basic canons of the ABET document, while others, such as ASCE, have expanded on them with its "guidelines to practice," which include such statements as, "Engineers whose professional judgment is overruled under circumstances where the safety, health and welfare of the public are endangered, shall inform their clients or employers of the possible consequences."

11. Several views of the significance of peer review were presented in amicus curiae briefs in the Bendectin case before the Supreme Court, *Daubert v. Merrell Dow Pharmaceuticals, Inc.*, 951 F.2d 1128 (9th Cir. 1991), *rev'd*, 113 S. Ct. 2786 (1993). *See, e.g.*, Brief of Amicus Curiae by Daryl E. Chubin, U.S. Office of Technology Assessment, et al. ("Although professional basketball referees must go to school to learn what is or is not a foul, peer-review journal referees receive no comparable training."); Brief for the American Association for the Advancement of Science and the National Academy of Sciences as Amici Curiae in support of respondent (courts should take into account the results of peer review in assessing the validity of scientific evidence); *see also* Thomas S. Burack, Of Reliable Science: Scientific Peer Review, Federal Regulatory Agencies, and the Courts, 7 Va. J. Nat. Resources L. 27 (1987) (discussing the current role of peer review and potential improvements in the process); David Bernstein, Out of the Frying Pan and into the Fire: The Expert Witness Problem in Toxic Tort Litigation, 10 Rev. Litig. 117 (1990) (discussion of suspect testimony). The Court's opinion stated that trial courts might rely upon peer review as one of many relevant factors in applying Rule 702 of the Federal Rules of Evidence. Daubert v. Merrell Dow Pharmaceutics, Inc., 113 S. Ct. 2796 (1993).

12. *See* David Bernstein, Out of the Frying Pan and into the Fire: The Expert Witness Problem in Toxic Tort Litigation, 10 Rev. Litig. 117 (1990) (discussing Judge Glasser's call to professional associations and learned societies to reexamine the criteria for qualifying expert witnesses); Paul C. Gianelli, Frye v. United States, 99 F.R.D. 188 (1984) (and other articles in this issue in the section "Symposium on Science and Rules of Evidence" concerning the probative value of scientific evidence and possible modifications to Rule 702 of the Federal Rules of Evidence). *But see* Jack B. Weinstein, Rule 702 of the Federal Rules of Evidence Is Sound; It Should Not Be Amended, 138 F.R.D. 631 (1991) (improvement in expert testimony depends on steps the scientific community and the bar and courts can take under the present rule).

13. The Vice President for Research at the University of Miami explains:

As money becomes less and less available, more people are going to be compromising their principles, compromising their time. . . . We can get to the point at some stage in this process where we're not research universities any longer but fee-for-service corporations— hired guns.

Universities' Reliance on Companies Raises Vexing Questions on Research, N.Y. Times, Mar. 17, 1993, at B9 (describing response of universities to declining government support of scientific research). The University of Miami requires $100 million in research support annually just to keep its research machine running. *Id.* Corporations, many of them foreign, are filling the gap. *Id.* See also Victoria Slind-Flor, Scientific Fraud and the Law, National L.J., Oct. 25, 1993, at 1.

Much of the problem is due to different viewpoint of lawyers and scientists and their different roles. *See generally* Peter H. Schuck, Multiculturalism Redux: Science, Law and Politics, 11 Yale L. & Pol. Rev. 1 (1993), for some of the reasons for each culture misjudging the other. See also David Nelken, The Truth about Law's Truth, Working Paper, University College of London, 1989 (to be published in 1994), at 4 ("clashes between legal and scientific conceptions of reality and methods of truth finding"). *See also, e.g.,* Gary Spencer, Court Allows Damages for Fear of Cancer, N.Y. L.J., Oct. 13, 1993, at 1 ("Elevating market reality over scientific theory in eminent domain proceedings, the Court of Appeals ruled yesterday that landowners who can show that public fear of potential health risks posed by high voltage power lines has devalued their land will not have to prove that the public's fear is 'reasonable'").

14. A recent study reported in the New England Journal of Medicine revealed that 27 percent of the scientists surveyed had personally encountered falsified or fabricated research. Close to half of the participants acknowledged that fraud was on the rise. Moreover, the vast majority of those who had recognized scientific misconduct admitted that they had done nothing about it. *See* John D. Dingell, Misconduct in Medical Research, New Eng. J. Med. 1610, 1633 (June 3, 1993). *See also* William Broad and Nicholas Wade, *Betrayers of the Truth* 214 (1982) ("Under the pressure of competition, some researchers yield to the temptation of cutting corners, of improving on their data, of finagling their results and even of outright fraud."); *id.* at 215 ("the celebrity system favors the search for personal glory over the search for truth); Robert Bell, *Impure Science, Fraud, Compromise and Political Influence on Scientific Research* (1992).

15. *See, e.g.,* Daubert v. Merrell Dow Pharmaceuticals, Inc., 113 S. Ct. 2786 (1993) (rejecting *Frye* rule of general scientific acceptance in the field); Frye v. United States, 293 F. 1013 (D.C. Cir. 1923). I have elsewhere indicated why I think the simplistic *Frye* rule is not the most

useful way of controlling the use of science in the courts. *See, e.g.,* Jack B. Weinstein & Margaret A. Berger, 3 *Weinstein's Evidence,* ¶¶ 701-1ff. (1992); Jack B. Weinstein, Rule 702 of the Federal Rules of Evidence Is Sound; It Should Not Be Amended, 138 F.R.D. 631 (1992); Jack B. Weinstein, Improving Expert Testimony, PLI Litig. & Admin. Practice Course Handbook Series No. 341, 1987; *see also* United States v. Sessa, 806 F. Supp. 1063 (E.D.N.Y. 1993). Admissibility of expert opinions that are based on inadmissible hearsay raises special problems of reliability and fairness. See Paul C. Gianelli, Expert Testimony and the Confrontation Clause, 22 Capital U. L. Rev. 45 (1993).

A more sophisticated analysis by the court of the appropriate mode of inquiry for the purposes of the case is required. *See, e.g.,* United States v. Downing, 753 F.2d 1224 (3d Cir. 1985); *In re* "Agent Orange" Prod. Liab. Litig., 611 F. Supp. 1223 (E.D.N.Y. 1985); *see also* Margaret A. Berger, Procedural and Evidentiary Mechanisms for Dealing with Experts in Toxic Tort Litigation: A Critique and Proposal, Consultant's Report for the Carnegie Commission on Science, Technology and Government (Oct. 1991); Brief of Carnegie Commission by Margaret A. Berger et al. as Amicus Curiae in Support of Neither Party in Daubert v. Merrell Dow Pharmaceuticals, Inc., 113 S. Ct. 2786 (1993) (testing the process of scientific inquiry); *see also* Lawrence B. Novey & Lawrence T. Gresser, Science in the Courtroom, Institute for Health Policy Analysis, Georgetown University Medical and Law Centers (1988); J. D. Hybart, Science, Technology and Decisionmaking, Sloan School of Management, MIT (1981); David M. O'Brien, *Courts and Science: Policy Disputes* (1987); Papers prepared for Task Force in Science and Technology in Judicial and Regulatory Decision Making, Carnegie Commission on Science, Technology, and Government (Oct. 15, 1992).

16. *See, e.g.,* Roger J. Porter & Thomas E. Malone, *Biomedical Research: Collaboration and Conflict of Interest* 166 (1992). I am grateful for the assistance on this subject of Professor Alan Wolf of Cooper Union, a student at Cardozo Law School, and a student intern of mine in 1993. In addition to being an expert on chaos theory, he has served as a peer reviewer on many occasions. His paper on file analyzes the limitations of peer review in great detail. *See* Alan Wolf, The Deficiencies of Peer Review (Mar. 1993) (unpublished, on file).

17. *See, e.g., In re* Paoli R.R. Yard PCB Litig., 916 F.2d 829, 857 (3d Cir. 1990), *cert. denied sub nom.* General Electric Co. v. Knight, 499 U.S. 961 (1991) (lack of exposure to peer review is inadequate ground for excluding testimony); Deluca v. Merrell Dow Pharmaceuticals, Inc., 911 F.2d 941, 954 (3d Cir. 1990) (same), *on remand,* 791 F. Supp. 1042 (D.N.J. 1992), *aff'd,* 6 F.3d 178 (3d Cir. 1993), *cert. denied,* 114 S. Ct. 691 (1994). The use of the *Frye* rule and such rules as those requiring certain risks and confidence intervals have been uti-

lized by the courts to give a mechanical air of impartiality to rulings, allowing cases to go to the jury or not when scientific testimony was the basis of the claim. This approach is not an effective substitute for a detailed analysis of the evidence and reasonable inferences to be drawn from it. *See, e.g.,* Jones v. Lederle Lab., 785 F. Supp. 1123 (E.D.N.Y.), *aff'd,* 982 F.2d 63 (2d Cir. 1992); *In re* "Agent Orange" Prod. Liab. Litig., 611 F. Supp. 1290 (E.D.N.Y. 1985), *aff'd,* 818 F.2d 210 (2d Cir. 1987), *cert. denied,* 484 U.S. 1004 (1988).

18. *See* Alan Wolf, The Deficiencies of Peer Review (Mar. 1993) (unpublished, on file).

19. An important first step was taken in November 1992 with the publication of the inaugural issue of Scientific Evidence Review, a publication of the Standing Committee on Scientific Evidence of the ABA's Section on Science and Technology.

20. *See, e.g.,* Carnegie Commission on Science, Technology and Government, *Science and Technology in Judicial Decisionmaking: Creating Opportunities and Meeting Challenges* (Mar. 1993).

21. Richard P. Nielsen, Changing Unethical Organizational Behavior, *The Academy of Management, Executive,* vol. 3, 123 (1989) (emphasizing the desirability of changing the organization rather than acting against those performing unethical acts). *See also* United States v. Williams, 583 F.2d 1194, 1198 (2d Cir. 1978) (noting professional organizations' standard governing spectrographic analysis).

22. *See* Fed. R. Evid. 706; *cf.* Edward V. DiLello, Fighting Fire with Firefighters: A Proposal for Expert Judges at the Trial Level, 93 Colum. L. Rev. 473 (1993).

23. Carnegie Commission on Science, Technology and Government, Science and Technology in Judicial Decisionmaking: Creating Opportunities and Meeting Challenges 49 (Mar. 1993).

24. *See* Letter to Helene Kaplan, Carnegie Commission on Science, Technology, and Government from Jack B. Weinstein, Feb. 16, 1993. For a suggested model employment agreement for a neutral expert factfinder see Joseph T. McLaughlin, Alternative Dispute Resolution, ALI-ABA Course of Study, Trial Evidence, Civil Practice, and Effective Litigation Techniques in the Federal Courts 442–48, Feb. 25–27, 1993; *cf.* Melissa A. Davey, Expert Witness Not Liable for Unfavorable Testimony, Legal Intelligencer, Nov. 5, 1993, at 4; Panitz v. Behrend, 632 A.2d 562 (Pa. Super 1993) (expert admitted on cross-examination that her testimony in prior trial could no longer be sustained).

25. *But see* Kenneth P. Coffey v. Healthtrust Inc., 955 F.2d 1388 (10th Cir. 1992), *appeal after remand,* 1 F.3d 1101 (10th Cir. 1993). The Court of Appeals held that an attorney's failure to disclose that other experts, who had made a study of the relevant geographic market in which plaintiff's expert relied, disagreed with plaintiff's expert's con-

clusion was not sanctionable under Rule 11 of the Federal Rules of Civil Procedure. Even if Rule 11 is not expanded to include experts who submit misleading reports, the lawyer and the expert who cooperates in misleading the trier ought, in my opinion, to be chastised for unethical conduct.

26. For a full discussion of the use of such experts see Joe S. Cecil & Thomas E. Willging, Federal Judicial Center, Court Appointed Experts: Defining the Role of Experts Appointed under Federal Rule of Evidence 706 (1993).

27. Consultation with ethics expert seeking help in setting up method of communication with clients has been increasingly utilized by counsel.

28. Plaintiffs' lawyers in mass tort cases, subject as they are to the many difficult ethical problems I have discussed and the prospect of potential disciplinary or malpractice actions, increasingly have sought protection in the form of formal ethical opinions from professional ethicists. *See, e.g.,* redacted letter from professional ethicists to plaintiffs' attorney in toxic site litigation, Apr. 28, 1988. One difficulty lies in the price that may be charged for this "protection." *See, e.g.,* Carole Bass, Hazard Navigates the Course on Ethics Business, Legal Times, May 14, 1990, at 12 (describing one professor's "one-man ethics business providing expert testimony, advocacy, and consultation" yielding $250,000 annually in fees); *see also* Emily Couric, The Tangled Web, A.B.A. J., Apr. 1993, at 64 (describing dramatic increase in malpractice suits based upon alleged violations of ethical rules).

Plaintiffs' attorneys who were criticized by some members of the bar for unethical conduct in a federal class action because they worked out a settlement for future claimants while also settling claims of present claimants took two different steps to protect themselves. One group retained a law professor "to advise them on ethical issues." Asbestos Litig. Rptr. (Andrews), July 2, 1993, at 27,829. The other group obtained a ruling from a state judge declaring "that the settlement agreements did not violate the West Virginia rules." *Id.* at 27,830. A national rule of ethics in national cases is essential. *But cf.* Preliminary Fairness Hearings in *Carlough* Slated for Aug. 23, 8 Mealey's Litig. Rpts., Asbestos 4, 6 (Aug. 20, 1993) (Center for Claims Resolution, in connection with its papers supporting approval of asbestos class action settlement, submitted affidavits by two academic experts on ethics supporting the settlement from an ethical standpoint); Ethics, Mealey's Litig. Rpts., Asbestos 5, 6 (Aug. 20, 1993) (some parties "highly critical" of ethical opinions on application of Rule 5.6 to a global settlement involving future clients).

29. This procedure does not avoid the need for a law firm accused of unethical practices, or seeking to avoid a charge of unethical practices,

to obtain an ethical opinion. At times the effort required warrants substantial compensation. For example, the opinion of one noted authority to a major law firm on charges by the office of Thrift Supervision was obviously required. A twenty-two-page summary of the opinion is in the author's files. Unfortunately, settlement of cases by the Office of Thrift Supervision against many law firms as a result of pressure from their clients, their banks, and their insurers has meant that no definitive court ruling on these issues has been available to the bar. This is one of the unfortunate aspects of alternate dispute resolutions by settlement and otherwise. *Cf.* John D. Feerick, Congress Must Curb OTS Power, Nat. L.J., Dec. 20, 1993, at 13 (criticizing Office of Thrift Supervisor's use of freeze order on law firm's assets forcing capitulation on dispute issue of obligations to clients and regulatory authorities).

CHAPTER 8

1. Courts are severely limited by lack of legislative support and the need to provide remedies given inappropriate substantive, procedural and choice of law rules. *See* Steven L. Schultz, Comment, *In re* Joint Eastern and Southern District Asbestos Litigation: Bankrupt and Backlogged—A Proposal for the Use of Federal Common Law in Mass Tort Class Actions, 58 Brook. L. Rev. 553 (1992).

2. This conclusion has been reached by one commentator in the Agent Orange context:

> I find the specter of Agent Orange in the courts so appalling—and, in like fashion, on more impressionistic evidence, the long journey of asbestos and Dalkon Shield claimants from the tort system into bankruptcy court sufficiently discouraging—that continuing resort to the tort system in these mass toxics cases seems indefensible.
>
> When process costs become the dominant characteristic of a system designed to allocate liability on corrective justice principles, tort law has lost its bearings. When closer inquiry suggests that the system is no longer even pursuing corrective justice ends, tort law has lost its *raison d'être* as well.

Robert L. Rubin, Tort System on Trial: The Burden of Mass Toxics Litigation 98 Yale L.J. 813, 829 (1989).

3. The current push for dramatic reform of our health care system reflects powerful pressures in our society for solutions to mass problems that reject case-by-case, "free market" approaches in favor of mechanisms that account for the needs of the entire national community. *See, e.g.*, Insurers, in Shift, Ask U.S. to Require Coverage for All, N.Y. Times, Dec. 3, 1992, at A1 (insurance industry calls for federal law to require

coverage for all Americans and contain costs); Robert H. Blank, Regulatory Rationing: A Solution to Health Care Resource Allocation, 140 U. Pa. L. Rev. 1573 (1992) (noting that while government involvement with health care rationing may be new, rationing of various sorts has long existed); Eric Lamond Robinson, The Oregon Basic Health Services Act: A Model for State Reform?, 45 Vand. L. Rev. 977 (1992) (Oregon Basic Health Services Act would provide 97 percent of state residents with basic health care rationed according to a prioritized list of services); *see also* Kenneth S. Abraham & Lance Liebman, Private Insurance, Social Insurance, and Tort Reform: Toward a New Vision of Compensation for Illness and Injury, 93 Colum. L. Rev. 75, 77 (1993) (arguing that "a clearer sense of the principles animating the institutional arrangements for compensation in the United States is an essential prerequisite to creating a more coherent system of protection and to assigning proper roles to tort law, private insurance and social insurance.").

New York Governor Mario Cuomo proposed an innovative solution to compensate parents of impaired children quickly and in greater numbers than the current tort system currently provides. His proposed Impaired Newborn Compensation Trust Fund would finance medical care, education, vocational training, and housing costs on a no-fault basis. Not surprisingly, trial lawyers have assaulted the bill as flawed and unfair. *See* Gary Spencer, Cuomo Outlines Proposed System for Compensating Injured Infants, N.Y. L.J., Apr. 21, 1993, at 1. In an unrelated move, Governor Cuomo has also proposed a product liability reform statute in an effort to stem the flight of manufacturers from the state. The measure, which limits manufacturers' liability under certain circumstances, is opposed by the plaintiffs' bar. The defense bar, in contrast, claims the bill does not go far enough. *See* Daniel Wise, Bar Splits into Predictable Camps on Cuomo Products Liability Bill, N.Y. L.J., Apr. 26, 1993, at 1.

4. The current debate over the supposed ills of our tort system as a whole and the alleged "litigation explosion" generally misses the mark when it comes to mass torts. *See generally* Walter K. Olson, *The Litigation Explosion: What Happened When America Unleashed the Lawsuit* (1991); *see also* Marcia Chambers, Quayle's Crusade, Nat'l L.J., Feb. 24, 1992, at 17 (discussing the former Vice-President's attacks on the tort system). The problems of which I speak stem from the unique character of mass tort cases, not simply their numbers. Perhaps the least interesting aspect of mass tort cases are the total numbers of claims they add to the legal system.

In any event, there is considerable doubt as to the empirical basis for the claim that our system suffers from a debilitating "litigation explosion." *See, e.g.,* Marc Galanter, Working Paper, The Debased Debate on

Civil Justice (Disputes Processing Research Program, Feb. 1992); Marc Galanter, Pick a Number, Any Number, Am. Law., Apr. 1992, at 82; Randall Samborn, In Courts: Caseloads Still Rise, Nat'l L.J., July 5, 1993, at 10 (1991 annual report by National Center for State Courts indicates that while filings have increased, much of rise is due to criminal cases and concludes "[t]he evidence points to tort litigation growing more slowly than civil cases generally"); Roxanne Barton Conlin, Litigation Explosion Disputed, Nat'l L.J., July 29, 1991, at 26; Andrew Blum, Debate Still Rages on Torts, Nat'l L.J., Nov. 16, 1992, at 1; *The Cost of Litigation: A New Perspective* (Nat'l Assoc. of Manufacturers, Sept. 1992); Geoffrey C. Hazard, Bush Report Not All That Controversial, Nat'l L.J., Dec. 16, 1991, at 13; Michael J. Saks, Do We Really Know Anything about the Tort Litigation System—And Why Not?, 140 U. Pa. L. Rev. 1147, 1183 (1992) (stating that a "great many potential plaintiffs are never heard from by their injurers or their insurers" and describing a California malpractice study that found that only 10 percent of negligently injured patients sought compensation); Milo Geyelin, Star of Legal Reform Kindles Controversy but Collects Critics, Wall St. J., Oct. 16, 1992, at C1 (reporting doubt about empirical basis for Peter Huber's calculations of cost of litigation to society).

5. Tort reform legislation to date has been characterized as follows:

Although more than forty states adopted tort reform legislation of some kind during the last decade, on the whole this legislation has merely tinkered with tort law doctrine and cannot be seen as fundamental change. The most common reforms include placing ceilings on the amount of pain and suffering damages recoverable, modifying the collateral source rule, and restricting the scope of joint and several liability.

Kenneth S. Abraham & Lance Liebman, Private Insurance, Social Insurance, and Tort Reform: Toward a New Vision of Compensation for Illness and Injury, 93 Colum. L. Rev. 75, 76 n.2 (1993) (citing Joseph Sanders & Craig Joyce, "Off to the Races": The 1980s Tort Crisis and the Law Reform Process, 27 Hous. L. Rev. 207, 217–23 (1990) (collecting measures enacted)).

One commentator's observations in the context of Agent Orange are apposite here:

If our horizons stretch no further than the no-fault model, grounded in the dominant influence of the workers' compensation regime, a causal nexus stands as a prerequisite to recovery, and the VA's responsibility to the *Agent Orange* claimants remains indeterminate at best. Only when disability becomes a sufficient condition for reparation—in other words, when a social insurance model is adopted—are the causal issues put to rest.

Robert L. Rabin, Tort System on Trial: The Burden of Mass Toxics Litigation, 98 Yale L.J. 813, 826 (1989).

6. *See, e.g.,* David A. Stoll, *Mass Tort Reform Act: A Proposal* (1993) (unpublished paper calling for a commission to control substantive as well as procedural law).

7. Implementation of such schemes is a highly difficult and complex matter beyond the scope of this paper. Many of the worthy attempts that have been made to date are not without serious problems and drawbacks. *See, e.g.,* Accident Compensation Act No. 43 (N.Z. Stat. 1972) (amended 1990) (comprehensive no-fault accident compensation scheme in New Zealand under rubric of administrative commission); N.Y. Workers' Compensation Law (McKinney's 1992). In Canada there is a strong network of social services and compensation schemes, and courts have capped general damages and rarely award punitive damages. Bruce A. Thomas, The Canadian Experience with Alternative Dispute Resolution in Products Liability Cases, 17 Can.-U.S. L.J. 363 (1991); *but see* The Bill Comes Due: Canada's Health Care Costs, N.Y. Times, Mar. 7, 1993, at A1 (cost of providing universal comprehensive health care in Canada is rising as rapidly as the cost of health care in the United States; Canada is moving toward fees and reduced services); *see also* Colloquy: An Administrative Alternative to Tort Litigation to Resolve Asbestos Cases, 13 Cardozo L. Rev. 1817 (1992) (symposium issue) (debate about Professor Lester Brickman's proposed administrative scheme to remove asbestos cases from the courts, including this author's general endorsement of such a project); New Bankruptcy Chapter among Options Suggested to Resolve Asbestos Crisis, 4 Bankr. L. Rptr. 254 (BNA) (1992) (reporting consideration of proposed "Chapter 14" of Bankruptcy Code by House Judiciary Subcommittee on Intellectual Property and Judicial Administration to provide for treatment of asbestos litigation under the bankruptcy laws); Robert L. Rabin, Tort System on Trial: The Burden of Mass Toxics Litigation, 98 Yale L.J. 813, 825 (1989) ("the search for an alternative outside the tort system turns out to be exceedingly complex").

Careful additional study is required before acting. *See* Deborah R. Hensler, Assessing Claims Resolution Facilities: What We Need to Know, 53 Law & Contemp. Probs. 175 (1990); Michael J. Saks, Do We Really Know Anything about the Behavior of the Tort Litigation System—And Why Not?, 140 U. Pa. L. Rev. 1147, 1189 (1992) (administrative systems that reduce barriers to recovery will result in many more claims, including likely quintupling of cases in certain areas of litigation).

8. *See, e.g.*, Peter Huber, Safety and the Second Best: The Hazards of Public Risk Management in the Courts, 85 Colum. L. Rev. 277, 335 (1985); *see also* Wolfgang Friedman, *Law in a Changing Society*, 168 (2d ed. 1972) (shift from tort to insurance).

9. I do not suggest that we would be better off with no tort system. While dramatic reform may be necessary, the principles underlying our tort system are vital to the health of our democracy for the interstitial areas where administrative controls are not yet in place. *See* David J. Rothman & Sheila M. Rothman, A Death in Zimbabwe, N.Y. Rev. of Books, Oct. 22, 1992, at 21 (describing efforts of Zimbabwean couple to hold medical profession accountable for death of their son caused by malpractice and concluding, "the Zimbabwean experience shows that when free-market economics provides the only controls on medicine, the quality of health care deteriorates.").

10. *See, e.g.*, Walter Gellhorn, *Ombudsmen and Others: Citizens' Protectors in Nine Countries* (1966) (seminal book on ombudspersons); Ford Foundation, *Conflict Resolution* 52 (1978) (describing Swedish consumer system); Wolfgang Friedman, *Law in a Changing Society* 438–41 (2d ed. 1972).

11. *See* Black Lung Benefits Act of 1972, *codified at* 30 U.S.C. § 901-945 (1986) (providing for death and disability benefits to coal miners totally disabled by pneumoconiosis and their eligible survivors). "The Department of Labor . . . awards benefits after adjudication by a deputy commissioner, and after review (if requested) by an administrative law judge . . ., the Benefits Review Board, and a Federal Court of Appeals." United States Dep't of Labor v. Triplett, 494 U.S. 715 (1990); *see also* Allen R. Prunty & Mark E. Solomons, The Federal Black Lung Program: Its Evolution and Current Issues, 91 W. Va. L. Rev. 665, 667 (1989) (seven years after its adoption in 1969, the Black Lung Benefits Act "was the only single industry, single disease compensation law ever attempted"; a task force evaluating the program "looked to the federal black lung program as the laboratory that would generate a good model for future handling of occupational disease claims."); *but see* Edward A. Slavin, Jr., There's No Defense for Insensitive Acts of Black-Lung Unit, Legal Times, Feb. 1, 1993, at 32 (describing high denial rate for benefits, frequent lack of counsel for claimants, "twisted burden of proof" under 1981 amendments, and complex regulations that "dying miners or their widows in Appalachia can be guaranteed not to understand"); Black Lung Bill Advances as NCA Cites Cost Study, Coal Week, Sept. 28, 1992, at 8 (describing HR 1637, which would make it easier for miners to prove their eligibility for benefits and address several other problems with the program).

12. *See* National Vaccine Injury Compensation Program, 42 U.S.C. §§ 300aa-10 to 300aa-34 (1991). Although the program allows fami-

lies to pursue a lawsuit, it establishes obstacles to discourage litigation and incentives to participate in the plan. The federal tort compensation plan does not require that claimants prove causation, thus avoiding long trials with many witnesses. Generous compensation, including up to $250,000 for pain and suffering, is available as a result of an excise tax on vaccines. Under the Act a claimant will receive compensation if he or she proves by a preponderance of the evidence:

> that the injured party (1) received a vaccine listed in the Vaccine Injury Table, Section 300aa-14 . . . , (2) suffered a listed injury within the specified time period following administration of the vaccine, (3) suffered the residual effects of the injury for at least six months, and (4) incurred unreimbursable expenses of at least $1,000, or died from receiving the vaccine and has not collected compensation for the injury or death from a civil suit.

J. Stratton Shartel, DPT Victim's Presence at Hearing Assists Vaccine Injury Case, Inside Litig., May 1990, at 1, 3 (describing administrative claims processing procedures). While a number of possible claimants have objected to the lack of publicity and the possibility of being barred by a short statute of limitations, the statute appears to have accomplished its purpose of overcoming excessive deterrence of research, development, and production in the vaccine field. *See* A Major Revival in Research on Vaccines, N.Y. Times, Aug. 22, 1990, at D7; Compensation Cutoff, Newsday, Sept. 10, 1990, at 2.

13. *See, e.g.*, Jerry L. Mashaw, *Bureaucratic Justice: Managing Social Security Disability Claims* (1983); Jack B. Weinstein, Equality and the Law: Social Security Disability Cases in the Federal Courts, 35 Syracuse L. Rev. 897 (1984).

14. Only federal consideration of the problems will ensure the necessary dialogue within the national community to answer the critical questions: "For how much justice is the American taxpayer prepared to pay? What, if anything, is the American public, in this age of population growth, technological leaps, and increased social expectations, willing to yield of its traditional system?" Bertram Harnett, *Law, Lawyers and Laymen* 307 (1984).

15. The Supremacy Clause is a powerful tool that could be utilized to supplant patchwork state tort law schemes with national ones. In the absence of satisfactory comprehensive federal schemes, however, explicit statutory preemption and implicit preemption doctrine have tended to insulate manufacturers from liability where more stringent safety standards would be appropriate. If federal safety laws preempt state tort and other laws, they should provide federal protections that are stronger and more efficient. *See, e.g.*, King v. Collagen Corp., 983 F.2d 1130 (1st Cir. 1993) (tort claim for harm caused by Zyderm, a cosmetic

device consisting of injecting cow tissue under the skin, preempted by the Medical Device Amendments of 1976, which provide for FDA regulation and approval); Slater v. Optical Radiation Corp., 961 F.2d 1330 (7th Cir. 1992) (tort claim against manufacturer for harm caused by implantation and removal of intraocular lens preempted by FDA "Investigational Device Exemption Regulations"), *cert. denied,* 113 S. Ct. 327 (1992); *but see* Burke v. Dow Chem. Co., 797 F. Supp. 1128 (E.D.N.Y. 1992) (tort claim against manufacturer of household insecticide was not entirely preempted by the Federal Insecticide, Fungicide and Rodenticide Act where savings clause indicated Congress's intent to leave state with powers to regulate pesticides); *see also* Amelia Jean Uelmen, Note, Trashing State Criminal Sanctions?, 30 Am. Crim. L. Rev. 373 (1993) (arguing that inadequate OSHA law should not be construed to preempt state criminal prosecutions of those responsible for unsafe workplaces).

Care would have to be taken to ensure that any uniform federal standards were adequate. *Cf.* Day v. NLO, Inc., 814 F. Supp. 646 (S.D. Ohio 1993) (in litigation involving Fernald nuclear production plant in Ohio, plaintiffs were permitted to seek establishment of medical monitoring program despite recent congressional enactment requiring Department of Energy to establish such programs since defendants failed to show that statute provided type of plan plaintiffs sought).

16. *See* 42 U.S.C. § 9631, *repealed,* Pub. L. 99-499, Title V, § 517(c)(1), Oct. 17, 1986, 100 Stat. 1774.

17. The problem of sometimes counterproductive deterrence in the tort system is captured in the following observation about development of contraceptives:

One factor that makes extensive research needed for development of such a [contraceptive or abortion] pill uneconomic in the United States is a widespread public misunderstanding of the effects of the prolonged use of any drug on a large population. Genetic diversity insures that there will always be some people in whom even the safest drug produces adverse effects. If the percentage of such people is substantial, then the adverse effects show up in clinical trials carried out on several hundred people before the drug is released on the market; but if the adverse effects manifest themselves in, say, one person out of 10,000, then the probability of their showing up in clinical trials is negligible. When the drug is later used by millions, and affected persons sue the manufacturers for negligence, then litigation and damages may cost that firm many millions of dollars. These costs and the accompanying adverse publicity are some of the factors that have discouraged further development of contraceptives.

M. F. Peretz, The Fifth Freedom, N.Y. Rev. of Books, Oct. 8, 1992, at

3. *See also* Suits Involving Defunct Bendectin Chill Development of Pregnancy Medications, Wall St. J., June 22, 1993, at B1 (describing how lawsuits stemming from unscientifically proved claims have "scared" drug companies away from research into drugs for women's health problems, particularly those relating to pregnancy).

18. For an excellent recent study comparing the myths and realities concerning the effect of the tort system on our economy and society, *see* Michael J. Saks, Do We Really Know Anything about the Tort Litigation System—And Why Not?, 140 U. Pa. L. Rev. 1147 (1992).

19. The commendable effort to develop a national health care system will require treatment of numerous problems of interaction with the tort system and other compensatory schemes. *See, e.g.,* Institute for Civil Justice, Conference Proceedings, *Health Care Delivery and Tort: Systems on a Collision Course?* (Rand Institute, 1991); Health-Care Plan May Cover Injuries on Job and Roads, N.Y. Times, May 8, 1993, at A1.

20. Tort alternatives may prove to work symbiotically with the tort system. *See* Kenneth S. Abraham & Lance Liebman, Private Insurance, Social Insurance, and Tort Reform: Toward a New Vision of Compensation for Illness and Injury, 93 Colum. L. Rev. 75, 99 (1993) ("[I]t is possible that with the advent of universal health insurance, reducing the scope of tort liability would find more political favor than at present, and that the savings from this reform could be used to help finance the health insurance system.").

21. 28 U.S.C. § 1407.

22. *See, e.g.,* Andrew Blum, Schwartz on Torts, Nat'l L.J., July 12, 1993, at 1 (describing battle over products liability bill in Congress and influence of lobbyists); Vicki Kemper, Lawyers on Trial, Common Cause, Fall 1993, at 14.

23. *See* Robert L. Rabin, Tort System on Trial: The Burden of Mass Toxics Litigation, 98 Yale L.J. 813, 827–28 (1989) ("Abandoning the tort system involves a trade-off of individualized treatment according to corrective justice norms—with particular emphasis on the assessment of intangible loss—for routinized, universal coverage under categorical rules of eligibility.").

CHAPTER 9

1. This chapter constitutes an expansion of remarks and a paper delivered by Jack B. Weinstein at the First International Conference on Equity, The Hebrew University School of Law, Mount Scopus, Jerusalem, Israel, June 1990. It was then expanded and published as Jack B. Weinstein & Eileen B. Hershenov, The Effect of Equity on Mass Tort Law, U. Ill. L. Rev. (1991). I acknowledge my debt to Theresa Gorski, J.D., Columbia Law School 1990, for her valuable

research on the equitable antecedents of class actions and consolidations, only a portion of which has been used in this chapter, and to my clerk, colleague, and coauthor, Eileen B. Hershenov of the New York Bar.

2. Stephen Subrin, David Dudley Field and the Field Code: A Historical Analysis of an Earlier Procedural Vision, 6 Law & Hist. Rev. 311, 345 (1988).

3. Attempts to pass federal legislation to reform the civil justice system, to provide for centralized treatment of multidistrict mass tort litigation, or to provide compensation for particular classes of toxic tort victims have thus far been unsuccessful. *See, e.g.,* Occupational Disease Compensation Act of 1985, H.R. 3090, 99th Cong., 1st Sess. (1985) (seeking to establish workers' compensation–type program for asbestos and other toxin-related injuries); Asbestos Workers' Recovery Act, H.R. 1626 and S. 1265, 99th Cong., 1st Sess. (1985). A bill providing federal district courts with original jurisdiction in mass tort cases where at least twenty-five persons sustained injuries resulting in damages exceeding $50,000 per person, Multiparty, Multiforum Jurisdiction Act of 1990, H.R. 3406, 101st Cong., 2d Sess., 136 Cong. Rec. H3116–3117 (1990) was passed by the House of Representatives, *id.* at H3119, but not adopted by the Senate. Congress did pass Senator Biden's Judicial Improvements Act of 1990, Pub. L. No. 101-650, 104 Stat. 5089 (1990), which attempts to address problems of case management in complex and other litigation. The Judicial Conference of the United States has drafted a fourteen-point plan for handling the problem of cost and delay in civil litigation. *See* Judicial Conference Approves Plan to Improve Civil Case Management, 22 Third Branch 1, 1-3 (May 1990) [hereinafter Third Branch]. In addition, the Federal Courts Study Committee chartered by Congress and consisting of members appointed by the Chief Justice recently issued a report in which it recommended that Congress amend the multidistrict litigation legislation to enable consolidation for trial, as well as for pretrial proceedings and to make other changes that would enable related state and federal cases to be consolidated in the federal courts. Report of the Federal Courts Study Committee 44 (1990). In September 1990 Chief Justice Rehnquist appointed an ad hoc committee composed of six federal district and appellate judges to recommend methods of addressing the asbestos mass tort backlog in the courts. *See* Third Branch, *supra,* at 1. Legal academics and judges also have advocated federal legislation. *See, e.g.,* Am. Law Inst., Complex Litigation Project, various drafts (1987–1990); Linda S. Mullenix, Class Resolution of the Mass Tort Case: A Proposed Federal Procedure Act, 64 Tex. L. Rev. 1039 (1986); Jack B. Weinstein, Procedural and Substantive Problems in Complex Litigation Aris-

ing from Disasters, 5 Touro L. Rev. 1 (1988) [hereinafter Disasters]; Jack B. Weinstein, Preliminary Reflections on the Law's Reaction to Disasters, 11 Colum. J. Envt'l. L. 1 (1986) [hereinafter Preliminary Reflections]; Spencer Williams, Mass Tort Class Actions: Going, Going, Gone, 98 F.R.D. 323 (1983). *But see* Robert A. Sedler & Aaron D. Twerski, The Case against All Encompassing Federal Mass Tort Legislation: Sacrifice without Gain, 73 Marq. L. Rev. 76 (1989) (opposing consolidation of mass tort litigation in single federal court on federalism and choice of law grounds). For a general discussion of the government's refusal to cooperate in mass tort litigation, *see* Kenneth R. Feinberg, In the Shadow of Fernald: Who Should Pay the Victims?, Brookings Rev., Summer 1990, at 41.

See generally 1 & 2 Am. Law Inst., Final Report, Compensation and Liability for Product and Process Injuries (Prelim. Draft No. 3, Aug. 15, 1990) [hereinafter Compensation and Liability]; 1 & 2 Report to the Congress from the Presidential Commission on Catastrophic Nuclear Accidents (Aug. 1990) [hereinafter Nuclear Accident Report]. *See* 2 Nuclear Accident Report, at 150–63 for testimony of Jack B. Weinstein.

4. *See* Black Lung Benefits Act of 1972, 30 U.S.C. §§ 901–945 (1989) (providing federal funds to those totally disabled by pneumoconiosis and their eligible survivors).

5. *See* Price-Anderson Act, 42 U.S.C. § 2210 (1988) (limiting liability to atomic power plant licensees at $7 billion and requiring President to develop compensation plan in event of accident); *id.* § 2210(l) (establishing President's Commission on Catastrophic Nuclear Accidents to study and recommend "means of fully compensating victims of a catastrophic nuclear accident" when aggregate claims exceed the $7 billion liability limitation of the Act).

6. *See* National Vaccine Injury Compensation Program, 42 U.S.C. § 300aa-10 to 300aa-34 (1988). Although the program allows families to pursue a lawsuit, it establishes obstacles to discourage litigation and incentives to participate in the plan. The federal tort compensation plan does not require that claimants prove causation, thus avoiding long trials with many witnesses. Generous compensation, including up to $250,000 for pain and suffering, is available as a result of an excise tax on vaccines. Under the Act a claimant will receive compensation if he or she proves by a preponderance of the evidence:

> that the injured party (1) received a vaccine listed in the Vaccine Injury Table, Section 300aa-14 . . . , (2) suffered a listed injury within the specified time period following the administration of the vaccine, (3) suffered the residual effects of the injury for at least six

months, and (4) incurred unreimbursable expenses of at least $1,000, or died from receiving the vaccine and has not collected compensation for the injury or death from a civil suit.

J. Stratton Shartel, DPT Victim's Presence At Hearing Assists Vaccine Injury Case, Inside Litig., May 1990, at 1, 3 (describing administrative claims processing procedures). While a number of possible claimants have objected to the lack of publicity and the possibility of being barred by a short statute of limitations, the statute appears to have accomplished its purpose of overcoming excessive deterrence of research, development, and production in the vaccine field. *See* A Major Revival in Research in Vaccines, N.Y. Times, Aug. 22, 1990, at D7; Compensation Cutoff, Newsday, Sept. 10, 1990, at 2.

7. Office of Special Masters Annual Report (Nov. 15, 1988–Jan. 31, 1990).

8. During the 1980s, the majority of states have enacted tort reform measures in an essentially ad hoc manner. Most of these laws capped damages and in general made it more difficult for plaintiffs to recover. *Cf.* George L. Priest, The Current Insurance Crisis and Modern Tort Law, 96 Yale L.J. 1521, 1523–24 (1987) (calling state tort reform laws "the most extraordinary state law development having national import since the states' unanimous adoption of the Uniform Commercial Code.").

9. Am. Bar Ass'n, Comm'n on Mass Torts, Report to the House of Delegates (1989) [hereinafter Comm'n on Mass Torts].

10. *See* Compensation and Liability, *supra* note 3, at 1.

11. *See, e.g.,* C. Bacon & F. Morse, *The Reasonableness of the Law: The Adaptability of Legal Sanctions to the Needs of Society* 187 (1924); H. Hanbury & R. Maudsley, *Modern Equity* 13 (10th ed. 1976) (in Britain, the nineteenth century was a period of great development of equitable jurisdiction because of enormous industrial, international, and imperial expansion); Stephen C. Yeazell, Collective Litigation as Collective Action, 1989 U. Ill. L. Rev. 43, 48-49.

12. *See* M. Halliwell, Equity as Injustice 1 (paper delivered at International Conference on Equity, Jerusalem, Israel, June 24–29, 1990) (forthcoming) ("Equity's lifeblood stems from its remedial capacity.").

13. *See generally* Owen M. Fiss, The Social and Political Foundations of Adjudication, 6 Law & Hum. Behav. 121 (1982) (describing structural reform litigation).

14. *See generally* Abram Chayes, The Role of the Judge in Public Law Litigation, 89 Harv. L. Rev. 1281 (1976) (modern civil procedure looks to equity for remedies in public law cases). *But cf.* Marc S. Galanter, Why the "Haves" Come Out Ahead: Speculations on the Limits of Legal Change, 9 Law & Soc'y Rev. 95 (1974); Mark Peterson & Molly Selvin, Mass Justice: The Limited and Unlimited Power of

Courts 123 (May 1990) (conference paper prepared for Modern Civil Procedure: Issues in Controversy, Program in Civil Liability, Yale Law School, June 15–16, 1990); Paul Rheingold, Tort Class Actions, What They Can and Cannot Achieve, Trial, Feb. 1990, at 59.

15. *See generally* Theodore Eisenberg & Stephen C. Yeazell, The Ordinary and Extraordinary in Institutional Litigation, 93 Harv. L. Rev. 465 (1980).

16. *See, e.g.,* Sindell v. Abbott Laboratories, 26 Cal. 3d 588, 611, 607 P.2d 924, 936, 163 Cal. Rptr. 132, 144 ("[T]he cost of an injury and the loss of time or health may be an overwhelming misfortune to the person injured and a needless one, for the risk of injury can be insured by the manufacturer and distributed among the public as a cost of doing business."), *cert. denied,* 449 U.S. 912 (1980); United States Dep't of Justice, Tort Policy Working Group, An Update on the Liability Crisis 54 (1987) [hereinafter Dep't of Justice]; James A. Henderson, Jr., Coping with the Time Dimension in Public Law, 69 Calif. L. Rev. 919, 931–39 (1981).

I do not discuss in this chapter the dissatisfactions of litigants with traditional modes of dispute resolution. For papers on this subject, *see* E. Allan Lind, R. MacCoun, P. Ebener, W. Felstiner, D. Hensler, J. Resnik, & T. Tyler, The Perception of Justice: Tort Litigants' Views of Trials, Court-Annexed Arbitration, and Judicial Settlement Conferences (1989) (Rand Corporation Institute for Civil Justice); Alan I. Widiss, R. Bovbjerg, D. Cavers, J. Little, R. Clark, G. Waterson, & J. Jones, *No Fault Automobile Insurance in Action* 20–21 (1977).

17. For a summary of aggregative and joinder devices, *see* Cutler v. The 65 Security Plan, 831 F. Supp. 1008, 1993 U.S. Dist. LEXIS 7024 (E.D.N.Y. 1993).

18. Fed. R. Civ. P., 308 U.S. 645 (1938).

19. Fed. R. Civ. P. 26–32.

20. Fed. R. Civ. P. 56.

21. Fed. R. Civ. P. 50.

22. *See* Terence Dungworth & Nicholas M. Pace, Statistical Overview of Civil Litigation in the Federal Courts 30 (1990) (Rand Corporation) (terminations after motions activity have become much more significant for contract, real property, and tort litigation; between 1971 and 1986 percentage rose from 21 percent to 30 percent for contracts and from 12 to 25 percent for torts); Marc S. Galanter, The Day after the Litigation Explosion, 46 Md. L. Rev. 3, 26 (1986).

23. *See, e.g.,* United States Government Accounting Office, Product Liability: Extent of "Litigation Explosion" in Federal Court Questioned 20–23 (1988) (asbestos cases accounted for half of growth in all federal tort cases between 1974 and 1986, with Bendectin and Dalkon Shield claims together comprising an additional 4 percent).

24. *See generally* Peter W. Huber, *Liability: The Legal Revolution and Its Consequences* (1988); A Product Dead-Ended by Liability Fears, N.Y. Times, May 19, 1990, at A50 (Monsanto decides not to produce "miracle fiber" as asbestos replacement allegedly because of fear of attracting lawsuits). *But see* A Major Revival in Research on Vaccines, N.Y. Times, Aug. 22, 1990, at D7 (suggesting that fears of liability are abating).

25. *See* Jack B. Weinstein, After Fifty Years of the Federal Rules of Civil Procedure: Are the Barriers to Justice Being Raised?, 137 U. Pa. L. Rev. 1901, 1906 (1989). Probably the vast majority of people with possible claims in such diverse fields as toxic torts and medical malpractice or civil rights violations never sue because of the difficulties, lack of knowledge, or a desire to make better use of their energies.

26. *See, e.g.,* Judith Resnik, The Domain of Courts, 137 U. Pa. L. Rev. 2219, 2227–29 (1989) (aggregation of cases indicates less willingness on part of federal courts to attend to small cases and individual problems); Roger H. Trangsrud, Mass Trials in Mass Tort Cases: A Dissent, 1989 U. Ill. L. Rev. 69, 87 ("Our civil justice system owes a twelve-year-old girl born with foreshortened limbs after her mother took a prescribed morning sickness drug the same due process it owes a thirty-two-year old man paralyzed when the brakes on his Chevrolet fail and his automobile slams into a tree.").

27. *Cf., e.g., In re* Colt Indus. Shareholder Litig. (Woodrow v. Colt Indus.), 155 A.D.2d 154, 553 N.Y.S.2d 138 (App. Div. 1st Dep't. 1990) (while there is no due process right to opt out of class action that seeks predominantly equitable relief, out-of-state class members with damage claims have a protected property interest).

28. *See* H. Hanbury & R. Maudsley, *Modern Equity* 4 (10th ed. 1976). Early American commentators, such as Joseph Story, also believed that equity's role was properly an auxiliary one, limited to correcting defects in the stricter common law. *See* Stephen N. Subrin, How Equity Conquered Common Law: The Federal Rules of Civil Procedure in Historical Perspective, 135 U. Pa. L. Rev. 909, 932 & n.123 (1987) (citing Gary McDowell, *Equity and the Constitution: The Supreme Court, Equitable Relief, and Public Policy* 76–79 (1982)).

A good example of this belief in the proper role of equity is offered by a Justice of the Indiana Supreme Court who observed one hundred years ago that

> equity follows the law, so far as the law goes in securing the rights of the parties, and no further; and, when the law stops short of securing this object, equity continues the remedy until complete justice is done. In other words, equity is the perfection of the law, and is always open to those who have just rights to enforce where the law is inadequate. Any other conclusion would show our system of jurispru-

dence not only a failure, but a delusion and a snare. Justice alone can be considered in a court of chancery, and technicalities never be tolerated except to obtain and not to destroy it. . . .

Isgrigg v. Schooley, 125 Ind. 94, 100–101, 25 N.E. 151, 153 (1890) (quoting Grand Lodge A.O.U.W. v. Child, 38 N.W. 1, 5 (Mich. 1888).

29. Randy E. Barnett, The Virtue of Redundancy in Legal Thought, Clev. St. L. Rev. (forthcoming).

30. John Locke, *Second Treatise on Civil Government: Two Treatises of Government* § 160 (P. Laslette ed., 1970).

31. *See infra* text accompanying notes 36–164.

32. *See infra* text accompanying notes 165–227.

33. *See infra* text accompanying notes 228–36.

34. *See infra* text accompanying notes 237–54.

35. *See infra* text accompanying note 255.

36. For a good example of this phenomenon as it affected the growth of group litigation in courts of equity, *see* Stephen C. Yeazell, *From Medieval Group Litigation to the Modern Class Action* (1987) (tracing changes undergone by group litigation in response to the erosion of feudal society, the industrial revolution, and finally modern-day entrepreneurial capitalism).

37. Peter H. Schuck, Introduction: The Context of the Controversy, in *Tort Law and the Public Interest* 3 (1990). Professor Schuck, without explicitly recognizing the analogy to equity jurisprudence, has the following to say about American tort law:

> For deep structural reasons . . . change has always been a driving force in tort law. The great landmarks of American tort law— *Rylands v. Fletcher, MacPherson v. Buick Motor Company,* Justice Traynor's concurring opinion in *Escola v. Coca-Cola Bottling Company, Ybarra v. Spangard, Sindell v. Abbott Laboratories*—represented important breaks with the past, breaks as sharp as the mythical continuities of common law adjudication would permit. In each of these cases, the pressure of social change contributed to the rupture. *Rylands* marked the passing of the dominant squirearchy in industrializing England, *MacPherson* foreshadowed the decline of localistic, face-to-face economic relationships and the rise of national markets and advertising, *Escola* and *Ybarra* explored the logic of enterprise liability in an era of mass production and the bureaucratized provision of health care, and *Sindell* mapped a strategy for preserving tort law deterrence and compensation in the face of the distinctive challenges posed by mass toxic exposures.

Id. at 2–3.

38. Stephen N. Subrin, How Equity Conquered Common Law: The Federal Rules of Civil Procedure in Historical Perspective, 135 U. Pa. L. Rev. 909, 921 (1987) (citing 1 W. Holdsworth, *A History of English Law* 425–28 (3d ed. 1944)); *see also* C. Christopher and B. Bowen, Progress in the Administration of Justice during Victorian Period, in 1 *Select Essays in Anglo-American Legal History* 524–27 (1907); Charles Rembar, *The Law of the Land: The Evolution of Our Legal System* 298–303 (1980); R. Walker & M. Walker, *The English Legal System* 31 (3d ed. 1972).

39. *Cf.* Stephen N. Subrin, How Equity Conquered Common Law, 135 U. Pa. L. Rev. 909, 925 (1987).

40. 3 William Blackstone, *Commentaries on the Laws of England* 436 (1768).

41. "The Commissioners who drafted the New York Field Code in the mid-nineteenth century . . . cited, drew upon, and applauded equity procedure." Stephen N. Subrin, How Equity Conquered Common Law, 135 U. Pa. L. Rev. 909, 912 (1987).

42. *See* Jack B. Weinstein, The Ghost of Process Past: The Fiftieth Anniversary of the Federal Rules of Civil Procedure and Erie, 54 Brook. L. Rev. 1, 4 (1988).

43. *See* Fed. R. Civ. P. 7–16.

44. *See* Fed. R. Civ. P. 26–37.

45. *See* Fed. R. Civ. P. 14, 18, 19, 20, 22, 24.

46. *See* Richard L. Marcus, Completing Equity's Conquest? Reflections on the Future of Trial under the Federal Rules of Civil Procedure, 50 U. Pitt. L. Rev. 725, 726 (1989) (contrasting common law trials with practice of courts of equity that had historically made decisions on basis of written materials obtained through discovery or submitted by the parties).

47. *See, e.g.,* Rules 67 & 68, Equity Rules of 1842, in J. Hopkins, *The New Federal Equity Rules* 56–57 (8th ed. 1933) (providing that the only method for taking testimony was by commission or deposition). In the next set of successor rules, however, the Supreme Court provided that "[i]n all trials in equity the testimony of witnesses shall be taken orally in open court." Rule 46, Equity Rules of 1913, in J. Hopkins, *supra,* at 249.

48. Rule 30(b)(4) of the Federal Rules of Civil Procedure authorizes the use of videotaped depositions. Fed. R. Civ. P. 30(b)(4).

49. *See generally* Edward Brunet, Experts in Summary Judgment Motions, in 16 Litig. 36 (1990) (liberalization of Rule 56's standards coincides with modern trend to encourage use of expert testimony); Terence Dungworth & Nicholas M. Pace, *Statistical Overview of Civil Litigation in the Federal Courts* 30 (1990). This trend represents a significant lessening of the courts' prior insistence that issues be put before

a jury. For instance, in the 1940s the Second Circuit's approach to summary judgment was to deny it if there was the "slightest doubt" on the merits. Richard L. Marcus, Completing Equity's Conquest?, 50 U. Pitt. L. Rev. 725, 735 & n.57 (1989) (citing cases). Today the Supreme Court has tried to promote summary judgment in several areas to solve perceived overlitigation problems. *See id.* at 737 & n.70, 739–42. Three Supreme Court cases from 1986 also exhibit the easing of formerly stringent standards for summary judgment. *See* Anderson v. Liberty Lobby, Inc., 477 U.S. 242 (1986); Celotex Corp. v. Catrett, 477 U.S. 317 (1986); Matsushita Elec. Indus. Co. v. Zenith Radio Corp., 475 U.S. 574 (1986). Moreover, some courts have found that summary judgment is particularly appropriate in complex cases. *See, e.g.,* Terry's Floor Fashions, Inc. v. Burlington Indus., 763 F.2d 604, 610 (4th Cir. 1985) (antitrust); Weit v. Continental Nat'l Bank & Trust Co., 641 F.2d 457, 464 (7th Cir. 1981) (antitrust).

50. *See* Federal Civil Cases Rarely Reach a Trial, Wall St. J., June 27, 1990, at B2 (reporting Rand study finding that 95 percent of private civil cases settle).

51. According to the Supreme Court the inquiry is twofold: "First, we compare the . . . action to 18th-century actions brought in the courts of England prior to the merger of the courts of law and equity. Second, we examine the remedy sought and determine whether it is legal or equitable in nature." Tull v. United States, 481 U.S. 412, 417–18 (1987) (citations omitted). A majority of the Court places a greater emphasis on the second prong of this test, the nature of the relief. *See also* Chauffeurs, Teamsters & Helpers Local 391 v. Terry, 494 U.S. 558 (1990) (worker bringing duty of fair representation case against union has right to jury trial because claim was analogous to old equitable action in which trust beneficiary brings suit against trustee for breach of fiduciary duty); Granfinanciera, S.A. v. Nordberg, 492 U.S. 33 (1989) (person who has not submitted claim against bankruptcy estate has Seventh Amendment right to jury trial when sued by trustee to recover allegedly fraudulent monetary transfer—despite fact that Congress allows such claims to be tried by a non–Article III bankruptcy judge). Former Justice Brennan has argued that the courts should dispense with the first part of this inquiry and concentrate solely on the nature of the relief sought. *Terry,* 494 U.S. at 571–79 (Brennan, J., concurring in part and in the judgment).

52. C. Bacon & F. Morse, *The Reasonableness of the Law* 204 (1924).

53. Fed. R. Civ. P. 23.

54. Fed. R. Civ. P. 42.

55. Fed. R. Civ. P. 18–20.

56. Fed. R. Civ. P. 22.

57. Fed. R. Civ. P. 24.

58. *See* Fed. R. Civ. P. 72–76.

59. Fed. R. Civ. P. 53.

60. 28 U.S.C. § 1335 (1988).

61. In particular, *see* Chapter 11 of the Bankruptcy Code, 11 U.S.C. §§ 1101–1174 (1988). By bringing all creditors—including numerous personal injury plaintiffs—together under the jurisdiction of the bankruptcy court, bankruptcy acts as a method of aggregation. *See, e.g., In re* A. H. Robins Co., 63 Bankr. 986 (E.D. Va. 1986) (Dalkon Shield IUD cases); *In re* Johns-Manville Corp., 36 Bankr. 743 (S.D.N.Y. 1984) (asbestos cases).

62. Multidistrict Litigation Act, 28 U.S.C. § 1407 (1988) (giving panel on multidistrict litigation power to order consolidation of tort claims scattered in different venues). There exists, however, no formal way to consolidate in a single court cases that are pending in two or more state courts.

63. 28 U.S.C. § 1404(a) (1988).

64. *See, e.g., Designation of District Judge for Service in Another District within His Circuit* (2d Cir. Jan. 23, 1990) (Oakes, C.J.) (copy on permanent file with University of Illinois Law Review) (designating Judge Weinstein as Southern District Judge); *In re* Joint Eastern and Southern Dists. Asbestos Litig. (Jan. 22, 1990) (Nickerson, J.) (copy on permanent file with University of Illinois Law Review) (assigning all New York Navy Yard cases to Judge Weinstein).

65. *See* Judith Resnik, From "Cases" to "Litigation" 37 n.78 (May 1990) (conference paper prepared for Modern Civil Procedure: Issues in Controversy, Program in Civil Liability, Yale Law School, June 15–16, 1990) (citing Stephen C. Yeazell, Collective Litigation as Collective Action, 1989 U. Ill. L. Rev. 43, 59–68, who differentiates between procedural and substantive collectivization).

66. Fed. R. Civ. P. 23.1. Members of the personal injury asbestos plaintiffs' bar established a still extant Asbestos Litigation Group in 1978. *See, e.g.,* Mealey's Litig. Repts., Asbestos (current documents and analysis of asbestos litigation including opinions, motion papers, verdict amounts, and gossip; also provides access to transcripts and depositions); Asbestos Litig. Reptr. (Andrews) (same). Combinations of asbestos manufacturers set up the Wellington Asbestos Claims Facility.

67. *See* Jack B. Weinstein, Disasters, *supra* note 3, at 8–10 (discussing criteria); *Preliminary Reflections, supra* note 3, at 1 (same); Jack B. Weinstein, The Role of the Court in Toxic Tort Litigation, 73 Geo. L.J. 1389 (1985); Russell J. Weintraub, Methods for Resolving Conflict-of-Laws Problems in Mass Tort Litigation, 1989 U. Ill. L. Rev. 129 (discussing need for simplified and unified choice of law approach as well as for unified products liability law).

68. Zacharia Chafee, Some Problems of Equity 200–201 (1950); *see*

also 1 J. Pomeroy, *Equity Jurisprudence* §§ 252–53 (4th ed. 1918); Zacharia Chafee, Bills of Peace with Multiple Parties, 45 Harv. L. Rev. 1297 (1932).

69. Stephen C. Yeazell, Group Litigation and Social Context: Toward a History of the Class Action, 77 Colum. L. Rev. 866, 877 (1977).

70. *Id.* at 878.

71. *Id.* at 873.

72. *Id.* at 881–82.

73. There is some indication that when they revised the class action rules the drafters had in mind suits brought by the NAACP.

74. *See generally* Judith Resnik, From "Cases" to "Litigation" 66–67 (May 1990) (conference paper for Modern Civil Procedure, Yale Law School, June 15–16, 1990) (noting contrast between substantial controversy that greeted 1966 revisions of class action rule and absence of objections to consolidation pursuant to Multidistrict Litigation Act); Robert L. Carter, The Federal Rules of Civil Procedure as a Vindicator of Civil Rights, 137 U. Pa. L. Rev. 2179, 2184–90 (1989).

75. Stephen C. Yeazell, Group Litigation and Social Context, 77 Colum. L. Rev. 866, 877 (1977).

76. *Id.* at 871.

77. *Id.*

78. *Id.* at 888.

79. *Id.* at 891.

80. *Id.* at 880.

81. *Id.*

82. *Id.* at 881.

83. Stephen C. Yeazell, *From Medieval Group Litigation to the Modern Class Action* 178 (1987).

84. *Id.* at 175, 209.

85. *Id.* at 218; *see also* Joseph Story, *Equity Pleadings* § 97 (3d ed. 1944); Note, Action under the Codes against Representative Defendants, 36 Harv. L. Rev. 89 (1922).

86. Stephen C. Yeazell, *From Medieval Group Litigation to the Modern Class Action* 218 (1987).

87. Note, Developments in the Law—Class Actions, 89 Harv. L. Rev. 1318, 1336 (1976).

88. *Id.* at 1332–43.

89. Zacharia Chafee, *Some Problems of Equity* 148–98 (1950).

90. Rogert H. Trangsrud, Joinder Alternatives in Mass Tort Litigation, 70 Cornell L. Rev. 779, 818 (1985). For cases denying bill of peace joinder for personal injury claims, *see, e.g.,* Southern Steel Co. v. Hopkins, 174 Ala. 465, 57 So. 11 (1911); Vandalia Coal Co. v. Lawson, 43 Ind. App. 226, 87 N.E. 47 (1909). In addition, *see* Yuba Con-

sol. Gold Fields v. Kilkeary, 206 F.2d 884 (9th Cir. 1953).

91. Roger H. Trangsrud, Joinder Alternatives in Mass Tort Litigation, 70 Cornell L. Rev. 779, 817 (1985).

92. Harry Kalven, Jr., & Maurice Rosenfield, The Contemporary Function of the Class Suit, 8 U. Chi. L. Rev. 684, 695 (1941).

93. *See, e.g.*, Bruce H. Nielson, Was the 1966 Advisory Committee Right?: Suggested Revisions of Rule 23 to Allow More Frequent Use of Class Actions in Mass Tort Litigation, 25 Harv. J. on Legis. 461 (1988); David Rosenberg, Class Actions for Mass Torts: Doing Individual Justice by Collective Means, 62 Ind. L. Rev. 561 (1987); *cf.* Arthur R. Miller, Of Frankenstein Monsters and Shining Knights: Myth, Reality, and the "Class Action Problem," 92 Harv. L. Rev. 664, 668 (1979) (describing "ferocious attack on the class action").

94. *But see* County of Suffolk v. Long Island Lighting Co., 907 F.2d 1295 (2d Cir. 1990), *aff'g* 710 F. Supp. 1407 (E.D.N.Y. 1989) (affirming district court's decision allowing a plaintiff to opt out of mandatory Rule 23(b)(1)(B) class under some circumstances); *In re* Temple, 851 F.2d 1269, 1272–73 n.5 (11th Cir. 1988) (suggesting possibility of opt-out of mandatory class).

The Advisory Committee on Federal Civil Procedure is now considering modifications of the class action rules. They would eliminate some of the present problems by reducing the importance of present classifications, making notification easier, and providing somewhat more discretion to the judge. Oral discussion of Sam C. Pointer, Chairman of the Committee at 26th Conference of Multidistrict Judges, Oct., 1993. These changes, if adopted, will make it easier to use class actions in the federal courts. Since the procedure of many states is based on federal rules, states could be expected to follow suit.

95. Fed. R. Civ. P. 23 advisory committee's note (1966 amendment).

> In various situations an adjudication as to one or more members of the class will necessarily or probably have an adverse practical effect on the interests of other members who should therefore be represented in the lawsuit. This is plainly the case when claims are made by numerous persons against a fund insufficient to satisfy all claims. A class action by or against representative members to settle the validity of the claims as a whole, or in groups, followed by separate proof of the amount of each valid claim and proportionate distribution of the fund, meets the problem.

Id.

96. *See, e.g., In re* School Asbestos Litig., 789 F.2d 996 (3d Cir.) (decertifying nationwide 23(b)(1)(B) class for punitive damages), *cert. denied*, 479 U.S. 852 (1986); *In re* Bendectin Prods. Liab. Litig., 749

F.2d 300, 307 (6th Cir. 1984) (issuing writ of mandamus vacating certification of Rule 23(b)(1) class); *In re* N. Dist. of Cal. "Dalkon Shield" IUD Prods. Liab. Litig. (Abed v. A. H. Robins Co.), 693 F.2d 847 (9th Cir. 1982) (reversing certification of 23(b)(1) nationwide punitive damage class), vacating 526 F. Supp. 887 (N.D. Cal. 1981), *cert. denied,* 459 U.S. 1171 (1983); Jenkins v. Raymark Indus., 109 F.R.D. 269, 276–77 (E.D. Tex. 1985) (district court refused to certify mandatory class on grounds that limited fund theory was too speculative), *aff'd,* 782 F.2d 468 (5th Cir. 1986); *see also* Linda S. Mullenix, Class Resolution of the Mass-Tort Case: A Proposed Federal Procedure Act, 64 Tex. L. Rev. 1039, 1054 (1986) (noting extensive judicial controversy surrounds the issue of the existence and ascertainment of the "limited fund" contemplated by the Federal Rule); *cf. In re* Temple, 851 F.2d 1269, 1271 (11th Cir. 1988) (dicta stating that certification of mandatory class in mass tort case "clearly implicates the Anti-Injunction Act"); *In re* Federal Skywalk Cases, 680 F.2d 1175, 1183 (8th Cir.) (vacating certification of mandatory class on grounds that it violated Anti-Injunction Act), *cert. denied,* 459 U.S. 988 (1982); Waldron v. Raymark Indus., 124 F.R.D. 235 (N.D. Ga. 1989) (denying certification of mandatory class in asbestos litigation on Anti-Injunction Act grounds). *But see In re* Joint E. & S. Dist. Asbestos Litigation, 982 F.2d. 721 (2d Cir.) allowing limited fund case to proceed as a non–opt-out class action so long as sub class representatives were appointed), *modified,* 993 F. 2d 7 (2d Cir. 1993); Dickinson v. Burnham, 197 F.2d 973 (2d Cir. 1952), *cert. denied,* 344 U.S. 875 (1952) (limited fund used to effect a pro rata reduction of claims); County of Suffolk v. Long Island Lighting Co., 907 F.2d 1295 (2d Cir. 1990) (limited fund RICO case); *In re* Drexel Burnham Lambert Group, Inc., 960 F.2d 285 (2d Cir. 1992), *cert. dismissed sub nom.,* Hart Holding Co. v. Drexel Burnham Lambert Group, Inc., 113 S. Ct. 1070 (1993); *In re* "Agent Orange" Prod. Liab. Litig., 100 F.R.D. 718 (E.D.N.Y. 1983) (certifying mandatory class for determining punitive damages), *mandamus denied,* 725 F.2d 858 (2d Cir.), *cert. denied,* 465 U.S. 1067 (1984). *See also In re* Joint E. & S. Dist. Asbestos Litigation (Eagle-Picher), 134 F.R.D. 32 (E. & S.D.N.Y. 1990) (power in limited fund class action to stay all cases, state and federal).

97. *See* Keene Corp. v. Fiorelli, et al., 14 F.3d 726 (2d Cir. 1993); Eagle Picher, 134 F.R.D. 32, also resulted in bankruptcy.

98. In 1985 Chief Judge Robert Parker of the Eastern District of Texas considered certifying a Rule 23(b)(1)(B) class in the asbestos case, but concluded at that time that such a class "was not certifiable because of the lack of evidence of a limited fund." Francis E. McGovern, Resolving Mature Mass Tort Litigation, 69 B.U. L. Rev. 659, 667 (1989) (citation omitted). Compare cases cited *supra* note 97 (Rule 23(b)(1)(B) cases certified).

99. *See* Califano v. Yamasaki, 442 U.S. 682, 700–701 (1979) (class action seeks to foster judicial economy and efficiency by adjudicating in a unified proceeding issues that affect many similarly situated persons).

100. Fed. R. Civ. P. 23(b)(3) advisory committee's note (1966 amendments) (citations omitted).

101. *See* Jack B. Weinstein, Revision of Procedure: Some Problems in Class Actions, 9 Buff. L. Rev. 433, 469 (1960).

102. There were some early experiments, however, in certifying mass accident suits under Rule 23(b)(1). *See, e.g.,* Hernandez v. Motor Vessel Skyward, 61 F.R.D. 558 (S.D. Fla. 1973) (655 personal injury claims of passengers due to contaminated water on board ship), *aff'd,* 507 F.2d 1278 (5th Cir. 1975); American Trading & Prod. Corp. v. Fishbach & Moore, Inc., 47 F.R.D. 155 (N.D. Ill. 1969) (twelve hundred tort claims for a fire at McCormick Place convention center).

103. *In re* A. H. Robins Co., 880 F.2d 709, 747 (4th Cir.) (affirming class certification), *cert. denied,* 493 U.S. 959 (1989).

104. *In re* "Agent Orange" Prod. Liab. Litig., 100 F.R.D. 718, 722 (E.D.N.Y. 1983), *mandamus denied,* 725 F.2d 858 (2d Cir.), *cert. denied,* 465 U.S. 1067 (1984).

105. *See, e.g.,* Jenkins v. Raymark Indus., 782 F.2d 468, 473 (5th Cir. 1986) (certifying class of nine hundred asbestos workers for purposes of determining common issues including state-of-art defense, product defectiveness, and punitive damages); *In re* School Asbestos Litig., 789 F.2d 996, 1009 (3d Cir.) (certifying nationwide mandatory class for punitive damages and opt-out class for compensatory damages), *cert. denied,* 479 U.S. 852 (1986).

106. *See, e.g., In re* "Agent Orange" Product Liability Litigation (Ivy v. Diamond Shamrock Chemicals Co.), 996 F.2d 1425 (2d. Cir. 1993), *cert. denied,* 114 S. Ct. 1125 (1994); County of Suffolk v. Long Island Lighting Co., 710 F. Supp. 1422 (E.D.N.Y. 1989), *aff'd,* 907 F.2d 1295 (2d Cir. 1990); *Jenkins,* 782 F.2d at 468 (703 asbestos cases); *In re* "Agent Orange" Prod. Liab. Litig., 725 F.2d 858 (2d Cir. 1984). *But see In re* Fibreboard Corp., 893 F.2d 706 (5th Cir. 1990) (granting defendants' petition of mandamus and vacating class of 2,990 asbestos claimants); *In re* Bendectin Prods. Liab. Litig., 849 F.2d 300 (6th Cir. 1984) (issuing writ of mandamus vacating certification of Rule 23(b)(1) class for settlement); *In re* Northern Dist. of Cal., "Dalkon Shield" IUD Prods. Liab. Litig., 693 F.2d 847 (9th Cir. 1982) (decertifying mandatory national punitive damages class and voluntary California class in IUD cases), *cert. denied,* 459 U.S. 1171 (1983).

107. *See generally* Lester Brickman, Contingent Fees without Contingencies: *Hamlet* without the Prince of Denmark, 37 UCLA L. Rev. 29 (1989) (arguing that contingency fees that exceed any legitimate risk

premium for the lawyer's anticipated effort constitute a breach of fiduciary obligations to the client).

108. A good example of the perversity and lack of uniformity that can characterize opt-out classes is the Bendectin litigation. Merrell Dow, the manufacturer of the antinausea drug that was prescribed to as many as thirty million women worldwide between 1957 and 1983, offered to settle all birth defect claims for $120 million. The company withdrew the offer, however, when a federal appeals court ruled that the settlement would not bind those claimants who wished to pursue suits on their own. Eventually a class of 1,200 plaintiffs brought and lost a class action suit when a jury found that they failed to prove causation. Most individual Bendectin suits have also been lost by the plaintiffs, although some have prevailed. *See* Stephen D. Sugarman, The Need to Reform Personal Injury Law Leaving Scientific Disputes to Scientists, 248 Science, May 18, 1990, at 823.

109. The Anti-Injunction Act, 28 U.S.C. § 2283 (1988), is no bar to resolving pending state cases in a federal class action. *See In re* Joint E. & S. Dists. Asbestos Litig. (*In re* Johns-Manville Corp.; Findley v. Blinken), 120 Bankr. 648 (E.D.N.Y. & S.D.N.Y. 1990) (memorandum on stays; Anti-Injunction Act does not prohibit federal court certifying Rule 23(b)(1)(B) class from enjoining concurrent state court actions); Martin H. Redish, The Anti-Injunction Statute Reconsidered, 44 U. Chi. L. Rev. 717, 754 (1977) ("necessary in aid of jurisdiction" exception).

110. *See In re* A. H. Robins Co., 880 F.2d 709 (4th Cir.) (plaintiffs' class action against Robins's insurer was resolved in context of Robins's bankruptcy proceedings), *cert. denied*, 493 U.S. 959 (1989).

111. *See infra* text accompanying note 236.

112. *See In re* N. Dist. of Cal., Dalkon Shield IUD Prods. Liab. Litig. (Abed v. A. H. Robins Co.), 693 F.2d 847, 852–56 (9th Cir. 1982) (reversing district court's certification of Fed. R. Civ. P. 23(b)(1) nationwide class for purposes of seeking punitive damages and Fed. R. Civ. P. 23(b)(3) subclass of California plaintiffs on grounds that proposed classes did not meet requirements of typicality or commonality under Fed. R. Civ. P. 23), *vacating* 526 F. Supp. 887 (N.D. Cal. 1981), *cert. denied*, 459 U.S. 1171 (1983); *see also In re* A. H. Robins Co., 880 F.2d 709, 712–14 (4th Cir.), *cert. denied*, 493 U.S. 959 (1989).

113. For instance, the claimants were only one of several groups of creditors—including shareholders, the Aetna Insurance Co. (Robins's insurer), future claimants, and trade creditors—all of whom had claims on the same fixed amount of assets. Once in bankruptcy the plaintiffs no longer had the option of seeking punitive damages. Under the Bankruptcy Code, the Robins management had a statutorily set exclusive time period to file a reorganization plan, thus getting first crack at

developing a resolution. Nor did the plaintiffs retain control over matters such as the makeup of the claimant creditors' committee, the value assigned to the claims as a whole, or the value given any individual claimant. Moreover, the judge had the power to confirm a plan even over their objections. *See generally* Francis E. McGovern, Resolving Mature Mass Tort Litigation, 69 B.U. L. Rev. 659, 677–88.

114. *See, e.g.,* 11 U.S.C. § 362(a)(1) (1988); *see also In re* Joint E. & S. Dists. Asbestos Litig. (*In re* Johns-Manville Corp.; Findley v. Blinken), 120 Bankr. 648 (E.D.N.Y. & S.D.N.Y. 1990) (utilizing rationales of both the Bankruptcy Code, 11 U.S.C. § 105(a) (1988), and Rule 23(b)(1)(B) limited fund class certification to stay all pending federal and state actions against the Manville Personal Injury Trust).

115. *See* 28 U.S.C. § 157(d) (1988). In bankruptcy actions:

[T]he district court may withdraw, in whole or in part, any case or proceeding referred under this section, on its own motion or on timely motion of any party, for cause shown. The district court shall, on timely motion of a party, so withdraw a proceeding if the court determines that resolution of the proceeding requires consideration of both title 11 and other laws of the United States regulating organizations or activities affecting interstate commerce.

Id.

116. *See* Francis E. McGovern, Resolving Mature Mass Tort Litigation, 69 B.U. L. Rev. 659, 676–77 & n.71 (1989) (after Robins filed its bankruptcy case in Richmond, Virginia, where it had its headquarters, Judge Merhige, on Robins's motion, entered order retaining non-core portions of proceedings).

117. N.Y. Civ. Prac. L.&R. § 6401(a) (McKinney 1980); *see also In re* New York City Asbestos Litig.; *In re* Joint E. & S. Dists. Asbestos Litig., 123 Bankr. 7 (N.Y. Sup. Ct. & E.D.N.Y. & S.D.N.Y. 1990) (joint federal-state memorandum in New York Navy Yard asbestos litigation noting existence of equitable and legal powers that might enable state and federal judges to exercise control over Trust).

118. Comment, Procedural Devices for Simplifying Litigation from a Mass Tort, 63 Yale L.J. 493, 501 (1954).

119. Zacharia Chafee, *Some Problems of Equity* 153–54 (1950).

120. *Id.* at 154.

121. *Id.* at 155.

122. 28 U.S.C. § 1407 (1988).

123. As Professor Resnik notes, the legislative history of MDL shows that the evil to be avoided was "'the possibility for conflict and duplication in discovery and other pretrial procedures.'" Judith Resnik, From "Cases" to "Litigation" 90 (May 1990) (Conference paper for Modern Civil Procedure, Yale Law School, June 15–16, 1990) (quoting H. R.

Rep. No. 1130, 90th Cong., 2d Sess. 4 (1968)).

124. Am. Law Inst., Complex Litigation Project, Tentative Draft No. 2 (Apr. 6, 1990).

125. *See* Am. Law Inst., Preliminary Study of Complex Litigation 48 (1987) ("Experience has shown that most actions consolidated under Section 1407 are not returned to the transferor forums, primarily because of the frequency of settlement.").

126. *See generally* Judith Resnik, From "Cases" to "Litigation" 53–54 (May 1990) (Conference paper for Modern Civil Procedure, Yale Law School, June 15–16, 1990).

127. *But see In re* Asbestos & Asbestos Insulation Material Prods. Liab. Litig., 431 F. Supp. 906, 910 (J.P.M.D.L. 1977) (Judicial Panel on Multidistrict Litigation heeded objections of attorneys and rejected consolidation of asbestos cases).

128. 28 U.S.C. § 1407(e) (1988).

129. Judith Resnik, From "Cases" to "Litigation" 53 (Conference paper for Modern Civil Procedure, Yale Law School, June 15–16, 1990) (citations omitted).

130. *See generally id.* Professor Resnik demonstrates how the "background of MDL grows out of the federal judiciary's concern, dating from sometime after World War II, about 'similar' and 'protracted' cases filed in district courts across the country." *Id.* at 45. In the 1960s the present MDL's predecessor committee was "'charged with developing methods for expediting' cases involving damages (mass accidents as well as antitrust cases seeking damages)." *Id.* at 44 (quoting Fed. R. Civ. P. 23(b)(3) advisory committee's note (1966 amendments)). The theme of judicial control emerges again and again. *Id.* at 45–46.

131. Stanley A. Weigel, The Judicial Panel on Multidistrict Litigation, Transferor Courts and Transferee Courts, 78 F.R.D. 575, 585 (1977).

132. Judith Resnik, From "Cases" to "Litigation" 76–83.

133. *See id.* at 83–94 (discussing specific proposals).

134. *See, e.g.,* Am. Law Inst., Complex Litigation Project Tentative Draft No. 1, at 85 (Apr. 14, 1989).

135. 304 U.S. 64 (1938).

136. *See* Judith Resnik, From "Cases" to "Litigation" 88.

137. *In re* E. & S. Dists. Asbestos Litigation, 995 F.2d 343 (2d. Cir. 1993) (reversing consolidated power house trials); *In re* Repetitive Stress Injury Litigation, Debruyne, et al. v. National Semiconductor Corp. et al., 11 F.3d 368 (2d. Cir. 1993) (granting mandamus against consolidation of carpal tunnel and other repetitive work syndrome cases).

138. *See, e.g.,* Brown v. Superior Court, 44 Cal. 3d 1049, 751 P.2d 470, 245 Cal. Rptr. 412 (1988) (consolidating group of sixty-nine DES-related cancer victims in which the California Supreme Court

ruled, because of the public interest in promoting development, availability, and reasonable price of drugs, pharmaceutical liability for defectively designed drug should not be measured by standards of strict liability).

139. *See* Lester Brickman, Contingent Fees without Contingencies: *Hamlet* without the Prince of Denmark, 37 UCLA L. Rev. 29, 127 (1989) ("Contingent fee setting today operates in a milieu substantially devoid of fiduciary oversight.").

140. Under this method the hours reasonably expended by counsel are determined and multiplied by a reasonable hourly rate. The resulting figure may then be increased (or decreased) based on several factors, including the contingent nature or risk involved in taking the particular case, the complexity and novelty of the issues, the quality of the attorney's work, the amount of recovery, the delays experienced, etc. *See generally* Johnson v. Georgia Highway Express, Inc., 488 F.2d 714, 717–19 (5th Cir. 1974) (setting forth twelve factors for consideration); Lindy Bros. Builders, Inc. of Philadelphia v. American Radiator & Standard Sanitary Corp., 487 F.2d 161 (3d Cir. 1973) (creating lodestar approach), *appeal following remand*, 540 F.2d 102 (3d Cir. 1976). The lodestar method has been criticized, however, as increasing judicial workload, failing to be either objective or uniform, giving the mistaken impression that the value of lawyers' work is subject to mathematical precision, promoting the padding of bills, providing disincentives to settle, and creating confusion. *See* Third Circuit Task Force, Court Awarded Attorney Fees, 108 F.R.D. 237, 246–50, 270 (1985).

141. The common fund doctrine follows traditional equitable practice. Under this doctrine a lawyer who recovers a common fund for the benefit of others or for his or her client is entitled to reasonable attorneys' fees from the fund. *See* Boeing Co. v. Van Gemert, 444 U.S. 472, 478 (1980); Alyeska Pipeline Serv. Co. v. Wilderness Soc'y, 421 U.S. 240, 257–58 (1975). This rule is premised on the equitable principles of prevention of windfall and unjust enrichment. *Boeing*, 444 U.S. at 478. Rather than charging one or a group of clients too much, the common fund doctrine enables a court with "jurisdiction over the fund involved in the litigation" to "[p]revent this inequity by assessing attorney's fees against the entire fund, thus spreading fees proportionately among those benefited by the suit." *Id.*

142. *See In re* "Agent Orange" Prod. Liab. Litig., 611 F. Supp. 1296, 1310 (E.D.N.Y. 1985), *aff'd in part and rev'd in part*, 818 F.2d 216 (2d Cir.) (comparing compensation on a contingent basis with compensation at an hourly rate), *cert. denied*, 484 U.S. 926 (1987).

143. *See* Thomas E. Willging, History of Asbestos Case Management (Federal Judicial Center staff paper prepared for June 25, 1990, National Asbestos Conference) (copy on permanent file with University of Illi-

nois Law Review) (although courts have consolidated larger and larger clusters of cases for trial or settlement, they have failed to keep pace with new filings in most districts) (citing Thomas E. Willging, *Trends in Asbestos Litigation* (Federal Judicial Center 1987)).

144. Comm'n on Mass Torts, *supra* note 9, app., at 4e (separate statement of P. Rheingold). Judge William W. Schwarzer, Director of the Federal Judicial Center, recently estimated that some thirty-three thousand asbestos cases—including both personal injury and property damage—are currently pending in the federal courts. W. Schwarzer, Asbestos Litigation: Some Thoughts concerning Possible National Strategies (June 14, 1990) (memorandum from Judge Schwarzer to participants in June 25, 1990, Asbestos Conference) (copy on permanent file with University of Illinois Law Review).

For example, as of the end of June 1990, 7,598 of a total of 10,818 pending civil cases in the Eastern Division of the Northern District of Ohio were asbestos cases. Memorandum from Judge Frank J. Battisti to all judges 1 & n.1 (July 9, 1990) (partial copy on permanent file with University of Illinois Law Review). In the District of Massachusetts, the number of pending asbestos cases nearly doubled between May 1984 and September 1985, from 1,723 to 3,236. Eagle-Picher Indus. v. Liberty Mut. Ins. Co., 829 F.2d 227, 236 n.15 (1st Cir. 1987). According to the Court Administration Bulletin, there was a dramatic increase in the number of asbestos personal injury product liability filings as of October 1990, despite an overall decrease in civil filings. Filings soared from 7,718 in 1989 to 12,822 by the fall of 1990—a 66 percent increase. Court Administration Bull. (Oct. 1990).

145. Francis E. McGovern, Resolving Mature Mass Tort Litigation, 69 B.U. L. Rev. 659, 673 & n.61 (1989) (citing Deborah R. Hensler, W. Felstiner, M. Selvin, & P. Ebener, Asbestos in the Courts: The Challenge of Mass Toxic Torts 84–85 (1985) (Rand Corporation, Institute for Civil Justice)).

146. Thomas Willging, History of Asbestos Case Management (Federal Judicial Center staff paper for June 25, 1990, National Asbestos Conference). As of the fall of 1990, over seven thousand asbestos cases have been pending for two to three years. Court Administration Bull. 2 (Oct. 1990).

147. The Manville Trust is the mechanism established in 1986 to enable Manville Corporation to emerge from four years in Chapter 11 bankruptcy and resume compensating asbestos claimants. *See In re* Johns-Manville Corp. (Kane v. Johns-Manville Corp.), 843 F.2d 636, 639 (2d Cir. 1988) (affirming plan). In recent years, it became clear that the Trust was inadequately financed and managed.

148. While attempts at a global settlement ultimately proved unsuccessful, and the state and federal cases severed to conduct concurrent

state and federal trials, pretrial preparation was greatly expedited, and as a result a majority of defendants settled before the trials.

149. In this regard they are similar to the Dalkon Shield cases that Robins had litigated for fifteen years prior to declaring bankruptcy in 1985.

150. In addition to Manville, UNR Industries, Amatex Corporation, Raytech (formerly Raybestos-Manhattan), Eagle-Picher Industries, and others have also filed under Chapter 11.

151. According to a Rand Corporation study, injured claimants receive less than 37 percent of the total amount spent on asbestos litigation. Deborah R. Hensler, W. Felstiner, M. Selvin, & P. Ebener, Asbestos in the Court: The Challenge of Mass Toxic Torts (1985) (Rand Corporation, Institute for Civil Justice). Experience of the senior author with the Manville case confirms this result. When court time is factored in, the Manville Trust transactional costs are in the order of 70 percent. Plaintiff attorneys' per-hour compensation probably runs into thousands of dollars per hour in large mass settlements. See generally Lester Brickman, Contingent Fees without Contingencies, 37 UCLA L. Rev. 29 (1989).

152. Spencer Williams, Mass Tort Class Actions: Going, Going, Gone?, 98 F.R.D. 323, 324 (1983); see also In re Allied Signal Inc., 915 F.2d 190 (6th Cir. 1990) (nullifying at least with respect to Sixth Circuit claims attempt of federal judges to aggregate and dispose of asbestos claims on a national basis).

153. In re Fibreboard Corp., 893 F.2d 706, 712 (5th Cir. 1990) (denying certification for trial of class of 2,990 asbestos claimants in Eastern Texas).

154. See In re Asbestos & Asbestos Insulation Material Prods. Liab. Litig., 431 F. Supp. 906 (J.P.M.D.L. 1977) (denying consolidation of 103 asbestos-related personal injury claims on the grounds that plaintiffs were from many different trades and their cases presented differing causation and medical issues). The MDL panel declined jurisdiction again in the personal injury cases in 1980 and in the school district cases in 1985. See In re Asbestos School Prods. Liab. Litig., 606 F. Supp. 713 (J.P.M.D.L. 1985); In re Asbestos Prods. Liab. Litig. II, MDL-416 (J.P.M.D.L. Mar. 13, 1980) (unpublished order). Asbestos claims have been consolidated within a single jurisdiction, but usually only after fairly stringent criteria for assessing the common issues are met. See, e.g., Johnson v. Celotex, 899 F.2d 1281, 1285 (2d Cir.) (criteria to consider when determining whether consolidation is appropriate include: "(1) common worksite; (2) similar occupation; (3) similar time of exposure; (4) type of disease; (5) whether plaintiffs were living or deceased; (6) status of discovery in each case; (7) whether all plaintiffs were represented by the same counsel; and (8) type of cancer alleged") (citations

omitted), *cert. denied,* 498 U.S. 920 (1990).

155. *See generally* Francis E. McGovern, The Cycle of Mass Tort Litigation (May 25, 1990) (conference paper prepared for Modern Civil Procedure: Issues in Controversy, Program in Civil Liability, Yale Law School, June 15–16, 1990) (copy on permanent file with University of Illinois Law Review) (discussing cyclical process of maturation of mass torts and suggesting that timing in consolidation is therefore a crucial element in ensuring an equitable global solution).

156. The author has met with both federal and state judges and has discussed the matter with staff of the MDL Panel and of the Federal Judicial Center.

157. *See, e.g.,* Cimino v. Raymark Indus., 739 F. Supp. 328 (E.D. Tex. 1990) (over three thousand asbestos cases joined in class action for purposes of eight-week Phase One trial determining, inter alia, which products were capable of causing harm in their application, use, or removal; which defendants' products were defective and unreasonably dangerous; on what date each defendant knew or should have known that insulators and their families were at risk of contracting asbestos-related injuries as a result of exposure to asbestos-containing products; and what amount of punitive damages, if any, should be awarded); Turley v. Owens-Corning Fiberglass Corp., Nos. 84-C-3321 et al. (Kanaway Co., W. Va. Cir. Ct.) (trial of common liability issues in 315 consolidated asbestos cases held in April–May 1989).

158. The development of a common database for the Dalkon Shield litigation "represented the largest and most expensive social science survey ever conducted under the auspices of a court." Francis E. McGovern, Resolving Mass Tort Litigation, 69 B.U. L. Rev. 659, 686 (1989). The process was a consensual one, conducted by the parties' experts, court-appointed neutrals, and subcontractors. The court-appointed expert who supervised the survey estimates that the costs could have been halved had the court-appointed experts rather than the parties' experts conducted the study. *Id.*

159. *See* Mark Peterson & Molly Selvin, Mass Justice: The Limited and Unlimited Power of Courts 27 (Conference Paper for Modern Civil Procedure, Yale Law School, June 15–16, 1990) ("Individual consideration for plaintiffs and defendants might be preserved even in mass litigation through techniques of sampling, statistics, neutral expertise and computer analyses."). Judge Robert M. Parker of the Eastern District of Texas has already pioneered some potentially powerful and innovative computer and video technology that allowed him to "dramatically shorten" a recent complex antitrust conspiracy case. ETSI v. Burlington N., Inc., C.A. No. B-84-979-CA (E.D. Tex.) (*described in* H. Reasoner, J. Murchison, & W. Tomlin, Innovative Judicial Techniques in Complex Litigation (paper prepared for American College of Trial

Lawyers' 40th Annual Spring Meeting, Mar. 4–7, 1990) (copy on permanent file with University of Illinois Law Review)).

160. United States Sentencing Comm'n, Guidelines Manual § 1.4 (1989).

161. See, e.g., In re A. H. Robins Co., 85 Bankr. 373, 378 (E.D. Va. 1988) ("[T]he requirements of Rule 23 may be more easily satisfied in the settlement context than in the more complex litigation context"), aff'd, 880 F.2d 709 (4th Cir.), cert. denied, 493 U.S. 959 (1989); see also In re Joint E. & S. Dists. Asbestos Litig. (In re Johns-Manville Corp.; Findley v. Blinken), 120 Bankr. 648, 656 (E.D.N.Y. & S.D.N.Y. 1990) (discussing appropriateness of negotiating settlement agreement prior to ruling on class certification); County of Suffolk v. Long Island Lighting Co., 710 F. Supp. 1422, 1424 (E.D.N.Y. 1989) (same), aff'd, 907 F.2d 1295, 1323-26 (2d Cir. 1990). But cf. Brent Rosenthal, When Opt-Out Class Actions Are Charades, Legal Times, July 12, 1993, at 23 (corporate defendants have learned that class actions can be highly advantageous in toxic-tort cases; but when an opt-out class action resolves claims for future injury, the results for plaintiffs can be unfair).

162. See, e.g., In re Joint E. & S. Dists. Asbestos Litig.; In re New York City Asbestos Litig., 129 F.R.D. 434 (S.D.N.Y. & E.D.N.Y. & N.Y. Sup. Ct. 1990) (joint federal-state appointment of Kenneth R. Feinberg, Esq., as Settlement Master-Referee in asbestos litigation); In re Ohio Asbestos Litig., OAL Order No. 3 (N.D. Ohio July 14, 1983) (copy on permanent file with University of Illinois Law Review) (order appointing Professors Francis E. McGovern and Eric D. Green special masters to manage asbestos litigation); see also Francis E. McGovern, Toward a Functional Approach for Managing Complex Litigation, 53 U. Chi. L. Rev. 440, 480 (1986); Report from Special Master Jack Ratliff to The Honorable Robert Parker (Sept. 20, 1989) (in Cimino v. Raymark Indus., No. B-86-0456-CA (E.D. Tex. 1990)). See, generally, Margaret G. Farrell, Special Masters: Defining the Role of Special Masters Appointed under Federal Rule of Civil Procedure 53(b), Federal Judicial Center, Temporary Edition (1993).

163. Fed. R. Civ. P. 53(b).

164. See, e.g., Francis E. McGovern, Resolving Mature Mass Tort Litigation, 69 B.U. L. Rev. 659, 669–71.

165. See Stephen N. Subrin, How Equity Conquered Common Law, 135 U. Pa. L. Rev. 909, 912–13 (1987).

166. See Curtis v. Loether, 415 U.S. 189, 196 (1974) (action for money damages was "traditional form of relief offered in the courts of law."). Where money damages are either restitutionary or incidental or intertwined with injunctive relief, they may be equitable. See Chauffeurs, Teamsters & Helpers Local 391 v. Terry, 494 U.S. 558 (1990); see also Albermarle Paper Co. v. Moody, 422 U.S. 405, 415–18 (1975)

(back pay awarded in Title VII action constitutes equitable relief); *accord* Title VII, 42 U.S.C. § 2000e-5(g) (1988).

167. United States Dep't of Justice, *supra* note 16, at 54–55.

168. *See* United Steelworkers of Am. v. United States, 361 U.S. 39, 60 (1959) (citing English cases from 1587 to 1799).

169. *See* Ramirez de Arellano v. Weinberger, 745 F.2d 1500, 1527 (D.C. Cir. 1984) (from early times, courts in equity considered injury to real property to be irremediable at law); Restatement (Second) of Torts § 821D (1977) (defining private nuisance as a "nontrespassory invasion of another's interest in the private use and enjoyment of land"); 2 Frederick Pollack & Frederick Maitland, *The History of English Law before the Time of Edward I* 53 (2d ed. 1903) (Nuisance is caused "by things . . . erected, made, or done not on the soil possessed by the complainant but on neighbouring soil. . . . Law endeavors to protect the person . . . in the enjoyment of those rights against his neighbors which he would be entitled to were he seised under a good title."); Edward Rabin, Nuisance Law: Rethinking Fundamental Assumptions, 63 Va. L. Rev. 1299, 1319 (1977) (nuisance involved interference with enjoyment of land). Public nuisances were defined by then Judge Cardozo as:

> the nuisance whereby "a public right or privilege common to every person in the community is interrupted or interfered with. . . ." Public also is the nuisance committed "in such place and in such manner that the aggregation of private injuries becomes so great and extensive as to constitute a public annoyance and inconvenience, and a wrong against the community, which may be properly the subject of a public prosecution."

People v. Rubenfeld, 254 N.Y. 245, 172 N.E. 485, 486 (1930) (citations omitted).

170. Weinberger v. Romero-Barcelo, 456 U.S. 305, 314 n.7 (1988) (citations omitted); *see also* Beatty v. Washington Metro. Area Transit Auth., 860 F.2d 1117, 1124 (D.C. Cir. 1988).

171. *See generally* Arvin Maskin, Overview and Update of Emerging Damage Theories in Toxic Tort Litigation 38 (Mar. 1990) (prepared for ALI/ABA course of study) (copy on permanent file with University of Illinois Law Review) (collecting cases).

172. *See, e.g.,* Sterling v. Velsicol Chem. Corp., 855 F.2d 1188 (6th Cir. 1988) (acknowledging nuisance theory as basis of liability but restricting its use to residents of affected area).

173. *See, e.g., In re* Johns-Manville Corp., 801 F.2d 60 (2d Cir. 1986); *In re* A. H. Robins Co., 89 Bankr. 555 (E.D.Va. 1988); *see also* Eagle-Picher Seeks Shield of Chapter 11, Wall St. J., Jan. 8, 1991, at A3, col. 3.

174. Corporate reorganization emerged out of the courts of equity as part of the response to railroad insolvencies of the mid-nineteenth century. Faced with multitudes descending to press their individual claims and threatening to dismember the functioning roads, these courts began to fashion a procedure that would satisfy the calls both of equity and of the interested community. To this end, the venerable common law property remedies of receivership and foreclosure were pressed into service. The result was a scheme that encompassed what are today the separate processes of liquidation and reorganization. Jeffrey Stern, Note, Failed Markets and Failed Solutions: The Unwitting Formulation of the Corporate Reorganization Technique, 90 Colum. L. Rev. 783, 783 (1990) (citation omitted).

175. As the Supreme Court recently noted, the Bankruptcy Code grants the bankruptcy courts residual authority to approve reorganization plans including "any . . . appropriate provision not inconsistent with the applicable provisions of this title." 11 U.S.C. § 1123(b)(5); *see also* § 1129. The Code also states that bankruptcy courts may "issue any order, process, or judgment that is necessary or appropriate to carry out the provisions" of the Act. § 105. These statutory directives are consistent with the traditional understanding that bankruptcy courts, as courts of equity, have broad authority to modify creditor-debtor relationships. United States v. Energy Resources Co., 110 S. Ct. 2139, 2142 (1990).

176. *See* Francis E. McGovern, Resolving Mature Mass Tort Litigation, 69 B.U. L. Rev. 659, 680–85 (1989).

177. Plaintiffs in the Dalkon Shield litigation had brought a class action against Aetna directly, charging that the insurer and Robins were joint tortfeasors.

178. *See* Stephen D. Sugarman, Serious Tort Law Reform, 24 San Diego L. Rev. 795, 797–98 (1987) (collecting cases).

179. The many debates that have raged around the effectiveness of the tort system as opposed to other means as a deterrent of corporate malfeasance, as well as questions involving the legal, social, economic, and moral desirability of punitive damages, are beyond the scope of this article. It is worth noting, however, that in limiting recovery to compensatory damages, retribution and deterrence are not completely lost; both often play a significant role in jury awards for pain and suffering, a compensatory, albeit nontangible, damage heading. I do not agree with the view that punitive damages may be regarded as compensation for "dignitary" losses sustained when a person is wronged by outrageous or malicious conduct. *See* Bruce Chapman & Michael Trebilcock, Punitive Damages: Divergence in Search of a Rationale, 40 Ala. L. Rev. 741, 768–69 (1989).

180. This is not to say that the manufacturers of asbestos, the

Dalkon Shield, or other harmful products are free of fault. The magnitude of the mass tort problem in this country is a function not merely of huge numbers of plaintiffs, but also of the increasing size of compensatory and punitive damages awarded by juries understandably incensed by the deplorable record of corporate malfeasance. I am therefore not necessarily advocating the complete elimination of punitive damages which respond to notions of culpability. *See generally* Paul Brodeur, *Outrageous Misconduct: The Asbestos Industry on Trial* (1985); B. Castleman, *Asbestos: Medical and Legal Aspects* 461–527 (2d ed. 1986) (describing manufacturers' long-standing knowledge of dangers of asbestos exposure); Morton Mintz, *At Any Cost* (1985) (describing the Dalkon Shield litigation). In the asbestos context, judges, too, have noted the decades-long attempts of the industry to suppress information about the health hazards of asbestos. *See, e.g.,* Billetz v. Johns-Manville Corp., No. 80-2976 (D.N.J. Apr. 17, 1984); *In re* Asbestosis Cases, 274 S.C. 421, 266 S.E.2d 773 (1980).

181. For an extreme example of this, *see* Beshada v. Johns-Manville Prods. Corp., 90 N.J. 191, 447 A.2d 539 (1982) (asbestos case in which court imputed knowledge to manufacturer of all that was known at time of trial and thus found defendant liable without regard to foreseeability or actual knowledge at time of production of or exposure to asbestos-containing products).

182. *But see* George L. Priest, Modern Tort Law and Its Reform, 22 Val. U. L. Rev. 1, 12, 35 (1987) ("A product or a substance should be regarded as the cause of an injury or a condition only where it is believed that to attach liability for generating the source will lead to a reduction in the accident rate.").

183. A majority of states, however, have interpreted the unreasonably dangerous language as requiring or allowing to some degree the introduction of negligence concepts into strict liability analysis. *See* James E. Beasley, *Products Liability and the Unreasonably Dangerous Requirement* (1980) (documenting diverse forms of strict liability in every state). Moreover, some strict liability states allow defenses such as contributory negligence or assumption of the risk to bar recovery. In comparative negligence states, even under strict liability theory, the amount recovered by a plaintiff may be reduced according to his or her degree of negligence.

184. *See* Beshada, 90 N.J. 191, 447 A.2d 539.

185. In the 1980s at least thirty states repealed or harshly restricted joint and several liability. American Tort Reform Ass'n, Legislative Reform 11 (1989).

186. *See, e.g.,* White v. Celotex Corp., 907 F.2d 104 (9th Cir. 1990) (finding California-type market share liability applied in DES cases inappropriate in asbestos litigation because: (1) asbestos fibers are not fun-

gible; (2) "[a]sbestos is put to numerous uses"; (3) "[s]ome of the products to which a plaintiff could be exposed would undoubtedly have been purchased out of state prior to the exposure of the plaintiff"; and (4) "[a] plaintiff may be exposed to asbestos over a period of many years, during which time some of the defendants will have begun or discontinued the making and marketing of asbestos products") (citing *In re* Related Asbestos Cases, 543 F. Supp. 1152, 1158 (N.D. Cal. 1982)); Sholtis v. American Cyanamid Co., 238 N.J. Super. 8, 25, 568 A.2d 1196, 1205 (App. Div. 1989).

187. This theory is sometimes labeled a civil conspiracy to commit a tort. *See In re* N.D. Personal Injury Asbestos Litig., 737 F. Supp. 1087 (D.N.D. 1990) (in context of establishing personal jurisdiction over out-of-state asbestos supplier, court finds that plaintiffs made a prima facie case that defendant engaged in concerted action to suppress information concerning health risks of asbestos—thereby depriving plaintiffs of warnings—through its membership in Asbestos Textile Institute, a trade organization for asbestos manufacturers).

188. Hall v. E. I. DuPont deNemours & Co., 345 F. Supp. 353, 378 (E.D.N.Y. 1972).

189. *See, e.g., In re* "Agent Orange" Prod. Liab. Litig., 597 F. Supp. 740, 819 (E.D.N.Y. 1984).

190. 26 Cal. 3d 588, 607 P.2d 924, 163 Cal. Rptr. 132, *cert. denied,* 449 U.S. 912 (1980).

191. In addition to California, three states, Washington, Wisconsin, and New York, have developed modified forms of market share liability. Washington has adopted a "market share alternate liability theory" that allows a plaintiff to bring suit against only one defendant. *See* Martin v. Abbott Laboratories, 102 Wash. 2d 581, 689 P.2d 368 (1984). Defendants are presumed to have an equal market share and are liable on a pro rata basis but may rebut this presumption by proving their actual market share, in which case they are liable only for that percentage of damages. *Id*. at 605–06, 689 P.2d at 383. The presumptive share of the defendants that are unable to establish market share is adjusted upward, accounting for 100 percent of the market. *Id*. Wisconsin has adopted a "risk contribution theory." *See* Collins v. Eli Lilly Co., 116 Wis. 2d 166, 342 N.W.2d 37 (1984). Here the plaintiff need only sue one defendant drug company, and that company need not constitute a substantial share of the market. *Id*. at 193, 342 N.W.2d at 50. If no others are impleaded, that company is liable for all the damages if it cannot prove by a preponderance of the evidence that it did not produce or market DES during the relevant period or in the relevant geographic market area. *See id*. at 193–98, 342 N.W.2d at 50–52.

New York developed its own version of market share liability utilizing a national market and apportioning liability to correspond to the overall culpability of each defendant as measured by the percentage of risk of injury each defendant contributed to the public at large. *See* Hymowitz v. Eli Lilly, 73 N.Y.2d 487, 511–12, 539 N.E.2d 1069, 1078, 541 N.Y.S.2d 941, 950 (1989). In New York liability is several only and is not inflated if all the manufacturers are not brought before the court. *Id.* at 512–13, 539 N.E.2d at 1078, 541 N.Y.S.2d at 950.

A number of other states have rejected market share liability. *See, e.g.,* Mulcahy v. Eli Lilly, 386 N.W.2d 67 (Iowa 1986); Zafft v. Eli Lilly, 676 S.W.2d 241 (Mo. 1984).

192. *Hymowitz,* 73 N.Y.2d 487, 539 N.E.2d 1069, 541 N.Y.S.2d 941.

193. *See, e.g.,* Brown v. Superior Court, 44 Cal. 3d 1049, 1074–75, 751 P.2d 470, 486–87, 245 Cal. Rptr. 412, 428 (1988). In effect, joint and several liability is relinquished in exchange for indeterminate defendant liability.

194. *Cf.* United States v. Monsanto Co., 858 F.2d 160, 167 (4th Cir. 1988) (court backs examination of involvement of the parties to arrive at equitable allocation of costs of cleanup of toxic dump), *cert. denied,* 490 U.S. 1106 (1989); *cf.* Dan Riesel, Private Hazardous Substance Litigation Seminar 25 (ALI-ABA Environmental Litigation Seminar) (discussing other apportionment doctrines in CERCLA context, such as relative toxicity of wastes involved, degree of care exercised by party, *caveat emptor,* and "as is" theories).

195. Ferebee v. Chevron Chem. Co., 736 F.2d 1529, 1534 (D.C. Cir.), *cert. denied,* 469 U.S. 1062 (1984). *See generally* Jack B. Weinstein & Robert Kushen, Scientific Evidence in Complex Litigation (Oct. 9, 1990) (unpublished manuscript).

196. Many cancers, for example, offer no physical evidence of the responsible agent but may be attributed to risk factors other than the defendant's product. Stephen Epstein, *The Politics of Cancer* 40 (1978). According to a 1984 National Research Council Report, there was no information available on the toxicity of approximately 80 percent of the nearly fifty thousand chemical substances that were in commercial use in the mid-1980s. National Research Council, Toxicity Testing—Strategies to Determine Needs and Priorities (1984).

197. *See, e.g., In re* "Agent Orange" Prods. Liab. Litig., 611 F. Supp. 1223, 1231 (E.D.N.Y. 1985) (epidemiological studies in that case are "the only useful studies having any bearing on causation").

198. Ferebee v. Chevron Chem. Co., 736 F.2d 1529, 1535–36 (D.C. Cir.), *cert. denied,* 469 U.S. 1062 (1984). *Accord* Christophersen v. Allied-Signal Corp., 902 F.2d 362 (5th Cir. 1990) (absence of epidemiological studies showing statistically significant link between colon cancer and exposure to nickel or cadmium fumes does not render expert's opinion on causation sufficiently unreliable as to warrant exclusion);

Wells v. Ortho Pharmaceutical Corp., 788 F.2d 741, 745 (11th Cir. 1986). *But see* Brock v. Merrell Dow Pharmaceuticals, 874 F.2d 307 (5th Cir.), *modified,* 884 F.2d 166 (5th Cir. 1989) (absent statistically significant epidemiological proof that Bendectin is human teratogen, plaintiff's proof that the drug caused child's birth defects held insufficient), *cert. denied,* 110 S. Ct. 1511 (1990).

199. *See, e.g., Ferebee,* 736 F.2d at 1535–36 (finding that "a cause-effect relationship need not be clearly established by animal or epidemiological studies before a doctor can testify that, in his opinion, such a relationship exists"); *see also Christophersen,* 902 F.2d at 366–67; Longmore v. Merrell Dow Pharmaceuticals, 737 F. Supp. 1177 (D. Idaho 1990) (declining to follow District of Columbia Circuit, First Circuit, and Fifth Circuit and finding that lack of epidemiological studies showing link between Bendectin and birth defects did not require entry of summary judgment as plaintiffs could show by chemical analysis and animal studies there could be a link); 1 Nuclear Accident Report, *supra* note 3, at 109–14 (discussing alternative approaches to causation such as "probability of causation" method, in which causation is attributed based on standardized characteristics such as age at time of exposure and manifestation, level of exposure, type of cancer, latency period, etc.).

200. *See, e.g.,* Allen v. United States, 588 F. Supp. 247 (D. Utah 1984), *rev'd on other grounds,* 816 F.2d 1417 (10th Cir. 1987) (reversing burden of proof once it was established that radiation exposure was substantial factor in inducing certain plaintiffs' diseases), *cert. denied,* 484 U.S. 1004 (1988); *see also* Richard Delgado, Beyond Sindell: Relaxation of Cause-in-Fact Rules for Indeterminate Plaintiffs, 70 Calif. L. Rev. 881 (1982) (favoring shifting burden to defendants and making recovery proportional to probability of causation).

201. *See, e.g.,* Steve Gold, Note, Causation in Toxic Torts: Burdens of Proof, Standards of Persuasion, and Statistical Evidence, 96 Yale L.J. 376 (1986).

202. For instance, one court adopted a "duration and intensity" theory requiring that the plaintiff only show that the "aggravation of the disease or . . . the exposure was of such duration and intensity that it generally causes the disease in question, even though actual causation or aggravation cannot be established in the claimant's case." Caudle-Hyatt, Inc. v. Mixon, 220 Va. 495, 500, 260 S.E.2d 193, 196 (1979) (asbestos); *see also* Ora Fred Harris, Toxic Tort Litigation and the Causation Element: Is There Any Hope of Reconciliation?, 40 Sw. L.J. 909, 938 (1986) (discussing duration and intensity theory); Ronald B. Lansing, The Motherless Calf, Aborted Cow Theory of Cause, 15 Envtl. L. 1 (1984) (advocating abandonment of causation requirement in favor of "consistency" rule).

203. David Rosenberg, The Causal Connection in Mass Exposure

Cases: A "Public Law" Vision of the Tort System, 97 Harv. L. Rev. 849, 862-66 (1984); *see also* 1 Nuclear Accident Report, *supra* note 3, at 110 (discussing proportionate recovery; "where proof falls short of a preponderance of the evidence, but the increased risk brought about by exposure to a particular toxin exceeds some threshold value . . . recovery is allowed in proportion to the increased risk").

204. For a critique of and elaboration on Rosenberg's technique, *see* Steve Gold, Note, Causation in Toxic Torts, 96 Yale L.J. 376, 397–401 (1986).

205. Causation of a specific disease was also discarded in the DDT settlement. *See* Francis E. McGovern, DDT Settlement Fund (paper presented before Conference on Mass Settlement of Mass Torts, Duke University, Apr. 1989) (settlement of DDT exposure class action litigation in Alabama compensated class members on basis of exposure alone rather than requiring diagnosis of designated specific harm linked to DDT exposure; those with higher exposure as measured by higher levels of DDT in their tissue were compensated at comparably higher rate).

206. For a general discussion of these new theories, *see* Arvin Maskin, Overview and Update of Emerging Damage Theories in Toxic Tort Litigation (Mar. 1990) (copy on file with University of Illinois Law Review). Much of the following text is based on this paper. *See also* 1 Nuclear Accident Report, *supra* note 3, at 107–14.

207. "Off-the-record" interviews with various experts and members of the bar by the author.

208. *See generally* Note, Claim Preclusion in Modern Latent Disease Cases: A Proposal for Allowing Second Suits, 103 Harv. L. Rev. 1989 (1990).

209. For example, according to leading epidemiological studies, approximately 15 percent of asbestosis sufferers later contract mesothelioma of the pleura—a cancer of the lining of the lungs. Irving J. Selikoff, Jacob Churg, & E. Cuyler Hammond, Relation between Exposure to Asbestos and Mesothelioma, 272 New Eng. J. Med. 560, 562 (1965).

210. A number of courts have found that claim preclusion applies in these "second injury" situations. *See, e.g.,* Graffagnino v. Fibreboard Corp., 776 F.2d 1307, 1308 (5th Cir. 1985) ("[E]xposure to asbestos can give rise to only a single cause of action for all injuries that are caused by that exposure, whether or not all the injuries have become manifest at the time the cause of action accrues."); Gideon v. Johns-Manville Sales Corp., 761 F.2d 1129, 1137 (5th Cir. 1985) ("[Plaintiff] could not split his cause of action and recover damages for asbestosis, then later sue for damages caused by such other pulmonary disease as might develop, then still later sue for cancer should cancer appear.").

211. *See, e.g.,* Silkwood v. Kerr-McGee Corp., 667 F.2d 908 (10th Cir. 1981) (applying Okla. law), *rev'd on other grounds,* 464 U.S. 615

(1984); Westrom v. Kerr-McGee Chemical Corp., No. 82-C-2034 (N.D. Ill. Oct. 4, 1983) (LEXIS, Genfed library, Dist. file) (Ill. law); Bennett v. Mallinckrodt, Inc., 698 S.W.2d 854 (Mo. Ct. App. 1985) (Mo. law), *cert. denied*, 476 U.S. 1176 (1986).

212. *See, e.g.,* Fusaro v. Porter-Hayden Co., 145 Misc. 2d 911, 917, 548 N.Y.S.2d 856, 859 (Sup. Ct. 1989) (New York allows recovery in increased risk claims only where that risk is put at greater than 50 percent), *aff'd,* 170 A.D.2d 239 (1st Dept. 1991); *see also* Sterling v. Velsicol Chem. Corp., 855 F.2d 1188, 1204 (6th Cir. 1988) (predicted future disease must be medically reasonably certain to follow from existing present injury); Jackson v. Johns-Manville Sales Corp., 781 F.2d 394, 412 (5th Cir.) (where jury found on basis of ample supporting evidence that plaintiff would "probably" contract cancer recovery for cancer itself was permissible), *cert. denied,* 478 U.S. 1022 (1986); Laswell v. Brown, 683 F.2d 261, 269 (8th Cir. 1982) (rejecting increased risk of disease and genetic damage claim of children of former servicemen exposed to radiation during nuclear bomb tests where claim was based on mere possibility of some future consequence), *cert. denied,* 459 U.S. 1210 (1983); Wilson v. Johns-Manville Sales Corp., 684 F.2d 111, 119 & n.44 (D.C. Cir. 1982) (traditional American rule requires proof that damage is more likely than not to occur); *cf.* Restatement (Second) of Torts § 912 comment e (1979) (recovery for harm that may result in future depends on establishing a "probability" that the harm will ensue); Pollock v. Johns-Manville Sales Corp., 686 F. Supp. 489, 492 (D.N.J. 1988) (precluding claim where expert testified that plaintiff had 43 percent chance of developing cancer as result of asbestos exposure because 43 percent does not rise to "more likely than not" standard). *But see* Valori v. Johns-Manville Sales Corp., No. 82-2686 (D.N.J. Dec. 11, 1985) (plaintiff allowed to proceed to jury for risk of contracting cancer where he offered statistical evidence that he was member of a class of which 43 percent would contract cancer).

213. In applying a "second-injury" rule to damage claims brought by a plaintiff who had contracted mesothelioma subsequent to filing suit for asbestosis, New York State Supreme Court Justice Helen E. Freedman wrote:

> It is precisely because courts have rejected claims by asbestos victims for increased risk of cancer on the ground that they are too speculative that the right to recover independently should a second injury develop has been recognized in other jurisdictions. It would be unfair to prohibit claims for increased risk of cancer for asbestosis sufferers and at the same time, hold that failure to bring a suit against any or all defendants when a plaintiff is suffering from asbestosis acts as a time bar to a future cancer claim. To ameliorate that potential

unfairness, it has been held that "the time to commence litigation does not begin to run on a separate and distinct disease until that disease becomes manifest."

Fusaro v. Porter-Hayden Co., 145 Misc. 2d 911, 917, 548 N.Y.S.2d 856, 859–60 (Sup. Ct. 1989) (quoting Wilson v. Johns-Manville Sales Corp., 684 F.2d 111, 112 (D.C. Cir. 1982)).

214. Consultants to the American Law Institute recently endorsed tort recovery for increased risk, stating that "[j]udicial refusal to treat risk as injury frustrates compensation and deterrence objectives." 2 Compensation and Liability, *supra* note 3, at 440.

215. *See, e.g.,* McAdams v. Eli Lilly & Co., 638 F. Supp. 1173, 1178 (N.D. Ill. 1986) (in DES case, showing of present bodily injury required for fear of cancer claim); Cathcart v. Keen Indus. Insulation, 324 Pa. Super. 123, 152, 471 A.2d 493, 508 (1984) (claim that wife "undoubtedly ingested" asbestos fibers when laundering husband's clothes was not sufficient where plaintiff demonstrated no physical manifestations of disease; "some physical injury or some medically-identifiable effect linked to her exposure to asbestos particles" is a prerequisite for recovery for emotional distress).

216. *Compare* Herber v. Johns-Manville Corp., 785 F.2d 79, 83–84 (3d Cir. 1986) (pleural thickening sufficient injury to support "fear of cancer" claim) *with* Webb v. Pfizer Inc., No. C28-32211 (S.D. Ohio Apr. 21, 1989) (fear of cancer claim rejected where only physical manifestation of injury was pleural thickening) and Burns v. Jaquays Mining Corp., 156 Ariz. 375, 377, 752 P.2d 28, 30 (Ariz. App. 1987) (pleural plaques and thickening deemed noncompensable).

217. *See, e.g.,* Laxton v. Orkin Exterminating Co., 639 S.W.2d 431 (Tenn. 1982) (ingestion by homeowners of "an indefinite amount" of contaminated water constituted sufficient physical injury to support award for mental distress); *cf.* Shields v. Eli Lilly & Co., 895 F.2d 1463 (D.C. Cir. 1990) (allowing case of DES-cancer daughter to go to jury even though there was no direct evidence of in utero exposure to drug); Sholtis v. American Cyanamid Co., 238 N.J. Super. 8, 568 A.2d 1196 (App. Div. 1989) (describing "frequency, regularity and proximity" test designed to focus on cumulative effects of the exposure).

218. *See, e.g.,* Rabb v. Orkin Exterminating Co., 677 F. Supp. 424 (D.S.C. 1987) (evidence of plaintiffs' fears properly excluded where plaintiffs failed to offer proof that they feared a specific disease). *But see* Stites v. Sundstrand Heat Transfer, Inc., 660 F. Supp. 1516 (W.D. Mich. 1987) (proof of definite concrete fears of acquiring cancer as result of toxic chemicals in water not necessary to allow factual issue to go to fact finder).

219. *See, e.g., In re* Moorenovich, 634 F. Supp. 634 (D. Me. 1986).

220. *See, e.g.,* Pollock v. Johns-Manville Sales Corp., 686 F. Supp. 489 (D.N.J. 1988).

221. *See, e.g., Laxton,* 639 S.W.2d at 434 (court found there was "sufficient 'injury' to plaintiffs from [pesticide contamination] to justify a recovery for their natural concern and anxiety for the welfare of themselves and their infant children"). *But see* Potter v. Firestone Tire & Rubber Co., No. 81723 (Cal. Sup. Ct. Dec. 31, 1987) (although court awarded plaintiffs damages for their fear of cancer claims, it rejected claims of emotional distress caused by increased risk of cancer in their children), *rev'd,* 863 P.2d 795 (Cal. 1993).

222. Arvin Maskin, Overview and Update of Emerging Damage Theories in Toxic Tort Litigation 40 (Mar. 1990) (copy on file with University of Illinois Law Review).

223. Sterling v. Velsicol Chem. Corp., 855 F.2d 1188 (6th Cir. 1988).

224. *See, e.g.,* Ayers v. Township of Jackson, 202 N.J. Super. 106, 493 A.2d 1314 (App. Div. 1985), *aff'd in part, rev'd in part on other grounds,* 106 N.J. 557, 525 A.2d 287 (1987) (upholding jury award of over $5 million to residents for "impact to quality of their lives" during twenty months when they were deprived of running water).

225. *See, e.g., In re* Fernald Litig., No. C-1-85-0149, 1989 WL 267038 (S.D. Ohio Sep. 29, 1989) (in settling federal class action, Department of Energy agreed to make funds available for medical monitoring of residents living near uranium processing plant; fund would pay for periodic cancer screenings and long-term epidemiological study of residents who have suffered psychological disorder called "informed of radioactive exposure complex"); *Ayers,* 106 N.J. at 609, 525 A.2d at 314 ("The public health interest is served by a fund mechanism that encourages regular medical monitoring for victims of toxic exposure."); *see also* 1 Nuclear Accident Report, *supra* note 3, at 90–91 (recommending prepaid medical monitoring program as "the most sensible approach to compensating those who have been exposed to predetermined levels of radiation"). For a helpful critical analysis, *see* Sheila L. Birnbaum & Gary E. Drawford, Tests Set for Medical-Screening Damages, Nat'l L.J., Nov. 29, 1993, at 16.

226. Wide disagreement as to remedies continues to characterize discussions of tort policy. *See, e.g.,* Am. Bar Ass'n Tort & Ins. Practice Sec., Tort Law and the Public Interest (May 31–June 3, 1990 conference pamphlet).

227. More may be implicated than adopting substantive tort law changes. For example, Professor Judith Resnik suggests that it may be worth investigating the possibility of fostering—or compelling—a market in life and health insurance policies as a specific response to the indeterminate and uncertain illness problems. *See* Stuart A. Schlesinger & Edward J. Sanocki, The Duty to Recall Defective Products, N.Y. L.J.,

July 18, 1990, at 3 (arguing that separate duty exists under law to recall harmful products, and that failure to do so in response to a directive from agencies such as the FDA and Consumer Product Safety Commission gives rise to tort liability).

228. In general, the transaction fees and attorneys' fees in mass tort litigation—which one study of the asbestos litigation estimated to be close to 60 percent of every dollar spent for costs or awards—are unacceptably high. *Cf.* Mark Peterson, Giving Away Money: Comparative Comments on Claims Facilities (Rand Corporation) (Apr. 1989). *See generally* Lester Brickman, Contingent Fees without Contingencies, 37 UCLA L. Rev. 29, 102–11 (1989) (discussing the noncompetitive market for legal services in the sale of tort claims).

229. Judge Robert Parker, dealing with a vast number of asbestos cases, has attempted a large number of creative techniques for dealing with the problem, including mass trials and trials of specific issues using representative cases. *See, e.g.,* Cimino v. Raymark Indus., 751 F. Supp. 649, 653 (E.D. Tex. 1990) (describing three-phase trial procedures); *see also, e.g.,* Thomas Willging, Trends in Asbestos Litigation (Federal Judicial Center 1987) (reporting on pretrial and trial management in various federal courts).

230. *See, e.g., In re* Joint E. & S. Dists. Asbestos Litig. (Loper v. Eagle-Picher Indus.; Liebson v. Raymark Indus.; Schaefer v. Celotex Corp.), 134 F.R.D. 32 (E.D.N.Y. & S.D.N.Y. 1990) (order appointing special master to hold hearings to determine whether limited fund exists); *In re* National Asbestos Litig., Nos. 1:90-CV-11,000, 1:90-CV-5,000 (Aug. 10, 1990) (1990 WL 135758 Westlaw, Allfeds library) (joint order issued by Judges Parker (E.D. Tex.) and Lambros (N.D. Ohio) (attempting to consolidate multidistrict asbestos cases into a Rule 23(b)(3) "settlement class," a Rule 23(b)(1)(B) litigation class, and excluding up to six "limited fund" defendants who may be certified as a class in Eastern District of New York), *vacated in part on jurisdictional grounds sub nom. In re* Allied-Signal, 915 F.2d 190 (6th Cir. 1990) (nullifying national order to extent that it was filed in the Northern District of Ohio and consolidated any Northern District of Ohio cases).

231. *See* Stephen B. Burbank, Of Rules and Discretion: The Supreme Court, Federal Rules and Common Law, 63 Notre Dame L. Rev. 693, 715 (1988) (litigants and courts need more guidance than federal rules, local rules, standing orders, and operating procedures provide; "[t]oo often they must turn to the judge herself" to find it) (citing Stephen B. Burbank, The Chancellor's Boot, 54 Brook. L. Rev. 31 (1988)).

232. *See supra* note 3 (discussing legislative proposals) and chapter 10, *infra*.

233. *See* 11 U.S.C. § 524(e) (1988).

234. Here the district court and affirming appellate court did not strictly abide by the Bankruptcy Code, which, for instance, does not provide for resolution of related litigation such as that brought directly by the plaintiff class against Robins's insurer, Aetna, whom plaintiffs charged was a joint tortfeasor. Appellate courts apparently feel that matters of equity—avoiding the burden to the courts and parties of reopening tens if not hundreds of thousands of claims and the value of closure in general—supersede the strict requirements of the Code and even of individualized due process rights. *See In re* A. H. Robins, Inc., 880 F.2d 694 (4th Cir.), *cert. denied,* 493 U.S. 959 (1989); *see also* Kane v. Johns-Manville Corp., 843 F.2d 636, 641–47 (2d Cir. 1988) (approving Manville bankruptcy reorganization plan and declining to adjudicate rights of future claimants).

235. Kenneth R. Feinberg, The Dalkon Shield Claimants Trust Claims Resolution Facility (Apr. 1989) (paper prepared for Duke Law School Mass Tort Settlement Conference). One should note, however, that some have faulted the A. H. Robins Plan for delaying paying out claims and "intimidating" some women from pursuing serious bona fide claims in the face of the deterrents erected to pursuing the litigation option.

236. *See In re* "Agent Orange" Prod. Liab. Litig., 100 F.R.D. 718, 722 (E.D.N.Y. 1983) (order certifying class), *mandamus denied,* 725 F.2d 858 (2d Cir.), *cert. denied,* 465 U.S. 1067 (1984).

237. For discussions of these problems and proposed solutions, *see, e.g., In re* Fibreboard Corp., 893 F.2d 706, 707, 711 (5th Cir. 1990) (noting that pendency of five thousand asbestos cases in circuit and predictions that filings will continue at same steady rate until the year 2000 constitute a crisis in judicial system); *In re* A. H. Robins Co., 880 F.2d 709, 725–27 (4th Cir.) (noting that mass tort suits present most important and difficult management problem facing federal court system), *cert. denied,* 493 U.S. 959 (1989); Judicial Improvements Act of 1990, Pub. L. No. 101-650, 104 Stat. 5089 (1990) (intended to reduce delay and expense in civil justice system); Multiparty, Multiforum Jurisdiction Act of 1990, H.R. 3406, 101st Cong., 2d Sess., 136 Cong. Rec. H3116-17 (1990); Report of the Federal Courts Study Committee 44–46 (1990); Alvin B. Rubin, Mass Torts and Litigation Disasters, 20 Ga. L. Rev. 429, 432 (1986) (noting human and economic costs of mass tort claims affect all of society); Spencer Williams, Mass Tort Class Actions, Going, Going, Gone?, 98 F.R.D. 323, 324 (1983) (state and federal trial judges being inundated); *see also* Comm'n on Mass Torts, *supra* note 9 (offering recommendations for dealing in fair and efficient manner with mass tort problem); Am. Law Inst., Complex Litigation Project Tentative Draft No. 1 (Apr. 14, 1989); Dep't of Justice, *supra* note 16.

238. *See, e.g.,* Dep't of Justice, *supra* note 16, at 54; George L. Priest, The Current Insurance Crisis and Modern Tort Law, 96 Yale L.J. 1521 (1987).

239. *See* Brown v. Superior Court, 44 Cal. 3d 1049, 1064, 751 P.2d 470, 479, 245 Cal. Rptr. 412, 421 (1988) (in DES case finding that strict liability should not be applied to pharmaceutical industry court cites reports of lifesaving vaccinations being withdrawn from market because of cost of liability litigation and unavailability of insurance); *see also* Jay Angoff, Insuring against Competition: How the McCarran-Ferguson Act Raises Prices and Profits in the Property-Casualty Insurance Industry, 5 Yale J. on Reg. 397, 413 (1988) (citing Insurance Information Institute's advice that insurance executives and agents tell media and policyholders that "insurers have no recourse but to cut back on liability insurance until improvements in the civil justice system will create a fairer distribution of liability, reduce the number of lawsuits, and create a climate in which insurance can operate more predictably").

240. *See, e.g.,* A Product Dead-Ended by Liability Fears, N.Y. Times, May 19, 1990, at A50 (Monsanto Company decides against producing fiber heralded as alternative to asbestos because of fear of "costly and unwarranted lawsuits").

241. *See* George L. Priest, The Current Insurance Crisis and Modern Tort Law, 96 Yale L.J. 1521 (1987).

242. For example, plaintiffs are being discouraged from bringing suits through Rule 11 sanctions. *See* Report of the Third Circuit Task Force on Federal Rule of Civil Procedure 11 (finding that Rule 11 sanctions are awarded almost three times as often against plaintiffs as against defendants and nine times as often against civil rights plaintiffs as against civil rights defendants); *see also* Cooter & Gell v. Hartmarx Corp., 496 U.S. 384 (1990) (holding that district court could impose Rule 11 sanctions after plaintiff voluntarily dismissed action). Advocates of restricted access also support limiting discovery, toughening summary judgment standards, stricter pleading requirements, the abolition of pendent jurisdiction in many cases, and increased standing barriers. *See* Disasters, *supra* note 3, at 2 & nn.1–7.

243. *See* Report of the Federal Courts Study Committee (1990).

244. *See* Robert L. Carter, The Federal Rules of Civil Procedure as a Vindicator of Civil Rights, 137 U. Pa. L. Rev. 2179, 2184–90 (1989). *See generally* James S. Liebman, Implementing *Brown* in the Nineties: Political Reconstruction, Liberal Recollection, and Litigatively Enforced Legislative Reform, 76 U. Va. L. Rev. 349 (1990) (discussing generally the disfavor in which so-called "countermajoritarian" solutions to systemic problems have fallen).

245. *See* A. Leon Higginbotham, Federal Jurisdiction: The Essential Guarantor of Human Rights, in *The Federal Appellate Judiciary in the*

21st Century 57, 61 (1989) (arguing that it is essential that federal courts retain their "human rights agenda" by retaining jurisdiction over civil rights and social security cases).

246. *See generally* Compensation and Liability, *supra* note 3.

247. The transcript of the oral argument before the Fifth Circuit of defendant's petition for mandamus decertifying an asbestos personal injury class certified by Judge Parker is instructive. One of the panel members observes:

> There's something being taken away from this. This is I'm sure an old-fashioned notion about jury trials, about what's being taken away when you take the person out of the courtroom. The individual plaintiff is not there. The questions have to do with causation . . . [but] [t]he jury never sees the individual. These jury-like judgments that we want from the jury are really sort of taken away. They're looking at dry numbers and not people and not looking at causation in this individual and making judgments about people. And I have a problem with that. . . .

Transcript of Oral Argument, *In re* Fibreboard Corp., 893 F.2d 706 (5th Cir. 1990) (Nos. 89-4937, 89-4945, & 90-4015).

In response to the Fifth Circuit's mandamus writ, Judge Parker issued an order, noting:

> This Order is a testament to failure—failure of the federal court system after ten years of trials and appeals to find a way to avoid the unacceptable costs of this repetitive litigation. . . . Yet another jury will now be asked to determine whether the same old products are unreasonably dangerous when all the world already knows the answer. We will, then, present to a succession of juries, the same witnesses, time after time, to explain the effect of asbestos fibers on the body and to show how the various disease processes result from exposure. We will repeat time and again which products were used [where]. . . .
>
> . . . .
>
> The Court's task appears to be insurmountable. However, the absence of resources to provide fair and efficient dispute resolution for these cases does not relieve the Court of its responsibility; these cases will not simply go away. The problem at hand is analogous to that where an East Texas farmer is compelled to hitch a Georgia stock to an old mule and replow the same row time and again while his neighbor uses a diesel tractor and jet airplanes fly overhead. Just as the farmer knows that the row is too long and that the mule won't last, this Court knows that many class members will not live to see

the end of this controversy. The effect [of the Court of Appeals ruling] will be to deny access to the courts for a significant portion of the class.

Cimino v. Raymark Indus., No. B-86-0456-CA, 1989 WL 253889 (E.D. Tex. Jan. 29, 1990) (order denying defendants' motion for a continuance) (copy on permanent file with University of Illinois Law Review).

248. See generally Deborah R. Hensler, Resolving Mass Toxic Torts: Myths and Realities, 1989 U. Ill. L. Rev. 89, 91–92 (1989) (discussing E. A. Lind et al., The Perception of Justice (1989) (Rand Corporation Institute for Civil Justice); see also In re N. Dist. of Cal., Dalkon Shield IUD Prods. Liab. Litig. (Abed v. A. H. Robins), 693 F.2d 847 (9th Cir. 1982) (class actions in mass torts prevent plaintiffs from selecting their own counsel and forum), cert. denied, 459 U.S. 1171 (1983).

249. See generally David Rosenberg, Class Actions for Mass Torts: Doing Individual Justice by Collective Means, 62 Ind. L.J. 561, 594 (1987) (arguing that mass tort class actions provide "better opportunities for achieving individual justice than does the tort system's private law, disaggregative processes").

250. See Deborah R. Hensler, Resolving Mass Toxic Torts, 1989 U. Ill. L. Rev. 89, 92–97 (1989).

251. See id. at 96.

252. See id. at 99 ("most frequently cited objective of lay litigants in adjudicatory proceedings was to 'tell my side of the story'").

253. Id. at 98 (citing James S. Kakalik, P. Ebener, W. Felstiner, G. Haggstrom, & M. Shanley, Variation in Asbestos Litigation Compensation and Expenses 19 (1984) (Rand Corporation, Institute for Civil Justice)).

254. See, e.g., Charles R. Richey, Rule 16: A Survey and Some Considerations for the Bench and Bar, 126 F.R.D. 599, 604 (1989) ("[C]ourts cannot always rely on attorneys to fairly represent to their clients the merits of a particular settlement.").

255. United States v. Leasehold Interest in 121 Nostrand Avenue, 760 F. Supp. 1015 (E.D.N.Y. 1991) (matriarchy resisting dispossession under drug laws; this form of family organization is becoming prevalent).

CHAPTER 10

1. This chapter is largely based on A View from the Judiciary, 13 Cardozo L. Rev. 1957 (1992), which in turn was based on remarks at the Administrative Conference of the United States, October 31, 1991. Permission to reprint has been granted by the Cardozo Law Review.

2. *See* Accident Compensation Act, No. 43 (N.Z. Stat. 1972) (amended 1990). This Act introduced a comprehensive no-fault accident compensation scheme in substitution for the previously existing common law rights and workers' compensation legislation and created the Accident Compensation Commission (now Corporation, as amended in 1988) to administer that scheme.

There is much to be learned from a comparative study of product liability. Most systems cannot be directly transposed because of differences in social, political, and legal systems and historical events requiring modifications if portions of another system are to be imported. *See* Geraint Howells, *Comparative Product Liability* (1993). *See also, e.g.*, Germany to Pay Victims in AIDS Blood Scandal, N.Y. Times, Nov. 13, 1993, at A6 (373 known persons were infected with AIDS as a result of negligence of a private company; those HIV positive would be paid by government funds $588 per month regardless of financial need, and those who developed AIDS would receive twice that amount).

Among the many excellent reviews of proposals to reform liability law are: William K. Jones, Strict Liability for Hazardous Enterprises, the Center for Law and Economics Studies, Columbia University School of Law, Working Paper No. 85 (1992); Mark Geistfeld, Towards A More General Theory of Products Liability Reform, The Center for Law and Economic Studies, Columbia University School of Law, Working Paper No. 77 (1992); Jules L. Coleman, *Risks and Wrongs* (1992).

The most important study is the two-volume American Law Institute, Reporters' Study on Enterprise Responsibility for Personal Injury (1991). *See* the extensive comments and analysis of the study in articles by many of the leaders in the field of torts, Tort Reform Symposium: Perspectives on the American Law Institute's Reporters' Study on Enterprise Responsibility for Personal Injury, 30 San Diego L. Rev. 213 ff (1993). It contains substantial references to other studies.

3. 335 U.S. 469, 69 S. Ct. 213 (1948).

4. *Id.* at 486, 69 S. Ct. at 223 (1948).

5. For a description of the organization of the Trust, *see In re* Joint E. & S. Dists. Asbestos Litig. (Findley v. Blinken), 129 B.R. 710, 767 (E. & S.D.N.Y. 1991).

6. Lester Brickman, The Asbestos Claims Management Act of 1991: A Proposal to the United States Congress, 13 Cardozo L. Rev. 1891, 1895 (1992).

7. For an estimate of asbestos exposure nationwide, *see* Paul Brodeur, *Outrageous Misconduct: The Asbestos Industry on Trial* 120 (1985) ("Millions of unsuspecting American workers—four and a half million men and women in the wartime shipyards alone—were left to undergo exposure to dangerously high levels of asbestos dust as they applied insulation products. . . .").

8. N.Y. Civ. Prac. L. & R. 214 (McKinney 1962), *amended by* N.Y. Civ. Prac. L. & R. 214-c (McKinney 1990).

9. For injury caused by the latent effects of exposure to any substance, the three-year statute of limitations is computed either from the date of actual discovery or the date the plaintiff should have discovered the injury through the exercise of reasonable diligence. N.Y. Civ. Prac. L. & R. 214-c (McKinney 1990).

10. *See, e.g.,* N.Y. Gen. Oblig. Law § 15-108 (McKinney 1990); N.Y. Civ. Prac. L. & R. 1601-02 (McKinney 1990), as applied in *In re* E. & S. Dists. Asbestos Litig., 772 F. Supp. 1380 (E. & S.D.N.Y. 1991) (molding verdicts into judgments in the Brooklyn Navy Yard cases), *aff'd in part, rev'd in part and sub nom. In re* Brooklyn Navy Yard Asbestos Litig., 971 F.2d 831 (2d Cir. 1992).

11. For a discussion of some of the moral conceptions of tort law as a nonutilitarian exercise seemingly mandating individual adjudicators of rights see, e.g., Stephen R. Perry, The Mixed Conception of Corrective Justice, 15 Harv. J. of Law and Public Policy 917 (1993) (discussing the views of Jules Coleman, Ernest Weinrib, and Perry); Stephen R. Perry, The Moral Foundations of Tort Law, 77 Iowa L. Rev. 449 (1992).

12. *See generally In re* Joint E. & S. Dists. Asbestos Litig. (Findley v. Blinken), 129 B.R. 710, 734–47 (E. & S.D.N.Y. 1991) (discussing manufacturers' and management's coverups and failure to warn workers of known dangers of asbestos exposure), *vacated on other grounds,* 982 F.2d 721 (2d. Cir. 1992), *modified,* 993 F.2d 7 (2d Cir. 1993). *See also* Paul Brodeur, *Outrageous Misconduct: The Asbestos Industry on Trial* (discussing Johns-Manville's and Raybestos-Manhattan's awareness of asbestos hazards and the deliberate efforts to conceal the hazards from workers and the public).

13. Findley v. Blinken, 129 B.R. at 908. Radiation injuries and other harms caused by "experiments" conducted by the government on people raise problems similar to those of Agent Orange. A schedule of payments for diseases which might have been caused by these activities similar to that for veterans claiming Agent Orange injuries as well as medical monitoring by the government seems sensible. No litigation should be required, and the government should concede liability. *See, e.g.,* U.S. Details Fees Paid to Fight Radiation Suits, N.Y. Times, Jan. 4, 1994, at A10; White House Criticizes G.O.P. on Radiation Data, N.Y. Times, Jan. 4, 1994, at A10; Pay Studied for Radiation Victims, Newsday, Jan. 4, 1994, at 4. In a sense these victims, though civilians, are veterans of the cold war.

14. *See* Ten Federal Judges Agree on Plan to Consolidate Asbestos Lawsuits, N.Y. Times, Aug. 11, 1990, at A1.

15. Judith Resnik, From "Cases" to "Litigation," 54 Law & Contemp. Probs., Summer 1991, at 5, 65. *See also* Myron J. Bromberg &

Anastasia P. Slovinski, Pay or Play in Mass Torts: Alleviate Backlogs with an Expanded System or Joinder Methods, 45 Rutgers L. Rev. 371 414–15 (1993). The idea that the tort system gives each person a day in court in mass cases is chimerical. Each person does not have a day in court when thousands of cases are settled at a time and much less than 1 percent go to trial. *Cf.* Robert G. Bone, Rethinking the "Day in Court" Ideal and Nonparty Preclusion, 67 N.Y.U. L. Rev. 193 (1992) (preclusion rules should be broader); Judge S. Arthur Spiegel, Settlement of Multidistrict Litigation, Speech at 26th Transferee Judge Conference, Oct. 5, 1993 (unpublished) (all his cases were settled, as was the case with almost every transferee judge).

16. *See, e.g.,* E. Allan Lind et al., The Perception of Justice: Tort Litigants' Views of Trial, Court-Annexed Arbitration, and Judicial Settlement Conferences (Rand Corp. Series No. R-3708-ICJ, 1989).

17. *Cf.* Jack B. Weinstein & Eileen B. Hershenov, The Effect of Equity on Mass Tort Law, 1991 U. Ill. L. Rev. 269, 284.

18. *Compare* Lester Brickman, The Asbestos Claims Management Act of 1991, 13 Cardozo L. Rev. 1891, 1907 (1992) (tit. I, § 103) *with* Mark A. Peterson, Giving Away Money: Comparative Comments on Claims Resolution Facilities, 53 Law & Contemp. Probs., Autumn 1990, at 113.

19. *In re* "Agent Orange," Ivy v. Diamond Shamrock Chemical Co., 781 F. Supp. 902 (E.D.N.Y. 1991), *aff'd,* 996 F.2d 1425 (2d. Cir. 1993), *cert. denied,* 114 S. Ct. 1125 (1994).

20. *See In re* Joint E. & S. Dists. Asbestos Litig. (Findley v. Blinken), 129 B.R. 710, 863–69, 956–69 (E. & S.D.N.Y. 1991).

21. *See generally* Samuel Issacharoff, Administering Damage Awards in Mass-Tort Litigation, 10 Rev. Litig. 463 (1991) (examining the procedures and circumstances for determining and allocating damages on a class basis and proposing a procedural mechanism which would establish liability on a classwide basis).

22. *See* Lester Brickman, The Asbestos Litigation Crisis: Is There a Need for an Administrative Alternative? 13 Cardozo L. Rev. 1819, 1834–40 (1992); Findley v. Blinken, 129 B.R. at 863 (E. & S.D.N.Y 1991); *see also* Lester Brickman, Contingent Fees without Contingencies: *Hamlet* without the Prince of Denmark?, 37 UCLA L. Rev. 29 (1989) (discussing the legitimacy of contingent attorney fees); Lester Brickman, Michael J. Horwitz, & Jeffrey O'Connell, A Procedure to Enforce Ethical Standards and More Promptly Compensate Personal Injury Claimants Represented by Contingent Counsel (1993).

23. Speech of Judge S. Arthur Spiegel, Settlement of Multidistrict Litigation, 26th Transferee Judges Conference, Oct. 5, 1993:

With the recognition of claims for emotional distress based on the fear of future ailments, fear of cancer (or cancer phobia), along with the possibility of punitive damages in instances of egregious conduct, an entire industry can be wiped out. Thus, certification of a defendant class should probably be given very serious consideration as a device to save an industry that created a risk potentially placing it in a precarious situation, where the industry produces other safe products of value to society. With the certification of a defendant class, wide ranging settlement agreements can be reached which provide for medical monitoring, funding for research and treatment, and damage awards similar to awards in workers compensation. Such innovative settlement agreements may save an industry before it is destroyed by plaintiffs picking off one company at a time through punitive damage awards. This would operate both to save the defendant class from industry-wide devastation, while at the same time forcing it to face the facts of its collective responsibility, and to create a pool of funds of such magnitude to realistically cover potential losses over time but put a cap on recoveries so that the industry can survive. I suspect that is the philosophy behind the breast implant reported potential settlement. Would that such an approach had been considered when the asbestos litigation began—a number of companies which produced many other products, as well as asbestos products, have gone "belly up," as they were hit by huge punitive damage awards defending their asbestos activity.

The mere fact of settlement discussions may have a large effect on the market value of a stock. *See, e.g.,* W. Kip Viscusi, *Reforming Products Liability,* 164–65 (1993). The SEC properly insists on publicly announced settlement negotiations because of their possible use by insiders, but the premature announcement creates conflicts among litigants and makes settlement more difficult. *See, e.g.,* Dow Corning Offers to Settle over Implants, Wall St. J., Sept. 10, 1993, at A3; Wall Street Welcomes Settlement Proposal, N.Y. Times, Sept. 10, 1993, at A16; Fund Proposed for Settling Suits Over Breast Implants, N.Y. Times, Sept. 10, 1993, at A16. A number of plaintiffs' attorneys objected privately to me that announcement of settlement in the breast implant case raised the hopes of their clients excessively, making it more difficult to "sell them" on a limited fund. Dow Corning Corporation was bound by its obligation to the market to publicly unveil its proposed settlement plan. *See* Big Cases May End in Small Settlements, N.Y. Times, Week in Review, Sept. 26, 1993, at 6; Andrew Blum, Some Grumble Over Implant Pact, Nat. L.J., Oct. 18, 1993, at 3.

24. Black Lung Benefits Act, Pub. L. No. 91-173, tit. IV, § 401, 83 Stat. 792 (1969) (codified as amended at 30 U.S.C. §§ 901–945 (1988)).

25. National Childhood Vaccine Injury Act of 1986, Pub. L. No. 99-

660, tit. III, § 301, 100 Stat. 3755, 3756 (1986) (codified at 42 U.S.C. § 300aa (1986)).

26. The basic thrust of tort reform in the United States assumes reliance upon a tort rather than an administrative system. *See* Geraint Howells, *Comparative Product Liability* 223 (1993).

27. 880 F.2d 694 (4th Cir. 1989); 788 F.2d 994 (4th Cir. 1986); *see* Kenneth R. Feinberg, The Dalkon Shield Claimants Trust, 53 Law & Contemp. Probs., Autumn 1990, at 79, 101 (two actions were undertaken by defendant A. H. Robins Co. "that ultimately enabled it to achieve a comprehensive and final resolution of all the personal injury claims").

28. For a consideration of some of the special problems in connection with such a court, *see* P. Richter, Note, Considerations Relating to the Enactment of Venue Schemes as Applied to Specialty Courts, 93 Colum. L. Rev. 1738 (1993).

29. Warren W. Eginton, Judicial Activism: A Response to Legislative Inaction, 2 Products Liability L.J. 61 (1991).

30. For an excellent critique of both strict liability and tort reform trends in the United States and support of a regime of regulation and social insurance see Anita Bernstein, A Model of Products Liability Reform, 27 Val. U. Sch. of Law 637 (1993).

31. *See, e.g.,* Manufacturer Admits Selling Untested Devices for Heart, N.Y. Times, Oct. 16, 1993, at 1 ($61 million fine for at least one death and twenty-two emergency heart surgeries; after indictment, the company's chief executive resigned). *See also, e.g.,* Chemical Week, Oct. 6, 1993, at 5 (EPA fines Chevron Chemical $17 million for failure to file premanufacturer notifications for six chemicals); Settlement for $371 Million by Prudential Unit Expected, N.Y. Times, Oct. 1, 1993, at D1 (SEC settled with Prudential for more than one hundred individual investors in limited fraudulent partnerships); N.Y. Times, Oct. 22, 1993; Fraud Accord Has Prudential Phones Ringing, N.Y. Times, Oct. 23, 1993, at Y16; Limiting the Statute of Limitations, *id.* (statute of limitations waived by Prudential leaving open-ended liability). Since there need be no legal fees for plaintiffs, the net awards received will probably be greater than would have occurred in a class action suit. The transactional costs in saved litigation costs should be substantial.

32. W. Kip Viscusi, *Reforming Products Liability,* 213–14 (1993) (Ford Motor company underestimated value in its Pinto decision by a factor of ten).

33. *Id.* at 215. *Cf.* G.M. Pickup Case is Taken Over by the Secretary of Transportation, N.Y. Times, Nov. 19, 1993, at A18 (recall of trucks with dangerous gas tanks would cost $300 million to $1 billion; petition was by the Center for Auto Safety to the National Highway Safety Commission).

34. W. Kip Viscusi, *Reforming Products Liability* 66, 212–15 (1993);

Stephen Breyer, *Toward Effective Risk Regulation* (1993); *see also* Daniel Mazmanian & David Morell, *Beyond Superfailure, America's Toxic Policy for the 1990s* (1992); Paul Slovic, James H. Flynn, & Mark Layman, Perceived Risk, Trust and the Politics of Nuclear Waste, Science, Dec. 13, 1991, at 1603.

The question of whether our tort system inhibits our foreign trade by making our products noncompetitive does not respond to a single analysis. *See* Yale Law School Program in Civil Liability, Centers for Studies in Law, Economics, and Public Policy, George L. Priest, Lawyers, Liability, and Law Reform: Effects on American Economic Growth and Trade Competitiveness (1993), at 4–5 ("[there is] no adequate theory for measuring the effect of the magnitude of lawyers on economic growth . . . [F]or the U.S. and for most modern nations, the number of lawyers is probably insufficient, rather than excessive. . . . long tail liability for products manufactured years before will not generally affect current product prices in competitive markets.").

The dangerous inhibiting effect of overdeterrence in the area of drugs and implants is well known. *See, e.g.,* Implant Industry Is Facing Cutback by Top Suppliers, N.Y. Times, Apr. 25, 1994, at A1 ("Giants like DuPont and Dow Fear They'll Be Drawn into Product Liability Suites").

35. *See, e.g.,* 31 U.S.C. § 3730 (false claims); United States v. Halpen, 490 U.S. 435, 444 n.5; Dick v. Long Island Lighting Co., 710 F. Supp. 1485 (E.D.N.Y. 1989), *aff'd,* 912 F.2d 13 (2d Cir. 1990).

36. United States *ex rel.* Barajas v. Northrup Corp., 1993 5 F.3d 407, 410, n.9 (8th Cir. 1993).

37. Despite the huge costs to health from exposure to lead, government regulation, e.g., by elimination of lead from gasoline, is the effective way of dealing with the problem. Private suits are unlikely to work. *See, e.g.,* Joseph J. Ortego & Josh H. Kordisch, Lead Paint Cases Raise Causation Issues, Nat. L. J., Nov. 8, 1993, at 19.

38. *See* Geoffrey C. Hazard, Jr., Communitarian Ethics and Legal Justification, 59 U. Colo. L. Rev. 721, 724 (1988) ("[T]he possibilities for creative interpretation in American law are such that *every* American lawyer carries new law in his pen."). Hazard has described the paradox that

> there are things that work in practice even though they do not work in theory. One thing that works more or less in practice is the process of resolving fundamental issues of right and wrong on a day-to-day basis without a satisfactory theoretical basis for doing so. The courts perform this task, often being troubled and confused, but they get the job done somehow.

Id. at 740.

39. "What really matters is this, that the judge is under a duty, within the limits of his power of innovation, to maintain a relation between

law and morals, between the precepts of jurisprudence and those of reason and good conscience." Benjamin N. Cardozo, The Nature of the Judicial Process, 133–34 (1921).

APPENDIX

The law and facts with respect to mass litigation continue to develop rapidly. The following additional changes would have been made between sending the manuscript to the printer in April 1994 and correcting page proofs in late August of that year.

p. xiv. Add to articles: Jack B. Weinstein, The Effect of *Daubert* on the Work of Federal Trial Judges, 2 Shepard's Expert and Scientific Evidence 1 (1994).

The public continues to overestimate the precision and speed with which science can answer questions the law poses in specific cases requiring immediate decisions and to underestimate some of the technicians' errors, even where the basic science is established. *Cf.* Naftali Bendavid, DNA: What the Code Won't Unlock: In Search for Evidence, Our Faith in Science Can Lead Us Astray, Wash. Post, Aug. 13, 1994, at C3. The spate of articles and decisions following *Daubert* provides the law and the science communities with a new opportunity and reason for cooperating. Interdisciplinary work is essential if we are to deal effectively with the huge physical flow of new biological, ethical, and other problems requiring cooperation.

p. 20. In the Agent Orange case New Zealand and Australian veterans were part of the plaintiff class. Korean veterans are now seeking Agent Orange funds. In the breast implant cases women from abroad are now seeking part of the multibillion-dollar settlement made for the benefit of United States consumers. *See* Jeanne D. Cooper and Michael Unger, Implant Inequity, Foreign Women Outraged by $4.25 Billion U.S. Settlement, Newsday, July 24, 1994, at A7.

p. 57. The court's power to review communications to prevent the misleading of clients cannot be restricted by secrecy or privilege claims. The privilege is the client's, not the attorney's. For a discussion of the need for a second opt-out period because of misleading letters from attorneys to clients *see* Mealey's Litigation Reports, Asbestos, June 3, 1994, at 4.

p. 64. Binding future claimants presents serious legal and ethical problems. My own experiences suggest that the courts can evaluate fairness best if there is a strong independent representative of the future subclass as well as an independent special master or consultant involved in critical settlement negotiations and fairness hearings. In the Agent Orange case I was fortunate to have had the assistance of Special Masters David Shapiro and Kenneth R. Feinberg to represent future claimants' needs. In the Manville case Leslie G. Fagen represented the future claimants as their appointed attorney while Mark A. Peterson, under the title of Consultant to the Courts, acted in effect as a special master.

p. 72. Where there is a substantial interest beyond that of the immediate parties, withdrawal of an opinion is almost never warranted. Trial court, as opposed to appellate, decisions are more readily withdrawn. *Compare, e.g.,* IBM Credit Corporation v. United Home for Aged Hebrews, 848 F. Supp. 495 (S.D.N.Y.) (withdrawn) with Cardinal Chemical Co. v. Morton International, 113 S. Ct. 1967 (1993) (patent's effect on market place) and Manufacturers Hanover v. Yanakas, 7 F.3d 310 (2d Cir. 1993). Since the opinion is part of the record, it should remain in the file even though "withdrawn."

p. 74. Evidence in the Manville case indicates that legal fees to lawyers representing some 10,000 claimants in Maryland will probably run over half a billion dollars.

p. 174 n. 4. Stephen Breyer subsequently became a member of the Supreme Court of the United States.

p. 175 n. 8. *See also, e.g.,* Steven Garber, *Product Liability and the Economics of Pharmaceutical and Medical Devices* (Rand Institute for Justice 1993).

p. 175 n. 16. *See also* Andrew Blum, The Talk of ATLA: Class Megatorts, Nat. L.J., Aug. 8, 1994, at 6. Case by case disposition seems to me to be unsuitable for what may be many thousands of stress disorder cases. *See* Barnaby J. Feder, A Spreading Pain and Cries for Justice, N.Y. Times, June 3, 1994, Bus., at 1. The Court of Appeals disagrees and has required disaggregation of the cases. *See* In re Repetitive Stress Injury Litigation, 142 F.R.D. 584 (E.D.N.Y. 1993), *vacated by mandamus,* 11 F.3d 368 (2d Cir. 1993), *reh'g denied in part,* 1994 U.S. App. LEXIS 20158 (1994), 850 F. Supp. 188 (E.D.N.Y. 1994) (cases transferred per appellate decision). The Court of Appeals has not, in my opinion, sufficiently considered the efficiency of having one decision on the science issues instead of, as in Bendectin, many decisions by trial and appellate courts all over the country. Expenses to plaintiffs are increased since each must pay a substantial filing fee. Control of discovery by many magistrate judges instead of one is duplicative and less effective; the work of many judges and magistrate judges is needed to control discovery. The Court of Appeals seems primarily concerned with not encouraging the bringing of marginal cases. This is a form of closing the courthouse door that represents a shifting of the balance of substantive law in favor of defendants. *See* Jack B. Weinstein, Procedural Reform as a Surrogate for Substantive Law Revision, 59 Brook. L. Rev. 827 (1993).

Contrasted with the restrictive view imposed by the Second Circuit on the Eastern District of New York is the view of Supreme Court Justice Stephen G. Crane, who is responsible for 500 stress syndrome cases in New York City. *See* In re New York County Data Entry Worker Products Litigation (Brooks v. International Business Machines Corp.), N.Y. L.J., Aug. 23, 1994, at 23; Edward A. Adams, Computer-Injury Suits Subject to 3-Year Rule, N.Y. L.J., Aug. 23, 1994, at 1. It would be desirable, as in the asbestos and D.E.S. cases, to have a single federal and a single state judge in New York jointly appoint a single Special Master-Adviser to handle all the New York stress syndrome cases cooperatively.

p. 176 n. 2. United States District Judge H. Russell Holland is trying the key Valdez cases expeditiously in three trials before the same jury. *See* Keith Schneider, With 2 Valdez Trials Down, Big One [on punitive damages] Is Coming Up, N.Y. Times, Aug. 14, 1994, at 34.

p. 179 n. 6. *See also* Matthew L. Wald, Out-of-Court Settlement Reached Over Love Canal, N.Y. State to Receive $98 Million, N.Y. Times, June 22, 1994, at B5 (cleanup to extend for decades).

p. 186 n. 27. *See also* George Brandon, Pulling Together in Electromagnetic Field Defense, Nat. L.J., Aug. 1, 1994, at B19 ("Defendants need a coordinated strategy for the mass tort some call the 'asbestos of the 90's'").

p. 191 n. 48. Indicative of how complex these cases can be is the Keene case, in which individual claims, suits against spun-off associated corporations, non–opt-out class actions, bankruptcy proceedings, and suits by the defendants against plaintiffs' counsel leave little money for the injured claimants. *See, e.g.*, Andrew Blum, Keene Truce Announcement, But Will It Hold?, Nat. L.J., July 11, 1994, at A10.

p. 193 n. 51. Congress appears unable to act. *See* N.Y. L.J., June 30, 1994, at 1: "The U.S. Senate, under pressure from trial lawyers and consumer groups, voted yesterday to block any changes in product liability laws . . . the 13th straight year it has taken that position . . . . Senators sympathetic to business failed to attract the 60 votes needed to end a filibuster . . . ."

p. 194 n. 55. *See also* Jack B. Weinstein, The Effect of *Daubert* on the Work of Federal Trial Judges, 2 Shepard's Expert and Scientific Evidence 1 (1994); Symposium, 15 Cardozo L. Rev. 1745 (1994).

p. 200 n. 80. The American Law Institute's proposal to consolidate mass cases and provide a rational choice of law provision has engendered great opposition among conflicts of law scholars. *See, e.g.*, Symposium, American Law Institute Complex Litigation Project, 54 Louisiana L. Rev. 833–1160 (1994) (articles by fourteen leading scholars, including professor Friedrich K. Juenger, and a judge). The complexity and differences in state substantive law with respect to relationships among plaintiffs and settling and nonsettling defendants made settlement of the Manville asbestos case exceedingly difficult. *See, e.g.*, 129 B.R. 710 (E. & S.D.N.Y. 1991); Gail Appleson, Asbestos Victims Get Only 10 Percent in Trust Pact, Reuters, July 28, 1994, BC cycle; Wall St. Journal, July 29, 1994, at B8.

p. 217 n. 5. *See also* Gerald Gunther, *Learned Hand* 398 (1994) ("Again and again, he spoke of the obstacles to the survival of the autonomous individual in an increasingly homogeneous mass society, considering how democracy might survive around the pressure towards conformity in twentieth-century America").

p. 225 n. 40. The proposal has been criticized in a Symposium, 54 Louisiana L. Rev. 833 (1994). *See also* Robert J. Martineau, Defining Finality and Appealability by Court Rule: Right Problem, Wrong Solution, 54 U. Pitt. L. Rev. 717, text at nn. 268 ff. (1993).

p. 229 n. 59. *See also* David M. Frankford, book review of David Sciulli, *Theory of Societal Constitutionalism: Foundations of a Non-Marxist Critical Theory,* 94 Colum. L. Rev. 1076, 1077 (1994) ("collegial organizations [are] the vehicles by which civil society can be constituted"); Robert D. Putnam, Social Capital and Public Affairs, Bulletin Am. Acad. of Arts and Sciences, May 1994, at 5, 7 (1994) ("working together is

easier in a community blessed with a substantial stock of social capital");
Peter H. Schuck & Robert E. Litau, Regulatory Reform in the Third
World: The Case of Peru, 4 Yale J. on Reg. 51 (1986) ("life in many
Third World states is more communitarian and less individualistic than
life in the United States . . . .").

p. 229 n. 61. In a sense the legal system itself may be denominated as a
community of communicators. *See* David Sciulli, *Theory of Societal Constitutionalism: Foundations of a Non-Marxist Critical Theory* 100 (1992)
("Habermas calls researchers (and actors) *communities of communicators*"; emphasis in original).

p. 230 n. 63. Communicatarianism "has much in common with some
aspects of feminist moral theory." Bailey Kuklin & Jeffrey W. Stempel,
Foundations of the Law, An Interdisciplinary Primer 22 (1994). The
feminist theory "emphasizes the importance of relations and interdependence among persons and the need to communicate." Id. at 21. *See
also* Carol Gilligan, *In a Different Voice* 30 (1982) (belief in communication as the mode of conflict resolution). *See generally,* Amitai Etzioni,
The Spirit of Community: Rights, Responsibilities, and the Communitarian Agenda (1993).

p. 233 n. 80. *See also* N.Y. L.J., Aug. 2, 1994, at 1 (eight-person steering committee approved on behalf of 661 claimants with 114 lawyers
who have filed World Trade Center suits).

p. 238 n. 20. This same attorney sent a videocassette to her clients in
the breast implant cases explaining the pros and cons of opting out of
the settlement, with an invitation to call her at her law office for further
information. *See Breast Implant Global Settlement Presented by Law
Office of Sybil Shainwald* (1994).

p. 245 n. 63. A consultant to the courts was also appointed. *See* text at
note 67. He was called a consultant rather than a special master because
of some doubt about the ability of a bankruptcy court to appoint a special master.

p. 249 n. 249. *See also* Banking Agency Setback, High Court Makes
Suits Against Professionals More Difficult, A.B.A. J., Aug. 1994, at 18;
Pansy v. Borough of Stroudsburg, 23 F. 3d 772 (3rd Cir. 1994) (press
entitled to intervene to obtain knowledge of settlement terms); Secrecy
Orders at Issue, A.B.A. J., Aug. 1994, at 32.

p. 257 n. 124. *See also* Cerise Anderson, Sealing Order Granted for Partial Settlement; Court Rebuffs Non Settling [repetitive stress syndrome] Defendants, N.Y. L.J., Aug. 9, 1994, at 1.

p. 260 n. 142. Hearings in Manville settlement and trial of Maryland issues, Aug. 2, 1994, United States District Court, Eastern District of New York (settlement of some 10,000 asbestos cases in Maryland at approximately $500 million, with projected revenues of well over one billion additional dollars and a contingency fee of 33 1/3 percent).

p. 260 n. 143. Most plaintiffs' lawyers in the Manville case, including those from Baltimore who have not yet settled, have agreed to a fee of 25 percent against Manville Trust payments. Some plaintiffs' attorneys have obtained orders from local courts for higher fees than the Eastern and Southern Districts of New York approved.

p. 266 n. 178. Some appellate courts have not fully appreciated the desirability of this kind of control, plus the opportunity to obtain better answers to science questions when consolidation rather than dispersion takes place. *See* Jack B. Weinstein, The Effect of *Daubert* on the Work of Federal Trial Judges, 2 Shepard's Expert and Scientific Evidence 1, 5 (1994).

p. 270 n. 1. *See* Arizona L. Rev., Dayton L. Rev., and American Judicature articles by Jack B. Weinstein on judges learning, speaking, and acting (all forthcoming in 1994).

p. 270 n. 3. Cf. *Report of Proceedings of the Judicial Conference of the United States,* March 15, 1994, at 27 (*Report of the Committee to Review Circuit Council Conduct and Disability Orders on Recommendations of National Commission on Judicial Discipline and Removal*).

p. 283 n. 93. Jack B. Weinstein, The Effect of *Daubert* on the Work of Federal Trial Judges, 2 Shepard's Expert and Scientific Evidence, 1, 6, (1994). The current surge of interest in joint science-law work should lead to an increasing emphasis on interdisciplinary study at law schools, already begun at institutions such as Columbia Law School.

p. 299 n. 27. *See* Monroe Freedman, Trials of an Ethics Expert Witness, Legal Times, May 23, 1994, op. ed. at 32.

p. 307 n. 22. *See also, e.g.,* David E. Rovella, Lawyers Are Big Boosters of Rosty Defense Fund, Nat. L.J., Aug. 8, 1994, at A6 (attorneys donate $136,000 for pending federal trial of Congressman Dan Rostenkowski).

p. 312 n. 25. The same exaggeration of the burdens of litigation are present in the securities field. *See* John C. Coffee, Jr., Security Class Actions: Myth, Reality and Reform, N.Y. L.J., July 28, 1994, at 5.

P. 312 n. 26. *See also* American Law Institute studies designed to restrict basis for design defect claims. A.B.A. J., Aug. 1994, at 24; Symposium, Touro L. Rev. (forthcoming 1994) (Proposals for Restatement of Torts [Third]).

p. 314 n. 42. *See* Jack B. Weinstein, *Reform of Court Rule-Making Procedures* (1977).

p. 333 n. 192. Based on this substantive law, I permitted jurisdiction to be obtained against any producer, even if it had not done business in New York. *See* In re DES Cases (Ashley v. Abbott Laboratories), 789 F. Supp. 552 (E.D.N.Y. 1992). The New York State Appellate Division, First Department, in an opinion by Justice Sidney H. Ash, extended jurisdiction on this basis, supporting the view of Supreme Court Justice Ira Gammerman, to whom New York City DES cases had been assigned. *See* Cerise Anderson, Jurisdiction Extended to Calif. DES Firm, N.Y. L.J., Aug. 19, 1994, at 1; In re New York County DES Litigation (Carrano v. Abbott Laboratories), 1994 N.Y. App. Div. LEXIS 8368 (1st Dep't Aug. 18, 1994).

INDEX

Abraham, Kenneth S., 260 n. 145, 301 n. 3, 302 n. 5, 307 n. 20
Acid rain, 20
Acton, Jan Paul, 219 n. 14
Administrative Office of U.S. Courts, 59
Agent Orange, 3, 4, 7, 8, 11, 12, 20, 41, 49, 55, 56, 58, 59, 61, 62, 65, 68, 75, 78, 85, 88, 94, 96, 103, 105, 107, 132, 145, 147, 153, 157, 158, 160, 161, 168, 170, 173 n. 1, 185 n. 27, 351, 352; advisory board, 105; aggregation of claims, 155, 161; aggregate settlement, 74; aid for families, 28; telephone answering, 3
Air pollution, 31, 210 n. 128
Airlines, 9
Aldock, John D., 218 n. 13
Alternative Dispute Resolution, 88
American Academy of Science, 115, 152
American Bar Association, 42, 72, 124, 138, 176 n. 2, 182 n. 7, 227 n. 50
American Law Institute, 9, 13, 24, 42, 44, 124, 138, 216 n. 2, 219 n. 15, 224 nn. 34, 35, 40
Anderson, William J., 179 n. 6
Angelos, Peter, 239 n. 23
Antonucci, Peter A., 174 n. 5
Apel, Karl-Otto, 229 n. 63
Arendt, Hannah, 235 n. 91, 272 n. 17
Arnold and Porter, 7
Asbestos, 11, 19, 20–21, 41, 49, 80, 87, 95, 139, 144, 164; Manville, 10, 12, 39, 51, 59, 62, 64, 65, 98, 164, 167, 352; in schools, 89; White Lung Associations, 56
Asbestos, Navy Yard. *See* Navy Yard
Ash, Sidney H., 357
Association of the Bar of the City of New York, 227 n. 50

Association of Trial Lawyers of America, 58, 254 n. 109
Atomic disaster, 170
Atomic energy, 123
Atomic weapons site pollution, 3
Austern, David, 279 n. 74
Australian veterans, 157, 351

Bacigal, Ronald J., 183 n. 21, 277 n. 59
Bacon, C., 310 n. 11, 315 n. 52
Bankruptcy, 57, 62, 106, 107, 120, 136
Bar Harbor resolution, 213 n. 146
Barnett, Randy E., 313 n. 29
Barney, Gerald O., 248 n. 75
Baron, Frederick M., 246 n. 69
Battisti, Frank J., 325 n. 144
Bazelon, David L., 283 n. 92
Beasley, James E., 331 n. 183
Behrens, Mark, 208 n. 116
Bell, Derrick A., 234 n. 87
Bell, Griffin B., 256 n. 118
Bell, Robert, 293 n. 5, 296 n. 14
Bellah, Robert, 291 n. 5
Bendectin, 3, 19, 188 n. 37, 353
Benhabib, Seyla, 6, 175 n. 10, 229 n. 63, 241 n. 29
Bennett, Michael J., 228 n. 52
Bentham, Jeremy, 6
Berger, Curtis J., 271 n. 14, 273 n. 24
Berger, Margaret A., 65, 218 n. 13, 297 n. 15
Bernstein, Anita, 348 n. 30
Bernstein, David E., 173 n. 1, 185 n. 26, 287 n. 110, 292 n. 3, 293 n. 4, 295 nn. 11, 12
Beverly Hills Supper Club, 16, 180 n. 7
Bhopal, 12, 16, 20, 98, 177 n. 3
Biblow, Charlotte A., 221 n. 29
Bidding for case control, 78